BETWEEN HARVARD AND AMERICA

Copyrighted by Chickering, Boston, 1904.

Between Harvard and America

THE EDUCATIONAL LEADERSHIP OF CHARLES W. ELIOT

HUGH HAWKINS

New York   OXFORD UNIVERSITY PRESS   1972

For
J. WALTER RICHARD,
humanist

Preface

How have universities originated, survived, and sometimes thrived
in American society, given their special values, which often conflict with widely shared public attitudes? In this book I have approached that question through the thought and action of a
single university president, hoping to gain something in concrete-
ness. The chosen angle of vision sets this study apart from others
on Eliot and Harvard.

In no strict sense is *Between Harvard and America* an institutional history or a biography, although a reader wondering about
the institution or the man will find much that speaks to his
curiosity. He will find a good deal about the concern of an upper-
class Bostonian for personal achievement through public service,
but even more about a university's problems in claiming a privileged place in society. Those problems were particularly severe
in a country where democracy, religion, and practicality all
overshadowed the pursuit of knowledge. This study attends
less to the man's psychological development than to his work
in the world and less to the university's internal restructuring
than to its external relations. This important part of academic
history has been generally neglected, while historians have con-

v

centrated on the complicated and vastly documentable inner histories of colleges and universities. My assumption has been that for external relations the view from the president's office is likely to be the most revealing.

For anyone seeking to study in depth the personal development of Charles W. Eliot, the two-volume biography by Henry James is available, and Samuel Eliot Morison has provided readers with both a survey of Harvard history over three centuries and a collection of detailed accounts of departmental affairs during Eliot's presidency. These volumes of the 1930s have become standard works of American educational history, and, like them, recent scholarship puts a high estimate on Eliot's importance.[1]

Although studies by Edward A. Krug and Theodore R. Sizer suggest how much can be learned through Eliot's activities in lower school reform, it is of course in higher education that Eliot's accomplishment is most memorable.[2] Frederick Rudolph's *The American College and University: A History* provides a rich analysis of Eliot's support for the elective system, along with some negative comments that indicate the Harvard president's continuing ability to rankle. Laurence R. Veysey's massive *The Emergence of the American University* includes more references to Eliot than to any other person and declares him "easily the most commanding figure among all the late nineteenth-century university presidents." Two scholars writing of the Gilded Age and the Progressive Era, Frederic Cople Jaher and Barbara Miller Solomon, have felt obliged to place Eliot among the exceptions to the anti-democratic or nativist strains they criticize in others of his class. Clearly, Eliot is of continuing interest to American historians.[3] Both those who picture him as a bureaucratizer erecting new organizational structures and those who see him as a devotee of an extreme version of individualism can find support in the record. This seeming conflict in what the man stood for invites further scrutiny.

Although Eliot occasionally appears as a symbol in current educational affairs, I have found that academics tend to confuse him with his cousin, Charles Eliot Norton, or with his successor, President Abbott Lawrence Lowell. The farther we get from our academic forebears, the more alike they seem, as with photographs of ancestors whose identities grow confused because they so commonly wore beards and all stared straight into the camera. As for the man in the street, he can scarcely be expected to recall Charles W. Eliot. Yet many survivors of the magazine-reading generations retain at least a hazy image of Eliot and his grandson immersed in a book, a picture widely circulated in advertisements for the Harvard Classics. A man lives on in such images, in anecdotes, and in those little prolegomena that give lecturers on current issues a historical running start. Eliot deserves more. In this book I hope to describe the most original and significant undertaking of his life: nurturing a university in a changing, sometimes hostile social environment.

In centering this book on the antagonisms between academic and other social values, I originally cast Eliot as "mediator." The label may still give some sense of the book, but Eliot was simply too energetically constructive, too firmly convinced of his own ideas, to be essentially a compromiser. Yet even such a man, caught between the intellectual ethos of a university and the equalitarian, religious, and utilitarian impulses of Americans, found himself necessarily seeking a *via media*. Eliot was early aware of the effect of such dilemmas on the presidential role. In 1869, in a passage of his inaugural address describing the president's duties, he declared:

> He must . . . influence public opinion toward the advancement of learning; and . . . anticipate the due effect on the University of the fluctuations of public opinion on educational problems . . . [and] of the gradual alteration of social and religious habits in the community. The University must accommodate itself promptly to significant changes in the character of the people for whom it exists. . . . In this mobile nation the action and reaction between the University and society at large are more sensitive and rapid than in stiffer communities.[4]

This social aspect of Eliot's administration at Harvard forms the major theme of the pages that follow.

I have used Eliot's years as student and teacher to reveal the academic practices and reform currents of the 1850s and 1860s. I then sketch the entire period of his Harvard presidency (1869–1909), first in its "university" aspects, then in its "collegiate" aspects, especially its record in expanding the elective system. The university's changing responses to religious, equalitarian, and utilitarian traditions of Americans are taken up in turn, followed by Eliot's efforts on behalf of lower school reform, which grew directly out of his concerns as a university president. I have also presented the ideas and strategies of the element within Harvard that objected to the effects of Eliot's program on undergraduate life, an element that increasingly gained power toward the end of Eliot's administration. In the epilogue I have briefly treated Eliot's public image during his post-presidential years.

I have sought to write critically, and not in celebration. But I want to register my awareness that I have written within a framework of liberal-progressive values. Ideologically, my approach to Eliot has been largely sympathetic. Like most practicing academics during the last decade, I have been dismayed by how much inhumanity and intransigence persist in liberal corporatism in general and higher education in particular. But in recent academic politics I have found myself among the left-liberal reformers and not among the radicals. I believe that there is immense promise for human fulfillment in American institutions of higher education, flawed as they may be. Such views have predisposed me to analyze sympathetically the era in which the American university was created.

H. H.

Plainfield, Mass.
June 1972

Acknowledgments

It is difficult to convey the extent to which a book like this one rests on the efforts of people other than the author. I cannot imagine having begun this study without a foreknowledge of the generosity of archivists, librarians, and scholarly friends.

At all the manuscript repositories visited, I received cordial assistance. But again and again I went to the Harvard University Archives, first for general perusal of the Charles W. Eliot Papers, later with quite special and perplexing inquiries. I could not have asked for more kindly and informed assistance. My thanks go to Kimball C. Elkins, Harley P. Holden, and the entire staff of the archives.

I have been merciless in calling on friends to read the manuscript of this book in various stages of development. The stages were several because each reader showed me where improvements were needed. In quite different ways, but always ways for which —without involving them in responsibility for my errors—I am happily indebted to them, the following readers of the entire manuscript contributed to its final form: Theodore Baird, Robert L. Church, Tilden G. Edelstein, Allen Guttmann, Robert C. Townsend, Laurence R. Veysey, and John William Ward. Additional thanks go to Professor Edelstein and Professor Veysey, whose critical readings of the manuscript were preceded by many helpful discussions of the direction the project should take. In the earliest stages of planning, Richard J. Storr gave me the benefit of his reflections on the most promising avenues open for the history of American higher education. I thank also Arthur Kaledin, David B. Potts, and J. Walter Richard, to whom I submitted portions of the manuscript with requests for aid, which were generously answered. Several friendly scholars shared with me discoveries about Eliot made during their own researches—Robert V. Bruce, Clifford E. Clark, Jr., Louis Harlan, and Fred Nicklason.

My reliance on the skills of librarians has been virtually constant. Joseph R. Anderson of the New York Mercantile Library helped in a variety of ways. The staff of the Robert Frost Library at Amherst College in particular has enhanced the satisfactions of research and writing. Of this able group, I single out Floyd Merritt and his associates in the reference department, where queries were answered and obscure publications obtained with sleuth-like ability and friendly concern. The Amherst College community, in fact, is a living refutation of those stereotypes which depict colleges as antagonistic to original investigation. I hope the members of this community will accept a general expression of gratitude. Deserving special thanks for help in moments of difficulty are Prosser Gifford, dean of the faculty, and Friederike Dewitz, secretary of the Department of American Studies.

It has been my good fortune at Oxford University Press to have the counsel of Sheldon Meyer and the editorial assistance of Caroline Taylor.

The initial year spent in research for this book was supported by fellowships from the Simon Guggenheim Memorial Foundation and the Trustees of Amherst College. A grant from the Ford Foundation aided in manuscript preparation. I thank all those individuals who showed faith in my project through these grants. I note with gratitude the assistance of Lois LaClaire and Eleanor

Starzyk, who performed the tasks of manuscript typing and re-typing, and of Rose Ann Richard and Nancy Tripp, in indexing.

In a somewhat different version, Chapter IV has appeared in the *Journal of American History;* its inclusion here is with permission of the Organization of American Historians. Permission to quote from manuscript sources in their possession (identified by location in the notes) is gratefully acknowledged from the following: the Harvard College Library; the Harvard University Archives; the Huntington Library, San Marino, California; and the Yale University Library. I thank also Charles W. Eliot 2d for permission to use material from his grandfather's papers in the Harvard University Archives, and Miss Frances Tetlow for providing a photograph of her father.

To authors of the many works cited in the notes, works without which this one would have been thin indeed, I offer thanks, not only for specific contributions, but for that continuing education which (as President Eliot observed) comes to persistent readers.

H. H.

Contents

BETWEEN HARVARD AND AMERICA

I

Harvard's Mr. Eliot

I think we had better pause for a few minutes and ask Mr.
Eliot to draft a resolution.

PRESIDENT JAMES WALKER,
at Harvard faculty meetings [1]

I

For Charles William Eliot, entering Harvard College as a freshman in 1849 was hardly leaving home. His father, Samuel Atkins
Eliot, was the college's treasurer and *ex officio* a member of the
Corporation; he had just published a history of Harvard.
Charles's grandfather, a highly successful import merchant and
possibly the richest Bostonian of his day, had endowed the college's Eliot Professorship of Greek in 1814. Two uncles by marriage, George Ticknor and Andrews Norton, were former Harvard professors, internationally recognized scholars, and leaders in
Boston-Cambridge intellectual circles. Harvard's new president,
Jared Sparks, was an intimate family friend. Two cousins entered
college with Charles, and weekends he could return (with his
laundry) to the family home on Boston's Beacon Street, next to
the State House. To enter Harvard, then, was only to shift location slightly within the family.[2]

The Eliot family was among those Oliver Wendell Holmes
dubbed "the Brahmin caste of Boston." In their eyes their wealth
obliged them to strive for personal achievement and social usefulness. With such ideals Samuel A. Eliot had trained at Harvard

Divinity School (though he was never ordained), and he did not allow his business pursuits to dominate his life. As mayor of Boston, he abolished the riotous volunteer fire companies, and as a member of the city school committee, he introduced music into the schools. He wrote on religious and political subjects for serious journals, and ghostwrote the original version of the life of the fugitive slave Josiah Henson, a work moderate in its antislavery sentiments yet destined to have great influence as a model for *Uncle Tom's Cabin*. He was also active in prison reform. Conservative Unitarians and pillars of King's Chapel, the Eliots believed, as Charles's father expressed it, that "excitement and agitation are things not encouraged by Christianity." [3] They rejected Emerson as a romantic anarchist, and they dreaded Garrisonian abolitionists, whom they considered to be unpatriotic and impractical. In fact, during a brief term in Congress as a Webster Whig, Samuel A. Eliot voted for the Fugitive Slave Law and consequently gained notoriety in the abolitionist press as "Samuel Abductor Eliot." [4]

The Eliots believed in institutions—families, governments, churches, schools. They were accordingly concerned for the development of Harvard University. Treasurer Eliot proved an adroit solicitor of funds: his public statements sometimes loosened pursestrings more effectively than the reports of the university's president did. Convinced that applied science was the route to national prosperity, Eliot took an active role in establishing Harvard's Lawrence Scientific School and finding its engineering professor. He argued against critics who saw any departure from liberal culture as a corruption of the university, but he was no philistine. Like his friends, he valued literary culture and pure science. No one thought of George Ticknor's history of Spanish literature or Louis Agassiz's fossil fish collection as useful, yet these two men were paragons of Boston society. Part of this drive toward cultural achievement was, or course, nationalistic. It rankled that Europe had universities superior to America's. Confident in his nation's political genius, the elder Eliot hoped that it could also obtain "the renown of a high degree of civilization," aided by such institutions as Harvard.[5]

Such a man looked closely after his own son's education. When Charles entered Harvard, it was with the confidence that he had received a preparatory education tailored to that institution's requirements—the Latin, Greek, mathematics, and ancient history of the Boston Public Latin School. But the Eliots had not let this curriculum set bounds for Charles's early education. He learned both the aristocratic arts of dancing and riding and the manual skills of carpentry, wood-turning, and type-setting.

Despite such careful instruction and the love lavished on an only son, Eliot remembered childhood as a time of vivid griefs and fears. He recalled the classroom canings he had witnessed at the Latin School and fights on the Boston Common with bigger Irish boys from the North End. Some of these fights grew out of taunts directed at Charles's disfigurement, for though tall and sturdy, he bore a birthmark which covered much of the right side of his face, extending to his lip and twisting it upward. At the age of ten, in a crisis of self-examination, he determined that he would not allow this infirmity to ruin his life. That dedication to self-discipline, plus the burden of near-sightedness, severely restrained his natural impulses to sociability. The fifteen-year-old who left the Latin School in 1849 was, he recalled, "reserved, industrious, independent and ambitious." [6]

The Harvard that Eliot entered was still at heart a traditional college. Its students' social homogeneity was scarcely challenged by the occasional farmer's son from Maine or scion of the Virginia aristocracy. Its curriculum was almost entirely prescribed. Experiments with student choice of subjects were labeled a failure in the inaugural address of President Sparks, who had been a Unitarian minister, editor of the *North American Review*, and Harvard's first McLean Professor of History. This renowned biographer of Washington defended subject prescription on the ground of symmetry in mental training, arguing for "thorough discipline of all the powers of the mind . . . in due proportions and in a variety of exercises." Under Sparks, students were allowed one elected subject a year as juniors and seniors, although a second could be taken as an "extra" for no credit. Sparks, who could write contentedly of the "Collegiate Department" as following its "ordinary routine . . . with its accustomed uniformity," seemed more concerned to note the absence of disorder than the presence of intellectual awakening.[7]

The resulting curriculum was undeniably inclusive. In effect, every student sampled all the recognized fields of learning and concentrated willy-nilly in either foreign languages or mathematics. The class of 1853 studied Latin, Greek, mathematics, rhetoric (composition, public speaking, and logic), history, chemistry, French, natural history, intellectual and moral philosophy, physics, political economy, constitutional law, and evidences of natural and revealed religion. There was no unwillingness at Harvard to introduce new subjects, but often the student learned no more than the contents of a simple textbook, and the heavy reliance on recitations discouraged independent thought. The Harvard of the 1850s suffered in alumni recollections, serving as a negative contrast to later reformed practices. Henry and Charles Francis Adams had little good to say for it, though Henry recalled it as simply the best college in the land. Even William Everett of the class of 1859, who recalled "a general high, keen, intellectual energy" among the students, admitted that the system had cramped those with special gifts.[8]

The collegiate department was the oldest, largest, and best-endowed division of Harvard, the center of presidential concern and alumni sentiment. But Harvard was more than a classical college. The title which President Edward Everett had insisted upon, "the University at Cambridge," was suitable, whether the name was taken to mean a confederation of specialized faculties or an institution dedicated to the advancement of knowledge as well as teaching. The medical school dated from the end of the American Revolution, and the divinity and law schools had emerged in the second decade of the nineteenth century under the presidency of John Kirkland. The observatory, founded by subscription in 1843, had installed a refracting telescope equal to the world's largest, and soon the Boston-Cambridge community prided itself on the discoveries of a third ring of Saturn and two comets.[9] At the Lawrence Scientific School, founded in 1847, technological impulses were dwarfed by the stature of its leading professor, Louis Agassiz, a volatile Swiss genius whose approach to zoology and geology was imbued with ideals of advancing science for its own sake. As to graduate education, a few "resident graduates" pursued desultory studies in Cambridge without special courses or an advanced degree as a goal. In none of the professional schools was any previous higher education an entrance requirement, though college graduates were often among their students. Thus Samuel A. Eliot had grounds for speaking of the A.B. program in 1850 as "preparatory." The Lawrence faculty debated establishment of a Doctor of Science degree in 1857, but settled for granting some of its S.B. degrees "with mention of original research." [10]

Harvard in the early fifties was experiencing one of its most intense periods of public criticism. This "child of the Commonwealth," the evangelicals charged, had fallen into the hands of a minority sect. Indeed, there was no denying that the Corporation was made up solely of Unitarians. The Sparks regime, admitting the departure from Congregational orthodoxy, though denying sectarianism, sought to set the divinity school adrift, a measure blocked by the state Supreme Court.[11] Whatever its liberal aberrations, the college still required students to attend morning and evening prayers and Sunday services, and to study the rational theism of Paley's *Evidences* and Butler's *Analogy*. Arguments against the existence of God were carefully answered in the classes of the Alford Professor of Natural Religion, Moral Philosophy, and Civil Polity. In an effort to reassure the religious public, in 1855 Harvard chose for the new position of Preacher to the University and Plummer Professor of Christian Morals, Frederic Dan Huntington, a Unitarian of evangelical leanings who had attended orthodox Amherst College.

A parallel accusation was that Harvard was controlled by the wealthy and accessible only to sons of the wealthy. Charges that Harvard kept out the poor boy were in part true. Room and instruction costs were double those at Yale and Brown. With the possible exception of the University of Virginia, Harvard was the most expensive college in the United States. Treasurer Eliot took this matter to heart. He admonished alumni to expand Class Scholarship funds and propagandized successfully for a state program of public scholarships applicable at Harvard, Williams, or Amherst.[12]

In 1850 new charges that Harvard fell short of "the just expectations of the people" came from a legislative committee headed by an ambitious young Democrat, George Boutwell, who was shortly to become governor by exploiting the division of the Whig Party on the slavery issue. The committee's chief objection was that Harvard failed to provide practical instruction and student freedom to specialize. The report argued for the elective principle with a heavy-handed application of the free-market analogy. President Francis Wayland of Brown University had just launched an effort to give curricular equality to applied science by means of broadened electives, and he had adherents in Massachusetts. They were irritated to observe Harvard backing away from the elective principle and priding itself on its rising entrance requirements. Harvard defended itself by pointing to its new scientific school, where students found easier admission than in the collegiate department and freedom to study in a single field.[13]

On one matter of institutional autonomy, the selection of professors, Harvard was sorely tested by the exuberant democracy of the early fifties. The Overseers, then including the entire Massachusetts Senate and Governor's Council *ex officiis*, refused to confirm the appointment of Francis Bowen as professor of history. Bowen had supported the Compromise of 1850 and had written disparagingly of Kossuth and the Hungarian revolution, thus offending both enthusiasts for "Young America" and anti-slavery forces. He had hoped to win a chair by truckling to Harvard's "aristocratic and monarchical Faculty," concluded the *Massachusetts Spy*. Taking advantage of the recent conviction of a Harvard professor for murder, the newspaper analogized that Bowen "goes into his study as did John W. Webster to his laboratory, and there enacts the murderous deed." Two years later, the Board of Overseers having been restructured to include only five public officials *ex officiis*, Harvard made Bowen Alford Professor.[14] In the midst of such conflicts Charles Eliot pursued his studies as an undergraduate. He thus observed early the problematical relations of an institution of higher learning and its environing society.

Without inconsistency, Eliot could criticize the Harvard College of his undergraduate years, seeing it as having declined from an earlier era, and yet speak highly of the education he obtained.[15] His own personality and his family's circumstances helped immensely in the self-instruction which is at the heart of any true education. A bright student of great regularity and application, Eliot had no taste for schoolboy pranks. Ambitious for high academic standing (well publicized in those days by the order of speaking at commencement), he carefully prepared even those subjects he thought dull or useless. Under the Scale of Merit, which included marks from every recitation in every subject and also registered lapses in deportment, he graduated second in his class.

During his first two years every subject was required. Edward Tyrrel Channing, who in the year before his retirement taught Eliot rhetoric, and his successor Francis J. Child may be credited with some of the clarity and power of Eliot's later writing and speaking; but the boy arrived at college with a remarkably strong and melodious speaking voice. In his sophomore year, Eliot studied natural history under Jeffries Wyman, who offered the subject during the absence of Asa Gray, to whom it was regularly assigned. Eliot recalled Wyman, who also presented required lectures in anatomy and physiology during the senior year, as his personal ideal of the qualities of a man of science—"lucidity, candor, sagacity, patience, modesty, and fairness." [16]

Required work in philosophy in his last two years brought Eliot under the instruction of James Walker, another Unitarian minister turned professor, who became president during Eliot's senior year. Here Eliot received the culminating interpretations with which the antebellum colleges crowned their curriculum. In mental and moral philosophy Eliot got a strong and apparently permanent innoculation of Scottish common sense. In the course on evidences of natural and revealed religion he was taught that both psychology and history proved man to be by nature a religious being. He later told Walker that he had learned more from him than anyone else except his parents. In his last semester, Eliot studied Wayland's *Political Economy* and Kent's *Commentaries on American Law* under the controversial Francis Bowen, whom he remembered as a man of unreliable judgment, but clear, incisive, and kind.[17]

In his junior and senior years Eliot did not hesitate to elect the mathematics courses of the world-famous Benjamin Peirce, a professor in both college and scientific school, whose teaching many students found unintelligible. Indeed, Eliot's competitor for first place in the class of 1853, Charles Carroll of Baltimore, who reputedly chose the electives most likely to raise his average, was disturbed to learn that Eliot was making the highest possible grades in mathematics. But a forecast of Eliot's later disagreements with Peirce occurred in class one day when infinitesimal variables was the subject. Eliot, who was developing empiricist leanings in his chemical studies, ventured the opinion that what was being said consisted of "theories or imaginations rather than facts or realities." The mathematician responded gravely, "Eliot, your trouble is that your mind has a skeptical turn. Be on your guard against that tendency or it will hurt your career."

Eliot appeared never to find it worthy of remark that he enrolled in a second, creditless elective. Possibly the practice was taken for granted among better students. Limited to the ancient and modern languages for this extra, Eliot chose Latin and enjoyed it.[18]

The influence that made Eliot's own undergraduate education

the sort that he later urged for all college students—"university" education—came from Josiah Parsons Cooke. Although Cooke, a Harvard graduate of 1848, had spent a year in Europe, he was a largely self-taught chemist. He was full of enthusiasm and dedication, eager to serve both the advancement of knowledge and the well-being of the college. As a tutor, even before he succeeded the hapless John W. Webster as Erving Professor of Chemistry, Cooke added to recitations from a chemistry textbook lectures in which he performed experiments before the class and excursions which he led to nearby factories to observe the principles of chemistry applied. During Eliot's freshman year Cooke's lectures were voluntary, but the entire class attended. "Then and there," Eliot recalled, "I, for one, first learned what Chemistry was about, and what was the scientific method in observing and reasoning." [19]

From his sophomore year on, Eliot was admitted to Cooke's private laboratory in the basement of University Hall. There he had "the advantage of what was really private instruction," a rare privilege among Harvard College students.[20] As his relationship with Cooke deepened into friendship, Eliot learned enough to help in the laboratory and the mineralogical cabinet. Cooke gave him reagents for use in a small laboratory which his family, in spite of their fear of fires, allowed him to set up at home. He jocularly dated a letter from "Beacon-hill Laboratory." In his junior year, complaining of logic as "a useless study of technicalities" and of the natural philosophy (physics) textbook as "very simple but dry," he reported that chemistry filled up any chinks in his schedule.[21]

A Harvard student far less perspicacious than Eliot could have seen that chemistry was rapidly gaining prestige. Students were joining the new Rumford Society, devoted to amateur chemical experiments. Unlike his predecessor in the Erving Professorship, Cooke was made a member of the college faculty, and he also taught at the scientific and medical schools. Praised by the president for his diligence, he was given leave so that he could purchase equipment in Paris. The applications of chemistry witnessed by the students on class excursions suggested infinite industrial possibilities. In the summer of 1852 Cooke and Eliot hiked across New England and New York, investigating mineral resources and every "application of chemistry to the practical arts" that they could get wind of. The young men observed a bustling, unfinished society, where many expected they would soon get rich. Such tours continued through 1857, and often Francis Humphreys Storer, a budding chemist who assisted in Cooke's laboratory, came along.[22]

Chemistry generally filled for Eliot the role that the extracurriculum played for many undergraduates. But he participated in some of the elaborate enterprises that revealed the inventiveness of antebellum students in counteracting the bland course of study. He joined the Natural History Society, arranged its cabinet of minerals, and prevailed upon the Corporation to give it $200. Believing the Porcellian Club given to dissipation, he declined membership, but he did join the Institute of 1770 (at that time still a literary and debating society) and the somewhat scientifically oriented Alpha Delta Phi.[23] Of the latter he was chosen president in his senior year, an obligation which he hoped would advance his resolution to become more sociable and communicative. He had by then decided, for all his academic striving, "that this continual effort to improve one's mind is too selfish and unfruitful to be very satisfactory, and that this everlasting digging can at best produce but a fruit with a stone at its heart." This resolution would have surprised one classmate, who wrote of Eliot soon after graduation, "He despised the class as a whole and as a whole they were not slow in reciprocating—indeed he was very unpopular." In spite of newly sociable intentions, as his college years drew to a close Eliot still thought of himself as "a stiff, pokerish, glum, unattractive young man."[24]

Just as Charles's entrance into Harvard had meant no significant departure from his family, so life in his father's house during the year after graduation marked no interruption in his education, though it now became more directly vocation-oriented. Besides taking private instruction in French and German, he pursued bookkeeping in a business school. He also tried out philanthropic activities akin to those which dominated his father's life. As a volunteer instructor in a church-sponsored evening school for working boys, he discovered that he liked teaching. He learned about public schools through his appointment to the Boston Primary School Board, a sprawling public body in which each member acted as visitor to a particular school.[25]

All these undertakings helped Charles in his hard thinking about his future during the winter of 1853–54. The old Puritan concern for a "second calling" was formalized in an Eliot family tradition, a letter to a parent announcing and justifying one's choice of a lifework. During his college years people had asked Charles, "What *are* you studying chemistry for? *Do* you mean to be a professor?!!!" He had replied that he did not know. Meanwhile, his father gently suggested the merits of a business career. He had argued effectively to his nephew Charles Eliot Norton that besides "the potentiality of becoming rich," business promised an unparalleled knowledge of the world and highly developed habits of accuracy. It was perhaps after hearing similar suggestions that Charles asked an intimate to suggest "some reasons why I should not be a merchant." [26]

Charles escaped the frustration experienced by those young Brahmins who felt that democratic society offered no place worthy of their background and aspirations.[27] Toward the end of his college years, when he had begun questioning his constant intellectual self-improvement, he had yearned to "be doing somebody good." But he feared no absence of opportunities to fulfill this wish in society. On the contrary, the rich variety of promising professions made him hesitate. Family wealth, far from filling him with lassitude, gave him the liberating sense that money-making need not bear importantly on his decision. Business and philanthropy in the style of his father appeared as a major possibility. But Charles recognized other ways to be "a man of influence, of reputation, and of usefulness." Teaching was especially honored in his community, he observed, and especially necessary since "the very maintenance of our free institutions depends on the education of the people." As to science, his summer excursions had heightened his awareness of the importance its applications would have in a developing nation, and he justified the study of science that had no practical bearing as "meat for the mind." He linked the prestige of the scientific scholar to a view of the country that was anything but pessimistic: "New Colleges springing up everywhere, government expeditions by land and water, mines and factories, all requiring scientific aid, and very few scientific men to meet all this demand. The scientific men of America will make their mark on the page of history within the next fifty years."

His decision blended concern for a constructive role in society with concern for self-development. The "high intellectual level" and self-improvement of the scholar attracted him. "When I left College," he recalled, "the thought that I should probably never know again as much science as I then knew, that I was to renounce such studies forever, was a very painful one to me." In a long, reasoned letter to his mother, based on the standard of glorifying God by being useful and happy, he announced his decision to become a student and teacher of science. He was just turning twenty.[28]

II

His profession decided, Eliot was glad to accept a tutorship in mathematics at Harvard College, a post he held from 1854 till early 1858, when he was promoted to the newly created rank of assistant professor and chemistry was formally added to his teaching responsibilities. Eliot began teaching at Harvard under the burden of a regulation that all unmarried tutors must live in college dormitories and take responsibility for order there and in the yard, a duty he found "unpleasant to perform, and unpleasant to shirk." Although eight printed pages of regulations gave an inescapable pettiness to the task, he of course did not shirk it. This activity, plus his natural constraint, put a barrier between "old Eliot" and the students. Tales of Eliot's coldness and tactlessness as a teacher were recounted by his students, yet they found that a certain power grew out of his reserve. "As he rarely proffers a remark, those which he does let fall have double weight," a student noted ruefully, after keeping a boil painted with iodine at Eliot's behest, and thereby further inflaming it. The sophomore of 1860 who called Eliot "cold as an icicle," placed more importance on his being "fair, gentlemanly, and pleasant." [29] In retrospect Eliot himself shrewdly assessed his limitations as a young teacher. "I had little range of observation, no breadth of experience, and small capacity for sympathetic imagination." He was somewhat humanized for students by his participation in Harvard boat races, which he entered in spite of qualms about his dignity. Nor was the student misguided who, when denied his degree because of a prank, turned to Eliot for a letter to his father. The young assistant professor gently put the escapade in perspective as a traditional college joke and explained the magic of late degrees, granted "as of" the student's original class year.[30]

Students respected Eliot as an effective teacher. His faculty colleagues recognized him as a reformer. After a single year in the straitjacket of daily recitation and daily marking, he tried new approaches. He had already sought to make his subject "as concrete as possible," illustrating principles with practical applications, and the logic of this method soon led out of the classroom. Obtaining surveying equipment, he took a volunteer group from his class and helped them apply the trigonometry they were learning in a thorough survey of the college yard and environs. Meanwhile, he and his fellow tutor James Mills Peirce assaulted the traditional oral examinations given before a committee of the Overseers. Offended by the dubious expertness and obvious absenteeism of the Overseers, the unequal difficulty of questions posed to different students, and the weight assigned to daily recitation marks, the young tutors obtained permission to substitute written examinations, which they graded themselves. The new arrangement had a strong appeal to faculty professionalism, and it rapidly spread to other departments. By increased reliance on written examinations in determining rank, the faculty freed class time from graded recitations.[31]

In 1858 Cooke and Eliot successfully proposed a new course in chemistry. Offered as an elective in the junior year, it extended the student's options beyond languages and mathematics. This made student laboratory exercises part of a Harvard College course, probably for the first time. There is reason to believe that such laboratory teaching was largely Eliot's idea, for at first Cooke clung to the recitation system in his half of this small elective. During the 1856–57 term Eliot had lectured in chemistry at the medical school, replacing Cooke, but now at last he was officially teaching chemistry in Harvard College. Meanwhile, Cooke's infectious enthusiasm for chemistry had aided the expansion of the Boylston Fund and the erection of Boylston Hall, despite protests from the medical faculty, who feared competition.[32]

Eliot's uniqueness on the faculty came not from his considerable abilities as a teacher, but from his genius for organization. This gift, which led to speculation among young alumni that he was "to be president of Harvard, bye and bye," proved especially helpful to the aging President Walker. The administrative tasks that Eliot performed ranged across duties which were later assigned to a whole retinue of university officers: registrar, secretary to the Corporation, secretary of the faculty, director of physical education, director of buildings and grounds, curator of mineralogy, librarian in charge of purchasing, alumni relations director, and development director. On his initiative, gas lights were installed in the dormitories and classrooms. Abolition of "evening prayers" soon followed, on the ground that lighted classrooms allowed the late afternoon to be used for recitations —a neat paradigm of the use of technology to unseat custom.[33] Before Corporation meetings Eliot regularly helped Walker prepare the agenda, and at faculty meetings the president would at times suggest, "I think we had better pause for a few minutes and ask Mr. Eliot to draft a resolution." Meanwhile, Eliot was getting more education from Walker, who hoped to make Harvard a place of "high and various scholarship." The fact that Eliot was virtually assistant to the president was recognized early in 1859, when the Corporation voted the twenty-four-year-old assistant professor an extra $300 a year. Young though he was, Eliot was already very much an institutional insider—"behind the curtain," said a fellow teacher. The Corporation directed queries to him on virtually any matter requiring prompt and complete information and reasoned proposals.[34]

Eliot's rage for order sometimes verged on New England busybodyism. His concern for the quality of the new Preacher to the University carried him close to pettiness. Convinced that Huntington was using old sermons ill-adapted to students, Eliot urged a mutual acquaintance to advise the newcomer to reform his ways. In his zeal to halt pilfering in the laboratory, he surprised and offended an innocent student whose book bag seemed suspiciously capacious. "Mr. Atkinson," Eliot brusquely ordered, "let me understand what you do with that bag." The student explained satisfactorily, but he told others of the incident with rancor.[35]

These excesses sprang from a deeply engrained sense of responsibility, a healthy refusal to let things ride. Eliot properly counted himself among those "who care about the general tendency and policy of the College." In this he apparently belonged to a minority. Although at faculty meetings he began to hear the language of change, he concluded unhappily, "The head-quarters of Conservatism are in the Colleges and other Institutions for teaching. The conservative spirit in politics is not nearly as stiff and invincible as literary conservatism." [36]

In spite of the time he spent in teaching and administrative tasks, Eliot felt the tug of research interests that were increasingly to characterize American university faculties. No one influenced him in this direction more strongly than Frank Storer, his ebullient hiking companion. A graduate of Lawrence Scientific School, Storer had studied chemistry abroad for two years before opening a private consulting laboratory in Boston. The collaboration of the two friends, which began in earnest about 1860, resulted in at least five published researches, the most important of which was a study of the impurities in commercial zinc.[37] With a professional's concern for priority, Eliot at one point warned a correspondent to "keep dark as to our results, for we are not quite ready to publish." He basked in the favorable reception of their reports and even thought he glimpsed the outlines of a new law of mineralogical classification. In fact, he began to resent the interference of other duties. "The College," he complained, "demands so much of my time that I can do original scientific work only by working up to the very limit of physical endurance and sometimes going a little beyond it." [38]

During this period, aided by Storer's broad scientific friendships, Eliot was beginning to form those extra-institutional connections with fellow specialists that marked the breaking up of collegiate parochialism. The closest of these was with George J. Brush of Yale's Sheffield Scientific School, who suggested procedure in the zinc study and urged Eliot to make his mark by becoming a good crystallographer and devoting himself to the physical characteristics of minerals. Eliot confidently sent off inquiries to any source, commercial or scientific, American or European, that he thought could help him with zinc samples or technical suggestions. [39]

Besides being a chemist among chemists, Eliot found himself an effective representative of scientists to potential benefactors. When Storer completed a dictionary of solubilities which appeared not to be commercially publishable, Eliot enlisted a group of Bostonians to risk five hundred dollars each "for the advancement of science." Adeptly he evoked for these laymen the volume's potential worth to scientists and promised to keep an eye on the business side of the matter. The touch of the mediator was evident. [40]

All these activities offered satisfactions, but Eliot's situation at Harvard in the late 1850s was not ideal for one who had determined to be a teacher and student of science and had begun to feel the impulse toward research. For one thing chemistry filled only about a fifth of his teaching time, and he found trigonometry classes increasingly dull. Properly to equip himself for chemical research, Eliot needed the European training that had transformed Storer and Brush into professional chemists. He did intend to study abroad in 1857, but he had to cancel his plans when his superiors decided that the college could not spare him.[41]

Something more than institutional exigencies was to disturb Eliot's life that year. The national economy, which had been bouncing along splendidly, in August suddenly lurched, bringing home to Eliot the uncertainties of life. The 1850s had started off brightly for business and agriculture. The new territories gained from Mexico, though exacerbating the slavery issue, had promised new resources (the Gold Rush was only a hint of more to come) and new markets, both in the newly settled West and across the Pacific. A transcontinental railroad was clearly in the offing. Americans had begun to mechanize their agriculture, and even as farm production boomed during the 1850s, manufacturing almost caught up with it in value of product. American industrial ingenuity was already recognized abroad, and foreign capitalists eagerly supported developing American enterprises. New England mercantile fortunes were also invested in new, or newly steampowered, factories, especially for textiles, boots and shoes, and clothing.

As so often before, the line between prudent investment and dangerous speculation proved hard to draw. Much of the nation's prosperity came crashing down in 1857, in a relatively brief but severe panic. Samuel A. Eliot was among the victims. He had become a silent partner in a firm of cotton factors, which was now caught overextended. The business went under, and though he might possibly have escaped by legal maneuvering, Eliot, the soul of probity, insisted that all his property and his wife's go into the settlement. Included in the forced sales were the family home and furnishings, though some of his wealthy relatives bid in a few items that he treasured. His life was radically changed. He was uncomplaining, but his health soon declined. Young Charles's prospects for a large inheritance vanished. Although new burdens fell on him, this exposure to the vicissitudes of American private enterprise appeared not to diminish in the least his faith in economic liberalism or in the nation's prosperous future.

Nor, happily, did the financial debacle prevent his marriage a year later to a childhood friend of his sisters, Ellen Derby Peabody, whose father had been minister of King's Chapel. Ellen's beauty and gentle gaiety brought into Eliot's life much that he had felt lacking in himself. He used part of a moderate legacy from his maternal grandfather to build a double house in Cambridge, the young couple moving into one half and Eliot's parents and three unmarried sisters into the other.[42]

Meanwhile, Eliot's relationship with Cooke had begun to change, and in 1859, a year of religious and scientific controversy in Cambridge, they ceased to be friends. Even before the publication of Darwin's *Origin of Species,* Louis Agassiz and Asa Gray were debating the credibility of the development thesis before the American Academy of Arts and Sciences. Cooke sympathized with Agassiz's concern for the effect of the theory on man's view of God. Eliot, like Gray, wanted to divorce scientific hypothesizing from theological considerations. He believed it was a detriment to science when Cooke gave public lectures on natural theology. The mounting disagreement attached itself to the case of Huntington's conversion from Unitarianism to Episcopalianism, which was in some eyes a threat to Harvard's religious liberalism.[43] After an explicitly theological quarrel, Cooke decided that Eliot had adopted a "changed view of life."

But various professional abrasions may have been more important. Some mutual friends spoke of Eliot as a rival of Cooke. How should credit be ascribed for a manual on which both had worked? How much independence should Eliot have in the laboratory? The upshot was that Eliot moved out of Boylston Hall to a separate laboratory which he set up at his own expense in University Hall. Apparently the dispute had reached the point of the two men's not speaking to each other before President Walker initiated a reconciliation. Admitting a share of the fault, Cooke declared he would welcome a return to the earlier association. Cooke suggested, however, that Eliot, for his own advancement, might turn "to some department of applied science." With a degree of exaggeration he added, "You are not at all identified with my department and have devoted so little time to it since you left College that it would be no loss to you to change your plans." [44] Their friendship was restored, though not the old intimacy. The episode revealed the difficulties of the pattern, found in both American colleges and German universities, that allowed only one professor in each subject. The new position of assistant professor was uncomfortably ambiguous; the very name suggested both subordination and control.

Luckily for Eliot, Harvard already had enough diversity that he could continue to be a chemist yet remain within the institution. His opportunity grew out of troubles in Lawrence Scientific School. Eben N. Horsford, the Rumford Professor, had been in charge of the Lawrence chemistry laboratory since it opened. Debts had accumulated, apparatus had been removed because of his carelessness, and he soon stopped troubling himself with lectures, being much involved in his own researches in food chemistry. Early in 1861 he decided—probably under Corporation pressure—to give up the laboratory, though not his chair. Eliot's organizational abilities and his awkward situation under Cooke made him appear just the man to take over the laboratory at Lawrence. A relieved Cooke could speak of the brightness of Eliot's "chemical prospects." [45]

But the prospects of the United States seemed to be dimming. War threatened to destroy a young nation still looked upon as a radical test of the democratic theory of government. For a later generation, it is difficult to understand the relatively mild impact that the coming of the Civil War had on Harvard and many other Northern colleges. In truth, life was not much changed in Cambridge. Most Southern students did not return after the winter vacation of 1860–61, but it took the fall of Fort Sumter to convince most Harvard men that there would be a war, and even then few imagined that it would be prolonged. Some students enlisted in the fall of 1861, but the Panic of 1857 had been followed by a sharper drop in freshman enrollments than occurred in 1861—or in any war year until 1864. President Lincoln's own son remained at Harvard until he graduated in 1864. It was generally considered no disgrace to hire a substitute if one was drafted. Ultimately, 1311 Harvard men did serve in the Union forces, and 138 lost their lives (of the 257 who served the Confederacy, 64 died in the war). Eliot's own class, that of 1853, counted 99 members (including those who did not graduate). Of these, fifteen served in the war, and one, Wilder Dwight, was killed.[46]

In April 1861, as flags appeared from dormitory windows, word came that the Cambridge arsenal had been deprived of its garrison. Eliot quickly organized a group of Harvard students for guard duty. From this undertaking developed the Harvard Cadets, a drill organization commanded by Eliot. By August 1861, he observed that war "fills up half our time and thoughts." In his letters, passionate accounts of the war's effects crowded out family news and academic shop talk.[47]

But Eliot, like many in the Harvard community, measured the question of participation in the war prudentially. In his case, he was virtually the sole support of his family—wife, parents, unmarried sisters, and by 1861 two children of his own. His parents both passed through grave illnesses in the winter of 1861–62, and in January 1862 his father died. His wife's father was also dead, and her two brothers were still adolescents. It would have been reckless for Eliot to have answered Lincoln's first call for volunteers. He would do what he could while remaining in the Boston-Cambridge area, such as aiding the Massachusetts Adjutant General's office in calculating town draft quotas. Although nothing came of Eliot's plan to reorganize Lawrence Scientific School for military training, its faculty and students took pride in the service of Dean Henry L. Eustis, a graduate of West Point, who became colonel of the Tenth Massachusetts Volunteers in the summer of 1862. Eliot collected contributions to assure his colleague a proper military outfit. He also took over Eustis's duties in the engineering department and became acting dean of Lawrence.[48]

In any case, it was not in Eliot to neglect his professional duties. At last master of a teaching laboratory, he had within a year accumulated a surplus to spend on apparatus and advertising notices. The young chemist boldly took on students asking for special instruction in "glass-making, copper and silver assaying, iron-founding, dyeing and calico printing, and the manufacture of common salt and Epsom salt from seawater." Even the brief announcement in the catalogue revealed that the program for the S.B. in chemistry was being thoroughly revised, with attention to firm grounding in chemical and mathematical fundamentals.[49]

Not a man to rest content within a single department, Eliot began to analyze the faults of the school as a whole—as the Corporation may well have foreseen. The widespread informality of teaching at Lawrence was the source of its effectiveness in the minds of many graduates. But such casualness was anathema to the new head of the chemistry laboratory. Lost apparatus and unqualified students were to Eliot symptoms of institutional laxness, and it was easy to discern his hand in the Corporation's order for an inventory of all books and equipment in Lawrence, to be followed by strict faculty accountability.[50]

The Lawrence faculty, in a reforming mood, had elected Professor Eustis to the deanship in place of Horsford and agreed to meet fortnightly. Even more promising was the creation of a special committee on school organization, consisting of Agassiz, Eustis, and Eliot. With Eliot taking the lead, the committee recommended an introductory general course which would be prerequisite to the degree examinations in a single science, and in April 1862 the Corporation backed the procedure by allowing payments of $100 to each professor participating.[51] But wholehearted support for the plan was lacking. Its only observable effects were among students under Eliot's control—those in chemistry and engineering. Eliot promised to serve students "who seek a scientific education, based mainly on Chemistry and Physics, but including the elements of several other sciences." He now prescribed for the chemistry and engineering programs written examinations on the work of each term. Thus Eliot ended for those enrolling in his departments the traditional Lawrence system by which students arriving with nothing more than a "good common English education" were allowed to specialize immediately and win degrees with as little as a year's residence.[52]

In the fall of 1862, as acting dean, Eliot renewed the drive for general studies. The reactivated committee on organization brought in a careful plan, largely Eliot's work, calling for written entrance examinations and a four year degree. The first two years would consist of a "regular system" of required general studies —mathematics, sciences, modern languages, and drawing— and the last two of specialized work. Although special students and students with advanced standing were allowed by the plan, so sharp a change in Lawrence's tradition threatened to undermine its attractions as a place to study with a single "great man." [53]

Such a change seemed especially directed at the teaching of Agassiz, who left students to their own devices in the laboratory, relying on the inspiration of his lectures, the excitement of his personality, and the shared vision of erecting a great zoological storehouse to reveal the order of nature. Such teaching, gratefully remembered by men as diverse as Simon Newcomb and Henry Adams, offended Eliot. Even Agassiz's famous spontaneous lectures seemed to him to suffer from dilution of thought. One lecture of Jeffries Wyman, Eliot declared, had "more thought in it than ten of Agassiz's." For a time Agassiz had appeared to favor a program of general introductory studies, but when Eliot brought in a detailed plan, Agassiz dragged his feet and then defiantly opposed the entire venture. With the backing of Benjamin Peirce, he was able to have it referred to the president.[54]

Agassiz apparently found the young chemist personally obnoxious.[55] Efficient and thorough, Eliot had an irritating way of imposing obligations on his institutional superiors. By Agassiz's lights, representatives of the Boston patriciate should admire him, contribute funds, perhaps become his scientific disciples—but they should not tell him how scientific students should be trained. Eliot's teaching style could hardly have been farther from Agassiz's. The younger man believed in rigid standards, written examinations, and conscientious teaching even of mediocre students. Moreover, since Asa Gray supported the reform proposal, Agassiz associated Eliot with his chief opponent in American scientific politics.

Agassiz had grown used to having his own way—at Lawrence, with the legislature, and with the governing bodies of Harvard.[56] He and Benjamin Peirce had helped win the presidency in 1860 for Cornelius Conway Felton, Agassiz's brother-in-law. When Felton died two years later, Agassiz and Peirce were leading supporters of the candidacy of his successor, Thomas Hill, the Unitarian minister, mathematician, and president of Antioch.[57]

Yet Agassiz's squelching of Eliot's plan to reform the S.B. program was based on more than personal antagonism or vanity. The proposed pattern for Lawrence threatened to interfere with the zoologist's ideas for university reform at Harvard. For a decade, a group of American scientists, calling themselves the Scientific Lazzaroni, had hoped to establish a university featuring advanced lectures by the nation's most creative scientists and scholars. Agassiz and Peirce were members of the group. Having failed to create such a university in New York or Albany, they now hoped to remold Harvard. Thus in rejecting the Eliot plan to restructure Lawrence, Agassiz could declare that he had a better idea—courses of lectures "of a character higher than those now given." Although it is conceivable that both proposals could have been adopted, President Hill pigeonholed Eliot's scheme and pressed for "University Lectures." [58]

This turn toward higher studies forecast the outcome of the competition for the Rumford chair, which Horsford vacated in January 1863. To Eliot the opening suggested his own promotion and the addition of Storer to the Harvard staff. To Agassiz this opportunity called for no less a scientist than his fellow Lazzarone, Wolcott Gibbs, a gifted and productive chemist who was then teaching at the Free Academy in New York.

When asked by a member of the Corporation for his reflections on the situation, Eliot admitted that to appoint Gibbs, whose name was being "vehemently urged" in some quarters, would bring to Harvard "undoubtedly the first chemist in the country," a man young enough to give his best years to the institution. But Eliot dwelt on Count Rumford's requirements for the chair he had founded: it should provide public as well as academic lectures and offer demonstrations of the utility of science for social well-being.[59] These obligations, Eliot declared, would not leave the Rumford professor time to manage the Lawrence laboratory. Perhaps too sanguinely, he announced that the laboratory was now profitable enough to support a second professor at the standard academic department salary of $2400 a year. If Gibbs were appointed to the Rumford chair, Eliot saw himself in this new professorship, retaining full control of the Lawrence laboratory; in fact, Gibbs should be allowed no part in it, since as an older man who "knows much more chemistry than I do," he "would not like to be *second* in the Laboratory." But if, as Eliot hoped, he himself were appointed Rumford professor, then his friend Storer would be ideal for the new professorship, and the two could carry on their fruitful collaboration in teaching and research.[60]

President Hill, faced with his first opportunity to show how Harvard could become a great university, believed that he must have Gibbs. But Eliot's rosy account of the chemistry laboratory's finances implied that Hill could also effortlessly retain Eliot. The Corporation took a somewhat more conservative position; after all, the war might cut the laboratory receipts of which Eliot was so proud. But it did offer Eliot promotion to professor, guaranteeing continuation of his present salary of $1500 (which would come from laboratory receipts if possible) and offering an additional $900 if laboratory income permitted it.

To lose the chance to make Storer his colleague was a disappointment, to be passed over for the Rumford chair a humiliation, but to be offered an under-salaried professorship where the exact income depended on his ability to draw students was an outrage. It would, Eliot insisted, encourage a system which poisoned student-teacher relations with commercial concerns. He characteristically informed the Corporation that it had recently resolved to end precisely such practices.[61]

Surprised by the forcefulness of Eliot's refusal, Hill undertook to raise money to assure a full salary—by asking for contributions from Eliot's relatives. Eliot promptly called a halt to the scheme. To retain a post because his relatives could afford a subvention was intolerable. Hill's second plan, in which Eliot pessimistically acquiesced, sought a large sum for permanent endowment of a new chemistry chair, without any previous assignment of it to Eliot. Wartime dislocations made the times unpropitious, however, and the hope for state support of new science professorships at Harvard was at best a distant one. Nothing came of Hill's efforts.[62]

Although such Harvard men as Josiah Cooke, James Russell Lowell, and James Walker supported Eliot for the Rumford chair, it went to Gibbs. After nine years as the youthful wonder of the faculty, Eliot's connection with Harvard ended. In New Haven, his friend Brush received both Storer's flamboyant version of the affair (Eliot victimized by the Napoleonic scheme of "that d——d Swiss adventurer") and Eliot's more moderate, fundamentally correct account ("The essential difficulty was in a lack of money to maintain two professors, and they chose Gibbs for the one"). But Eliot also recognized the work of the Lazzaroni group and included a list of the authors of his downfall, indicating their varying proportions of responsibility. Brush, who was no enemy of Gibbs, believed that Eliot, after creating "at least one of the best laboratories in the country," had been shamefully wronged.[63]

Hill's "mad scheme," as Storer called it, involved creating a university by filling professorships with the most creative minds available, even if they belonged to "outsiders." Hill, who was not unaware of Eliot's administrative talents, quite accurately concluded that Eliot was inferior to Gibbs in potential contribution to scientific knowledge. But foreshadowings of "university" standards also appeared in Eliot's reaction to the crisis. Merit, not family connections, should determine academic advancement, he had maintained.

In mid-1863, the twenty-nine-year-old chemist, for all his administrative promise, faced the immediate necessity of providing for a wife and two children. Eliot's achievements at Harvard supported the observation of his family that he possessed skills suitable to a business career. His brief tenure at Lawrence had been, if nothing else, a financial success. Storer was convinced that Eliot would be forced into business, and his lamentations evoked a response from Brush, who tried to assure Eliot that science offered greater comfort and happiness than the mercantile life. "As to changing my profession," Eliot responded, "there is but one inducement to such a grievous operation. Unfortunately that is a strong one viz.—a support for wife and babies. I know too well the suffering which comes on the family of a *poor* teacher, to be willing that the daily comfort of my wife and children should be restricted, or converted into struggling and anxious discomfort, because I happen to like Chemistry." This was perhaps the closest Eliot ever came to speaking as Economic Man.[64]

At the height of his occupational quandary, in June 1863, he received from Governor John A. Andrew the offer of a lieutenant colonelcy in a new cavalry regiment. Here was a tempting opportunity to take a more direct part in what he called "the great war which we are waging for freedom." The fact that he was a good horseman heightened the attraction of the offer. He deliberated for a week and tried to get better spectacles to correct his extreme nearsightedness. But given the dependence of his family on his earnings, he decided he should not voluntarily hazard his life. He cannot be counted among the romantic, self-searching young Brahmins who welcomed the war as a personal testing ground. Free from the torment of self-doubt, he was already a member of a rationally chosen profession, in which he had made a small but significant contribution.[65]

Must he desert that profession for a career in business? No, said some of his friends, urging instead that he go abroad. From cousins who had spent time in Europe came letters telling him not to look on travel as a luxury but to consider it as part of his education, a way out of "Cambridge ruts, which, after all, are pretty deep!" The residue of Eliot's legacy from his mother's father had been invested in the Suffolk Bank, which prospered as a clearing house for other New England banks. In mid-1863 it declared a

100 per cent dividend. With this windfall Eliot could go abroad with his wife, children, and a nursemaid. After a farewell visit to Brush in New Haven, he felt "squared up generally" and "quite afloat on the world already." He and his family sailed in September 1863.[66]

III

Eliot went to Europe armed with letters of introduction and commissioned with errands by friends at home. The errands he performed with dispatch, even one for his antagonist Louis Agassiz, but he was restrained in utilizing the entrées Cambridge and Boston furnished into European intellectual circles. For the most part he sought out scientists, men like Charles Lyell and Robert Wilhelm Bunsen. Most Americans living permanently in Europe struck him as "objectless and forlorn." He was not likely to adopt their pattern of life. Although he visited cathedrals and art museums, he sought also details of working-class life and political affairs and made strenuous efforts to visit industrial enterprises.[67]

Eliot cited two principal objects of study for his trip—educational institutions and chemistry. Settling first in Paris, he made the former his chief concern. To family queries as to why he studied "education in general" and not chemistry, he responded that Parisian chemistry lectures were elementary and the laboratories inferior to those in Cambridge and New Haven. He immersed himself in details of the vast range of French scientific and educational institutions—from an elementary school conducted by the Christian Brothers to the Conservatoire des Arts et Ateliers. He read regularly on such institutions in the Bibliothèque Nationale and attended various public lectures, though he was more interested in their form than in their matter. His habits of application, his energy, and his excellent memory made these self-designed investigations immensely instructive. Both the range and the high quality of French scholarship impressed him, and he sought "to understand how it is that France supports such a large body of scholars in every department of knowledge who not only teach, but also find time and means to prosecute entirely new researches." But most especially, he wrote home, he was investigating schools that trained young men "for those arts and trades which require some knowledge of scientific principles and their applications." [68]

Deciding after some hesitation that he could afford a second year abroad, Eliot chose to go to Marburg, describing it to his family as "a small town containing a small university among whose professors is an eminent chemist named [Hermann] Kolbe." Kolbe proved accessible and hospitable, and Eliot, who plunged into the study of German, found he could follow his lectures. Kolbe's laboratory he declared "something new and decidedly instructive," and he worked there intensely for seven weeks —less, it seemed, to complete a research than to learn laboratory ways that he might imitate in America. Plans to move to Tübingen for the spring term were upset by his children's illnesses, and he remained five months in Marburg, taking side trips to other German universities and polytechnical schools, meeting chemists, examining laboratories, and obtaining copies of regulations and course listings.[69]

An American in Europe during the Civil War gained a heightened nationalism, and Eliot was infuriated by the sympathy he found for the Confederacy, especially in Great Britain. Observing a Confederate flag displayed alongside the Union's at a hotel he was patronizing, he promptly removed his family, even though the offending banner was taken down. But when the occasional pro-Union Englishman, such as Goldwin Smith, was honored in America, Eliot was not better pleased. Such attentions suggested to him "the old hankering for the gracious praise of foreigners." [70]

Eliot's faith in the justice and ultimate triumph of the Union cause never wavered. Unhappy about his abstention from military service, he vowed that if drafted he would not hire a substitute. Reflecting on the battle death of Charles Russell Lowell and the military ordeals of his cousin Theodore Lyman, he concluded, "Studying chemistry is all very well, in common times, even though one does not know how or where or when one will be able to make it of some use to his fellow men, but in these days a nobler work calls devoted laborers." It was small consolation to take part in the organization of a Paris branch of the United States Sanitary Commission.[71]

Eliot saw the war as a vindication of republican government and American liberties. He defended expansion of government activities and even condoned the concomitant rise in corruption. These were necessary evils accompanying a great good. Proud of Harvard men's roles in the war, he wanted his cousin Theodore, returning after serving as a colonel, to go at once into politics. But he did not imagine that all the nation's future leaders would come from his own social class. He saw Lincoln as a prophetic figure, a model public servant, living proof that out of simple people leaders could emerge. In his memory the Civil War remained a "revelation of the nation's capacities." [72]

Quite aside from the war, his experiences in Europe made him feel more intensely American. "The sight of the burdens and suffering of these old nations makes me long to do something to confirm and strengthen our liberty at home." With supererogatory ideological statements in letters home, he articulated the axioms of American democratic liberalism. America differed from all previous republics by embracing principles of religious liberty and popular education. America gave its people freedom, which "makes men think for themselves, and thinking is living." With the solid bourgeois values that had established his grandfathers' fortunes, Eliot hoped the war debt could be paid off within twenty-two years. That would teach the world "the true relations of universal suffrage and national credit." [73]

In his national comparisons, stimulated by the lectures in Paris of the political theorist Laboulaye, Eliot's sense of America's strength was chastened by a heightened consciousness of its inadequacies. Americans, he decided, were "altogether too well satisfied with their system of Public Instruction." The merits of their lower schools were not equaled in higher education, in special and applied teaching, or in adult education. Economically, Americans were too prone to rely on "the fruits of mere muscle or of a virgin soil"; they could learn much from the French, who exported "productions of skilled labor, taste, and science." The increasing American importation of manufactured goods he found humiliating. "American inferiority in the technic arts," he wrote a cousin, "is not an accident or an exception but a necessary result of the present stage of our Republican institutions. Science, whether pure or applied, is not yet naturalized in the United States—we have not the institutions which Europe has obtained through the patronage which Kings and absolute governments have bestowed for centuries upon the arts." He forecast an "equivalent, but republican, method," yet wondered if it could emerge in his generation.[74]

Although he recognized disadvantages which equalitarian society imposed on the life of the mind, Eliot remained ambivalent about European learning. Too often it flourished "in seclusion and quiet, apart from the strifes which are the price of liberty." "The duties of an American citizen," he observed, "—voting, attending political meetings, serving on school-committees etc. —interfere with such exclusive devotion to Science as that of my friend Dr. [Emil] Erlenmeyer." But this Heidelberg professor knew "Chemistry and nothing else," and Eliot could not approve of his ignorance of contemporary social problems.[75]

Insulation from public responsibilities was not the only cause Eliot found for the scientific achievements of German professors. Unlike their American counterparts, the Germans were not devoured by pedagogical routine or burdened with supervision of student behavior. Eliot stopped short of the position of Henry Philip Tappan, who, in the 1850s, had hoped to model the University of Michigan directly on German universities. Instead, Eliot advocated selective importation of German ways. American college students were too young for the freedom the German university allowed, he concluded, and they did not have the sustaining motivation provided by German professional examinations. In an exchange of letters, Eliot found Asa Gray agreeing with him that features of the German university, rather than the full system, should be copied. In regard to the comparative unproductiveness of Americans in pure science, which Eliot noted, Gray explained his own predicament. He was tied down to irksome elementary teaching and lacked time to form and publish generalizations from his vast botanical collections. Yet precisely because the teaching was rudimentary, he had failed to train anyone to take his place.[76]

In May 1865, toward the end of Eliot's stay in Europe, he was involved in an episode which was so often recounted in later years by him and his admirers that one suspects mythic significance. He was offered the superintendency of the Merrimack Mills, a leading textile company in Lowell, Massachusetts, at twice a professor's salary. He felt competent for the position and knew of no other with which he could support himself on his impending return home. Yet after several days' consideration he declined, declaring that he would stay with his chosen profession of education.[77] The symbolic meaning was evoked by Eliot soon after he announced his decision: "Beyond a competency such as I have heretofore had, I have no desire to be rich, and if I were obliged to turn to money making as a profession, I should feel that I had exchanged a direct usefulness for an indirect one." The change in profession would not be "manly." Here spoke the transcendent Yankee, who performs the noblest of sacrifices—turning down money.[78]

The actual occurrence was a good deal more ambiguous. Eliot first knew of the offer only indirectly, through his mother. His original response was that if an immediate answer were required she should say yes. But he looked on Lowell, for all its industrial innovation, as "a *one-horse* place." He soon learned that the position would neither allow leisure to pursue chemical studies nor draw on the chemistry he already knew. From the beginning it troubled him to think of sacrificing the eleven years he had "invested" in his profession. Noting that the offer itself improved his general prospects, however, he directed his mother not to make a secret of it.[79]

Within seven weeks of his negative decision, a different offer arrived, inviting him to remain in his chosen profession and to pursue it in his native city. William B. Rogers, president of the Massachusetts Institute of Technology, wanted Eliot to accept a professorship of chemistry when the school opened that fall. Rogers, one of those accomplished general scientists who matured before the age of specialization, had been faculty chairman at the University of Virginia. In 1853, attracted by the city's cultural and scientific life, he had moved to Boston. There he married into established society and became a leader in the area's scientific organizations. Since the mid-1840s Rogers had been arguing the benefits of polytechnical education and the suitability of Boston as a site for a school, and in 1861 he had obtained a charter for the Massachusetts Institute of Technology.[80] With Yankee practicalism vindicated by the display of industrial prowess during the war and immense possibilities of industrial development glimpsed ahead, the year 1865 seemed ideal to open such a school, and the necessary funds had gradually been obtained. The Massachusetts legislature voted it land in newly filled Back Bay and assigned it three-tenths of the state's land-grant aid under the Morrill Act. Three state officers were placed on the Board of Governors *ex officiis*. But Rogers assured Eliot, who asked about the school's financial prospects and independence, "Of assistance from the State further than already given we make no calculations, nor should we desire it if accompanied by legislative control and political management." In fact, M.I.T., like many nineteenth-century American enterprises, represented a blending of public and private support. The legislature had granted the charter only after promises of private donations had been made. A timely bequest from William J. Walker, an alienated Harvard alumnus, and indirect support from the Lowell Institute, would allow the new school to open in 1865 with a faculty of ten at salaries equivalent to those of Harvard.[81]

Relations between the infant technological school and the institution in Cambridge were problematic. In the early stages of planning Rogers had barred a proposal for merger, and he had outmaneuvered Harvard interests in getting the Morrill funds. Rogers feared Harvard's absorption of the new school partly because he had seen the halting progress at Lawrence in providing technical training. As a member of the school's visiting committee, he had been an ally of Eliot's in the vain effort to broaden the training of S.B. candidates.[82]

But Eliot, whose attachment to Harvard remained strong, did not despair of the future of the applied sciences there. He hesitated to accept Rogers's offer, hoping that he might be wanted at Harvard for one of the new Hooper professorships in geology and mining. He also queried John A. Lowell, a leader on the governing boards of both Harvard and M.I.T., about the dangers of the new institution's injuring Lawrence. Lowell assured him that the potential competition promised to be healthful. Besides, he observed, the new venture was "designed for a class of students who rarely find their way to Cambridge." From Eliot's friend Ephraim Gurney, assistant professor of Latin at Harvard, came similar evaluations, approving the new school, but implicitly claiming Harvard's superiority. The Institute, far from lacking support, Gurney declared, was the darling of Boston, and it promised to be fruitfully experimental. But even as he tempted Eliot with the idea that he might succeed the ailing Rogers, Gurney held out the yet more tantalizing possibility of the presidency of Harvard; in fact, he vowed himself determined to see Eliot in that office.[83]

At M.I.T. Eliot would be assured of Rogers's good opinion and of the warmth of a restored collaboration with Storer, who had already joined the faculty. Not all the new professors, however, held a favorable view of Eliot. At informal faculty gatherings Storer heard distinctly unflattering comments about his friend. Some critics alleged a rigidity in teaching, others an obnoxious way of urging ideas; but most threatening was the talk of Eliot as a man with a lust for power, who probably imagined himself quickly replacing Rogers in the presidency. Storer strenuously combated such tales, and wrote to Eliot about them.

Receiving Storer's report just at the time he accepted Rogers's offer, Eliot wrote home that he would "be happy to be put on a shelf where friends need not overpraise me, nor antagonists attack my good fame." But there was nothing passive about his reaction. "I am well sick of being fought about—if there is to be fighting let me be one of the parties not their target." By September 1865 he was again in the thick of institutional labors, if not combat.[84]

With Eliot the professor of analytical chemistry and metallurgy and Storer the professor of general and industrial chemistry, the two friends set to work. Together they planned the chemical laboratories in the new Institute building, where they accepted both degree candidates and a wide variety of special students. Their teaching was decidedly laboratory-centered, for both were convinced that "chemistry can only be learned tools in hand." The professor should not perform experiments before a large class. Every student should be in the laboratory, learning what it was to see with his own eyes, record his experience, and draw inferences from it.[85] In this view, they were in full accord with the announced pedagogical theory of the Institute. "A high value is set upon the educational effect of laboratory practice," announced the first catalogue, "in the belief that such practice trains the senses to observe with accuracy, and the judgment to rely with confidence on the proof of actual experiment." In this dedication to the development of young empiricists, the Institute embraced a variant of the theory of mental training. But it proposed to inform as well as train, and the information supplied was to be predominantly practical. Accordingly, the chemistry professors promised always to pay special attention "to the description of those substances and processes which are of importance in common life or in the useful arts." [86]

The two colleagues published no joint research (in fact Eliot published none during his M.I.T. years), but they produced a textbook of major influence—the landmark *Manual of Inorganic Chemistry* (1867). This book, in whose originality of temper Eliot took justifiable pride, discouraged memorization and presented no theories or definitions without concrete examples. Eliot the teacher was acutely sensitive to the level of student attainment. He had instituted a return to mathematical and chemical fundamentals at Lawrence; now in his new post he was willing to make directions for experiments "painfully minute," since a good laboratory manual met students at the point of their actual capabilities.[87]

Back in an arena of faculty debate, Eliot found discussions lively, even turbulent, as befitted an institution still in formation. The most important controversy concerned how single-minded the Institute should be in providing specialized professional training. Eliot joined those favoring required general education for degree candidates. Eliot and Storer's *bête noir* was John B. Henck, head of the civil engineering department, who argued for a narrow definition of the Institute as a professional school. In an early victory for Eliot, the faculty put his language into the first catalogue: "Up to the end of the second year, the studies are the same for all regular students; each thus obtaining such an acquaintance with the whole field of practical science as is needed for the further pursuit of the studies of the School, in any of its departments."[88] The degree programs at M.I.T. gave an even greater role to general education than Eliot's Lawrence proposal, for they required several studies—mostly outside the natural sciences—in the junior and senior years. The school originally scouted any role for the classical languages, but in 1868 it shifted its stand. It strongly recommended Latin as a preparatory study, and included classical schools as suitable preparatory institutions. Eliot, believing that Latin provided good mental training, and hoping to improve the quality of entering students, supported the change.[89]

In addition to serving on curricular committees, Eliot put his business skills to use, setting up a system of student bonding to guarantee against loss of books and laboratory apparatus. He also sat through a number of painful discussions of student misbehavior, many dealing with required military drill. In spite of early hopes that the Institute would escape collegiate disciplinary problems, the experience was an impressive reminder, which he scarcely needed, of a major stumbling-block for American scholarship. Disruptions in the chemistry laboratories were marked in 1867–68, when Storer took full charge while Eliot was absent on leave in Europe, trying to restore his wife's failing health. On Eliot's return, printed regulations for the chemistry laboratories were issued, and, though there were grumblings about long chemistry lessons, the disruptions subsided.[90]

IV

Even as a professor at a rival institution, Eliot retained a proprietorial concern for Harvard. In spite of his continuing certainty that Lawrence was a school on a false plan, he believed Harvard to be the best of the American colleges, and he praised the liberal temper of Cambridge. While still in Europe Eliot had heard that the college faculty was turning to reform. With a leaven of young men, and aggressive debating by Benjamin Peirce, it was successfully expanding the elective system. About President Hill, who stood with the reformers but lacked decisiveness, Eliot was understandably ambivalent.[91]

Hill's last annual report, that of 1868, was an impressive document, as Eliot doubtless realized. It recorded a variety of new beginnings and was informed by the vision of a great university. Though noting with satisfaction the enlarged choice of studies after the freshman year, Hill refused to dwell on collegiate matters, turning instead to the possibilities of Harvard's becoming "a university of a high order." He detailed the needs of the professional schools—including the recently created dental school and school of mining, the projected Bussey Institution (for agricultural science), and the Department of Ethnology and Archaeology (provided in the bequest of George Peabody). The report was revolutionary in the importance it attributed to resident graduates, a category of students officially recognized since the Ticknor reforms, but tolerated rather than nurtured. According to Hill, future graduate students would be ambitious "to advance science, rather than to receive knowledge and diffuse it," and they should be encouraged by a program of fellowships and a new higher degree. It was more important, he maintained, to provide teaching at the highest level of knowledge, even for two or three students, than to add large numbers to the learners from textbooks. In his program of University Lectures, Hill recommended provision for both nonresident lecturers of established reputation and young scholars eager to test their abilities. Harvard was the country's nearest approach to a true university, he argued, and support for it was the surest way to national achievement in higher education.[92]

Hill raised these aspirations in a time of general concern for American higher education. Reform hopes, frustrated in the 1850s, were reborn among certain college officers and alumni. Who knew what good might follow the Morrill land grants, especially at institutions like Cornell and M.I.T., where they were linked to large private philanthropy? The frontier ideology of equal opportunity seemed ready to transform the gentlemanly quietism of state universities. At Columbia College, President Frederick A. P. Barnard was arguing for less stringent control of student behavior. Women, farmers, and manufacturers were demanding new avenues of learning, while nationalists were urging creation of American universities so that ambitious students would not need to study abroad. A Baltimore merchant, Johns Hopkins, promised half his fortune to a new university, leaving its definition to its trustees, one of whom suggestively noted that the American educational structure was "a temple without a dome." Emerson caught the mood in a journal entry of 1867: "The treatises that are written on University reforms may be acute or not, but their chief value to the observer is the showing that a cleavage is occurring in the hitherto firm granite of the past and a new era is nearly arrived." [93]

Many reformist treatises were written by Harvard alumni. One of these, Jacob Bigelow, first holder of the Rumford chair and a vice-president of M.I.T., argued that mental training could come as effectively in useful subjects as in useless ones, and he linked Harvard's required Greek with England's system of special privilege. Frederic Henry Hedge, professor in the divinity school, addressing his fellow Harvard alumni in 1866, compared the attitude of their *alma mater* unfavorably with "the liberal scope and cosmopolitan outlook" of the University of Michigan. Picturing

Harvard as essentially a school for boys, where professors were "task-masters and police-officers," he called for an end to rigid control of students' intellectual development and behavior and suggested higher qualifications for admission.[94]

John Fiske, a recent Harvard graduate of positivistic bent, objected to the college's tendency to inculcate doctrine when it should be teaching intellectual method. He argued for a required minimum in each subject, then specialization, followed—for the more ambitious—by examinations equivalent to Oxford triposes. Also needed, Fiske observed, were a postgraduate course and a system of fellowships. Thomas Wentworth Higginson put much greater emphasis on the need for advanced study, recommending that the college shrink into a preparatory department. He deplored the failure of the scientific school to become what Everett had originally intended, a seat of advanced training in both science and literature. To concentrate solely on utilitarian concerns would leave the nation culturally provincial, he warned, insisting that though the community sought wealth, it was also prepared to respect literary culture and abstract science. Francis Parkman, who was concerned for the quality of government as much as of culture, called for "a class of strong thinkers" to elevate the country above mere money-making and rescue it from "social and political charlatanry." A "powerful re-enforcement of higher education" might counteract the dominant mediocrity and philistinism, Parkman argued, but scholars could not remedy social ills unless they forsook the reclusive ways of their academic predecessors.[95]

In the postwar years Harvard seemed especially susceptible to reformers' plans—it had just been released from legislative control. Alumni pressure in the right places and general respect for Harvard men's role in the war contributed to the passage of a new law in April 1865. The long-standing dispute over the makeup of the Board of Overseers was settled by an arrangement that made Harvard more distinctly a "private" institution. Public officials lost their *ex officiis* positions on the board, and the legislature surrendered its right to elect Overseers. That power was transferred in 1866 to alumni of the college (A.B.'s, A.M.'s, and honorary degree holders), who voted in person in Cambridge and who were restricted in their choice of candidates to men who were residents of Massachusetts.[96]

Freshened by the change in electorate, the Overseers early in 1867 established a committee to report on the needs of the college. After nearly two years of deliberation the committee, chaired by James Freeman Clarke, pastor of the liberal Church of the Disciples, and including Eliot's former mentor James Walker, produced a thorough rationale for reform. Facing the competition of "the vigorous technological schools everywhere springing up," Harvard must end mere routine and adopt "all the best practical methods of education, whether they have been customary or not." The already established elective system should be extended, inasmuch as it was the chief distinguishing characteristic of a university. The rise in the average age of entering students was an opportunity for lessened constraint, and the trend could be accelerated by assigning the studies of the freshman year to preparatory schools. The newly provided "honors" for graduating students properly encouraged ambition for distinction in a specialty. To promote graduate study, honorary and "in course" degrees should be abandoned. In the committee's vision of the future, the university would become a place of original investigation, its students mature and its professors scholars of high reputation. Heidelberg was a model of what a university should be. The committee was optimistic about public support for this ambitious venture. The Overseers themselves would keep the university in touch with the outside community, and the new learning would become public property for the benefit of all.[97]

Eliot won election to this new and confident Board of Overseers in 1868, along with such worthies as Francis Parkman and Ebenezer Rockwood Hoar. Although he attended meetings conscientiously and performed committee chores, it was not in the role of Harvard Overseer that Eliot made his main contribution to the flourishing discussion of higher education. During the fall of 1868, having returned from a year in Europe spent in a fruitless effort to check the tuberculosis that had turned his once-vibrant wife into an invalid, Eliot poured himself into writing "The New Education: Its Organization," a two-part article which appeared in the *Atlantic Monthly* early in 1869. Eliot had written a few brief reviews for the *Atlantic* and the *Nation* since 1865, but this undertaking was a major effort, which James T. Fields, the *Atlantic*'s editor, welcomed in spite of Eliot's self-depreciating suggestion that the subject was "not an entertaining one, besides being rather worn just now." In fact, Eliot's essay ranked high among those treatises whose prevalence Emerson had noted. Longer than most, it was both more factual and more argumentative. "The new education" promptly became a reform slogan. Although the presidency of Harvard fell vacant during the time Eliot was writing the article, it bore little resemblance to a campaign document. It was a defense of separate polytechnical schools, and its tone, as Eliot later put it, was "rather saucy." [98]

The article began by describing the perplexity of a father looking about for a "practical" education for his son, one that would suit the young man's nonliterary bent and open up for him the vast opportunities of a free, resource-laden country. Judging social experience a better guide than "still-born theories," Eliot identified "the new education" with recent attempts "to organize a system of education based chiefly upon the pure and applied sciences, the living European languages, and mathematics, instead of upon Greek, Latin, and mathematics, as in the established college system." He attempted to prove that a separate technical school, such as the Massachusetts Institute of Technology, was superior to a scientific school attached to a College (such as Lawrence Scientific School, of which he spoke so harshly as to bring a rejoinder from Wolcott Gibbs) or a parallel scientific course within a college (such as Union College had long offered, though with declining popularity, to judge from falling enrollment figures).[99] Although Eliot's central argument for segregating technical education was unconvincing, the article abounded in acute observations on the nature of American society and the problems of American education. The writer's biases were undisguised, and his argument tipped with epigram.

The ideal which Eliot raised for the American college was rigidly nonutilitarian. The college should be dominated by the ideas of "formation and information of the mind," broad culture, and "the love of learning and research for their own sake." This remarkable amalgam included the discipline-and-furniture rationale developed in the Yale Report of 1828, traditional humanism, and even the research ideal. But one thing the college was not: it was not practical or utilitarian. Eliot argued at one point as if the chief reason for separate technical schools was the preservation of the nonutilitarian college.

For both technical schools and colleges, Eliot's ideal curriculum combined an initial core of required studies with freedom in the later years for the student to choose a specialty. This avoided the "loose and exaggerated elective system," with which President Francis Wayland had supposedly brought Brown to grief. Eliot was surprisingly unconcerned about the elective principle. He appeared undisturbed by the possibility that within his chosen specialty a student might face a second prescribed program, as was generally the case at M.I.T. He defended the curriculum he had helped shape at the Institute as "neither loose, superficial, nor one-sided" and able to give as much mental discipline as the traditional college course.

The article began and ended with a discussion of the country's material development and the need for engineers, architects, chemists, and manufacturers. Throughout, Eliot revealed his certainty of American uniqueness. Such peculiarities as the labor shortage and the great territorial expanse rendered impractical the labor-intensive, relatively immobile industrial techniques taught in Europe.[100]

This conviction of American difference underlay a prophetic passage in which Eliot looked above both the college and technical school to "the American university," which he argued had not yet appeared. Its essential characteristics would be provision for teaching on a high plane and of great variety. In fact, in "a real university" the practical and liberal subjects could exist together without danger to each other. The closest America had come to such a university, Eliot believed, was at Yale, where the Department of Philosophy and the Arts (which, in spite of broader aspirations, consisted chiefly of the scientific school) offered an "unpretentious but genuine" program to "a few real students" and where a new degree for America, the Ph.D., had been given thirteeen times since 1861. Noting the recent loss of status by the professions, Eliot suggested a partial remedy in the elevation of professional training to the postgraduate level, and he suggested that such a pattern also might characterize the American university.[101]

The animus with which Eliot in "The New Education" referred to clergymen who took college presidencies and thus robbed "the profession of education . . . of its few prizes" suggested that he thought of himself as an academic president—some time, somewhere. But in later recollection he was to maintain that he had not foreseen himself as president of Harvard University in 1869.[102]

From College to University

Universities have three principal, direct functions. In the first place, they teach; secondly, they accumulate great stores of acquired and systematized knowledge in the form of books and collections; thirdly, they investigate, or, in other words, they seek to push out a little beyond the present limits of knowledge, and learn, year after year, day after day, some new truth.

CHARLES W. ELIOT (1891) [1]

I

Rarely in Harvard history had so much been at stake in the selection of a president. The Overseers, when informed officially that President Hill had resigned on September 30, 1868, withheld immediate permission for the election of a successor and drew the Corporation into a joint investigation of the duties of the office. It was generally agreed that a new position under the president —such as a deanship—was needed to relieve him of routine duties. The next president, accordingly, could expect greater freedom of action than his predecessors had had, for they had been hampered by such persistent distractions as student discipline.[2]

The proposed redesigning of the presidential office was least significant to those supporting the candidacy of the acting president, Andrew Preston Peabody, Preacher to the University and Plummer Professor of Christian Morals. A Unitarian clergyman, Peabody was expected to guarantee a religious spirit at Harvard. He had already shown an ability to win the affection of undergraduates and an eagerness to play the paternal role. In fact, Peabody found the presidential duties not overburdensome, and he proposed to continue teaching if elected. The professional schools, he believed, were in good condition and should simply be let alone.

To academic reformers Peabody's candidacy appeared menacingly reactionary. During the winter an anonymous anti-Peabody campaign enlivened the press. Liberal journalists like E. L. Godkin, editor of the *Nation*, even if they were not Harvard men, sought to influence the outcome of the crisis. Readers were warned that the success at Harvard of the "higher view," which was faring so well in Ithaca and Ann Arbor, required the defeat of a backward-looking minority that hoped to capture the presidency. Indeed, the *Nation* suggested ruling out any clergyman who had graduated more than twenty-five years earlier, a formula tailored to exclude Peabody.[3]

Some of the barbs against candidates of advanced age may have been directed at Charles Francis Adams, recently returned from his brilliant ambassadorship to Great Britain. Adams was a national hero, but he was sixty-one years old. The Corporation offered him the presidency informally—perhaps reflecting that Harvard could use the skills of a diplomat—but he promptly refused.

Then, early in March 1869, the Corporation decided to nominate Eliot, to the surprise of many. The discussion at once grew acrimonious, though the candidate himself described it as "courteous and edifying." Eliot obviously did not fit the ministerial, paternal ideal. In fact, there was suspicion that his theological liberalism verged on skepticism, since he was not among those scientists who dwelt on Nature's revelations of God's purpose. But apart from religion, did his scientific background not make him a threat to the classics, and were not his technological concerns directly opposed to liberal education? Those asking such questions preferred some young reformer from among the humanists, a man like Ephraim Gurney, who (though himself a supporter of Eliot) was the model for the qualities recommended by the *Nation*.[4]

Many Harvard scientists were no friendlier to Eliot's candidacy than the worried humanists were. They judged him by standards of original investigation, and found him wanting. Did he, they wondered, really grasp the ideals of pure science? Especially among scientists, Eliot's attention to general education and his textbook writing raised the objection (echoing criticisms made during the Rumford controversy in 1863) that he was a "College" rather than a "University" man.

There were more personal objections. Recollections of his officious manner as a Harvard faculty member were only partly assuaged by reports that his wife's illness and her death, which coincided with his nomination, had softened him. Other grounds for opposition were his youth, and his family connections which seemed to some suspiciously "aristocratic" and to others a wire-pulling "machine." [5]

In the New England tradition of plain-speaking, many opponents told Eliot their views, and Eliot himself agreed with those who pointed to Gurney's appropriateness for the office. But two other Overseers, Theodore Lyman, Eliot's cousin and confidant, and James Walker, the former president, assured him that his doubts about his own suitability were groundless. Lyman's view of Eliot's capacity for the task ahead, as well as his limitations, was prophetic. "He will succeed and will advance the college, by his firmness, indomitable labor, entire method, and by his justice. Popular he will be only moderately; for his is a cold disposition, save to intimates. At times he will lack breadth, but will make up in intensity." [6]

What had made the Corporation decide to nominate Eliot? Younger than any man who had ever become president of Harvard, the thirty-five-year-old chemist had been judged unworthy of the Rumford chair only six years before, and then he had been allowed to leave the university. But this was a different position, one calling for distinctly administrative talents which no one doubted that Eliot possessed. Two members of the Corporation, John A. Lowell and Francis B. Crowninshield, had been instrumental in offering him the superintendency of the Merrimack Mills. His refusal had shown them how determined he was to apply his talents in the field of education. Lowell, a vice-president of M.I.T., had seen the young chemist's effectiveness there. Eliot's loyalty to Harvard now had the valuable counterweight of a look at its inadequacies from the outside, and his election as Overseer indicated respect for him among alumni. "How *could* those old gentlemen have done so good a thing as this!" one young alumnus wrote in his diary upon hearing the news.

Although some of Eliot's fellow Overseers were immediately favorable to his selection, one group remained determined to have Professor Peabody as president in order to preserve collegiate values, and others simply could not imagine a president of Harvard with Eliot's abrasive personality. By a narrow vote the Board on April 21 returned the nomination to the Corporation. In 1862 this same strategy had failed to prevent the election of President Hill, and this time also the Corporation firmly laid its nomination before the Overseers again, persisting in the belief that Charles William Eliot's election was in "the best interests of the University." Meanwhile, Walker, who knew intimately both Eliot and the nature of the presidential office, took the lead in changing the Overseers' minds. On May 19, 1869, the Board concurred in Eliot's election, by a vote of sixteen to eight. His presidential activities began at once.[7]

The inauguration, held on October 19, 1869, was traditional in its ceremony: a hierarchical procession into the First Parish Church that lasted half an hour; a Latin salutatory by a senior; a Latin song by the chorus; prayers; and a long address of installation by former Whig Governor John Henry Clifford, president of the Overseers, who handed Eliot the seal, keys, and charter. But Eliot's inaugural address itself was not traditional: in it he foretold change and experiment. He called for a broadened curriculum, reformed teaching methods, higher standards, and attention to individual differences. Both rich and poor students were to be sought, and women's admission to the advanced University Courses was presented as a promising innovation. His opening sentences struck through a tangle of academic antagonisms to a confident prediction of their solution:

The endless controversies whether language, philosophy, mathematics, or science supplies the best mental training, whether general education should be chiefly literary or chiefly scientific, have no practical lesson for us to-day. This University recognizes no real antagonism between literature and science, and consents to no such narrow alternatives as mathematics or classics, science or metaphysics. We would have them all, and at their best.

This challenge set the tone for the entire address. The audience alternated between hushed attention and strong applause. People left the church with a conviction succinctly expressed by John Fiske, "We are going to have new times here at Harvard." [8]

Accession to office in 1869 placed Eliot among a group of young university presidents who were destined to be cast as heroes in the classic accounts of the transformation of American higher education. An array of small colleges was developing into a more coherent system that extended upward to more inclusive and advanced universities. In 1868 Andrew Dickson White had delivered his inaugural address at newly opened Cornell University, urging close union between liberal and practical instruction and resistance to any denominational controls. At the University of Michigan the installation of James Burrill Angell in 1871 brought to office a man who successfully attracted the pride— and the tax dollars—of the state to an institution viewed as the apex of its educational system. In 1876 Daniel Coit Gilman presided over the opening of a new private foundation, the Johns Hopkins University, directed toward research and the teaching of advanced students. It was not in isolation, but among such leaders as these that Eliot sought to fulfill the aspirations voiced in the late 1860s for the creation of American universities.

II

Ironically, the resistance within the Harvard community to Eliot's election strengthened his hand as president. By refusing to withdraw his name, the Corporation deepened its commitment to educational experiment and executive vigor. None of the Fellows who had elected Eliot—all old enough to be his father —left office during the first six years of his term. To a complaining faculty member, they might at times soothingly grant the wisdom of "Festina lente," but Eliot's recollection was of their unswerving support. Indeed, at the end of Eliot's first meeting with the Fellows after his election, when he said that he had no further business, every member hurried out, delighted at the order and control demonstrated by the young man in whom they had placed their faith.[9] It was a standing joke around Harvard that when Eliot referred to something as necessitated by the will of the Corporation, it was his own will that was in fact operating. One satirist in the lively tradition of Harvard light verse painted an Eliot protesting, "We are seven," in spite of the fact that "six of them are never here." The Overseers were another matter. Though they too felt the fresh wind and were startled by special meetings called at Eliot's instigation, they tended to dig in their heels. By 1872 Eliot was gently mocking them as "Her Majesty's opposition." [10]

Eliot had imagined the ideal president for a new polytechnical school as one who gave "steady, careful, and kindly administration," but who was aggressive enough to make the school largely his own creation. The differences between heading a new institution and directing the oldest university in the land were considerable. But Eliot did not hesitate before traditions which he believed needed altering. Observers quickly noted his penchant for the new, his industry, and his commanding presence. Oliver Wendell Holmes of the medical school, who at first felt that the Corporation would need to restrain Eliot, was soon heaping praise on the young leader who, "with an organizing brain, a firm will, a grave, calm, dignified presence," took to his new duties "as naturally as if he had been born President." Outside the university, E. L. Godkin, hearing Eliot's first address to New York alumni, also chose the phrase "born president" to describe Eliot's self-confidence. His first annual report was praised by the

Independent for "the spirit, the energy, the *élan*, the youth in the blood which it exhibits." [11]

The new head of Harvard defied easy classification as either an "inside" or "outside" president. Clearly Eliot was not the old-style insider; he did not teach or preach, and he delegated student discipline to the dean. Perhaps the young president is best described as an insider who attended to structure more than to persons. A reviewer of his second annual report objected that amid the accounts of organizational and financial gains one caught not a glimpse of "the mental, moral, and physical condition of the young men." Students did not expect to know him, and young John Jay Chapman would mischievously shake his hand when they passed, in the belief that such human contact pained the president. Barrett Wendell of the faculty complained that a plan for change could catch Eliot's attention, but simply to do one's best was to be ignored. Apparently Eliot had little gift for personal gestures of encouragement. Toward such "inside" matters as buildings, curricular extension, and creation of committees, however, he directed steady and effective attention. His inaugural address revealed his willingness to import into education the rationalizing practices of other institutions: "The principle of divided and subordinate responsibilities, which rules in government bureaus, in manufactories, and all great companies, which makes a modern army a possibility, must be applied in the University." The Corporation's appointment of Gurney to the new deanship of Harvard College and Eliot's insistence that each professional school have a dean were early examples of this practice. Even to Bliss Perry, who arrived on the faculty late in Eliot's tenure, he appeared "primarily an organizer and administrator, with an imperial grasp of fact." [12]

Only for his first dozen years in office, however, was Eliot conspicuously an "inside" president; thereafter he turned increasingly to the world beyond the university, first in the field of education, then more widely. By the time of his retirement he was distinctly a national figure. The internal transformation itself pushed Eliot beyond the university because the new-modeled institution required interpretation and defense before the American people. As he nurtured the university, he grew to be as keen in predicting business trends as the ablest stock market speculator and as shrewd about power relationships within government as an elder politician. After first depaternalizing the presidential office and making it a rationalized superintendency of a complex organization, Eliot proceeded to transform it further, making it, in George Herbert Palmer's phrase, the post of Foreign Secretary. A president of Yale summed up Eliot's achievement in this "outside" role: "To him more than any other man . . . America owes it that her system of higher education is no longer a thing apart by itself, a sort of 'Ark of the Covenant' too sacred to be touched, but a normal part of the life of the nation as a whole." [13]

III

Eliot's career as a university president was almost coterminous with a period of peculiar openness in American higher education. In that era, an educator's definition of "university" could not be taken for granted. Although Eliot at times spoke of a "real" or "true" university, his language was usually nominalist. His thought owed little to Plato, much to Jeremy Bentham, Herbert Spencer, and Charles Darwin. Partly because of his empirical habit of mind, partly because the concrete example of Harvard was so much a part of his life, he never embraced the romantic university ideals which imbued many American educators. Even the metaphors of his early report from the University of Marburg were folksy and deflating: "A German University would suit the 150 young men who enter Freshman [at Harvard] every year, about as well as a barn-yard would suit a whale." Probably the most striking passage he ever wrote on the problem of creating American universities appeared in his *Atlantic Monthly* article, "The New Education," in 1869:

> The American university has not yet grown out of the soil.
> . . . A university, in any worthy sense of the term, must grow

from seed. It cannot be transplanted from England or Germany in full leaf and bearing. It cannot be run up, like a cotton-mill, in six months, to meet a quick demand. Neither can it be created by an energetic use of the inspired editorial, the advertising circular, and the frequent telegram. Numbers do not constitute it, and no money can make it before its time. . . . When the American university appears, it will not be a copy of foreign institutions, or a hot-bed plant, but the slow and natural outgrowth of American social and political habits, and an expression of the average aims and ambitions of the better educated classes. The American college is an institution without a parallel; the American university will be equally original.

He could hardly have made it clearer that for him there was no pre-established model in Europe. A worthy university suited its social environment.[14]

Yet a generic definition was implicit in Eliot's many discussions of universities. A university to him was an inclusive, elevated teaching institution, which also preserved and increased knowledge. "No subject of human inquiry," he said before his election to Harvard's presidency, "can be out of place in the programme of a real university," and he later cited with approval Ezra Cornell's dictum: "I would found an institution in which any one may study anything." But Eliot qualified the comprehensiveness of a university by specifying an advanced level of learning. "Every subject should be taught at the university on a higher plane than elsewhere." The instruction in Yale's unique Ph.D. program represented "a really high level" to Eliot in 1869, and to better deserve the name "university," American institutions of higher education should follow that example.[15]

To the professorial mind, especially among natural scientists, research was becoming the *sine qua non* of a university. In contrast, as if forgetting the importance he had once ascribed to original work, Eliot often seemed to see the faculty exclusively as a teaching body, and he was surprisingly slow to develop institutional devices to promote research. Yet that function appeared at least rhetorically in his early presidential statements on the university, for instance in 1872: "The University does not forget that it must do more than teach,—that it must learn, that it must explore as well as guide, and enlarge knowledge as well as diffuse it." Much later, in a letter of 1895, he called universities "teachers, store-houses, and searchers for truth," noting that the last was "quite as important as either of the other two." [16]

Whatever definitions university leaders carried in their heads in the late nineteenth century, the most characteristic change in the design of American higher education during their day was the appearance of "the graduate school," a program that encouraged the pursuit of liberal studies beyond the baccalaureate course. Inclusion of such a program was made the defining requirement for admission to the American Association of Universities when it appeared in 1900. To imply that Eliot looked on the advancement of such studies as the essential change at Harvard would misrepresent his multiform, developmental approach to university reform. Yet from the first year of his presidency Eliot sought to promote graduate work.

Harvard already invited graduates of other colleges to become "resident graduates," although only Harvard alumni could take a second degree in arts (the A.M.), and that did not require residence, but only good character, the passage of three years' time after the bachelor's, and the payment of a five dollar fee. One of Eliot's first actions as president was to schedule the termination of this degree procedure. He had recently deplored the failure of the Lawrence Scientific School to persevere in its original goal of postgraduate teaching (although he admitted that for some the S.B. constituted a second earned degree). He found evidence of "a small but steady demand" for instruction that was "higher than that of the ordinary college course, and yet different from that of the law, medical, and theological schools." Students were going abroad for such study since they could not find it at home.[17]

Eliot hoped to develop this aspect of university education through the University Lectures, begun in 1863 under President Hill. These miscellaneous lectures, open to the general public whose fees were the lecturers' only remuneration, offered little contrast to the public series of the Lowell Institute. Within a month after his election Eliot was seeking to raise the standards of this program. Labeling the venture an experiment, he invited some professors at Yale to join scholars in the Boston area to "teach their best to a few," with a guaranteed remuneration. In 1869–70, under this plan, Harvard offered, in addition to old-style University Lectures, two "University Courses of Instruction" for "graduates, teachers, and other competent persons (men and women)." Above all else, Eliot emphasized the advanced level. These were not to be lectures of the lyceum style, and undergraduates were not to attend.

In the University Courses of 1869–70 there were two series of lectures, one in philosophy and one in modern literature. Distinguished scholars gave several lectures each: visiting Yale professors spoke in both series, as did such non-faculty intellectuals as Emerson, Charles Sanders Peirce, and William Dean Howells. The fee was $150, examinations were given, and "honors" promised. Although the lectures were moved to Boston, the attendance was so small that the project was not repeated, and 1870–71 saw only many short courses with small fees. Eliot openly admitted the failure of his experiment. It neither kept Harvard graduates in Cambridge for systematic study nor attracted students from elsewhere. For the "profound, continuous, and systematic teaching" desired by advanced students, the university must rely on "resident, paid, professional teachers." [18]

Eliot and his associates now shifted ground radically. In January 1872 they established the "Graduate Department," which was to give earned degrees of A.M., Ph.D., and S.D. Nominally under the guidance of the "Academic Council" (all professors and assistant professors in all faculties), the department's real leader was the Secretary of the Academic Council, James Mills Peirce, once Eliot's fellow tutor and now University Professor of Mathematics. The new arrangement, Eliot told alumni, gave the "organization and definite goals" that the nonprofessional postgraduate instruction had previously lacked. After 1872, the "in course" master's was not given, and in 1873 the first doctorates—two Ph.D.s and one S.D.—were granted. To enhance the new degrees, no honoraries were given that year.[19]

Although the graduate department shared much of the nonutilitarian ethos which Eliot had envisioned for the college in 1869, he increasingly referred to advanced liberal studies as "professional." Such studies, after all, served as preparation for secondary school teachers and college professors, and both groups were increasingly claiming status as professionals. In 1872 Eliot described the new graduate work as having "a distinct pecuniary value" to those proposing to be teachers. The scholar, he ultimately claimed, was no longer "an accidental product," but "a well-equipped professional man, systematically produced in and for the higher institutions of education." [20]

Partly because the president's deepest concerns lay elsewhere, the program for advanced study in the arts and sciences remained underorganized. One incubus was the occasional implication that a student simply remained as a graduate to take electives that he had not been able to crowd into his undergraduate course. This discouraged students who felt the A.B. should mark a distinct change in the nature of study. Nor was there much success in attracting non-Harvard graduates. In the program's first year, twenty of twenty-three graduates taking courses held Harvard bachelor's degrees, and only fifteen were candidates for a degree. "We sometimes had to shut our eyes very close to the obvious fact that many of our graduates were below many of our best undergraduates in scholarship," William Watson Goodwin recalled. No separate courses for graduates were at first organized. They simply took more electives and did a great deal of private reading with the occasional help of a faculty member. The university's first Ph.D. in English (1876) recalled, "To all intents I taught myself," but he found that he could work with pleasure and enthusiasm.[21]

The years 1888–90 were another period of self-criticism and reorganization for Eliot and others concerned with the graduate program. This was caused partly by comparisons with the flourishing graduate work at Johns Hopkins. In 1888, when Eliot himself raised the question at a faculty meeting, he touched off a barrage of faculty complaints about the program. Edward Channing was among those who were dissatisfied: "With our great resources in teachers, money and 'plant' we should draw graduate students from all parts of the country. We do not and that one fact, to my mind, shows that something is wrong with our system of instruction, our organization, or both. I believe the last to be the case." Part of the trouble was that Hopkins had a generous fellowship program, whereas Harvard, with fewer grants, usually limited them to its own alumni, insisted on need, and often encouraged their use for study abroad. Eliot had long argued for financial need as a prerequisite for fellowships, and he continued to oppose "the business of hiring students to pursue advanced studies." [22] Another persistent problem was Eliot's conception of the college itself as the locus of "university" studies. Partly because of the age of American undergraduates (only slightly under that of German university students), he contended that much of their study should be of an advanced nature and not significantly different from work leading to post-baccalaureate degrees in arts and sciences. To the immense disadvantage of Harvard's graduate department, Eliot tended to overlook the differentiating training in research that properly characterized graduate education. His own research interests had developed independently of any graduate work, through a special relationship with a teacher while he was an undergraduate, through financial ability to pursue his scientific interests, and through comradely work with Storer.

Under the plan of 1890, the "Graduate Department" became the "Graduate School" with a dean and administrative board of its own, operating under the newly created Faculty of Arts and Sciences (which combined the Harvard College and Lawrence faculties). Courses were now categorized as "Primarily for Undergraduates," "For Graduates and Undergraduates," and "Primarily for Graduates." The last gave a previously lacking prestige to research, some items in this category being additionally labeled "Courses of Research." With new concern for graduate work within the departments and an increase in fellowships, the number of advanced students began to grow. By 1900 the number of doctorates granted exceeded that at Johns Hopkins for the first time since 1878, but not until 1904 were more than half the graduate students products of other colleges.[23]

When the academic world thought of Eliot's Harvard, it thought first not of graduate studies, but of the elective system at the collegiate level. It was symptomatic that a faculty member, advocating the privat-docent system in 1894, argued the need "to make the Graduate School something higher than an appendix of the College, controlled by the College spirit." [24] Eliot bluntly declared in 1904 that "neither the serviceableness nor the prestige of the University is determined by the work of the Graduate School in Arts and Sciences." Some allowance should be made in this case for exaggeration springing from Eliot's laudable desire to widen the membership in the American Association of Universities by permitting admission of differently structured institutions. The statement showed, nevertheless, that at least in the university's external relations Eliot believed the graduate program to be of subordinate value.[25]

IV

The aspect of Harvard to which Eliot turned his most persistent attention during the first half-dozen years of his presidency was the quality of the established professional schools. Observing the superior quality achieved by European professional education, he had become convinced that America's professional elites were suffering from the inroads of a misdirected equalitarianism. In a long footnote in "The New Education," beginning, "The term 'learned profession' is getting to have a sarcastic flavor," Eliot had detailed the inadequacies of the training given lawyers, physicians, and ministers in "the hastily organized, fast-growing American communities." Citing the laxness of such controls as the bar examination and ordination, he had concluded that universities must become the principal guarantors of professional standards.

This view fitted the distinction Eliot had drawn, in his inaugural address, between liberal studies and those that were "professional or utilitarian." He had criticized the University of Michigan for having so few holders of preliminary degrees in its law and medical schools, but he knew that conditions at Harvard were not much better.[26] To elevate the three main professional schools until they all required a bachelor's degree for admission as a degree candidate was a goal attained first in the divinity school and finally, in 1901, in the medical school. The new standard served several purposes: it provided society with better-educated practitioners than before, it strengthened the colleges by channeling through them those who planned to enter the professions, and it provided an institutional rationality agreeable to Eliot's orderly mind. The admission changes at the professional schools proved one of the hardest of Harvard reforms to export. In a debate of 1885 with President James McCosh of Princeton, Eliot found his counterpart blandly equating law, medicine, and liberal arts as three departments among which an entering student might choose. In 1902 such university leaders as Arthur Twining Hadley of Yale and William Rainey Harper of Chicago were still arguing that less than the full bachelor's course was enough preparation for professional school.[27]

The drive to raise professional school standards was the most personal of Eliot's early reforms. It was not, like electivism, a movement already underway before he took office. For many years Harvard presidents had not troubled to call meetings of the professional faculties or to attend them. In a rare word of censure for the Fellows of 1869 Eliot once recalled that they had not seen the importance of professional education to the university as a whole. Besides urging higher admission standards, Eliot sought higher graduation standards at the schools: improvements on the three years of residence without examination at the divinity school, three terms (eighteen months) without examination at the law school, and two terms with lenient oral examinations (plus a certificate of three months' work with a practitioner) at the medical school. Besides raising such standards, Eliot insisted on graded curriculums to replace the merry-go-round system, in which there were no beginning courses, simply a cycle of lectures which students entered at the beginning of any semester. These changes threatened to repel prospective students, but Eliot called for the reforms "at whatever sacrifice," certain that higher quality would ultimately attract students.[28]

In seeking improvement in teaching methods at the professional schools, Eliot knew better what he was against than what he favored. For him the vision of the yellowed manuscript from which Dr. Jacob Bigelow of the medical school lectured year after year symbolized the status quo. Even the "catechetical method," Eliot judged, would be an improvement. At least it interrupted "the flow of dull reading which came from the professor's mouth." In time, clinical, laboratory, and case methods developed, well suited to Eliot's empirical spirit and his activist learning theory.[29]

The new deanships which Eliot required at each professional school were at first underestimated, and this was to his advantage. Dr. Henry J. Bigelow, long the chief power at the medical school, tapped the underrated Calvin Ellis for the deanship, thus giving Eliot an able ally in a strategic position. At the law school, the two senior members made the newcomer Christopher Columbus Langdell dean, as Eliot had secretly hoped they would. At the divinity school, the post went to Oliver Stearns, a doctrinal moderate whose main concern was the advancement of theological scholarship.[30]

In the medical faculty, Henry Bigelow, for all his earlier friendship with Eliot, was determined to preserve his de facto control and the relative financial prosperity the school had already attained. Holmes sided with him in the early encounters with Eliot, who called medical faculty meetings and presided at them. The discussions were vivid, Eliot recalled; they "more closely approached a fight than anything else to which I have been a party in the University." At times "mercenary, cynical and selfish" objections were raised. How was it, Bigelow asked one evening, "that this Faculty has gone on for eighty years managing its own affairs and doing it well,— . . . and now, within *three or four months*, it is proposed to change all our modes of carrying on the School . . . ?" Eliot's bland reply has been immortalized in academic lore: "I can answer Dr. Bigelow's question very easily: there is a new President." About the time of this exchange, Holmes confided to the new leader that he was getting out from under Bigelow's thumb. By the fall of 1871 changes had been made all along the line. The medical program consisted of a three-year course, arranged progressively and systematically. All subjects must be passed in order to attain the M.D. Tuition was raised, the school's finances were placed under the control of the Corporation, and the faculty went off the fee system and onto salary. The autopsies and clinical work which ambitious students had earlier undertaken quite apart from the medical school course became a standard part of work toward the degree. Similar elevation of standards and rationalization of structure occurred, though less dramatically, at the other professional schools.[31]

V

Although the college faculty of 1869 included some pedants and drillmasters, it was on the whole a distinguished company, including Benjamin Peirce, Asa Gray, Francis James Child, and James Russell Lowell. Partly to free such scholars for advanced teaching, partly to represent new fields of learning, Eliot pressed for new faculty. His inaugural plea for outside examiners implied, moreover, that the faculty might require enlightenment on the question of standards.

It was not blind materialism to conclude that more money could improve the situation. In Eliot's first year the salaries of professors were raised from $3000 to $4000, utilizing new endowments and newly increased tuition. Eliot hired additional tutors and assistant professors, and although hidebound professors complained that this was dilution of the faculty, Eliot recalled with pleasure that James Russell Lowell was "no longer called upon for elementary or routine work." In the new professorial appointments made during the first three years, the most conspicuous areas of growth were applied sciences, modern languages, and medicine. In addition, there were new appointments in law and theology.[32]

In choosing the new faculty, the old faculty had almost no power, although there was some consultation, especially with those personally close to Eliot or the Fellows. The Yale and Cornell faculties had a greater role in selecting their associates, as Harvard men were aware. Consultation increased over the years, approval of the professors in the affected department usually being obtained, but the nominating power always remained with Eliot. "There have been cases at Harvard," one faculty member observed, "where Mr. Eliot has appointed professors from outside without the advice or consent of the departments, much to the good of the department in question." [33]

It became increasingly clear to Eliot that the best scholars on the Harvard faculty had not trained students who could fill their places, nor, generally speaking, had they even trained students who could come in to serve them as seconds. To hire an intelligent young graduate and send him to Europe for two or three years, as had been done in the cases of Ticknor and Everett, was a slow process, but as late as 1889, Harvard still resorted to it to let Arthur R. Marsh prepare himself in comparative literature.[34]

In his attempts to improve the faculty, Eliot adopted a method which was to become traditional—raiding other schools. Despite vigorous efforts, he failed to win away two Sheffield professors, his friend George J. Brush and William D. Whitney, the Sanskritist.[35] In raids on M.I.T., however, he won Ferdinand Bôcher for modern languages, Storer for agricultural chemistry (at the Bussey Institution), and Edward C. Pickering to head the Observatory.

The failure to win Sheffield men and the relative success with M.I.T. men revealed what was generally true of Eliot's early faculty building: his greatest resource was the Boston-Cambridge community itself. Here Puritan respect for a learned clergy had survived the emergence of mercantile fortunes, a Unitarian and Transcendentalist liberation of the mind had stimulated social re-

formism, profits of the industrial revolution early found their way
into philanthropies of intellectual value, and Europe seemed at
least as close as the American frontier. But since provincialism
was one of Harvard's ill, such local dependence was not a satisfactory long-range solution to the problem of staffing.

Eliot sought scholars of the new professional vintage, but he
was willing to let a mature journalist grow into a professor.
Charles F. Dunbar, editor of the Boston *Advertiser*, became professor of political economy, his "soundness" having been demonstrated in his editorials.[36] Forced to employ men who had never
taught, Eliot made some brilliant selections, none of greater consequence than the appointing of Langdell, a virtually unknown
lawyer who had impressed Eliot during their slight acquaintance
in student days. Although Henry Adams did not think himself to
be an especially appropriate teacher of medieval history, since he
knew nothing about it, Eliot met his doubts with a bland smile,
saying, "If you will point out to me any one who knows more,
Mr. Adams, I will appoint him." The remark, which Adams recalled as neither logical nor convincing, persuaded this creative
teacher to join faculty ranks. "Good men" were invited with
considerable indifference to the area of learning they might represent. Failing to win James Bradley Thayer in 1872 to a professorship of English, the Fellows tried again in 1873, offering him
the Royall Professorship in the law school, and they were successful.[37] The graduate department provided an early harvest of
faculty. Of the first twenty-six winners of the Ph.D. and S.D. degrees, half remained, or shortly returned, as staff members.[38] Not
until the 1890s did Eliot begin to appoint European scholars to
professorships.[39]

In short, by enlarging the faculty during his first years as president, Eliot sought to lighten the teaching burdens of the ablest
professors, to introduce new subjects, to challenge the sleepier
teachers with competitors in their fields, and to bring sophistication into the counsels of the university. This last, putting a sort
of premium on worldly wisdom, was a marked characteristic of

the early recruitment efforts. It suggests Eliot's conviction that a developing university would be deeply involved with other social institutions.

Eliot did not sharply differentiate the inquiry of the student from that of the mature scholar. In fact, his early use of the term "research" was usually connected with students. He was slow to rank faculty research equal to teaching. In "The New Education" Eliot had claimed as essential for the ideal faculty not "high reputation," but "conscientiousness in the discharge of routine duties, fair talents well improved, and a genuine enthusiasm." Gurney tried to enlighten him. In the view of the new dean, Harvard was "in danger of overvaluing improved machinery, important as that is, in comparison with what must be the driving-power at last, the enthusiasm of the teachers in acquiring as well as imparting knowledge." [40]

The president labored with the idea of pure scholarship, making awkward gestures of appreciation, as in 1874, when he supported broad faculty library privileges, since "every College needs research on the part of its Professors." But Eliot did not encourage Harvard's young chemist, Charles Loring Jackson, in his wish to drop one course temporarily in order to pursue certain investigations, for, Jackson later reminded Eliot, "you did not see how it could be of practical advantage to the University." The secondary importance Eliot ascribed to research was starkly revealed in 1881, when he wrote to Edwin H. Hall, a recent Johns Hopkins Ph.D. whom he was appointing to an instructorship, that he hoped his "activity in physical research would not entirely cease." The letter implied that research was suitable for summer vacations, when it would not undermine teaching. Hall's work in electromagnetism was favorably known among European scientists; indeed, it had already led to his discovery of the "Hall effect," praised by James Clerk Maxwell as equal to the achievements of Faraday. In 1884, when Hall asked for promotion to assistant professor, stressing his original work as justification, he was refused. Eliot kept him waiting till 1888. [41]

At first Eliot prized textbook writing as highly as original investigation. Sensitive to the limitations of American colleges and preparatory schools, he stressed the duty of university faculties to provide help as he had with his path-breaking chemistry manual. As late as 1898 Eliot outraged a Harvard professor by suggesting as reasons for not promoting George Santayana that he did not "lay bricks or write school books." The professor assured him that such a spirit smacked of the "old college level"; Harvard must be infused by "a spirit which means university work and of which you yourself were so often the inspiring interpreter." Indeed, by that time Eliot was forcefully on record concerning the university's duty to find new truth as well as to train young men.

One source of instruction was the Johns Hopkins University. Although Eliot had solemnly assured its trustees in 1874 that graduate training was only a distant prospect for their institution, Johns Hopkins opened two years later, with fifty-four graduate students and twelve undergraduates, and promptly redirected Eliot's thinking on the nature of university faculties. Johns Hopkins offered Harvard professors larger salaries and lighter and more advanced teaching assignments, a threat Eliot successfully countered. It furnished young scholars for the Harvard faculty, but they required guarantees of academic freedom and such lures as the new sabbatical system. And after Johns Hopkins achieved an international reputation through scholarly publication, Eliot received long, serious letters from his own faculty, arguing that there was something lacking at Harvard.[42]

On reading the letters, Eliot promptly asked for further, detailed suggestions. One result was the reorganization of the graduate department. Another was a changed image of professors in his public statements. In the closing decade of his administration, Eliot's matured evaluation of the professor's scholarly role acknowledged that "in a university the most influential professors are those who have creative or inventive capacity, and themselves contribute to the progress of knowledge and art." [43]

In 1901 the University of Göttingen offered a professorship to Harvard's Theodore Richards, who was still an assistant professor in spite of his widely recognized work in determining atomic weights. Responding to the challenge, Eliot quickly obtained Richards's promotion and worked out "an arrangement of his work which will leave him a teacher, and yet give him time and facilities for chemical research, and for creating a school of chemical investigators." At this point, Eliot predicted without complaint the development of research professorships. But during his administration he not only wanted all professors to remain teachers, he also advised against any professor's offering only small graduate classes: he should keep one large class to recruit for his small ones.[44]

Eliot never lost his interest in teaching and teaching methods. In his inaugural, he discussed both lectures and recitations. Lectures served "for inspiration, guidance, and the comprehensive methodizing which only one who has a view of the whole field can rightly contrive." But he also recognized limitations: "The lecturer pumps laboriously into sieves. The water may be wholesome, but it runs through. A mind must work to grow." As to recitations, at their best they served "for securing and testifying a thorough mastery on the part of the pupil of the treatise or author in hand, for conversational comment and amplification, for emulation and competition," but they could "readily degenerate into dusty repetitions." Although at times he could speak as if all good teaching embraced the methods of the inductive sciences, he warned a correspondent who thought of literature as a science, "Have we not all seen good literature spoiled as nutriment for young people by the attempt to convert it into scientific philology?" Increasingly aware that a wide range of personalities could make good teachers, Eliot appointed and promoted so unorthodox a candidate as the eccentric Barrett Wendell, in English, and he serenely tolerated the flamboyant and egotistical psychologist Hugo Münsterberg.[45]

In the economic redefinition of the career of university teaching, Harvard, sometimes nudged by ambitious newer institutions, took the lead. The salaries and perquisites of the profession were systematized and enhanced. There was a general salary rise in 1869, when Eliot took office, and another in 1890, when the university faced new competition from Clark, Stanford, and Chicago. A third increase came in 1905, when alumni raised a Teachers Endowment fund after financial retrenchment had led to the loss of several able young men.[46]

In 1880 Eliot assured a prospective faculty member that Harvard professors had life tenure. Indeed, the statutes of the university had long stated that professorships were "held without express limitation of time," though professors, like other officers, were subject to "removal for inadequate performance of duty, or for misconduct." As part of an economy drive in 1894, Eliot and the Fellows made peremptory use of the removal power by forcing the resignations of two professors presumed to be "dead wood." One of them had held that rank since 1881, the other since 1885.[47]

Although neither of the excluded professors was particularly old, the thought of their limited teaching capacities undermined by senility may have argued against their continuance. The guarantee of life tenure called for a pension system. Otherwise professors without independent incomes might continue meeting classes until they died. In fact, professors were bluntly drawing the attention of alumni groups to the faculty's need for both higher salaries and pensions. Harvard's pioneer pension scheme, launched in 1880, was limited to special cases until 1899, when it went into full effect, offering pensions to those with at least twenty years' service as assistant professor or professor. The scheme paid between one-third and two-thirds of the teacher's salary of his last active year. Under this system, Eliot commented, "the dignity, independence, and repose of the calling are increased," since "officials who have become too old for the effective discharge of their duties can be displaced in an honorable and considerate way." After 1906, Harvard professors were included in the pension program of the Carnegie Foundation for the Advancement of Teaching.[48]

Like pensions, the sabbatical year was a Harvard innovation in America. It was established by the Corporation in 1880 as part of an effort to attract scholars from other institutions. Leaves of absence for one year at half pay not more than once in seven years were made available to professors and assistant professors, whose object might be "health, rest, study, or the prosecution of original work in literature or science." [49]

In 1880 Eliot appointed three professors from outside who had done work of highly specialized scholarship. This was a shift from earlier acceptance of general culture as adequate qualification for appointment, and the Harvard community was set abuzz by the new approach. There was of course a period of overlap with an earlier style of general teaching. In the philosophy department, every member at one time or another taught psychology, but the appearance of Münsterberg in the nineties made the subject clearly one man's bailiwick. In 1896 Eliot celebrated the separation of mineralogy from chemistry (two fields which his own M.I.T. professorship had combined): "Thus disappeared another of those professorships which the late Professor Oliver Wendell Holmes, alluding to his own professorship of anatomy and physiology, described as not chairs but settees." [50]

An awareness of loss as well as gain from faculty specialization underlay an anonymous essay by an alumnus which appeared in 1898. He imagined two students, one complaining, "The time is coming when there will be a Professor of Perispomes and another of Proparoxytones, and so on, and none of them will know anything outside of his specialty. What will become of Greek literature then? No, sir, this specializing and these departments will kill culture." The student of opposite persuasion said, "We are still very superficial, of course, for the same man who treats of Coleoptera has Hymenoptera and Diptera; but the time is coming when it will be recognized that a single insect, the *Scarabaeus geotrupes*, for instance, is worthy to take up a professor's whole time. By this subdivision, we shall at last arrive at absolute truth." But the essay displayed only a mild animus against specialization. It approved the enthusiasm aroused in students by teachers who specialized, and it suggested that alumni romanticized the broad, wise teaching of bygone faculty members.[51]

Specialization had followed inevitably from the elective sys-

tem's proliferation of courses and the rising status of original research. When, at the behest of the Overseers, a faculty committee
in 1906–7 examined the many small courses to see if some could
not be eliminated, it boldly announced not only that all courses
given could be well defended by the departments concerned, but
that more teachers and more courses were in fact needed. Dean
Briggs doubted that a university faculty could have been built in
any other way than by assuring newly appointed professors that
they could teach the parts of their subjects to which they had
given special attention.[52]

The committee's report notwithstanding, the last years of
Eliot's administration saw increased sentiment against specialization among Harvard's humanists. "Modern scholarship suffers
from over-specialization," Professor Kuno Francke announced at
the opening of the Germanic Museum in 1903, and he expressed
the hope that a museum could form bonds among various studies.
George Herbert Palmer described the growing tendency to fear
that somebody might know more about a given subject than one-
self as "a kind of intellectual terrorism," and he praised Norton as
a representative of "wholeness," whose methods were "superbly
out of date in our specialized time." Eliot himself supported such
interdepartmental programs as "history and literature" and comparative literature.[53]

The ending of leisured institutional simplicity and intellectual
generalism was brought into sharp focus by the death of Nathaniel Southgate Shaler, in 1906. Shaler had led the expansion of
Lawrence Scientific School as its dean, and he had successfully
developed the summer school. He had also published philosophical essays and a cycle of poetic dramas. Scorned by Alexander
Agassiz as no true scientist, and humiliated by the exposure of his
"soft" lecture course by a faculty committee in 1903, he had convinced Gordon McKay to bequeath the university millions of dollars for the benefit of Lawrence, only to see the gift used to abolish the school (under a plan of obvious structural superiority).
The weaknesses of the man had been criticized in his lifetime, but
with his death his equally authentic strengths were recalled, and

they were identified with a dying order. William R. Thayer, an editor of the *Harvard Graduates' Magazine* who kept its pages open to critics of Harvard, was himself a strong supporter of the Eliot reforms. But on Shaler's death, he observed failings in the reshaped faculty, with its professional academics and its entrenched departmentalism: "As our universities grow large, their teachers grow timid. Much of the work is done by routine men, and much is done by men who know very nearly all that is to be known on some restricted specialty, and know very little besides. The result is an increasing atmosphere of commonplaceness. The younger men are naturally the disciples of the heads of their departments, and discipleship imposes reticence upon them. Even the heads lord it in a small domain only; outside of that, they prudently hold their peace, for fear of being found fallible." As Eliot went about assuring the public of the merits of the new universities, doubts were developing within the institution itself.[54]

A man whose watchword was "liberty," Eliot could scarcely avoid applying the ideal to the Harvard faculty. In the portion of his inaugural specifically addressed to the Corporation, he had proclaimed that above all a university must be free. "The winnowing breeze of freedom must blow through all its chambers. It takes a hurricane to blow wheat away. An atmosphere of intellectual freedom is the native air of literature and science." This was Eliot aphorism at its most compelling, but his practice at first fell short of his precept. In 1870 he joined the rest of the Corporation in directing Francis Bowen to remove from an economics textbook he was about to publish, either his support for repaying the national debt below par or all mention of his Harvard connection. Bowen himself had asked for the Corporation's judgment.[55] Apparently Eliot and the Fellows believed that textbooks had so direct and powerful an effect on the minds of the young that they might require censoring. That directive, a sad deflation of Eliot's promises of faculty liberty, led to this clumsy passage in a letter to a prospective professor: "The Corporation have no thought of interfering in the remotest manner with the writings or speeches of any person employed by them, unless indeed these writings are College textbooks. A professor here is free to think or say what he pleases." [56]

The flowering of Eliot's theory of academic freedom came in the 1890s, after the university had broadened its constituency. He made clear that such liberty included a teacher's speaking his mind either within or without the university. In 1893, writing to a candidate for faculty appointment who was then at the University of Berlin, Eliot promised "an absolute freedom from all restriction—governmental, academic or social—on freedom of thought and speech." In fact, he believed Harvard could outbid Berlin in precisely this regard. A professor who found himself criticized in the newspapers was assured by Eliot that "Harvard professors are quite independent of the newspapers, and are entitled to take comfort in that independence." As the election of 1900 neared, Eliot, who was to vote for McKinley, wrote an influential alumnus: "I cannot agree with you that it will do Harvard University the slightest harm for a considerable number of Harvard men to vote for Mr. Bryan. Nearly half the voters in the United States will go that way in any event, and there will be found in that party hundreds of thousands of sensible and conservative men." And when a fellow university president, E. Benjamin Andrews of Brown, was asked to resign because of his economic views, Eliot joined in a campaign to enlighten the Brown governing board. [57]

The ideal of freedom had firm grounding in Eliot's theology and social philosophy, but he also argued pragmatically for a free university. A despotic president, Eliot told David Starr Jordan of Stanford, sacrificed his opportunities to get "independent and responsible advice" from his faculty. Nor could there be effective teaching without faculty freedom. "Teaching which is not believed to be free," said Eliot, "is well-nigh worthless." [58]

Academic freedom was the subject of Eliot's Phi Beta Kappa address at Cornell in 1907. Recalling the Bowen episode, he made clear his regret at having pressed Bowen to modify his book. But even this considered view of the affair left some ambiguities. He appeared to believe that Bowen's "sense of duty and honor" had made him suppress the offending section and that such an attitude among its faculty was "the best defense of an institution against abuses of academic freedom." Even in 1907, Eliot did not see the dangers of cautious institution-mindedness on the part of scholars. "The teacher in a school," he maintained, "or the professor in a college or university, may properly abstain from saying or doing many things which he would be free to say or do if it were not for his official position." It was an uncritical institution-mindedness in Eliot himself that enabled him to say, "Any slight interference with academic freedom which time will certainly cure may be endured with equanimity for a season, in consideration of great counter-balancing advantages." Academic freedom as presented by Eliot was subject to prudential limits.[59]

But the Cornell address, taken as a whole, was one of the most sympathetic treatments of academic freedom to come from a university president at a moment of widespread faculty concern. Such academic gadflies as Professor J. McKeen Cattell of Columbia had recently begun assaulting university presidents as "autocrats," but they sometimes noted Eliot as an exception. The "General Declaration of Principles" of the newly formed American Association of University Professors, issued in 1915, gave a conspicuous place to Eliot's criticism of trustees who exercised "an arbitrary power of dismissal." The founders of the association were willing to lean on Eliot's prestige and accept his championship of academic freedom, without recalling his past offenses and ambiguities.[60]

VI

In the 1890s concern for structure gained such strength in American universities that it threatened the eclipse of intellectual ideals. The elaborately layered organization which William Rainey Harper projected for the University of Chicago was the most fitting symbol for this development.[61] Harvard, too, experienced a structural elaboration in 1890. The faculties of the college, the graduate department, and the scientific school were combined into the Faculty of Arts and Sciences, each of the three "schools" having its own dean and administrative board. In addition, eleven standing committees dealt with such matters as special students, public entertainments, and freshman advisers. The reorganization was followed by a rise in faculty morale, and Josiah Royce, always sensitive to the health of the intellectual community, concluded that the new structure enhanced university ideals.[62]

Although the new organization freed faculty meetings from details, members found themselves still involved in applying policy as members of committees, boards, and departments. William James believed that the scrupulously organized "machine" risked "overwhelming the lives of men whose interest is more in learning than in administration." Dean Briggs observed how the clustering of administrative duties at the opening of the year left the teacher "struggling, against nature, to transform himself into a man of business." Committee assignments came to be generally dreaded as "a serious interruption . . . to original work, not only from the time taken by the meetings, but also because of the break in the train of thought and the fatigue from this exacting and different work." [63]

Eliot had a strong concern for faculty participation in institutional government, and he yielded somewhat slowly to pleas for relief. By 1903 he was willing to consider whether the number of faculty committees and the size of each might not be reduced. Encouraged by the Overseers, a special faculty committee reported in favor of reduction in administration by teachers. Five committees on admission were combined into one, the committee on financial aid to undergraduates yielded its functions to two deans, and the membership on the college administrative board was reduced from fifteen to nine, and then to seven. At the same time departments and divisions asked for clerical aid. At Harvard, the professors more than the president desired the creation of new administrative offices and increased powers for the administrative staff.[64]

Eliot had once spoken of administrators as having the humble role of "mechanics of colleges." But toward the end of his presidency he concluded that since professors preferred research to administration and since some were administrative incompetents, a professor who became a dean deserved his extra pay. Shortly after leaving the presidency, Eliot included in an evocation of the freedom appropriate for professors, the freedom to lead an "undistracted life." This conclusion, suggested by his experience in Europe in the 1860s, had been confirmed by the desires of the Harvard faculty.[65]

It was in large part because of administrative expansion that the Faculty of Arts and Sciences, which by 1909 numbered 164, remained capable of effective debate on significant institutional questions. The faculty did not become a rubber stamp for its committees. The careful plans of committees were shattered in faculty discussions, reported Dean Briggs, while committee members met their fate "with a calmness that is almost Oriental." Although generally conversational in style, faculty meetings became notoriously long-winded. Eliot was uncomplaining. Critical while at M.I.T. of President Rogers's unwillingness to allow extended faculty argument, Eliot firmly believed in the faculty's "high value as an agency for conference and discussion, and for the selection of the best measure among several." Such was the faith of a true parliamentary liberal.[66]

Openness of discussion served to educate the president in academic affairs and gave him opportunities to observe the style of individual faculty members. "Some of us have thought," Dean Briggs recalled, "that in your tolerance of prolonged and tiresome debate there was more than patience; there was research." Bliss Perry, arriving in 1907, was shocked at the contrast between the punctilio of Princeton faculty meetings and the indecorum at Harvard. Professors straggled in, teacups in hand, during the first fifteen minutes of the meeting, and members did not trouble to rise when making motions.[67]

Beginning in 1891 twelve divisions—broad fields of studies that sometimes included only one department, sometimes two or three—controlled honors degrees and graduate programs. More fundamental curricular matters, however, were settled in the departments, which had existed since the Ticknor reforms of the

1820s, though they had generally been very loosely organized. These "little Faculties," as one professor called them, soon took on independent life: "They hold many and hotly contested meetings; they issue pamphlets; they edit publications; they examine candidates for honors and higher degrees." They did not, however, elect their own chairmen; these were chosen by the president and deans. Eliot had originally looked optimistically on departments, judging them protectors of faculty coherence since they allowed the delegation of responsibilities. By 1900, however, he concluded that departments undermined faculty unity: "To every active Department in a university its own interests appear supreme." Another danger cited by Eliot was that within these smaller domains the older members wielded too much influence; single departments often lacked the democratic qualities of the faculty as a whole.[68]

Division and subordination of the responsibilities of the presidential office, promised in Eliot's inaugural, continued throughout his administration. "When he began," Frank Taussig observed of Eliot, "everything centered in the President's office, and it is not much beyond the truth to say that everything was done by him in person." When Taussig became the first presidential secretary in 1880, Eliot still wrote most of his letters in his own hand. During his forty years, Taussig said, the president moved from "superintending" to "engineering." The shift was made possible by the creation of deanships, secretaryships, and other specialized offices that took over functions once performed by the president, such as those of the inspector of grounds and buildings and the publication agent. Particularly effective in rationalizing administrative procedures was Frank Bolles, a law school graduate and former newspaperman, who held the title "Secretary to the University" from 1886 till his death in 1894.[69]

When Eliot took a two-month trip during the school year 1891-92, one Boston newspaper declared him an organizing genius, an academic general who had developed a retinue of able subordinates. But the truth was that the untiring Eliot's taste for detail sometimes delayed the administrative staff expansion which the growth of the university suggested. He was somewhat resistant to the Overseer-originated idea of a new office of Secretary to the President (later Secretary to the Corporation), created in 1901. Although the appointee, Jerome D. Greene, was at first given so little to do that he found himself inventing tasks, in time he became virtually Eliot's alter ego, writing letters indistinguishable from the president's.[70]

Expressing an undercurrent of dissatisfaction with Eliot, the Overseers in 1906 urged creation of a joint committee of Overseers and Fellows to consider changes "in the organization and administration of the University." Eliot served on the six-member committee, and the results were largely to his liking. Its report, which concluded that "the President does not need to be relieved of any function he now performs; but he ought to be relieved of details," strongly supported the institutional role Eliot had created. "The functions of the President, as they have been developed during the growth of the University since the Civil War, are of high value, in that they tend to unify the University, and to place the experience of each Governing Board and every Faculty at the service of the whole institution." Dissents came from Overseers Charles Francis Adams, who called for more comprehensive measures, and James J. Storrow, who insisted that Harvard's administrative organization was "cumbersome and somewhat ineffective." Minor reforms followed: an assistant was hired for Greene, clerical help was given to the chairmen of divisions and departments, and there was further reduction in the size of faculty committees and boards. The report advised committees and boards to take final action whenever precedents or standing rules provided guidance, and "when good judgment suggests that an exception be made" to do so without referring matters upward. This was the enlightened bureaucratism of the day; it emphasized flexibility and expert adjustment to unpredictability in the flux of human activity.[71]

In 1911 J. McKeen Cattell sought views from professors of the natural sciences on his proposal for enlarged faculty powers, including faculty election of presidents for limited terms. Many of the Harvard respondents resisted his plan; in fact, among the universities concerned only Wisconsin had a larger percentage favoring approximately the status quo. Nine of twenty-six Harvard teachers gave virtually complete support to standing practice, which one labeled "tempered autocracy." The theme of most comments—including those opposed to the existing system— was the importance and difficulty of finding a wise man to exercise the necessary presidential power.

One Harvard scientist, who did not want "the powers of a well-chosen, well-qualified president stinted," remarked of Eliot, "I have seen a great president content year after year to lay his most cherished projects before a large faculty and labor year after year to bring this faculty to his own way of thinking, convinced that in this assembly he had, on the whole, the most intelligent and most fair-minded body of men in the world, for his purposes." Throughout all the delegations of responsibility and growth of departmental power, the faculty had "remained a fairly coherent body, members generally, old and young, feeling that, when certain questions of general policy were up, each man of them was expected to do his duty, though comparatively few, as a rule, took an active part in the debates. . . . Individuals who, from temperament or from departmental affiliations, must differ, could at least differ more intelligently than if they had not known each other by sight." Harvard's combination of "a masterful but considerate president, strong enough and fair enough to invite frank counsel, with a faculty willing to give this counsel in a broad spirit of loyalty" was a pattern this professor did not care to change.[72]

Eliot's own administrative gift and addiction to work allowed Harvard to erect a relatively slight administrative apparatus. Harvard in 1909 was not an over-rationalized or inflexibly bureaucratic institution. The faculty meetings in which Eliot was deaf to cries of "Question, question!" and in which he did not halt debaters who wandered from the subject revealed his characteristic stance toward the university. "A school or college must be a machine in some degree," he once remarked. "Let it be to the least possible degree."[73]

VII

In 1877, when Eliot was forty-three and his two sons had grown to adolescence, he married Grace Mellen Hopkinson, a resident of Cambridge twelve years his junior who sang in a church choir and enjoyed performing in amateur theatricals. Eliot insisted to Theodore Lyman that this new relationship was "love and not an arrangement of any cool and sensible sort." His private life was gladdened, but for some time those who knew him only in an official capacity continued to think of him as austere, if not frigid.[74]

Eliot never courted popularity among his faculty. His characteristic reserve, whatever its relation to his facial blemish, was heightened by his knowledge of strong opposition to many of his reform plans. When William James was in one of his episodes of depression, the thought of Eliot's "cold figure at the helm" would remind him how little he cared for Harvard. Anti-Eliot feeling probably reached a peak in the mid-eighties, when his successful assaults on required Greek had alienated the traditionalists and yet his relative insensitivity to scholarship still nourished resentment among the research-minded. But Eliot's willingness to develop his appreciation of research, his weathering of threats to the system of student freedom at the end of the eighties, and his successful restructuring of the university in 1890 dissolved many faculty antagonisms toward him.[75]

The ratification of these changing attitudes came in 1894, at the twenty-fifth anniversary of Eliot's election to the presidency. It was an occasion that could have been ignored or marked with dutiful formality. But Harvard men appeared to have been waiting for such an opportunity. The faculty gathered on June 7, 1894, the anniversary of the first faculty meeting at which Eliot had presided, and offered this tribute:

> It is the period of the present administration that will be remembered hereafter as the epoch in which the University was

first fairly able to take its place among the great seats of learning of the world, and to adopt as its foremost purpose, not simply the regulation of more or less unwilling youth in the last years of their schooling, but the nurture, discipline, and inspiration of men destined to devote their whole future to scholarship, science, philosophy, criticism, or art, and of students laying serious foundations of lifelong culture,—the leaders of the coming generation in the search for new knowledge, the establishment of new standards, and the creation of new intellectual forms.

At the commencement dinner that year the alumni presented Eliot a specially struck medal, and in the pages of the *Graduates' Magazine* various articles recounted the achievements of the preceding quarter-century. Among many personal letters of congratulation was one from William James. He expressed fear of the day when Harvard must have someone else as president. Although for a time uncomfortable with the visible friendliness of audiences—it seemed like a loss of stimulus—Eliot soon adapted. As his biographer recounts, "he became less reserved, more forth-going, more conversable, more ready to betray his wistful desire to come nearer to people." [76]

The epic battles for the university were now in the past. There would be new struggles with the shortcomings of the elective system, new growth for the graduate school, new professional schools to found, and always friction with other social institutions, but the remaking of Harvard College into a university had been accomplished. Some disagreements between president and faculty lay in the future, but they would generally occur as part of a relationship that went beyond mere mutual respect. Professor Charles Grandgent of the Romance Languages Department, trying to identify the new emotion, felt he needed the "new word" that James M. Barrie's characters had struggled for—"love." [77]

III

The System of Liberty

The elective system has been described by its opponents as a wide-open, miscellaneous bazaar, at which a bewildering variety of goods is offered to the purchaser, who is left without guidance, and acts without any constant or sensible motive. Nothing could be farther from the facts than this description.

CHARLES W. ELIOT (1908) [1]

I

It was a tribute to Eliot's effectiveness as a spokesman for academic reform that the public associated his name with student freedom of course election as if the idea had been uniquely his and the reform uniquely Harvard's. Actually, electivism had been tried at several colleges, and at Harvard it was in partial effect before Eliot's presidency.

In the colonial colleges, the size of faculty and the range of conventional knowledge had dictated a single curriculum for all students. Until 1767 at Harvard, and later elsewhere, the same tutor had taught an entire class in all subjects for its first three years.[2] The dominant rationale of collegiate education had justified prescription. The classic formulation of this theory was the Yale Report of 1828, an elaborate answer to a request that the faculty consider making the ancient languages elective. "The great object of a collegiate education, preparatory to the study of a profession," a faculty committee under the leadership of President Jeremiah Day responded, "is to give that expansion and balance of the mental powers, those liberal and comprehensive views, and those fine proportions of character, which are not to be found in him whose ideas are always confined to one particular channel." The classics were supposed to be doubly valuable: their content furnished "those elementary ideas which are found in the literature of modern times," and their form insured "the most effectual discipline of the mental faculties." Indeed, study of the classics employed every faculty of the mind—"the memory, judgment, and reasoning powers, . . . the taste and fancy." Modern languages could not fill this need because they were too easy.

The Yale Report was a remarkable intellectual product; in fact, it was one of the most thorough presentations of a theory of higher education ever produced in America. The repeated charges that it justified required subjects only on the basis of mental discipline (strengthening mental functions) are not correct. It raised other aims for higher education, including the imparting of information and the building of character. Its stress on balance, though partly referring to mental development, also stood for a wide representation of the intellectual achievements of mankind, in the sciences as well as in literature. Nor was it a document that objected to all change. The faculty, it assured the public, would recognize new subjects and adjust the curriculum to include them. In fact, the report was not totally antagonistic to student choice of subjects. Yale already allowed students to exercise certain options, beginning in the junior year, and was willing that this practice be increased.[3]

Its very moderation made the Yale Report an imposing conservative bastion. The many Yale men who became college presidents and teachers relied on its arguments in creating traditional classical colleges outside New England, but the poverty of these institutions made them less likely than Yale to moderate the required curriculum. At Yale itself, the arguments of the report, sometimes in the very same language, appeared again fifty years later, when the great battles over the elective principle were fought.

The challenge that evoked the Yale Report was part of a movement in the 1820s to give the student more control over his education. Thomas Jefferson, with European models in mind, planned the University of Virginia in such a way that a student chose a "school" (comparable to later departments) upon entering, and after receiving the diploma of a school, became a "graduate" of the university. "Every student shall be free to attend the schools of his choice," a regulation adopted in 1824 read, "and no other than he chooses." Beginning in 1831, the university gave a degree, the M.A., to students who gained diplomas in five schools: ancient languages, mathematics, natural philosophy, chemistry, and moral philosophy. This program limited Virginia's influence as an exemplar of the elective principle since it was virtually identical with the traditional baccalaureate curriculum.[4]

Jefferson's design for the University of Virginia helped inspire George Ticknor, who, after four years of study in Europe, had returned to America in 1819 to take up his duties as professor of French, Spanish, and belles-lettres at Harvard. Ticknor, alone of the small crop of German-trained teachers then at Harvard, showed the skill and patience to win reform. Aided by an alarming breakdown in student discipline and non-renewal of the annual legislative grant, he managed to stimulate a reassessment of Harvard education by the governing boards and the faculty, and in 1825 a new set of statutes went into effect. Although these statutes brought more rigorous supervision of students, they also allowed a certain amount of upper-class election (and even, according to a rule passed early in 1826, gave freshmen the privilege of substituting modern languages for half the required work in Greek and Latin). Since few of the Harvard faculty shared Ticknor's ideals, establishment of elective courses was made optional for each department (departmental organization being part of the new plan). Soon electives at Harvard were virtually limited to the modern languages. But there were thenceforth always advocates of the elective system at Harvard.[5]

Among methods by which the antebellum college allowed students to express their preference for certain fields of learning were the "partial course" and the "parallel course." The partial course, offered as early as 1796 at Princeton, let students with scientific interests largely avoid the ancient languages, but it awarded them only certificates of proficiency, not degrees. The parallel course was a more ambitious attempt to break the classicists' monopoly on academic respectability. It was usually a single, prescribed course called the "scientific" or "English scientific," and it led to a degree, usually the Ph.B.

The failure of the nonclassical courses to attract large numbers of students proved that those who cared to undertake college attendance sought the prestige or the educational values attributed to the long-established classical curriculum. In many ways the scientific course was inferior. At Yale it lasted only three years, and at Dartmouth it was on the level of secondary education. Union College was unusual both in awarding the A.B. for the scientific course and in attracting large numbers of scientific students. But against it were hurled accusations of academic chicanery.[6]

A graduate of Union undertook a more radical experiment with the elective principle in 1850. Francis Wayland had been president of Brown since 1827 and had earned a national reputation through his textbooks in economics and moral philosophy. His sudden burst of academic innovation after so many years in office took the educational world by surprise. Wayland had long been alarmed at the decreasing proportion of American youth who attended college. With a threat to resign, he forced a dramatic application of the elective principle at Brown, hoping to find the remedy. The reforms at Brown, besides emphasizing applied subjects and welcoming students who did not seek a degree, set up four separate paths to the baccalaureate. Three plans, each including at least one ancient language, led to the A.B.; the Ph.B. required two modern languages and included several applied subjects. Within each course plan, the original announcement promised, the student would have "a large liberty of choice."

But there were actually too few subjects to offer much election. Disheartened by declining enrollments, Wayland resigned in 1855, and except for retaining the Ph.B., Brown reverted to tradition. What defeated Wayland's reforms was less the depar-

ture from the required curriculum than the "cheapening" of the
A.B. by offering it in three years. Such degrees became objects of
derision from competing institutions. Another reason for failure
was Wayland's refusal to extend his ideal of student liberty to
dormitory life and study schedules. As a result, students failed to
advance beyond schoolboy attitudes, and two new professors of
applied science, resenting their policing duties, departed for
Yale's scientific school. Eliot was never accurately informed
about Wayland's reforms or their fate. In 1869 he called them
"loose and exaggerated." Thirty years later his praise was excessive: he judged Wayland to have been "about two generations in
advance of his time." [7]

When Cornell University opened in 1868, its students were
presented with the "group system," which President Andrew
Dickson White had admired at Yale's scientific school. Under this
arrangement a student elected one of several curriculums
("groups"), but within the group he had little if any choice. The
faculty could thus assure each student both a general education
core and specialization in a single subject, whose name the group
usually bore. There was, however, an "optional" course, a feature
borrowed from Henry Philip Tappan's Michigan, where White
had taught. The optional course allowed a student to construct
his entire course however he chose from among the university's
offerings. The priority in establishing a free elective system,
White later maintained, belonged to him, and he denounced its
ascription to Eliot. But the optional course was generally played
down at Cornell, and while White was still president, students in
the course lost the right to be candidates for a degree.

Although the groups continued to be loosened by allowing
more election within each, it was not until 1896 that Cornell
adopted a free elective system. More thorough-going than Harvard's, it left all courses to the student's free choice, except for
military drill and hygiene, which were required of freshmen.
Cornell also went beyond Harvard in this reform by granting the
once narrowly guarded A.B. for all courses in arts and sciences. [8]

An important variant of the elective system was the "major-subject system," developed by David Starr Jordan, an early graduate of Cornell, first as president of Indiana University and more fully as president of Leland Stanford Junior University, which opened in 1891. Under the Stanford arrangement, there was only one collegiate degree, the Bachelor of Arts. Only one course, English composition, was required. Each student selected a major professor, who could prescribe up to one-third of the student's total work in his department, including collateral minors in related departments. The rest of the student's course was freely elective, and he could even elect more of his major subject if he chose. A call for change by the trustees in 1905 was successfully resisted by the faculty, who staved off proposals for a "general course" that would not require students to specialize. Although the faculty set forth the desirability of half a student's work being done "outside the major and closely related departments," it refused to make this a fixed rule. With this scheme of liberty-plus-required-specialization went departmental independence and power, and a hope, not always fulfilled, that the major professor would enter sympathetically and constructively into a student's course planning.[9]

The group system at Cornell and the major-subject system at Stanford stopped short of the free elective system found at Harvard. But what made people think of electivism as a Harvard contribution to educational progress was less any uniqueness of the Harvard practice than the articulateness of its president and his willingness to bring academic controversy before the public.

II

The debates over the elective system threw into sharp relief the psychology of learning adhered to by participants. As frequently as his opponents, Eliot used the vocabulary of "mental faculties," which psychologists have since discarded as a naïve reification. The concept of mental faculties—used as early as Plato's time —arose from analogy with the senses and sense organs. Thus, ability to remember was considered traceable to the "faculty of memory." Among nineteenth-century educators and mental philosophers the lists of faculties varied widely. An unusually long inventory of "powers of the mind" was given by Princeton's President James McCosh in 1885, in a defense of course requirement. In naming "the senses, the memory, the fancy, judgment, reasoning, conscience, the feelings, the will," McCosh simply approximated most textbook lists, but he incorporated for good measure equivalents of the traditional curriculum—"the mathematical, the metaphysical, the mechanical, the poetical, the prosaic." [10]

Phrenology carried the belief in faculties to a physiologically precise absurdity, and the pedagogy which dwelt on developing each faculty through exercise deserved its eventual obloquy as "the muscle theory of mind." Faculty psychology, however, was not necessarily the adjunct of any single view of mind or of any single type of pedagogy.[11] The language of mental faculties had, in fact, an open-endedness that made it a more flexible instrument than certain later vocabularies, such as that of stimulus-response bonds. In many lists, the faculties named resembled what a later generation would call mental functions or mental processes. This was generally true of Eliot. Although permanently influenced by the mental philosophy of Thomas Reid, which he had studied as an undergraduate, Eliot named fewer faculties than Reid and most of his contemporaries did. Eliot's favorite list was a distinctly functional triad that led from environment to mind and back to environment: observation, reasoning, and expression.[12]

Although the vocabulary of mental faculties has died out, the dispute over mental discipline persists. Mental discipline (also called "mental training" and, especially by its detractors, "formal discipline") views learning as a strengthening of the mental ability of students. It can be sharply differentiated from the view that learning aims to impart knowledge or information. In the nineteenth century, as in the twentieth, most educators took a commonsense position between these two. Thus, in 1828 the Yale Report visualized the goal of college learning as both "the *discipline* and the *furniture* of the mind; expanding its powers, and storing it with knowledge." In 1869, Eliot similarly spoke of "the best formation and information of the mind." Those leaning one way or the other usually cast aspersions upon "mere drill" or "mere information." [13]

When Eliot defended the modern subjects, he generally emphasized their contributions to the student's mental training, not to his knowledge. The natural sciences, for instance, would "develop and discipline those powers of the mind by which science has been created and is daily nourished." E. L. Youmans, a reformer close to Eliot in time and temper, claimed (like Eliot) as much disciplinary value for the new subjects, especially the natural sciences, as for the long-established classical languages and mathematics. But Youmans, truer to Herbert Spencer, took great pains to show that science served "both for knowledge and discipline," and stressed that the knowledge provided should suit "the duties and work of the age in which we live." By comparison, Eliot was conservative in both his emphasis on mental discipline and his faith in the trained mind as the chief social utility of education. He stood even further from the American Herbartians, men like Charles De Garmo, who saw learning as a matter of apperception through association of ideas and hence stressed "content." [14]

None of these theorists brought forward experimental data to support his views. Edward Lee Thorndike did undertake studies in experimental psychology, however, and it was that grounding which gave such wide acceptance to his learning theory. Experimental results, which Thorndike began publishing in 1901 with Robert S. Woodworth, indicated that there was very little transfer of training from one intellectual task to another. Such transfer as did occur the two psychologists attributed to the presence of "identical elements." "There is no reason to suppose," they concluded, "that any general change occurs corresponding to the words, 'improvement of the attention,' or 'of the powers of observation,' or 'of accuracy.' " [15] A similar objection against too easy assumption of convertibility of mental skill had been directed specifically against Eliot in 1893 by Burke A. Hinsdale of the University of Michigan.

Eliot had often assumed a transfer far broader than the Thorndike-Woodworth experiments would allow. For example, in 1892 he wrote: "The field within which the power [of observation] is exercised may be narrow or special; but these words do not apply to the power." Yet it is hard to declare that Eliot was wrong when he spelled out what he believed to be transferable. In this case, he did not speak vaguely of "observation," but specified that the student should learn "how hard it is to determine with certainty even an apparently simple fact" and "to distrust the evidence of his own senses." [16] Those seeking to reassert the possibility of broad transfer of training turned to an idea remarkably similar to one Eliot had expressed as early as 1869. Charles Judd and his followers, beginning about 1908, pronounced "generalization" and "consciousness of method" as something which teaching could emphasize and which would strengthen transfer of training.[17]

In short, among educators and psychologists there have always been men of reputation and power who supported mental discipline as an educational aim. In the elective struggle of Eliot's day, both sides made mental discipline the chief educational value. His successor, in fact, put the case more emphatically than Eliot did. "Any special knowledge may fade away," President Lowell argued, "but the man's cultivated faculties remain, to be used throughout his life." [18]

At the time of his election to the Harvard presidency, Eliot's psychology of learning was essentially the self-assured eclecticism of the Yale Report. It is well exemplified by his defense of Latin as an appropriate study for the secondary schools. He defended the subject as knowledge: from it the student's mind would become "furnished with a literary stock of the best quality." Leaving no doubt that he was raising a cultural defense, Eliot cited Latin literature's "wonderful influence over the modern civilized communities." But he defended this subject as knowledge in another sense than the cultural: it imparted "knowledge of language as a vehicle of thought," and did so better than "less regular and less inflected languages." A second range of ideas was involved here—the theoretical or methodological rather than the cultural or historical—a range not considered in the Yale Report. In fact, to refer to such knowledge of a "vehicle of thought" pointed out a way in which information could become intellectual skill. Here as in later writings Eliot came close to transmuting both "formation" and "information" into a notion of method, which later curriculum-makers have often found a satisfactory guiding principle. But in spite of these intimations of new educational goals, Eliot was still vigorous in his defense of Latin as a source of traditionally transferable mental discipline: "It is not true that the man loses the mental habits which the boy acquired in studying Latin. . . . Most of the ways of thinking which become natural to him [while he studies Latin] will be applicable to other subjects of thought."

Though he saw knowledge as an acceptable educational goal, Eliot believed firmly in mental training and was ready to single out particular subjects as superior to others in their potential for such training. He believed in "transfer" of the resulting mental skill. But Eliot claimed no timeless superiority for Latin. Other languages might eventually serve the same purposes. Latin merely promised the most, given the "actual state of educational appliances." This characteristic relativism in Eliot's application of theory to curriculum appeared also in the opening sentence of his inaugural, where he downgraded the controversy over which subjects provided the best mental training.[19]

Eliot continued through most of his life to use the language of faculty psychology, and he shared with critics of the elective system the assumption that the chief aim of education was mental discipline. But he departed from traditional psychology of learning in his opposition to certain versions of mental discipline and to certain of its pedagogical applications. Eliot was among those who added to their belief in mental training an emphasis on individual differences. All minds were not alike, either in degree of ability or, more important, in the nature of abilities. The ideal of symmetry, dear to some who grew obsessive about their lists of mental faculties, had little appeal for Eliot. He denounced the round-mind theory of countless college inaugurals and catalogues. "Faculties are not given by God impartially," he contended, "—to each round soul a little of each power, as if the soul were a pill, which must contain its due proportion of many various ingredients. To reason about the average human mind as if it were a globe, to be expanded symmetrically from a centre outward is to be betrayed by a metaphor. A cutting-tool, a drill, or auger would be a juster symbol of the mind." Even pre-collegiate education should seek the discovery of individuals' natural asymmetries more than uniform development of uniform minds. To maintain that no faculty should be dwarfed did not mean that each must be equally developed. "For the individual," Eliot said in his inaugural, "concentration, and the highest development of his own peculiar faculty, is the only prudence." Yet the student need not equate his "bent" with some faculty found in a list in a textbook of mental philosophy. There was too much mystery in man for that. A student might find that a certain teacher, or courses taught by a certain method, were most effective for him. If so, Eliot believed, he should be free to choose accordingly.[20]

In addition to his attacks on "symmetrical development," Eliot opposed those advocates of mental discipline who emphasized the difficulty or repellence of a subject as a source of its value in mental training. Artificial difficulty was for Eliot the unpardonable educational sin. Without quibbling over fine points, he simply reversed the long-standing version of mental discipline which held that a young man built up his will by doing what he did not like. Eliot in effect merged the "interest" and "effort" schools by maintaining that the student developed his will by doing what he liked, not what he disliked; for then he would be truly doing it, not seeking ways of evading it, or wasting effort in hating it. "The thinking process must spring from within, must be motived from within," he said. "The pupil's own will must be brought into play; he must see in the process something of interest, or profit for himself. In child or adult thinking involves willing." He advised new students at Harvard to choose studies "which will, through your interest in them, develop your working power." By this line of reasoning, although it looked to mental training, a student should be free to take what interested him, what offered delights, even what "came easy." [21]

Eliot argued that a student should develop the mental faculty with which he was naturally best endowed, but without noting the contradiction, he came more and more to contend that there was a generalized mental power which all liberal subjects strengthened. Although he continued to associate certain subjects with particular faculties (and who could call him wrong in saying, for instance, that the study of English composition strengthens the power of expression?), he tended in his later years to avoid the narrow identification of ability with subject. After all, in intelligent conversation mental processes worked together— "all in a flash." The generalized mental power that Eliot stressed appeared sometimes to be an amalgam of will, work, and productivity. At other times it was "constructive imagination." "Argument," he said at one point, "the logical setting forth of a train of reasoning—that is almost the consummation of education." [22] Such holistic views of intellect supported Eliot's determination to leave the choice of studies up to the student. Even in the days when Eliot lay greatest stress on specific faculties, however, he had maintained a healthy sense of the unknown nature of learning, its complexity, and its unlooked-for rewards. All three views—specific faculties trainable by specific subjects, generalized mental ability, and psychological agnosticism—were used by Eliot to justify free course election. Apparently, institutional considerations or an ideology that went beyond education, and not any consistent theory of learning, dictated his advocacy of the elective system.

III

Before his election to the presidency of Harvard, Eliot did not conspicuously advocate freedom of students to choose their courses. Early in 1869 he expressed belief in a required core of studies distributed among various fields of learning. The system at Lawrence Scientific School aroused his scorn for offering "no common discipline, and no general course of co-ordinated studies which all candidates for any degree must pass through." He opposed overspecialization, depreciating the degree given at Lawrence to young men "densely ignorant" of everything except a single science, and he advocated a system that provided both breadth and a limited degree of specialization. This "balanced" system was the pattern at M.I.T. which Eliot had earlier tried to establish at Lawrence.[23]

By the time of his inaugural, Eliot's view had changed. He now pushed breadth back toward the pre-college years. "Through all the period of boyhood the school studies should be representative; all the main fields of knowledge should be entered upon. But the young man of nineteen or twenty ought to know what he likes best and is most fit for." Specialization dominated his new view of the college years. "When the revelation of his own peculiar taste and capacity comes to a young man," he proclaimed, "let him reverently give it welcome, thank God, and take courage. Thereafter he knows his way to happy, enthusiastic work, and, God willing, to usefulness and success." Midway in his first year as president, Eliot would admit only one tenable objection to the elective system, "like most things worth having,—it is costly." "With regard to the college proper," he wrote in 1872, "the one thing which we are doing at Cambridge is the introduction of a true University freedom of studies under the name of the 'elective system.' . . . I believe that Harvard is doing a great service to American education by leading the way in this reform. All other issues are comparatively unimportant." [24]

How can Eliot's conversion be explained? Partly, of course, by a shift of institutional setting. He continued to maintain that for a technical school the M.I.T. group system was best. At Harvard the faculty already had elective reforms underway. The anti-elective mood of the 1850s had passed, and Ticknor was once again a curricular hero. The governing boards were sympathetic; money was available. The Overseers' committee on the needs of the college had equated Harvard's becoming a "true university" with an end to the prescribed curriculum and had called for new funds for that purpose. The new president was expected to continue the elective advance.[25]

But Eliot was no institutional functionary. Much of his conversion came from continued reflection on the problems of collegiate education. In the summer of 1869 he did some of the hardest thinking of his life. Examining the elective system that had emerged through forty years of practice at Harvard, he found striking deficiencies. Wider learning in the university seemed dictated by the rapid expansion of human knowledge. Through a recent increase in tuition, and certain benefactions, he was in the happy position of being able to increase the faculty. The elective system could free students to pursue newly represented fields and newly offered advanced work in established fields. Indeed, in later years, the graduate school was looked upon by those most knowledgeable as the direct outcome of the elective system.[26]

An often overlooked source of Eliot's electivism was his concern with teaching method. "The actual problem to be solved is not what to teach, but how to teach," he told his inaugural audience. The surest way to improve the quality of teaching, he concluded, was the elective system. A teacher who was himself pushing out the boundaries of a subject would be most interested and most compelling when he taught classes advanced enough to be near his own area of exploration, and any teacher would teach elementary classes better when the students were there by desire and not by compulsion. Another point, which Eliot made less often but which may have figured importantly in his thinking, was that course election gave blunt evidence of student judgment of teachers and thus put the teachers on their mettle.[27]

A young man could learn to discipline himself, Eliot argued, only if he were released from external controls and only if he were interested enough in some goal to see the worth of self-discipline. His picture of his son Charles's career showed how he viewed this effect of the elective system. Charles enrolled at Harvard in 1878, where in a fully required freshman curriculum, he found himself largely continuing "his uncongenial school studies." At the end of his freshman year, he recorded "a thanksgiving that his 'classical education' was at last ended." Entering the elysium of voluntary studies, he found all of his electives to his liking. Although as a college student he had no idea what his profession would be and his choice of electives appeared incoherent, he chose courses remarkably appropriate to his later needs as a landscape architect. Eliot's belief in the elective system's benefit to students deepened until he looked on it as a student "right." In 1907, when most spokesmen for American higher education, including faculty members, ignored any student participation in academic freedom, Eliot carefully included both faculty and students in his advocacy of that ideal.[28]

This freedom was not a matter of educational expediency. "The elective system is, in the first place, an outcome of the Protestant Reformation. In the next place, it is an outcome of the spirit of political liberty." Eliot looked on American culture as peculiarly pervaded by liberty—in religion, in political life, in economic affairs. He began his advocacy of electives shortly after the Civil War, when the extension of liberty to oppressed groups had the prestige of the nation's greatest military effort, and he brought that advocacy to its culmination in the Progressive Era. "When the student of history reviews the great achievements of the human race," he said in 1908, "he comes to the conclusion that those achievements which have brought deliverance from some form of terror or oppression, or have been gains for some sort of freedom, have proved to be institutionally the most durable achievements,—one might almost say the only durable." He defined the Harvard free elective system with words central to Liberalism: "individuals exercise freely their spontaneous diversity of choice." The elective system was more than a technique to accommodate the expansion of learning. It was one of the fullest expressions of a rising ideology.[29]

IV

The ease with which the advance of the Harvard elective system can be sketched conceals the struggle that brought it about.[30] Teachers of required courses, loath to surrender the ascription of special value to their fields, poured out their anguish in seemingly endless faculty meetings. Eliot recalled various faculty objections that slowed the expansion of electives in his early years: the college could not afford the requisite increases in faculty, expanding the curriculum would force the college to hire many young and inexperienced teachers, students would come with motives other than a yearning for "hard intellectual work."[31] Only in retrospect did the system's advance appear inexorable.

In 1868–69, the last year before Eliot's accession to the presidency, all freshman studies (later called "courses") were required, as were half of the sophomore studies, and slightly fewer than half of those for juniors and seniors. Upperclassmen could choose their nonrequired studies from short lists, each strictly limited to a particular class. Almost as important as the remission of requirements was the gradual move away from identifying each course with a class and toward the new practice of listing courses by department name and number. In 1872 the catalogue announced that any course was open to a student of any class if he could convince the instructor he was qualified. A year later at least one course included representatives of all four classes. This phase of university rationalization undeniably promoted individual freedom. By 1875 Eliot could announce that only "a few fragments" remained required outside the freshman year, and in 1884 Harvard became, its faculty believed, the first college in the country to extend electives to freshmen (in any sense other than an option between two courses).[32] This was not done halfheartedly. Every freshman requirement was removed except English, weekly lectures in chemistry and physics, and either French or German, and these could be "anticipated" in preparatory school. The lectures in physics were dropped in 1890, and those in chemistry in

1894. When the requirements for sophomore themes and junior forensics were dropped, in 1899, the elective system reached its apex at Harvard.[33] The 1899 liberation was "welcomed everywhere," an undergraduate commented, "for a prescribed course is always disliked." [34]

Two earlier dates were more significant than 1899, however —1872, when seniors were freed almost totally from requirements, and 1884, when partial election for freshmen was introduced.[35] That undergraduates might in any year pick all their courses and that neophytes fresh from secondary school might be allowed to pick any were two departures radical enough to cause scandal in the American academic community.

Virtually every college except the poorest allowed some student election by the 1880s; thus, college leaders generally failed to realize until 1884 how radically the elective principle was being applied at Harvard. When the truth dawned, academic conservatives undertook a campaign to expose the apostasy at Cambridge. Most claimed that this new student freedom needed counterbalancing controls and that in failing to provide them Harvard set a bad example. This confrontation between Harvard and other colleges had an importance beyond curricular policies. It marked a movement away from collegiate parochialism toward regular inter-institutional communication that involved mutual criticism but suggested avenues for cooperation. It was an intellectual parallel to the generally friendly rivalry of the new intercollegiate athletic contests.

It is not the advance of the elective system at Harvard that calls for explanation; rational justifications for it abound. The difficulty comes in understanding its uncompromising application and Eliot's continuing adherence to its radical form. In retrospect it appears to have been a reform that succeeded too well. As early as 1881 Eliot predicted that the elective principle would soon apply to all courses. He later urged that the principle be expanded to allow a spontaneous diversity of choice that reflected the "infinite" diversity of human mind and character. Professor George Herbert Palmer, one of Eliot's converts, argued that to have the early college years required and the later years elective would "contaminate" both, that the elective principle once introduced could not be resisted, and that this irreversibility was a good thing.[36]

There were occasional debates on the elective principle at the meetings of the American Institute of Instruction and the National Education Association, and there was an important exchange on the subject between Eliot and President James McCosh of Princeton before a private club in 1885. Serious magazines of the day, such as the *Andover Review*, the *Independent*, and the *Nation*, published some polemics as furious as old abolition-proslavery exchanges. It became common to hear that a decline in student misbehavior or a rise in enrollment at a speaker's own college proved the wisdom of precisely its degree of electivism. Debaters at times revealed a lack of acquaintance with the actual system in the institution being criticized. Although Eliot prided himself on the openness of the experiment at Harvard, his critics spoke of the Harvard catalogue as if it were printed in secret code.[37]

Among leading critics of Eliot and Harvard were Yale's President Noah Porter and Professor George T. Ladd; Princeton's President James McCosh and Professor Andrew F. West; from younger institutions, Oberlin's Professor William G. Frost and California's Professor George H. Howison. West, who taught Latin at Princeton from 1883 to 1928, often exerted more power than the presidents he served under. His criticisms of Harvard's elective system, which he began to publish in 1886, continued for decades. At times, West spoke like a rigid mental disciplinarian who believed he knew which course did what to which youthful mental process. He distinguished between "the heavy studies, the chief subjects of discipline and instruction, the very stock and staple of American education," and another group, "the studies of information or accomplishment, rather than of training." Harvard students under the elective system had turned away from the first and toward the second, he claimed, and he used Eliot's annual reports for evidence.[38]

West's certainty about the pre-eminent disciplinary value of certain subjects obviously contradicted Eliot's educational theory. No less opposed to Eliot's ideas was the high value West set on symmetrical mental development. In West's opinion, Harvard tempted students to become premature specialists, bypassing genuine liberal education and sound intellectual training. West struck directly at Eliot's doctrine of individual differences. The Harvard president, he said, was so concerned with "the 'infinite diversity of mind' in secondary traits," that he ignored "the 'infinite' unity of all educable minds in their essential characteristics." To West the corrective for dilletantism was not specialization, or even (as some were beginning to suggest) a certain depth in every subject studied, but rather requirement of the "solid" subjects. The most promising alternative, West insisted, was the one practiced at Princeton, "a substantial required training in prescribed studies which promote general culture, supplemented by freedom of choice in elective studies." As actually practiced at Princeton in the 1880s, this meant no election in the first two years and considerable requirement in the last two.[39]

In the mid-eighties Eliot took cognizance of criticisms of the elective system and answered them in detail.[40] But in 1899 a new college president failed to find any recent discussions of the elective system and asked Eliot whether his "strong opinions" like "Prussia's boots" had silenced the discussion. Eliot did not deserve the accusation of Prussianism. He had, for instance, urged one anti-elective critic to publish, saying, "I believe absolutely in public criticism and discussion. I have been ready to take my part in them for the last twenty-two years; and I still am." It is true, however, that after the crescendo of the mid-eighties, public argument over electives died down for a time. Colleges such as Yale and Princeton gradually increased the amount of election allowed, though in a spirit decidedly different from that at Harvard and with a cautious reliance on controls. But by the turn of the century, the question was in the air again. In an attack on Harvard's electivism a Jesuit academician was able to enhance his argument with recent quotations from the presidents of Yale, Chicago, Western Reserve, and Hamilton.[41]

Eliot's reaction to the increased electives at Yale was a mixture of satisfaction, misinterpretation, and pique. "Yale is simply repeating the precise steps which succeeded each other here in the development of the elective system, but she is repeating them at the interval of from twenty-five to thirty years, during which she has lost a great deal of ground in the university race. The most curious fact about it is that the men concerned with these changes at Yale seem to have an impression that they have themselves invented them." [42] At the turn of the century Eliot was blandly confident of the success and worth of the free elective system. "It has by no means wrought out as yet all the good it can do; but it is firmly established throughout the country." But in 1908, having felt the strength of renewed criticisms, he presented a careful rejustification of Harvard's system in one of his Harris Lectures at Northwestern. [43]

V

There were three salient concepts in the criticism of the free elective system: coherence, the idea that certain combinations or sequences of courses fitted together rationally and should be prescribed; breadth, the idea that there was a minimum range of particular subjects which every student should study; and depth, the idea that the student should pursue some subject well beyond the level of superficial acquaintance.

Those most emphatically calling for coherence were the leaders of institutions whose curriculums were arranged in the "group system." Eliot agreed that this system was suitable for technological schools. He had favored it while teaching at M.I.T., and it characterized the Lawrence Scientific School after 1871. With a definite professional object already in view, he reasoned, it was possible to tell the young man what subjects best fit him for it, and since these subjects might fill up most of his course, it was also appropriate to tell him how most directly to get nonprofessional breadth.

This very association of the group system with technological schools may have strengthened Eliot's opposition, inasmuch as he insisted that all Harvard College subjects were liberal. But he mainly objected to the system's apparent arbitrariness, its neglect of individual diversity. Neither students nor subjects came in pre-established patterns, he argued. Generally, he felt that sequential demands within departments met any legitimate need for coherence, and he once suggested that courses which made bad combinations when taken simultaneously be preventively offered at the same hour.[44]

West accused Eliot of concentrating his attack on the group system to such an extent that it appeared to be the only alternative to the free elective system, and, indeed, Eliot's objections to the group system grew more elaborate as the system became less prevalent. (Cornell abandoned it in 1896.) In his lecture of 1908 he summarized his opposition. The group system blocked spontaneous diversity, it demanded too early a commitment by the student, it deprived the teacher of the sense that his course was freely chosen, and it compelled specialization. Eliot admitted that there had been some loosening up within the groups. Perhaps he hoped to administer a *coup de grace*.[45]

From among those who objected to the loss of breadth in the free elective system came the observation, "The elective system . . . dazzles us with the rich variety of electives, and somehow produces the impression that a student can take them *all* in the four years. Its advocates . . . studiously conceal the fundamental and essential branches which the student may omit." Eliot's mind did seem to leap from the observation that it was "impossible for one mind to compass more than an insignificant fraction of the great sum of acquired knowledge" to the unstated conclusion that it was therefore wrong to select any of it as suitable for a required minimum. He admitted himself "fundamentally a complete skeptic as to the necessity of any subject whatever as an element in the education of a gentleman and a scholar." Critics of the free elective system produced widely differing lists of subjects which should be prescribed. This very uncertainty about what should make up a core helped Eliot to ignore their argument. A plan that posed a greater threat, however, was the looser area requirement adopted by Cornell in 1905. Ending the free elective system, Cornell required that out of the one hundred and twenty hours of course work required for graduation, twenty-four should be chosen in an arrangement that guaranteed distribution in four different areas of knowledge. It was a modest but important shift, and it made Eliot's position at Harvard harder to maintain.[46]

Eliot not only opposed requiring courses that would give a "broad general foundation," he attacked such architectural metaphors as misleading. After the battles to dislodge Greek, Latin, and mathematics, it seemed foolhardy to invite representatives of the disciplines once again to vie for recognition as "that without which no one is an educated man." The elective reform had sought to loosen a grasp. "Requirement" was the enemy. If some of the new subjects had less general relevance than the old ones, it was better to let students discover this for themselves than to risk restoring the curricular straitjacket. The tenacity of requirements once instituted had been painfully proved. It was better to let sleeping—or at least drowsy—faculty jealousies and vanities lie. Besides, by the 1890s students seemed to have discovered on their own certain "culture courses," which most of them elected. It was regrettable but not disastrous that such special student favor was won by no natural science (except one easy course which taught "all the geology necessary to a gentleman"). Curricular openness, Eliot implied, was particularly beneficial at the stage reached by American colleges in the late nineteenth century. That all branches of "sound knowledge" were equally valuable for "mature students" was the appropriate view for his generation at least, he contended, since so many new fields had just been given academic recognition.[47]

To arguments based on the nature of the student rather than on the state of human knowledge, Eliot had equally ready answers. Yale and Princeton educators often argued that a student should be given time to adapt to being away from home or some home-like preparatory school. They dreaded the "headlong plunge into freedom," which came with free electives in the freshman year.[48] Even granting the new richness of the curriculum, might the authorities not better select for the neophyte what he should take the first year (or first two) while he gained in sophistication and acquaintance with the college's offerings?

Eliot admitted that there might be temptations for a young student in a university environment, but he believed that "the wise decision is to withdraw [the youth] betimes from a discipline which he is outgrowing, and put him under a discipline which he is to grow up to." Eliot saw the American eighteen-year-old as a rather mature, self-knowing young man. "At eighteen the American boy has passed the age when a compulsory external discipline is useful." To tell him what subjects to take would simply preserve the customs of the school in what should be a free university. Why encourage in any way the continuation of schoolboy immaturities in the new environment?

Yes, a certain range of subjects was beneficial to a youth, and some of these subjects could be readily specified. But this, Eliot averred, was the task of secondary education. The schools could provide the representative education in the "great subdivisions of elementary knowledge," and the colleges should require that the lower schools do so, rather than preserve part of this core work in the early collegiate years. Such an arrangement would elevate the character of the work done at both levels. "The Elective system will not work well unless the preparatory training of the young men who are to be subjected to it is good," Eliot admitted in 1874. "A young man does not know what to choose unless he has had a glimpse of the main fields of knowledge." At this time he pictured the college as still obliged to provide part of the "broad foundation" during the freshman year, though he counted on rising admission standards to change the situation. As a matter of fact, Harvard's entrance level already demanded work equivalent to many colleges' required freshman year.[49]

In valuing depth Eliot shared a good deal of ground with the critics of the free elective system. Indeed, the superficiality of the old required curriculum had been one of his principal objections to it. His concept of individual bent suggested concentration in an area suited to the student's natural abilities. Even Eliot's seemingly contradictory belief in generalized mental discipline placed high value on concentration, since the pursuit of one subject in depth developed broadly applicable intellectual power. Eliot's social ethic also justified depth. Only by concentrating could the student reach the state of useful productivity. Thus would he answer those who spoke of the elective system's asocial individualism.

Yet Eliot refused to require concentration. The device of the major subject, developed by Jordan at Indiana as early as 1885, never won support from the Harvard president. It would be superfluous, he maintained, since "there is a prevailing tendency on the part of every competent student to carry far any congenial subject once entered upon." The elective program, furthermore, built character by letting the student make mistakes. If his mistake was that of dabbling, he should be allowed to make it; it was to be hoped that he would come to his senses at some point in his college career. If he never came to his senses, then he had proved himself one of the unworthy, of less concern to the college than the serious, competent student was. Eliot believed, however, that even the unambitious student who took an "all-round" course worked harder under the free elective system. Fundamentally, Eliot did not want to let the camel's nose of requirement back into the tent. He insisted that colleges must grant the student freedom "to specialize early in his course, or not to specialize at all." [50]

Although unwilling to require concentration, Eliot supported devices that encouraged it. Shortly before he became president, the faculty had developed a system of "honors," which Eliot praised to alumni during his first year. By 1885, honors usually required six full-year courses in a department, plus a special examination and thesis. Under Eliot, in 1879, a lesser form of concentration-plus-quality, called "honorable mention," was devised. It usually required three courses in the same department and (like honors) an average in this work of 80 per cent. This latter form, Palmer testified, had been accepted to such a degree that it was "not quite the thing" to graduate without it. The more extended honors program, however, was chosen by very few. Eliot described these programs as "opportunities," with no suggestion that their element of concentration might set a general standard.[51]

Eliot had favorable words for both of the educational objectives that his successor was to make obligatory—concentration (depth) and distribution (breadth). Of the two, Eliot leaned toward depth. His own satisfactions came from concentration of ability and energy, and he imagined others to be likewise constructed. A wide-ranging education suggested the trivial and unproductive, or to speak in a more characteristic Eliot vein, the "unserviceable." Nevertheless, he had occasional good words for the emerging "culture courses" at Harvard. He hoped students would study landscape design, which would "open the eyes to natural beauty and the mind to the principles of harmony, contrast, and proportion in scenery, whether natural or artificial." In other words, the subject was of value to nonspecialists. It pleased him to think of Harvard graduate students as "men of general cultivation besides being specialists." [52]

Institutionally, distribution aided horizontal expansion and thus widened the variety of studies, a process which Eliot welcomed. But there was at least as much to be gained from having students concentrate. The more courses they took in a single department, the more that department would have to extend its offerings and the more specialized its faculty could become. If a university offering advanced study were to develop at Harvard, this route was necessary, for graduate students to populate advanced courses appeared very slowly.

Although his free elective system guaranteed neither breadth nor depth, Eliot saw merit in both. His greater emphasis on depth can be understood in part as a tactic he used for overthrowing the old pattern of curricular prescription. That pattern was most assailable because of the dabbling it required in a variety of subjects. To force the student to touch on the entire range of subjects in the name of breadth had cheapened them all, depriving them, Eliot argued, of their potential contribution to mental training. "To study the conquests of great minds in any field of knowledge must be good training," Eliot believed. But to get near the great minds required continued work in one field. Thus Eliot praised the elective system primarily for the support it gave to concentration. It offered students, he claimed, a chance for that delight which came only with the sense of mastery.[53]

Eliot's case against uniformity he almost always won, and the verdict of later educators is largely in his favor. But his case against compulsion he ultimately lost. The two controls that were later adopted generally throughout American higher education, the required distribution of subjects among various fields and the required pursuit of one subject in considerable depth, were not part of Eliot's Harvard. Concentration he favored and stimulated, and he welcomed students' trying out different subjects and taking "culture courses," but his emphasis on the free individual restrained him from enforcing these patterns. "If Harvard College is an 'inchoate chaos,' " he responded to a critic, "it is a chaos through which hundreds of young Americans yearly steer each his own profitable way." [54]

VI

The college entered as fully into Eliot's plan for reform as any other part of the university, but it was perhaps the least tractable. His *Atlantic Monthly* article of 1869 had named "the enthusiastic study of subjects for the love of them without any ulterior objects" as a dominant collegiate ideal. In his inaugural he repeated this theme. "The choice offered to the student [in Harvard College] does not lie between liberal studies and professional or utilitarian studies. All the studies which are open to him are liberal and disciplinary, not narrow or special." By 1885 some distinctly special subjects, including Old Iranian and Comparative Osteology, were included in the Harvard College curriculum, but Eliot still stressed nonutilitarianism, approximating his definition of liberal studies to the research ideal. Liberal studies, he then asserted, are those "which are pursued in the scientific spirit for truth's sake." [55]

This effort to identify special studies as liberal indicates Eliot's lack of sharp distinction between collegiate and graduate training. Admission to college, not the attainment of the bachelor's degree, was to him the major transition. The maturity of the student was the criterion, and he insisted that eighteen, not twenty-one, was the age by which character was formed. He repeatedly named eighteen as the ideal age of college entrance, whereas the Yale Report had suggested fourteen and President McCosh sixteen.[56]

This blurring of the distinction between undergraduate and graduate studies, this talk of university freedom for eighteen-year-olds, raised a storm of protest. Critics charged Eliot with importing a misconstruction of the German university, ignoring the parallels between the American college and the German Gymnasium and the French lycée. When he boldly spoke in his inaugural of elevating secondary schools to the level of the Gymnasium and making the American college resemble the German faculty of philosophy, he did indeed give the impression that the college was to become a school of advanced studies and cease to purvey general education. But if such an aim were achieved, would any meaning remain for the A.B.? Would it make any sense to require Americans to finish a college course before entering law or medical school, as Eliot recommended? After all, German law and medical faculties did not require their students to pass first through the philosophical faculty. From Yale especially came objections that Eliot was inconsistent. At Harvard itself, Overseer Francis Cabot Lowell complained of finding undergraduates in narrowly specialized courses.[57]

Eliot's best response would have been to picture the college as an institution which aided the student in a transition from general studies to special studies. His failure to do so can be traced partly to his fear of preserving schoolboy standards in college and partly to his recollection of his own undergraduate experience. His ideal for Harvard College drew on a vision of himself, working enthusiastically and of his own free choice in Professor Cooke's chemistry laboratory. But in the remaking of the college during Eliot's administration, this ideal became only one of several options for the Harvard undergraduate.

As a student Eliot had worked unusually closely with a faculty member and become his friend; at the same time he had been cold toward his classmates. This personal history was predictive of the Harvard he sought to design, emphasizing faculty-student relations and letting student social life take care of itself. At his inaugural he warned that "repression of genuine sentiment and emotion" was carried too far at Harvard, and he advised the undergraduates, "When you feel a true admiration for a teacher, a glow of enthusiasm for work, a thrill of pleasure at some excellent saying, give it expression. Do not be ashamed of these emotions." In spite of such views, Eliot was labeled "the spiritual father of the glacial era." "Oh, how we hated him!" recalled President William DeWitt Hyde of Bowdoin, a Harvard graduate of 1879, who was later a great admirer of Eliot. Much of this antipathy is attributable to Eliot's formal bearing. John Jay Chapman, who coined the "glacial era" phrase, preserved the highly external image of Eliot as "the martinet who stalked across the yard." Eliot often took personal interest in some undergraduate who was in financial straits, or ill; for instance, he once moved a student suffering from smallpox into his own house. But even though students heard such stories, they did not change their picture of Eliot as Harvard coldness personified.[58]

There is abundant testimony to the lack of warmth between students and faculty of Harvard in the 1870s and 1880s. An undergraduate during the first four years of Eliot's tenure recalled the "formal or neutral terms" between students and instructors, "affabilities between the Faculty and the students" not being in fashion. The Reverend Andrew P. Peabody, until his retirement in 1881, had willingly played a paternalistic role akin to that of small college presidents. He was recalled as "the heart of the College," offering students "the affection, emotion, and friendship of college life." In keeping with the spirit of older paternalism, Peabody's required course in ethics made few demands on the students' intellects.[59]

Aware of his own austere manner, Eliot continued to strive for greater intimacy between students and faculty. He once called the moral influence of teacher on student the "essential element in any academic system." At an alumni banquet in 1886 he observed, "The great problem of education—correctly understood—is the bringing of a young, fresh, ambitious mind into intimate contact with a mature, master mind. When I became president of the university I found this old attitude of antagonism. It has been a difficult task to change all that, but I think the younger men here will bear me out in saying that much has been done toward it." [60] Actually, a conference committee of students and faculty initiated the year before had soon collapsed. During the late 1880s some subject-oriented societies were formed in which students and faculty stiffly discussed serious subjects, and after 1889 each freshman had an adviser, a relationship that proved highly perfunctory.[61] Better success came with the appointment in 1891 of LeBaron Russell Briggs as dean of Harvard College.

Eliot, observing that students were going to this youthful-looking assistant professor of English for counsel, decided to make him dean, to the dismay of faculty who wondered how such a "pink-faced boy" could perform the college police duties. But soon the college was no longer on a police basis. In Briggs the students found a friend, to him they told the truth, and even those penalized admitted his fairness. He had an uncanny way of recognizing the student in need of reassurance, or cash. From the English department came also the famous "Copey," Charles Townsend Copeland, who became an instructor in 1892, lived in dormitories, welcomed visitors, and turned a wide range of students into his friends, or, some believed, into his sycophants. Eliot declined to promote the "unproductive" Copeland to an assistant professorship.[62]

Eliot was not much concerned with the loosening of ties among students. Until about 1885, fraternal sentiment among those entering college together continued strong; after that, the end of the common freshman year and the rapid increase in numbers lessened such class allegiance. A drastic social split ensued. The "right" group became that element from particular preparatory schools who lived in the elegant private dormitories of the "Gold Coast" and were invited to social events in Boston. Family background remained conspicuous, since a student's family was often near by, in Boston. The college was divided between society men (members of selective clubs) and nonsociety men. Among the latter there was a great deal of personal isolation. Friendships thrived within coteries, but loneliness could be the lot of a student who was a child of the new immigrants, poor, and hyper-studious. Albert Bushnell Hart described the transition: Harvard had once had the intimacy of a village; after the Civil War it became like a town, where one might know everybody, but friendship was a matter of a social set; finally, by the 1890s, the college experienced "the city's absolute indifference to next-door neighbors." [63]

Eliot revealed limited sensitivity to the sources of student comradeship, as when he commented, "There is no better starting-point for a college friendship than sympathy in an intellectual pursuit, or than a common devotion to an interesting subject or an interesting teacher." He admitted the "undue luxury" of the private dormitories of the Gold Coast, but was not certain that such contrasts of rich and poor were injurious. "In this respect, as in many others, the University is an epitome of the modern world." As to college dormitories, he judged them a bad investment. In the early nineties, after William Lloyd Garrison, son of the abolitionist, publicly denounced the sadistic burning of his son's arm during the initiation ceremony of a Harvard club (D.K.E.), newspapers took up his charge of "dissipation and immorality, bearing the stamp of fashion" among Harvard students and depicted Eliot as largely indifferent to the uglier aspects of student behavior. Henry Ware Putnam, an Overseer, joined the attack, declaring that recent controls had been instituted despite Eliot's opposition and his "do-nothing policy." [64]

The Harvard Union, an elaborate imitation of a gentleman's club, which both students and alumni could join, was built next to the Yard in 1901, the culmination of several proposals and the benefaction of Henry Lee Higginson. Eliot of course supported the new institution, hoping that class spirit would be replaced by the preferable "university spirit," which the Union sponsored. The Union proved a convenient place for meetings, but it was somewhat off the beaten track. Men from the Gold Coast joined but never warmed to it. It proved little more than a palliative for "the social question," and during 1903 and 1904 its membership decreased alarmingly, to be restored only by appeals that made it look like a charity. In 1900 faculty wives began holding Friday afternoon teas in Phillips Brooks House. The gesture revealed the general worry about isolation, but fell far short of curing it.[65]

Whereas many expressed alarm at the decline of united action and college spirit, William James in 1903 presented a warm defense of the side of Harvard life that made it least like a family or a club. He pointed to "the outside men," whose loyalty to Harvard was subtler than "the clubhouse pattern." These admirable students came to Harvard "because they have heard of her persistently atomistic constitution, of her tolerance of exceptionality and eccentricity, of her devotion to the principles of individual vocation and choice. . . . You cannot make single one-ideaed regiments of her classes." [66]

Friendship among classmates in earlier days had been in part a comradeship of the oppressed. Eliot's administration began with a rapid repeal of petty rules for student behavior. By 1877 a rule book of nearly forty pages had been reduced to one of five. When Eliot advised proctors simply to stay indoors during student bonfires in the yard, he successfully undermined the pranksters. Although his "liberty in education" found its most conspicuous fulfillment in the elective system, he carefully made freedom from the rigid discipline of the old college part of the new dispensation. A student's disciplinary record lost its effect on his rank in class, and in 1886 letter grades replaced percentage grades, which had had the implication of close measurement by some perfect standard.[67]

Eliot attributed the schoolboy spirit at colleges to "enforced attendance upon recitations, lectures, and religious exercises." Such regulations might have had merit when students had come to college at fourteen or fifteen, he observed, but the average entering age had risen to eighteen. He denounced the *in loco parentis* theory as "an ancient fiction which ought no longer to deceive anybody," and called the weekly academic rankings at West Point a threat to self-reliance. The "genuine university method" made no pretense of maintaining "parental or monastic discipline over its students." In America, at least, the individual must govern himself, and self-control was learned only through liberty. Thus the "voluntary system" at Harvard came to include voluntary attendance at classes. As early as 1873 Eliot was questioned about rumors that Harvard had no required class attendance, and a bright sophomore of 1884 who attended a weekly class only twice before the final examination passed without any sign of disapproval. Under a new rule adopted in 1886 students could regulate their own class attendance, a teacher retaining the right to exclude a student doing shoddy work.[68] Educators at other institutions often seemed more shocked by Harvard's freedom of class attendance than by its freedom of course election.

For a halcyon three years of "discretionary supervision," students had for all practical purposes unlimited cuts; then the virtuosity of student hedonism returned to haunt Eliot and his faculty. The discovery by a father that his son, a full-time student, was vacationing in Havana publicized the dangers of the new dispensation, and the faculty in the spring of 1889 adopted measures "to secure more frequent examinations, the prompter return of absences, and the quicker detection of cases of neglect of duty." The Overseers, who had at first demanded a morning roll call, were mollified. A professor returning that fall from a year's leave felt himself "cramped and belittled by the new regulations," while his students got "recitation room results." [69]

But evasion of class attendance remained easy. Students could "sign-off" with feigned illness when they wanted to cut classes. Dean Hurlbut acidly observed, "No sane man can accept as sufficient the great body of excuses handed in by students who ask to be treated as men,—weak eyes, . . . colds, headaches, stomachaches, and that intestinal trouble whose most serious havoc is in the orthography rather than the bodies of its victims." [70] This malingering brought moralistic comparisons with the standards of business life in the president's annual reports and calls by the college physician on students reported ill.

The tightening of the rules in 1889 was an admission, unusual for the Eliot era, that institutions should sometimes coerce individuals. But this check to liberty in education did not change Eliot's central educational theory that the desired growth of character and mind came only when the student himself was free to choose. The theological grounding of this theory was that free will was meaningless if it did not involve freedom to sin. For Eliot academic freedom for students was more than the elective principle. It meant that "the student ought to find himself free to determine the method of his daily life with no more restrictions than the habits and customs of civilized society necessarily impose." Some Eliot-supporters could give the devices of the voluntary system vast ethical overtones, Palmer, for instance, arguing that freedom to choose one's courses "uplifts character as no other training can, and through influence on character it ennobles all methods of teaching and discipline. . . . The will is honored as of prime consequence." [71]

Eliot often spoke about developing character. His inaugural included reassuring passages on the safeguards in college life against "sloth, vulgarity, and depravity," and in a homily to the entering freshmen of 1905, he urged a "spotless reputation" won "by living with honor, on honor." But he never revived the old-time college shibboleths that elevated character by belittling intellect. Not for him the pronouncement of President Nathan Lord of Dartmouth, that "the very cultivation of the mind has frequently a tendency to impair the moral sensibilities." The daily regimen Eliot recommended to students revealed his hierarchy of values: "sleep, 8 hours; meals, 3 hours; exercise, 2 hours; social duties, 1 hour; study, 10 hours. Sundays, no work." His negative phrase for social life was appropriately linked to the smallest time allotment. He could bluntly downgrade mere good manners. His ideal of a ten-hour work day was probably not far from his own undergraduate habits, but it showed little grasp of the realities of later Harvard College life. "Hard Money and Soft Electives" read a transparency carried in undergraduate torchlight processions.[72]

Loafers could be found in the college, Eliot admitted, but his view of "the careless, indifferent, lazy boys" was that they could not do worse under the system of liberty than they had under the old compulsory system, and at least they might lose their sense of grievance. Although he hoped they might pick teachers who would stimulate them, he could say dismissively, "It really does not make much difference what these unawakened minds dawdle with." [73] This attitude might be called Social Darwinist were it not that the academically unfit found survival at Harvard made easy.

Until 1893 a student could receive the bachelor's degree with D's in three-quarters of his courses; then the limit was lowered to one-half. The students' attitudes toward teachers were often cynical. Private tutors could cram a student for a passing mark in a course he seldom attended, and they could occasionally even win him an A. A thesis ghost writer informed Eliot that there were always about one hundred students who came to Harvard determined to do nothing, yet managed to get diplomas. Even a professor's son, a senior, believed that what constituted a university was a large variety of student activities. He confidently proclaimed in 1899 that Harvard had attained that level.[74] With such tendencies thriving, the Harvard bachelor's degree became alarmingly indeterminate as an indicator of intellectual achievement. Since Eliot had so strongly linked work to the intellectual aims of the college, this was a failure of considerable importance.

VII

Few developments revealed the limits of Eliot's control over life in Harvard College as clearly as the rise of intercollegiate athletics did. A persistent critic of exaggerated attention to sports and of the very nature of football, Eliot presided at Harvard during the era when intercollegiate football, initiated in the 1870s, rose to spectacular mass popularity. Frederick Rudolph links the football mania to the industrial and imperialistic aggressiveness that characterized the nation. Laurence Veysey sees it as combining the romantic and the simplistically practical impulses of students of Eliot's day. Clearly the students found something in the muscularity, the competition, the mass excitement that met a need. Through a failure of imagination Eliot never grasped what it was. The distant, objective tone of this statement was characteristic: "While spontaneous applause for good playing on either side is an exhilarating feature of competitive sports, continuous, pumped cheering during good and bad playing alike is absolutely unnatural, and has no counterpart in the contests of real life." [75]

The faculty first assumed oversight of intercollegiate athletics in 1882, with a committee soon reconstituted to include alumni and undergraduate members. This committee, a far better control than many universities created, was not vigorous enough in combating athletic excesses to suit Eliot. After initially greeting the new interest in sports as building "perseverance, resolution and self-denial," he shifted his stance. Again and again his annual reports attacked the injuries, overtraining, cheating, and distraction from intellectual concerns that resulted from intercollegiate competition. He saw the lesson taught by football as "driving a trade or winning a fight, no matter how." But the prestige of the game mounted. An alumnus of 1841 who lived in Cambridge complained in the mid-nineties that in both town and university he found only athletes discussed, rather than eminent scholars or thinkers, as in an earlier day. Eliot never succeeded in obtaining the suspension of football, although twice, in 1895 and 1905, such action was seriously considered.[76]

In response to the first of these attacks, Senator Henry Cabot Lodge, at the commencement dinner of 1896, testified: "The time given to athletic contests and the injuries incurred on the playing-field are part of the price which the English-speaking race has paid for being world-conquerors." The spirit of victory involved was to be treasured, since it subordinated the individual to the group. Eliot did not forget the challenge, and when war broke out two years later, he quickly checked the figures and announced that "men who take part in the highly competitive athletic sports" were no more inclined to enlist than ordinary healthy students. Nor was anything more unlike actual fighting than "the bodily collisions which take place between foot-ball players." An earlier bit of research had convinced him that athletes tended toward mediocrity in scholarship.[77]

When scandalous physical injuries brought suspension of football at several universities in 1905, Harvard reformed without suspending. Its most famous alumnus called the football authorities of Harvard, Yale, and Princeton to the White House to discuss elimination of dirty play. But though Theodore Roosevelt was against underhandedness, he did not mind the roughness of the game. For Harvard to suspend, he insisted, would be "doing the baby act." Like Lodge he contrasted the spirit of football favorably with the extreme individualism that many associated with Harvard. Eliot sought to enlighten the President about the brutality of football, and a rumor circulated that Roosevelt had called Eliot a mollycoddle.[78]

Just before the rowing competition with Yale in 1908, two Harvard oarsmen, caught removing a reserve book from the library and then lying about it, were dropped from the crew. A telegram to Eliot from Roosevelt and Robert Bacon, his classmate and assistant secretary of state, suggested some alternative punishment that would let the two row. Eliot's answering telegram, majestically moral, specified the nature of the misconduct and concluded, "A keen and sure sense of honor being the finest result of college life, I think the college and graduates should condemn effectively dishonorable conduct. The college should also teach that one must never do scurvy things in the supposed interest or for the pleasure of others." Through no wish of Eliot's, both telegrams reached the newspapers, and shadings were added to the public's image of both presidents. Eliot had raised doubts about the caliber of honor that the sports enthusiasts claimed for their version of college life. As a bonus for Eliot, Harvard won the race.[79]

A principal source of the exaggerated attention to intercollegiate athletics was the sense of unity it gave, a feeling increasingly hard come by at the city-like university whose creation Eliot directed. This interpretation, which Abbott Lawrence Lowell cogently presented, seemed not to occur to Eliot. He valued sports as a defense against the "bodily deterioration" threatened by urban life, and he could always find a good word for rowing. But although he recommended daily exercise to undergraduates, he failed to recognize the promise of budding intramural sports. After all, it was ultimately up to the individual.[80]

VIII

Some considered Eliot to be an enemy of the college because he strongly and persistently advocated reducing the baccalaureate course from four to three years. He was, in fact, among the leaders in a national movement for shortening the college program. A desire to segregate general and special education was the motive of some advocates of this change. John Burgess of Columbia, recalling how unsympathetic his colleagues at Amherst had been when he undertook advanced teaching akin to that of German university seminars, forecast the demise of the college, with general studies going to the preparatory schools, which would gradually rise to the level of the German Gymnasium, and special studies going to universities, also designed on the German model. In the same vein, President Richard H. Jesse of the University of Missouri asked in 1892, "If . . . the high schools and academies continue to advance their instruction, may not three years of the college curriculum be some day shortened to two, and finally abolished altogether?" As the professional schools gained in stature, they began to stress the purely pre-professional aspects of undergraduate training.[81]

Eliot, by contrast, chose to defend the college as a center of general or liberal education. He was glad to see undergraduates specialize according to their bent, but by his lights they were thus strengthening their mental capacities, fulfilling the chief aim of general education. With undergraduates and graduates sitting together in many classes, Eliot was eager to blur the demarcation between general and special studies in arts and sciences. He thus belonged with those who were chiefly interested, not in separating general and special education, but in saving time for the student. Through raising both college and professional school entrance requirements, Eliot helped lengthen the time a student spent in formal education. With his faith in youth and his emphasis on social service, however, he judged twenty-six or twenty-seven as too late an age for the trained professional to begin work. He thought he discerned a dangerous increase in the age of attaining the bachelor's degree and a decline in the proportion of youth seeking it.[82] An early admirer of Sheffield's three-year course, Eliot knew too of the three-year B.A. in English universities.

The acceleration movement at Harvard began in 1881–82, when students were allowed to "anticipate" certain freshman courses by their performance on admission examinations. Later in the decade, when the medical school asked that its first year be counted as the fourth for the A.B. (a plan similar to one then in use at Columbia), Eliot appointed a committee to consider "in all its relations the general subject of shortening the College course." [83] The idea of sharing the senior year with the professional schools never won support from the college faculty, but after heated debate, it voted in 1890 to reduce the number of courses required for graduation from eighteen to sixteen. This would have allowed relatively easy completion of the college course in three years. Though this plan was vetoed by the Overseers, students still managed, by taking extra courses and by anticipating, to obtain the earlier degree. Without a formal three-year system, the practice grew up "through continuous but indirect pushings by ambitious students." Certain reductions in graduation requirements occurred, owing more to the faculty's antipathy to required courses than to its interest in accelerated graduation. Between 1896 and 1900 one-sixth of those graduating with the A.B. did so in three years.[84]

Eliot patiently propagandized for the three-year degree in his annual reports and elsewhere. Summer school courses should be counted toward the A.B., he said. Five weeks of vacation was plenty. A student would develop efficiently if his training were "more continuous and more strenuous." The shorter course would allow earlier marriage, thus increasing the fecundity of Harvard graduates, whose failure to reproduce had begun to alarm Eliot.[85] Noting how early George Washington had become an effective member of society, Eliot insisted that modern youth were kept too long in school. His addresses before the Associated Harvard Clubs were effective, and a special study committee of these alumni reported in 1906 in favor of "a straight three years' course as the normal one for the degree of A.B." Even the Overseers expressed sympathy for formal recognition of the three-year course for "students of unusual diligence or marked mental capacity." [86]

Had the three-year program been financially profitable, it might have swept away all objections. Unfortunately for Eliot's hopes, the taking of early degrees contributed to Harvard's financial difficulties, which mounted steeply after 1901. With accelerated graduation came a shrinkage of the senior class and thus of total undergraduate tuition payments. Eliot blamed the financial troubles on lack of a counterbalancing growth in the freshman class, traceable to the "obscure conditions under which the three years degree has been developed," but to no avail. A setback for his plan came in 1906, when the college began requiring extra tuition from students who took more than four courses a year. Eliot wistfully suggested that the three-year degree saved the student money even if he did have to pay for extra courses, since it eliminated a year's board and lodging in Cambridge.[87]

The peak year of the movement proved to be 1906, when 36 per cent of those taking the A.B. did so in three years. The extra expense may well have been decisive, but as Eliot recognized, social and athletic considerations led many students to prefer four years of residence. For all the activity of Eliot and his widespread collaborators in the Economy of Time movement, none of their recommended abbreviations were generally incorporated into the pattern of American education.[88]

Eliot denied allegations that he was an enemy of the liberal arts college. To one critic who accused him of believing the college should disappear, he responded, "The task before me during the first twenty years of my presidency was to develop a university out of a college without doing the college anything but good, and just that is what I believe to have done." Indeed, the college might have disappeared if Eliot's generation had not remade the classical, semi-monastic institution of the mid-nineteenth century. By advancing the A.B. as a requirement for entrance to professional schools, Eliot reinforced the position of the college. In the structure that Eliot proposed for American education the college was securely in place. But if the A.B. was to be made a single road between secondary and professional schools, then, he insisted, "the road to such a degree should be as smooth and broad as possible." [89]

The college survived, but with its inner life fundamentally altered. One of these changes was the decline of the paternal role of the president. William Lawrence, Episcopal bishop of Massachusetts and a Harvard graduate of 1871, maintained in 1904 that Eliot had taken the place once occupied by Andrew P. Peabody in the students' hearts. He exaggerated. But there had been a shift in the undergraduates' views of Eliot. His advancing age made him less fearsome, and accumulated legends made students feel that they knew him. On his seventieth birthday the undergraduates gave him a reception which evoked warmth on both sides. With the honesty of youth a junior summed up Eliot's relations with undergraduates:

> He has not been a president who came into intimate relations with the students; very few knew him personally, but all were familiar with his figure, and nearly all knew the kindly recognition which was always forthcoming when one greeted him first. To the students President Eliot has stood as the embodiment of the official hostility to athletics; so it is all the more remarkable that none regards him otherwise than with respect and admiration. Not all agree with his ideas on student affairs; but all honor his fearless stand on every question brought before him.[90]

IV &

Christo et Ecclesiae?

Instructors who are authorities on scientific or literary subjects but who do not worship God ought not to instruct the children of men and women who do.

PRESIDENT CHARLES A. BLANCHARD,
Wheaton College (1891) [1]

I

For participants in the university movement the threat from many varieties of religious thought bore on their efforts with an immediacy that later generations can understand only with difficulty. Andrew D. White found his plans at Cornell attacked by presidents of church colleges, who "insisted that an institution not belonging to any one religious sect must be 'godless.'" By declaring to an Episcopal bishop that he cared not if the new engineering professor be a Buddhist, White evoked an expression of doubt as to "whether laymen had any right to teach at all, since the command to teach was given to the apostles and their successors." When Johns Hopkins University invited Thomas Huxley to give a lecture at the opening of its first academic year in 1876, no prayer was given even though the perspicacious President Gilman had thought one might be wise. The university found religious periodicals virtually inviting the godly to pray for the failure of the Baltimore venture.[2] In the last third of the nineteenth century the religion that had nurtured the colleges appeared as one of the greatest antagonists of the universities. It was only partial consolation that leading clergymen often actively mediated between faith and science and that "modernity" was on the rise in the denominations.³ For the university president who found himself between the faith of the community and the scientific naturalism of faculty members the need to establish a modus vivendi was pressing. In this battle, Harvard had the advantages of wealth and age, but it suffered from widespread popular suspicion and an institutional rigidity that made maneuvering difficult.

To a faculty member who wrote approvingly of Eliot's reliance on "the Eternal," he responded: "I belong to the barest of the religious communions, and I am by nature reserved except with intimates and even with some of them. I feel glad that what has been, I believe, a fact in my inner life these thirty years past has been visible to a close observer in my official career. I should not like to have it said by the next generation, as has often been said by my contemporaries, that I was a man without ideals and without piety." Eliot was not without piety, but it would have rung false—probably even in his ears—to have called him a pious man. There was a recognizable this-worldliness to a man who regarded prayer as "the highest achievement of the human reason" and who could say that "no cherished ideal of our race has undergone a more beneficent change during the present century than the ideal of God." ⁴ He did not look on the work of churches as the saving of souls, and to his doubts about the existence of immortality he added doubts about its desirability.⁵

Eliot's associates on Harvard's governing boards were charged in 1871 with showing "but a languid interest in [Harvard's] theological and religious prosperity." The Corporation, which had once been attacked for its unanimous Unitarianism, had changed by 1880; it then included only one Unitarian (Eliot), plus one Orthodox Congregationalist minister, one Episcopalian, and "four men whose religious convictions are indefinable." In 1877, with the departure of the single clergyman, it had seemed proper to choose another, but when the latter resigned in 1884, a lawyer replaced him. A clergyman did not again join the Corporation until 1913. This change was not made with impunity: a faculty member commented in 1894 that the university would be better off if the Corporation added one or two members "from outside the regular Boston, brahmin, agnostic, populace-defying gang." Meanwhile, on the alumni-elected Board of Overseers, still called "the Reverend," the number of ministers dropped from six in 1875 to one in 1895.[6]

Harvard was not church-dominated even in 1869. Still, four of Eliot's five immediate predecessors, though they had not come to the presidency directly from the pulpit, had been Unitarian ministers, and among his closest competitors for the presidency had been Andrew P. Peabody, Plummer Professor of Christian Morals and Preacher to the University.[7] The collegiate ideal of making "Christian gentlemen" still hung about the institution.

The forces of religious orthodoxy, far from powerless, feared Eliot as a scientist. A forecast of his difficulties came when John Henry Clifford, former Whig governor of Massachusetts and president of the Board of Overseers, took it upon himself to give public words of warning at Eliot's inauguration. The impression they left was summarized by Theodore Lyman, himself an Overseer: "This was the sound of it:—'Look here, you *very* young man: I know you! You are a chemist; therefore you have a powerful tendency to be an Atheist: because all scientifics are very bad Atheists; and yet that won't keep them from dying, and therefore they don't get ahead of us very pious persons.' " [8]

Unmistakably, Eliot was in league with the Lymans of the day, and not the Cliffords. Indeed, in his inaugural he said next to nothing of either the divinity school or the religious welfare of undergraduates. In complimenting Eliot on his inaugural, one clerical Overseer, Edward Everett Hale, welcomed his "plan of a University" with its inclusive curriculum and its open-mindedness, since it would offer a "fair field" in which religious truth would inevitably win over "the empiricism of mere science." [9] But Hale was a Harvard man and a Unitarian. Eliot had to worry about the more typical representatives of religious institutions in America, evangelical Protestants, battling Darwinian ideas and the new Biblical criticism and fearing that mere science might not be so mere as it once was.

Although the evangelicals were fighting a rearguard action during most of Eliot's presidency, they were fighting hard. In one frame of mind Eliot felt it his duty as an institutional representative to keep out of the battle, but his temperament constantly pulled him toward the firing line. He laced his writings with anticlerical statements and questionings of the ways of organized Christianity. Although not yet a university president when he wrote, "A really learned minister is almost as rare as a logical sermon," he surpassed that observation with another, written in 1883. "Millions of thoughtful men," he said, including himself, believed "that ministers, as a class, and as a necessary consequence of the ordinary manner of their education and induction into office, are peculiarly liable to be deficient in intellectual candor." [10]

Institutional Christianity continued its tradition of giving Harvard a bad pulpit and a bad press. The downgrading of the "Christo et ecclesiae" motto by guaranteeing an equal place on the seal for the university's older motto "Veritas" served a Haverhill clergyman as a sign of the evil times. Early in the 1890s an Episcopal rescue mission published a tract, *Saved by a Sandwich*, in which a former Harvard student told of joining nine classmates in a boarding club, at whose table he took his "first drink of liquid damnation." Four years later, he recounted, "Harvard University vomited out upon the world ten drunkards, of which number to-day, five are mouldering in drunkard's graves, three are inmates of inebriate asylumns." Two had been saved—but not by Harvard. Although Eliot forced a private retraction from the convert and an end to his recounting of his tale at mission meetings, the offender was nonetheless promoted in the Episcopal Church Army. A faculty member traveling in Europe in 1886 found the impression widespread among Americans "that Harvard College is a hotbed of atheism & of dissipation." That the information was usually "fourth hand" made it the more revealing of public opinion.[11]

The religious-oriented colleges of the country provided one fertile source of these fourth-hand opinions. These institutions, often clinging to existence, with few students and little income, had much to lose if Eliot's ideal of an unsectarian college sharing by means of the elective system the curriculum of a complex university gained general acceptance. Nor had Eliot's 1869 comments on the inadequacy of a clerical career as preparation for a college presidency endeared him to the typical president of these institutions.[12] Two encounters demonstrated the continuing antagonism.

The first was with President James McCosh of Princeton. More flexible than some of his Presbyterian colleagues, and effective in renovating Princeton after he became its president in 1868, McCosh did not sympathize with the extent of Eliot's ideals of liberty, either in the curriculum or in student religious life. When the two presidents debated the elective system before the Nineteenth Century Club of New York in February 1885, one of McCosh's criticisms was that it made the colleges less fit to prepare ministers. The denominations could protect their own colleges, but McCosh feared the future might bring "an unfortunate division of colleges into Christian and infidel." It was not hard to fathom on which side Harvard would fall. Aside from its failure to assure the production of ministers with sound classical backgrounds, Eliot's "new departure" threatened general moral development. A Harvard student might elect nothing but science, and "everybody knows that science alone is not fit to form or guard morality." At this point McCosh issued a challenge to a second debate on "the new departure in the religion of colleges." [13]

Eliot opened the second debate, held in February 1886, by classifying colleges not as Christian and infidel, but as denominational, partially denominational, and undenominational. Most colleges gradually passed from the first type to the last by a process of evolution, in keeping with the growing heterogeneity and tolerance in their constituencies. Harvard had reached the most advanced stage. An undenominational university, Eliot admitted, might "appear to be indifferent to religion, instead of impartial." But he evoked "the history of the civilized world" as proof that religious liberty did not extinguish interest in religion. He suggested standards to be followed by colleges of whatever type: respect toward all religious opinions, support of the student's attachment to the communion in which he was born, and encouragement of the voluntary attachment of all students to some religious body. Eliot appeared to concede a great deal to McCosh and to undercut his own praise of Harvard's courses in ethics when he observed, "Nobody has as yet shown how to teach morality effectively without religion."

Indeed, Eliot shared with McCosh the thought that religion was in some danger, but he felt that narrow sectarianism and a narrow curriculum contributed to the danger. "The widespread opinion," he warned, "that there is an opposition between the fundamentals of religion and modern science—an opinion which religionists on one side and socialists on another have industriously spread—is one which in the present temper of the popular mind does infinite harm to religion." He pronounced it the duty of all colleges to "demonstrate that modern science is creating a very spiritual idea of God" and that no true opposition existed between religion and science "although the religious imagination and the scientific imagination do not set forth precisely the same images of the omnipresent Deity they both adore." But the freer program of Harvard, he implied, was most likely to convince students of this divine compatibility.[14]

In an address in Chicago five years later, Eliot went beyond his undenominational college ideal of 1886 and pictured the "true university," which by its very nature could not be conducted as a strict denominational organization. He did not speak of the impossibility of teaching morality without religion; he said rather that "conduct has very little to do with creed, or at least is not dependent upon theological opinion." By demonstrating this truth, Eliot now asserted, the university softened denominational asperities.[15]

The speech goaded into action President Charles A. Blanchard of Wheaton College (Illinois), successor to his better-known abolitionist father and inheritor of his father's controversialist bent. At a "parlor conference" in a Chicago home, Blanchard took direct issue with Eliot and later sent his remarks to Eliot and a few other educators. Blanchard began, as had McCosh, with an attack on the elective system, seeing it as contributing to the religious debasement of students: "Early specialization which shuts men up to one small corner of the world and bids them delve, is not only a cause of narrowness and intellectual paralysis, but of infidelity and spiritual death as well." He gave a fair summary of Eliot's address: "In speaking of the work of a University he said that its offices was [sic] to teach, to create storehouses of learning and to investigate. In addition to this the great school, he said, would unify the nation, prevent religious and political antogonisms [sic] and thus prove helpful to the people." But to this ideal Blanchard took exception: "It seems to me that such work as is above indicated if devoid of positive christian teaching would injure rather than benefit a nation."

Blanchard included both practicalist and equalitarian criticisms of Eliot's university ideal, but his chief reason for wanting "a multitude of Colleges widely distributed" rather than "a few great schools" was this: Christian character was worth more than intellectual development. "Instructors who are authorities on scientific or literary subjects but who do not worship God ought not to instruct the children of men and women who do . . . ," he maintained. "Every Christian should pray for, give to, and patronize schools where the true purpose of education is sought."

An exchange of letters between the two presidents forcefully evoked the difference between the religious-oriented liberal arts colleges and the new universities. Eliot affirmed that Harvard cared just as much about educating the conscience and promoting righteousness as did Wheaton and forced an admission of illiberal faculty-hiring policies from Blanchard. But Blanchard posed the dilemma that Eliot's institution must be either untrue to its denominational benefactors or insincere in claiming not to be denominational, and he insisted that, like Harvard, Wheaton did not proselyte. The exchange concluded with Eliot's observation that Blanchard's paper was typical of the many—with Harvard often the target—in which one college's representatives "criticise and condemn and do injustice to the methods and policies of another." He counseled a broad tolerance, returning to the sentiment of his speech in 1886, that the country had room and need for all its educational endowments. Blanchard answered, not without accuracy, that Eliot had himself displayed intolerance, since his Chicago speech had tended to discredit church colleges as incapable by their very nature of imparting the fullest culture. For all his effort to be broad-minded, this was what Eliot believed, and the belief had tinctured his address.[16]

University-builder though he was, Eliot preserved much of the interest of earlier college presidents in developing character. There is as much pathos in his assurances to his Midwestern counterpart that they stood on common ground as there is in the vain efforts of Blanchard to turn back the university movement. The new urban-industrial culture must have its universities and science must have its fortresses, but Eliot had been sincere in claiming that Harvard continued to give religion a place in education. Some of his hardest struggles had been to preserve that place in an increasingly secular university.

II

In shaping the religious life of the university Eliot steadfastly maintained, first, that Harvard should be unsectarian, and second, that its loyalties to standards of scientific truth should not be harmful to religion. It is not hard to understand why Eliot, like White and Gilman, strove to present his institution to the public as nondenominational. Competition among the denominations had led to an overproduction of colleges, and continued bitterness after colleges were established had levied a heavy price on their energies and achievements. Even though Harvard had generally been considered a Unitarian institution, its large measure of self-satisfaction and aloofness had saved it from such exhausting interdenominational struggles as the South and West had witnessed.[17] This distance from sectarian quarrels Eliot was eager to extend. In answer to a Bureau of Education circular, he placed the period when Harvard could have been considered a denominational institution as 1810 to 1850, limits so minimal as to be inaccurate. The increasing religious heterogeneity of New England and Harvard's increasing desire to draw students from the whole nation provided new grounds for Eliot's policy of nonsectarianism.

Whenever a choice opened, Eliot chose the interdenominational path. As early as 1869, he and the Fellows listened sympathetically to a plan for the endowment of a chair of Swedenborgian theology at the divinity school. The gift of a residence hall with half its income to aid students intending to become Episcopal ministers was accepted in 1870, and in 1881 the post of Plummer Professor of Christian Morals and Preacher to the University was offered to Phillips Brooks, an Episcopalian. Eliot informed the public that no denomination had a majority among the students and that candidates for the faculty were not asked their religious opinions. "Yale represents Congregationalism," he assured a critical Harvard alumnus in 1872, "—Harvard is truly liberal and catholic in religion." [18]

Eliot gave cordial support to various student religious organizations, including one for Catholics founded in the 1890s and one for Jews founded early in the new century. He encouraged the Harvard YMCA to violate the evangelical membership limitation set by the International Association, contending that loss of all connection "would be by no means an irreparable misfortune." On a Western tour during 1892 he spoke with satisfaction of the presence of "a Mormon colony" at Harvard, and thereby aggravated anti-Mormon sentiment. His comparison of the Mormon migration to that of the Puritans heightened the uproar. Even Eliot's son Samuel, then a Unitarian minister in Denver, doubted his discretion and urged, "I hope that you will avoid newspaper abuse in California. Stick to your educational gospel and let the *Chinese* question alone." Eliot did not budge. "Religious liberty is for people we do not agree with," he told an interviewer in San Francisco.[19]

But Eliot had to admit that nonsectarianism did little to ease the university's relations with the religious public. Everything possible had been done to free the college from sectarianism, he wrote an alumnus in 1890, but to little avail: "I observe that a policy of impartiality between denominations is almost as objectionable to a strict denominationalist as a decided denominational policy not his own, the idea of equality between the different Christian denominations being very repulsive to a devoted sectarian." [20] Worse, nonsectarianism was widely interpreted as antagonism to all religion.

The main charge of antireligion, however, came less from Harvard's nonsectarianism than from a long tradition of freethinking among Harvard faculty members and graduates and from the fact that as it grew into a university it more and more justified itself on grounds of the scientific method and scientifically grounded truth. Eliot's second guiding principle in his mediation between the university and the religious community—establishing compatibility between science and religion—was the more urgently needed.

Speaking at Daniel Coit Gilman's inauguration as president of Johns Hopkins, Eliot assured the audience that scholarship filled men with "humility and awe, by bringing them on every hand face to face with inscrutable mystery and infinite power. The whole work of a university is uplifting, refining, and spiritualizing." He stoutly forecast that Johns Hopkins, nonsectarian by will of the founder and oriented toward science by will of Gilman and the trustees, would be a seat of piety as well as learning.[21] Of the scholarly fields, the most feared as antagonistic to religion were the natural sciences, now being elevated far above their cramped role in the required curriculum. Eliot scouted any such threat in his debate with McCosh, insisting, furthermore, that the danger was least where "there is a great variety of teaching and research." For such institutions, he had detailed praise:

> They can show how physics, with its law of the conservation of energy, chemistry with its doctrine of the indestructibility and eternal flux of atoms, and biology with its principle of evolution through natural selection, have brought about within thirty years a wonderful change in men's conception of the universe. If the universe, as science teaches, be an organism which has by slow

degrees grown to its form of to-day on its way to its form of to-morrow, with slowly formed habits which we call laws, and a general health which we call the harmony of nature, then, as science also teaches, the life-principle or soul of that organism, for which science has no better name than God, pervades and informs it so absolutely that there is no separating God from nature, or religion from science, or things sacred from things secular.[22]

Theologians might recognize the threat to Christian faith of such near-pantheism, but many Christians found it comforting to think that the busy scientists in the universities were chiefly glorifying God. The danger to religion in Eliot's assertion became clear, however, when he turned to discussions of method. With God and nature coterminous, the method of the natural sciences was the appropriate method for knowing God. "In every field of study," he observed approvingly, "in history, philosophy, and theology, as well as in natural history and physics, it is now the scientific spirit, the scientific method, which prevails." [23]

The shift from religious to scientific standards, which Eliot and Harvard shared with many other sources of American values, benefited freedom of thought. The tendency of empirical science to suspend judgment made condemnation of unorthodox views less likely. Eliot had good reason to judge the development of academic freedom as gain. He had begun his career as a chemist at the time when Columbia refused to employ Wolcott Gibbs because of his Unitarianism, and he recalled that being a Unitarian was once "a serious drawback for a teacher in New England." Although there were questionable decisions in matters of academic freedom during his administration, at the opening of his presidency he took a notable opportunity to uphold the liberty of the scholar against ecclesiastical opposition. He maintained to the Board of Overseers when it balked at the appointment of Positivist John Fiske as instructor of history that a man's religious opinions should not be considered in judging his fitness to teach.[24]

During his long administration Eliot was to have more than one occasion to support this particular side of academic freedom.

An Episcopal headmaster who thought Josiah Royce guilty of "energetic hostile teaching in opposition to much that Christians hold reasonably sacred and vital" was gently urged to read Royce's books. And when Hugo Münsterberg's support of alcoholic beverages brought abusive letters, usually from religious advocates of total abstinence, Eliot assured the professor of psychology that such protests had been ignored. "You will, of course," wrote the president, "feel perfectly free to express your views with entire frankness either in public or in private."[25] But to uphold freedom in the university was only part of a university president's obligation. At his best he would try by influencing society to remove the threats to freedom. This duty Eliot did not shirk.

He had no doubts of the power of religion, and he even declared religion and "domestic affections" to be "through all governmental and industrial changes, the supreme forces in human society." Such a belief made seemingly all the more important both for society and for universities the potential effect of universities on religion. They should strive to "enlarge and sweeten" its conceptions and "bring about modifications of obstructive dogma and ritual in organized religion." In a more immediate way, Eliot hoped that the dearth of able Protestant clergymen, which by 1882 he could call widely acknowledged, might be corrected by shifting theological training from "isolated denominational seminaries" which repelled "young men of independent spirit and mental virility" to universities characterized by diversity of intellectual activity and "academic freedom for teacher and pupil." The choice of the liberal George Gordon as minister of Boston's Old South Church, a turning point for Orthodox Congregationalism, was probably initiated by Eliot's recommendation.[26] Much of Eliot's hope that Harvard could elevate American religious life and make it more hospitable to university ideals came to center in the divinity school.

Eliot's plans for the divinity school differed little from those he had for the rest of the university. He wanted it to be undenominational and scientific. These standards, he hoped, would lessen both sectarian hostility and secular indifference.[27] Emphasis on the historical approach and selection of German-trained scholars were Eliot's principal techniques for making the school scientific. In this way he hoped to shape it for survival in "the modern world," which "respects only the scientific method, which admits of no settled convictions except those which rest upon thorough previous investigation." Even though two Baptists had been added to the divinity faculty, Eliot had to admit in 1900 that the experiment of an undenominational theological school was merely holding its own.[28] The school's union with Andover Theological Seminary in 1908, made possible by a liberalized Congregational clergy, did not reflect any broad attainment of interdenominationalism.

The experiment in scientific theology, however, produced noteworthy scholarship and, in 1908, a new theological journal. By keeping theology in the university as a respected intellectual discipline Harvard Divinity School in Eliot's day made its greatest contribution. This Cornell and Johns Hopkins and the state universities could not do.[29]

Ironically, he who had been feared by the devout came himself to fear that his successor might not foster the divinity school. A lack of interest in religious matters among the younger men from among whom the new president would be chosen, Eliot wrote in 1908, might weaken the school. He was therefore eager to leave it "as solid as possible."[30]

Since the mere fact that Harvard included a theological school helped calm religious fears about the university, the school can be counted an advantage which came to Eliot as a university-builder on a long-established foundation. But another heritage—compulsory attendance at prayers—brought chiefly difficulties. At Cornell, White had early developed a voluntary morning service, and when Sage Chapel opened there in 1875 he resisted the suggestion for a resident chaplain and instead established a system of services conducted by visiting preachers of various denominations and faiths. Gilman, whose university had few undergraduates, himself daily conducted a voluntary religious ceremony. Eliot, though unhappy with a phase of college life which he feared branded Harvard as sectarian and which comported ill with his ideals of student liberty, seemed hesitant to advocate the alternatives of multi-denominationalism and voluntary attendance at chapel.[31]

Compulsory attendance at prayers was a Harvard tradition of a quarter-millennium, and it proved tenacious. The gingerly handling of this matter and the elaborate compromise that emerged in 1886 indicated the pressures felt by Eliot and other university officials. When for the first half of the 1872–73 term repairs on Appleton Chapel forced suspension of morning prayers, Eliot pointed out in his annual report that there had been "no ill effects whatever on college order or discipline." [32] Encouraged by this hint and sympathizing with student antagonism to the requirement, the faculty recommended four times, beginning in 1873, that attendance at prayers be made voluntary. But on this question the Corporation chose to follow rather than lead the Overseers, judging that the larger body, elected by alumni, "fairly represented public opinion in all its different shades."

Emphasizing the need for public readiness, Eliot acquiesced in repeated rejections of the faculty's proposal. It was, after all, "a matter which easily stirs strong sentiments and passions." "The abandonment of a custom so salutary and so characteristic, as well as time-honored," one college president warned a Harvard Overseer, "would be fraught with most serious consequences to the whole fabric of our civilization." Eliot lamely justified compulsory morning prayers in an undenominational college as "a short service without any homily, or other opportunity for dogmatic teaching." In words that might have been expected from his opponent rather than himself, he averred during his second debate with McCosh, "In view of the prodigious flux of religious opinion which is upon us, College authorities are justified in resisting, rather than stimulating demands for changes in their customs and prescriptions." [33]

Loyal to the decisions of the governing boards, Eliot was not truly satisfied with the status quo. In 1880–81 he polled students' families as to their own practices regarding daily prayers and published his finding that five-sevenths did not follow the custom. He repeated without comment the delightfully transparent excuse that suburban fathers had to catch early trains. Unhappy with this survival from the *ancien régime* but hesitant about pressing for its destruction, Eliot felt the sting of faculty, parental, and student criticism. Professor George Herbert Palmer declined to conduct morning prayers so long as the governing boards refused to "treat religion as a matter capable of interesting a man who is not forced." A father wrote of his shock at finding his son on probation for not attending "*compulsory* prayers, . . . a degradation of a very sacred service to . . . the purpose of a roll-call suitable for school-boys." In 1885 students petitioned for abolition of this "remnant of ancient encroachments on civil liberty." In the face of the Overseers' obduracy, the issue was kept alive by a zealous grandson of William Lloyd Garrison.[34]

It was someone other than Eliot who had the imagination to work out a compromise in a spirit that mediated between university and religious ideals. Francis G. Peabody, Parkman Professor of Theology and Eliot's brother-in-law, played the role which would have done honor to Eliot. Peabody, one of the earliest spokesmen for the Social Gospel, achieved renown in the 1880s for his teaching of Christian ethics to students in both divinity school and college. Scarcely a year after the Overseers had rejected the "ancient encroachment" petition and upheld the status quo by a twenty to four vote, a new series of student petitions reached them. Peabody was then drawn into the matter by a request for his suggestions from Phillips Brooks, a member of a special Overseers' committee. In answer Peabody worked out an elaborate plan linking the protests against compulsion with means for "enriching and dignifying worship so that it can bear the strain of liberty." [35]

Since Andrew P. Peabody's retirement from the Plummer Professorship in 1881, various ministers officially connected with Harvard, including non-Unitarians, had been conducting prayers. The service had been enlivened by music, congregational participation, and a later hour. These reforms of 1881, which owed much to Eliot, Peabody drew into his new scheme. He urged the establishment of an interdenominational Board of Preachers whose members would successively take up residence at the college to counsel students as well as lead morning prayers. It was tacitly understood that the first board would recommend that prayers be made voluntary.[36] Peabody was willing to fill the Plummer Professorship if that chair, instead of being linked to the position of "Preacher to the University," were to involve participation on the Board of Preachers as *primus inter pares*.[37]

Although Peabody justly resented the frequent ascription of the plan to Phillips Brooks, the role of the Episcopal divine was of major importance. The most magnetic religious leader in New England and Eliot's first choice for the Plummer Professorship, Brooks had the prestige to convert his fellow Overseers. Indeed, had there not been a figure such as Brooks to still public outcry and, as a member of the first Board of Preachers, assure a large voluntary attendance, the plan would probably not have been tried. Although no one found the new program more congenial than did Eliot, it was not exhilaration but a sure touch for the religious pulse of the community that shaped his announcement: "It was only when they were urged by men of strong religious spirit in the Faculty, in the Board of Overseers, and among the Alumni to make the change for the sake of religion itself, that the governing boards consented to alter the ancient statute."

When a series of services supported by student contributions and addressed by members of the Board of Preachers was held in Boston's Globe Theater, press coverage was all that a university president could have desired. The *Congregationalist* called the meetings "a long step in the direction of redeeming the reputation of Harvard with the general public from the appearance of indifference to religion which many have mourned." The Boston *Herald* credited the activity to the new voluntary system.[38]

Eliot did not deny in his annual reports that the services were never attended by "a large proportion of the total body of students"—sometimes as few as sixty appeared on Mondays—but he hailed the healthier religious atmosphere and the wider opportunities for religious counselling. In 1901 he shrewdly suggested to an alumnus who found the services satisfactory in neither attendance nor "heartiness" that he visit Yale's compulsory chapel. The resulting observations vindicated Eliot and the Harvard system.[39]

Perhaps most important for Eliot's mediatorial role was the opportunity to show Harvard to ministers from various denominations and regions. Thus a New York Baptist minister could write of his admiration for the "simple and democratic" life he had found at Harvard, where "things of the spirit have larger place." From a Methodist came a hint that an invitation to someone of his denomination would be gratifying. At the Baptist-supported University of Chicago, President William Rainey Harper hoped to imitate the rotating interdenominational features of the Harvard plan, and he brought Peabody to his campus with that aim.[40] An unctuous article in the *New England Magazine* entitled "Harvard's Better Self" praised the new plan, as did a more sober report in the *Andover Review*. In 1895 the *Catholic Family Annual* presented the religious life of students at Harvard sympathetically. In short, the reform—less drastic than abolition but less rigid than the stance Eliot had taken before the Nineteenth Century Club—succeeded from nearly every point of view.[41]

As visiting members of the Board of Preachers learned the ways of the emerging university, Harvard students and faculty members had a chance to meet leaders of religious opinion in easy social interchange. The response varied. Brooks had one hundred student callers his first year on the Board. George Gordon of Old South Church had only two callers the same year, and though one of these sought only the way to the Bursar's Office, the other asked the way to the Kingdom of Heaven. Another member of the Board comforted a student who feared he had lost his faith by confiding that he did not himself believe in a six-day creation of the earth.[42] The necessary restriction to ministers who would attract a voluntary attendance tended to narrow the variety of points of view. Henry Van Dyke's moderate Presbyterianism was probably the most conservative theological position included.

The early lists of preachers, including Lyman Abbott and Washington Gladden, read like a directory of leading modernists of the day. Harvard students received no forewarning of *The Fundamentals* from their visiting religious mentors. During his last year in office, Eliot sought an endowment for the morning service to protect it from any "gusts of adverse public opinion" which might lessen its liberality and to cope with any indifference that might "prevail temporarily in the Governing Boards" and threaten abolition. He stated his support for the program eloquently: "There is no more characteristic feature of Harvard University than the conduct of its religious services. It expresses its liberality as regards opinions, its devotion to ideals, and the preciousness in its sight of individual liberty." Yet his statement showed that it was in part as mediator between a learned institution and the religious community that he prized the program of student worship: "It refutes the saying so common among Evangelical Protestants in this country that Harvard is irreligious." [43]

By the mid-1880s, having experienced internal reform of the university in the name of liberty, students and faculty chafed under religious forms that seemed anachronisms. Yet Eliot hesitated, asking whether America had changed enough to let the religious practices of the university conform to its individualistic ethos. Liberal clergymen, among them Francis G. Peabody and Phillips Brooks, showed him the way out. The reform of morning worship succeeded, and never again was religious opinion so strong a consideration in forming university policy. "The gradual alteration of . . . religious habits in the community" which Eliot had foreseen in 1869 had progressed further by the mid-1880s than he guessed. By the time of his retirement in 1909 he felt, perhaps to his own surprise, obliged to shore up the divinity school and voluntary religious service against future indifference.

Eliot's nonsectarian ideal helped win for Harvard a national stature and constituency suitable to its position as the country's oldest and richest university. Catholics, Jews, Mormons, Swedenborgians, agnostics, and atheists studied at Harvard, certain that no official creed would hinder their religious or intellectual pursuits. Even the university's near creed of science, feared by so many religionists, Eliot often managed to equate with a freedom and reach of imagination not inimical to faith. In fact, in an atypical moment of fideism he went so far as to observe of scientists, "They firmly believe and accept doctrines which they never have proved and never can prove. That is, their imagination outruns their reason, and their beliefs their knowledge." [44]

Yet there remains justice in the charge that after Eliot had increased the scholarly stature of the divinity school and the variety and beauty of the morning religious service, he left both lacking in richness and substance. What he called nondenominationalism was often, as critics charged, Unitarianism raised to the nth power. He was too confident that he understood those who differed with him on religious matters and that they were well provided for at Harvard.

V $\approx$

The University and Democracy

> The first half of the nineteenth century saw the development
> of individualism, the last half of collectivism. The generation
> to which I have belonged has had experience with both prin-
> ciples, and has found each wanting without the other.
>
> CHARLES W. ELIOT (1905) [1]

I

Political life was not foreign to Eliot, for it seemed virtually one
of his family's prerogatives. His father and his mother's brother
had been mayors of Boston and members of the state legislature,
and his father had gone to Congress. Before he was twenty years
old, the younger Eliot held his first public office, membership on
the Primary School Committee of Boston. In the 1860s he was
elected to the Common Council of Cambridge, where he was recalled as "very forward." [2] Accepting the presidency of Harvard
brought his withdrawal from public office, but not from politics.
In the election of 1882 Massachusetts sent to Congress two reformers pledged to a new civil service law. One was Eliot's
cousin Theodore Lyman; the other, the candidate from Eliot's
own district. Some political observers believed Eliot himself
would have accepted a draft to run for Congress that year. Cambridge, in fact, proved one of the richest seedbeds of the Mugwump movement. In this ferment, Eliot participated formally as a
vice president of the Cambridge Civil Service Reform Association
and informally as friend and counsellor of various leaders. Among
these was Cambridge's mayor, William E. Russell, who typified

the best of the reform impulse of the eighties and went on to three terms as reform governor in the nineties. Russell was a Harvard graduate of the Eliot era, and his addresses were said to be like Eliot's in their straightforwardness.[3]

The traditional birth-year of Mugwumpery is, of course, 1884, and the precipitating event the Republican nomination of James G. Blaine. Eliot, who was of Whig extraction, had voted Republican regularly in national elections since 1856.[4] But, like many others in the G.O.P., he was troubled by Blaine's reputation as a less than honest legislator. At a formative meeting held June 13, 1884, to denounce the Republican choice and urge Democratic nomination of a reform candidate, Eliot expressed his hope for a new political party. He did not neglect the importance of party and party organization, judging that "political progress is to be made only by a conflict of national parties, and, as a rule, of two national parties." Nor did he want a mere "Independent" alliance. He condemned such balancing between the parties as too weak a course, arguing that a new party could "look forward to a national triumph." [5]

Eliot hoped that the National Conference of Independents and Republicans, which met in New York in July, would take steps to organize a party and adopt a platform. In fact, Eliot himself framed a platform for a "New Party." But when the conference limited itself to support of the Democratic candidates he grew discouraged, and he took little part in the campaign. Although giving Cleveland faint praise by calling him the lesser of two evils, he drew up a forceful statement supporting him, but for some reason refrained from publishing it. His pro-Cleveland position was generally known, however, and it angered some Harvard alumni.[6]

Eliot's draft platform of 1884 was probably the fullest political statement he ever made. It showed him a confirmed Liberal, distinctly of the Mugwump stripe. The platform turned out to be a fair prediction of the next dozen years of American political reform. It comprised a list of principles, to be maintained "by speech, press, and ballot." These included integrity in office-holders, merit civil service, lower tariffs and other taxes, no currency depreciation, an end to "unearned pensions and bounties," immigration "without distinction of race, nationality or religion," "strict observance of constitutional limitations," and in foreign affairs "sobriety and candor." The strong implication was that the best government governed least.[7]

His strategy for a new party having been bypassed, Eliot stuck by his advocacy of party allegiance and declared himself a Democrat. At home he had the sterling Russell to support, and Cleveland as President proved much to his liking. In the campaign of 1889, Eliot addressed the Democrat's Bay State Club on "Three Reasons Why I Became a Democrat." He spoke the language of the Mugwump: "I will stay in a political party only so long as that party stands for the political principles which I believe in." Yet it was a rousing, distinctly partisan speech that struck wittily at the opposition's soft spots.[8]

As a Cleveland Democrat, Eliot made no radical break with his Harvard constituency. Although the majority of Harvard men presumably remained Republicans, at least two members of the Corporation were conspicuous Democrats: William Crowninshield Endicott, secretary of war in Cleveland's first cabinet, and Eliot's classmate John Quincy Adams, repeatedly candidate for governor and Vice Presidential candidate on the "straight-out" Democratic ticket in 1872. The defeat of Henry Cabot Lodge when he was a candidate for re-election as Overseer in 1890 showed Mugwump strength among the alumni. Civil service reform appealed to members of a minority class that mistrusted party machinery and the power of numbers, and lower tariffs suited both Boston's mercantile interests and its railroad developers. With increasing reliance on imported raw materials, New England manufacturers also found attractions in tariff reform.[9]

Eliot was more willing than most university presidents to take a stand on public issues. Part of his justification was that he thus set for Harvard students a proper example of an educated man's social involvement. When the Corporation voted in 1894 to ban political party meetings from college halls, Eliot sought to put the decision in the most permissive light, saying that only political rallies were banned and that there was no wish to lessen discussion of social and political problems. Nevertheless, this divorce of serious discussion from electioneering suggested the apolitical doctrine that wholesome discussion was one thing and vote-winning another. It forecast a lessening of Eliot's own direct involvement in politics.[10]

Although Eliot was called "king of the mugwumps," he actually stood somewhat apart in the Mugwump movement by his authoritative self-assurance and his willingness to declare a party allegiance. But true to the breed, he found the course of the Democratic Party in 1896 insupportable. He opposed free silver, of course, but when he applied the touchstone of morality to the Democratic platform, it was not the currency plan that he found "fundamentally immoral." More offensive to him were the platform's attacks on the Supreme Court and on Cleveland's use of troops in the Pullman Boycott. Eliot did not dally with the Gold Democrats, where some sound-money Democrats found harbor. He voted for McKinley.[11]

Both sides sought his endorsement in 1900, and after contradictory rumors began to circulate, he announced that he would vote again for McKinley. He did not find the Philippine issue strong enough to lead him back to the Democrats and doubted if Bryan would in fact modify foreign policy. "In view of the fact," he commented, "that there has been a new and wide-spread tendency to public disorder and violence since 1893, I should not wish to contribute by any political action this year to the weakening of the Supreme Court." [12]

Soon after the election Eliot expressed the hope that McKinley would live out his term because "Roosevelt as President would be dangerous." With the quick frustration of his wish, Eliot and Harvard were thrust into a different relation to the presidency and national politics. Eliot shared some of the university's pride in the new Harvard-trained President and supported him in 1904. But he managed to have enough public differences with Roosevelt to reinforce the public view of Harvard as a place of independence and dissent.[13] Eliot was never won over to the man, but during Roosevelt's term he began to speak more sympathetically of governmental intervention in society. He did not believe himself without influence on the President. He sent him letters of advice sprinkled with social philosophy, once likening Roosevelt's office to his own in the difficulties it posed in accurately gauging public opinion. In 1904 Eliot sent a proposed plank for the Republican platform which would have committed the party to replace in the Philippines "an American government with Filipino assistance" with "a Filipino national government with American assistance." [14]

In 1907 a New York *World* editorial suggested either Eliot or Woodrow Wilson as a scholar candidate for the presidency on the Democratic ticket. Eliot rather immodestly judged such a nomination unlikely because of "the average American's distrust of the expert." The nomination of Taft he found admirable. Both Taft and Wilson, whom he supported in 1912, offered him the ambassadorship to Great Britain, but both times he declined, doubting that modern diplomats had enough genuine independence to suit his ways.[15] In neither elective nor appointive office was Eliot to advance his political ideas. As a national sage, however, he spread them widely.

II

Although Eliot took political candidates and platforms seriously, he was more deeply concerned with the expression of a general social philosophy. Rarely original, he hewed to the line of nineteenth-century Liberalism, but he added a touch that was peculiarly personal and American. He drew on John Stuart Mill and Herbert Spencer, but Emerson was the philosopher on whom he most often relied. He kept a complete set of Emerson's works in both his Cambridge home and his summer home on Mount Desert Island. Darwinist social thought of the late nineteenth century he judged as largely a reassertion of Emersonianism in biological language.[16]

The vision of man which underlay Eliot's social thought accorded fully with his Unitarian theology. Like his co-religionists, he saw man as a creature of natural dignity and worth, part of "the original, unbroken and universal community of nature, man and God." Far from being a fallen race, humanity was "meant for progress, capable of holiness, and in the main improving from the beginning, though weak and wandering." In keeping with his view of man, social process almost inevitably meant progress.[17]

Although he saw man as a reasoning creature, Eliot when speaking of society almost always linked reason with sentiment, which he saw as man's primary motivation. Such sentiment as he noted was usually beneficent, and "happiness" often appeared as his supreme social good. Even though he recognized "the fierce passions of the multitudes," Eliot believed that the masses were amenable to individual innovation and leadership. Social process began in "human thought and feeling proceeding from individuals, seized upon and cherished by multitudes, and gradually carried into action both domestically and institutionally." [18]

Such a world view made liberty Eliot's central social value. The starting point of progress, individual thought and feeling, functioned best in freedom, and the culmination of progress, the achievement of "noble human character," was impossible without freedom. The theological ground was plain. God had given men free will. "That is what the world was made for, for the occupation of men who in freedom through trial win character. It is choice which makes the dignity of human nature." Accordingly, an organization benefited society to the extent that it gave "freer and freer play to the infinite diversity of human faculty and aspiration." [19]

Eliot's emphasis on liberty led him to reject another value of his age—equality. Although in 1875 he sought to praise a social institution by saying that it tended "to equalize the conditions of life," Eliot did not want the free individual sacrificed in attempts to enforce equality. To him a society with "no varieties of condition" would be "unnatural, monotonous, stupid, and unprogressive. Civilization means infinite differentiation under liberty." Such differentiation need not preclude unity. In his attempt of 1896 to rewrite the motto of the French Revolution for American purposes, Eliot changed "liberty" to "freedom" and "fraternity" to "brotherhood," replacement of Latinisms rather than changes in meaning. But for "equality" he substituted "unity." "Unity" could represent a sense of common interests, he claimed, since everyone gained from differentiation, but the notion that men are equal was "plainly false." Nor did he find equality of possessions a worthy aim for republican institutions.[20]

Eliot once called it a delusion to think of the golden age as in the past. In his most fully expressed Utopian vision, he made the university his model.

> [The best ultimate form of human government] is a government in which there is no use of force. There is some police inspection, and a constant watchfulness against disease, fire, noise, and similar evils, but no prison, no physical punishment, the least possible interference with the personal conduct of the governed, and a generous amount of good-will between all members of the community. . . . The government is not arbitrary, and yet it possesses large elements of discretion. It habitually acts under rules and usages, yet it is progressive; it does not permit a perverse individual to injure the main body, but its dealings with the individual are always in the direction of reformation, education, and recovery from downfall, and exile is never resorted to until many efforts at recovery and reformation have failed.

Good societies were instruments of education. In them, man would "enjoy a life of reason." This phrase, one of Eliot's happiest, captured his positive evaluation of both the emotional and rational qualities of man.[21]

The outcome of the Civil War having put a triumphal stamp on popular government, Eliot saw democracy as the inevitable governmental form of the future. Impatient with Victorian critics of democracy, he scoffed at Henry Maine's view that under democracy the many would prevent the few from achieving reform and progress. For Eliot this notion was "completely refuted by the first century of the American democracy." He had similar disagreements with his fellow Liberal E. L. Godkin, attributing to him the dark view of the habitual critic and rejecting his despair over the necessity for the good to work with the bad in politics.

In an article of 1892, Eliot parodied the "independent man's" doubts of democracy, especially his self-indulgent pessimism about public education because its products read trivial literature, consulted fortune-tellers, and called for fiat-money.[22]

The fact that from 1860 to 1916 he was on the losing side of a presidential election only once (in 1888) bolstered Eliot's belief in the wisdom of the electorate. Yet there were limits to his faith in the people. As early as 1875 he advocated the combination of compulsory elementary education with a literacy requirement for voters. By 1904 he believed it expedient to apply both educational and property qualifications for voting. He saw greater political virtue in the farmers, fishermen, and mechanics of the Revolutionary era than in the factory workers of the nineteenth century. Manhood suffrage he once likened to freedom of the will—"the only atmosphere in which virtue can grow, but an atmosphere in which sin can also grow"; he did not recommend it for young nations.[23]

Going beyond the suffrage question, Eliot sought to define American democracy through its "openness." When Prince Henry of Prussia visited Harvard, Eliot lectured him on the nature and success of American democracy, taking Massachusetts as his example, "with no class legislation, feudal system, dominant church, or standing army to hinder or restrain it." He could also put this openness positively, citing "public schools, democratic churches, public conveyances without distinction of class, universal suffrage, town-meetings, and all the multifarious associations in which democratic society delights." Though praising the virtues of this society, he took a Tocquevillean view of its perils, notably the abuse of power by temporary majorities. He found the tyranny of public opinion worse than the despotic will of a single tyrant because "it affects the imagination more, because it seems omnipresent, merciless, and irresponsible; and therefore resistance to it requires a rare kind of moral courage." One aristocratic value especially—honor, which he identified with self-respect—Eliot hoped could be extended throughout democratic society. Here too he shared an idea of Tocqueville's.[24]

Particularly discouraging to Eliot was the quality of political leadership in the Gilded Age. The balance between reason and sentiment was lost when political leaders contemptuously appealed only to the people's "prejudices, their cupidity, and their passions." He hoped that the country could find men like those who led the Revolutionary generation: "men of education, men of property and men of honor." Where were such leaders to come from? Partly from old family stocks, from that hereditary aristocracy which had somehow grown up and survived in America's open society. Believing that "durable families" ought to be nurtured, Eliot deprecated the tendency of families not to stay in one permanent home, and he welcomed new methods of setting up trusts to perpetuate inherited wealth. But he also looked beyond established families for leadership. He knew enough "old families" himself to know the possibilities of decay.[25]

Eliot's phrase for the elite in a democracy was less often "natural aristocracy" than "the educated classes." His regular use of the plural is suggestive, for the category included not only the offspring of "old families," who characteristically saw to their children's education, but also individuals from "undistinguished" families. The only difference between him and themselves, he once told an audience of immigrants, was that his family had valued education; they were free to do the same. Although he spoke of gifted children from poor families as "sports," implying that they were biological accidents, his position was far more hopeful than that of the rising eugenics movement with its dreadful vision of the inbred, idiotic Jukes. At his most exuberant Eliot saw democratic society "perpetually exchanging members up and down." And if biology influenced this mobility, educational institutions also had a role of importance. It is perhaps the implication of formal schooling that distinguishes the term "educated classes" most sharply from the term "natural aristocracy." Holding this view, Eliot liked to dwell on the emergence of the Adamses from rural obscurity in the eighteenth century through the elevating influence of Harvard College.[26]

Eliot once observed that though titles were not hereditary in

America, culture was. His "educated classes" clearly included the aristocracy of culture, whose self-conscious members, well exemplified by Charles Eliot Norton, believed themselves guardians of moral, aesthetic, and intellectual values. But an aura of political insufficiency hung about this group in the Gilded Age, as Henry Adams realized all too painfully. Before the small successes of Mugwumpery cheered him on the subject, Eliot had declared, "The educated classes have always been apt to grease the wheels of demagogues when they meant to upset their chariots." But part of the appeal of the category "educated classes" was that it included men of various family backgrounds who were trained for public service. In the trained expert Eliot increasingly placed his hopes, once going so far as to say that the professions controlled the country. The two groups, cultured men of old families and men trained for social service, were never rigidly separated in Eliot's thought. The college was not to turn out vulgar experts. It instilled culture in the gauche provincial besides giving him technical preparation for a public career, and no good Brahmin should consider himself educated without training for "service." [27]

Colleges and universities thus had a central role in Eliot's view of the proper working of democratic society. With public opinion taught (in the lower schools and through experience with the ballot) to respect expertise, and with experts properly trained and imbued with ideals of service (in the colleges and universities), democracy would flourish. Throughout society, the Napoleonic ideal of the career open to talents should apply, and part of that openness would be the readiness of the colleges to train the gifted, no matter what their class origins.

III

John Jay Chapman's assertion that Eliot was America's representative man between the Civil War and World War I exaggerates his typicality.[28] But Eliot was representative in his gradual relinquishment of the more extreme aspects of his individualism. In keeping with his younger fellows in the Progressive movement,

Eliot began in the early years of the new century to redefine liberty in light of industrial realities.

In the early years of his presidency Eliot was a doctrinaire advocate of laissez-faire. He found support in his friends among the English Liberals and such American economists as Edward Atkinson and Charles F. Dunbar. In a private letter of 1873, Eliot wrote:

> The fact is that the enlargement of the functions of the General Government is the great political sin and danger of these times, and it is to be hoped that the people will soon begin to see and understand the threatening evil. Not a week passes without the promulgation of some new scheme for adding to the activities and powers of the central government. Most of our public men, instead of holding by the American doctrine of leaving the people to take care of themselves, seem to be thoroughly inoculated with the European doctrine that it is the duty of government to help the people to what is good for them—to more railroads, and more canals, better savings-banks, more various industries and better schools.

Eliot did not restrict such views to private discussion. In 1874 he urged the Young Men's Christian Union to hold a debate on Emerson's "pregnant sentence": "The reliance on property, including the reliance on governments which protect it, is a want of self-reliance." [29]

Eliot's youthful allegiance to the Whig party did not make him an advocate of positive government during the Gilded Age. Later he rejected the Populists' ideas for widened government activity, but some of the municipal and state extensions of government in the era of Governor Russell won his support, notably the establishment of the Metropolitan Park System of Boston, in which his son Charles played an important role. After the accession of Theodore Roosevelt to the presidency, Eliot became a national spokesman for Progressivism. Especially during the years 1903–5 he elaborated a theory of government that was far from the individualism of his early years as Harvard's public spokesman.

Looking back in 1905, Eliot observed that his generation, having lived through first an era of individualism and then an era of collectivism, had discovered each wanting without the other. Neither alone could attain what Eliot regarded as the persisting goal of a democracy, "the greatest good of the greatest number." He saw origins of the new collectivism in the market revolution, citing "the extraordinarily increased dependence of each individual in the community on supplies and resources, which come to the individual from afar and from strangers." To a question he posed in 1904, "Is the individual free to act his own will in any modern community, independently of his neighbors?" Eliot's answer was, "By no means: the very opposite is true. Industrial, commercial, and political life is only to be carried on by combinations of many men working to common ends." In large groupings of men the greatest evil might be, not lack of freedom, but "incompetent administration." [30]

As persuasive examples of necessary growth of governmental power, Eliot chose conservation, regulation of business, or, most often, preventive medicine. One of his most complete descriptions of industrial society linked every aspect to public health: "The factory system with its smoke and foul air, rapid transit with its noise and hurry, and the quick despatch of business with its nervous strain work their injurious effects on the public health wherever population is concentrated, and nothing can offset these effects except collective measures to secure a tolerable supply of light and air, reasonable hours of labor, wholesome food, and the means and opportunities of recreation." In time he could speak of "the indispensableness of government interference." [31]

Eliot's shift away from individualism should not be exaggerated. Although he grew comfortable with the term "democratic collectivism," he denounced socialism, under which "the state would become a vast charitable institution, exercising a universal despotic benevolence," a plan destructive of the family unit, personal ambition, and the fine arts. Ministers who embraced socialism and advocated redistribution of property aroused his concern.[32] He saw dangers in private as well as governmental collectivism. In an address to the Boston Central Labor Union, Eliot observed that democratic society, having undergone "some revulsions of feeling with regard to personal liberty," seemed willing through both labor unions and employers' associations "to abridge the liberty of the individual for the supposed collective benefits of his class." It was in this context that he declared the scab "a fair type of hero." He was convinced that "the labor union monopolies are really much more threatening social and industrial evils than the capitalistic monopolies." In the National Civic Federation, a conservative reform organization that sought to bring employers, labor, and the public together, Eliot was perhaps the most outspoken critic of the closed shop and the union label. In a vigorous exchange at an NCF meeting he sought to convince Samuel Gompers that his unionist goals threatened liberty. Eliot could still assert in 1907 that "the great strength of a democracy is in the individual initiative," though he admitted such initiative was less possible than a generation earlier. What he hoped would emerge from the era of reassessment was "collectivism which does not suppress individualism." [33]

His insistence that in an industrial democracy opportunity persisted for "the play of individual will" was not always convincing. When he asserted, "There remains the freedom to choose among leaders, to choose a service, and to determine the kind of service the individual will render, generous or grudging, high-minded or mean, enlarging or shrinking as life goes on," he came close to saying that one had freedom under the new collectivism to like it or not. Even at the most individualistic stages of his thought, Eliot had valued community, duty, and self-sacrifice and had warned that liberty must not be mere selfishness. [34]

Perhaps never did Eliot evoke so strong an awareness of social bonds as he did in wartime. Talking to students during the Spanish-American War, he insisted that—though family obligations took precedence—there were legitimate motives for enlistment, notably "the sense that every member of human society is mainly indebted for his own character, resources, and happiness to the slowly developed qualities and slowly accumulated resources of the particular society into which he was born; that each of us is what he is, because the society of which he is a member is what it is." The more civilized the society, the more emphatic the debt became. This Burkean regard for prescription was a far cry from Emersonian self-reliance. To the young men debating their role in the war, Eliot repeated a Biblical passage that he often used when in an anti-individualistic mood: "No man liveth to himself, and no man dieth to himself." There had been strong foreshadowing of this effort to mark the limits of individualism in Eliot's early and persistent concern for family ties.[35]

IV

The change between the Eliot of the Gilded Age and Eliot of the Progressive Era can also be traced in his attitude toward government-supported higher education. He had come into office just as Harvard won release from vestigial state control, and he always judged this a happy liberation. Although his agreement with Herbert Spencer did not extend to an insistence on private lower schools, in the 1870s he applied laissez-faire ideas vigorously to higher education.

In what has been called "one of the shabbiest episodes in American academic history," Eliot in 1873 joined James McCosh in opposing efforts to increase the Morrill land grants for higher education. To help block such increases, the Princeton president privately circulated a letter from Eliot which maintained that such public aid would spread higher education too thin and "array class against class, and sect against sect." Eliot had earlier praised the effect of Morrill support at the Sheffield Scientific School and had taught at M.I.T., another recipient, but he now judged that the grants had borne little fruit.[36]

Toward Massachusetts Agricultural College, another Morrill beneficiary, Eliot displayed extreme antagonism. Plans to give it part of the annual dog tax threatened, he claimed in 1879, to make the school "a perpetual pensioner of the state." His ideal solution was to transfer the agricultural school to privately controlled Amherst College. Denying that it was inconsistent for him to support tax exemptions for institutions of higher education while opposing tax support, Eliot maintained in the early 1870s that "the cheapest and best way in which the State can get [churches, colleges, and hospitals] is to encourage benevolent and public-spirited people to provide them by promising not to divert to inferior public uses [i.e. by taxing] any part of the income" of the benefaction. He truculently differentiated earlier state support of Harvard from the later pattern of state universities. Harvard students had always paid "a very fair tuition fee," he observed. "It was reserved for the present generation in our Western States to insidiously teach communism under the guise of free tuition in State colleges." 37 In a rather cold reply to a proposal for cooperation, from William Watts Folwell, the new president of the University of Minnesota, Eliot wrote him in 1870 that "State aid to education is a most difficult subject which is not yet thought out." Questioned about the University of Michigan four years later, he responded that it had a very bad organization which left it strongly influenced by politics. In fact, he once suggested that Western state universities might be a transitional stage, that state support would end as the universities gained strength and accumulated endowment. As late as 1907, Eliot's description of state universities with "their hands deep in the state treasuries" had at least a hint of "fingers in the till." 38

The question of founding a national university gave Eliot preeminence among opponents of government financing for higher education. The national university plan, which its supporters traced back to George Washington, gained renewed vigor after the Civil War through the efforts of the indefatigable John W. Hoyt, an editor and educator who was to become territorial governor of Wyoming and first president of its state university. Hoyt used committees of the National Education Association to gain prestige for his plan, under which the federal government would found and support in the nation's capital a graduate university, a capstone of American education. In making his case, Hoyt noted the limitations of such universities as Harvard. Eliot's response at the NEA meeting of 1873, apparently the first open attack on

Hoyt's plan, remained the classic refutation of the national university idea.[39]

Eliot offered specific criticisms of Hoyt's promotional methods and of the cumbersome provisions of the bills then pending in Congress, and he did not spare Washington's climate and culture. But his chief argument drew on his idea of American exceptionalism. The national university plan was "of European origin, being a legitimate corollary to the theory of government by divine right." The United States, a modern republican confederation, viewed governments as "purely human agencies with defined powers and limited responsibilities." Eliot saw a particularly important relationship among government, learning, and national character:

> If the people of the United States have any special destiny, any peculiar function in the world, it is to try and work out, under extraordinarily favorable circumstances, the problem of free institutions for a heterogeneous, rich, multitudinous population spread over a vast territory. We indeed want to breed scholars, artists, poets, historians, novelists, engineers, physicians, jurists, theologians and orators; but, first of all, we want to breed a race of independent, self-reliant freemen, capable of helping, guiding and governing themselves. Now the habit of being helped by the government, even if it be to things good in themselves—to churches, universities and railroads—is a most insidious and irresistible enemy of republicanism; for the very essence of republicanism is self-reliance.

He called for support of "the genuine American method—the old Massachusetts method," namely, local support and control of lower schools, but for higher instruction he wanted endowments administered by trustees. This method, he predicted, would in time give several great universities to America.[40]

Eliot's address approached the intemperate. Western educators responded with expressions of faith in government as the agent of the people, residents of Washington spoke up for its climate and scientific resources, and McCosh expressed fear that Eliot's views represented antagonism to the principle of free public education (a charge Eliot quickly disclaimed). At the NEA meeting a year later, Hoyt branded Eliot's address "a blind attack upon the whole policy of government aid to education," while Andrew D. White, revealing a distinctly superior awareness of the educational needs of the nation, attacked Eliot's "undue extension of the *Laissez Faire* argument." [41]

Yet the Eliot position seemed vindicated. For a decade and a half, the national university idea languished. When it was revived in 1889 by some citizens alarmed by the founding of the Catholic University of America in Washington, Eliot defended the Catholic effort and declared that he had never seen a plan for a national university "that was in any degree promising." In fact, "nothing could be worse in an institution of learning than political management and the spoils system." [42] Yet when Hoyt renewed his efforts in the nineties, Eliot admitted that civil service reforms weakened one of his objections. Hoyt sought to moderate Eliot's continuing criticism: "He stands for the oldest, if not the greatest, of American collegiate institutions, with a natural pride of supremacy, and has been taught to cherish something of a prejudice against public education." The remark showed insight into Eliot's motivation, but it failed to consider an important change in his argument. Rather than condemning government aid, Eliot now invited it for universities already in existence. [43]

As for state universities, Eliot could not deny that their development had had no such debilitating effect on national character as he had prophesied. Although he failed to give full credit to the achievements of Western state universities when he visited them in the early 1890s, he developed friendly relations with such presidents as James B. Angell of Michigan, Richard H. Jesse of Missouri, and Charles R. Van Hise of Wisconsin. At the time of Jesse's retirement, Eliot judged his tenure at the University of Missouri "an admirable illustration of what the American democracy is capable of doing for public education, and of what public education is capable of doing for the democracy." This was a changed Eliot from the cocksure individualist of the 1870s. Gradually he had worked out a theory that made room for both state and private universities. He concluded that since private universities were "more enterprising and forward looking," they were valuable as pace-setters and competitors for the state universities.[44]

It became ever clearer to Eliot that private universities were also obliged to obtain public goodwill, including the goodwill of state legislatures. Faced with renewed legislative proposals to tax Harvard property, he found himself arguing in 1906 that mixed public and private support was in fact the general American pattern, to which Harvard as well as state universities conformed. His friendly exchanges with state university presidents, especially Van Hise, strengthened his willingness to associate Harvard's purposes with those of the public universities. Though he continued to perceive greater freedom at private universities, Eliot could say in 1909, "It is important that every university, endowed as well as state, should serve the people directly and indirectly and that that service should be recognized by the common people." [45]

V

In a letter to Eliot a young classicist once deplored scholars who were "too disdainful or forgetful of the great world outside their respective studies and laboratories,—to come down into the forum and state adequately from time to time the larger results . . . which they have to offer for the general good." [46] Such criticisms were more likely to come from outside the university, but in any case it was unwise to ignore them. Genuine scholarship might require indifference to the public, but a disaffected public had ways of injuring the university. It could refuse to send students. It could pass restrictive legislation. When Eliot took office many Americans were still alive who had voted against John Quincy Adams, thinking of him as a former Harvard professor, and less than two decades had passed since George Boutwell's attack on Harvard for its distance from the people. Eliot came to consider it one of his duties to win public respect for the scholar who cared nothing for such approval. In an address of 1891 in Chicago, he drew a portrait of the "very peculiar and interesting kind of human being—the scientific specialist," whom universities cherished. "He is an intense and diligent worker; but the masses of mankind would think he was wasting his time. He eagerly desires what he calls results of investigation; but these results would seem to the populace to have no possible human interest. He is keen-scented, devoted, and enthusiastic, but for objects and ends so remote from common topics that he rarely possesses what is called common sense. The market-place and the forum are to him deserts." [47]

Some faculty members were attractive to the nonintellectual public. The energetic Albert B. Hart joined in local public affairs and reveled in visible good works. Thomas N. Carver, a farmborn Midwesterner, rode horseback through the Corn Belt and New England chatting with farmers about their problems and gathering data for his Harvard course on agricultural economics.[48] But Eliot had to think also of single-minded scholars, men like the philologist Frederic DeForest Allen and the medievalist Charles Gross. It was for them that Eliot tried to win understanding through his Chicago address.

The two-hundred-fiftieth anniversary of Harvard's founding was made an occasion to call the public as well as learned institutions to witness its worth. Clerical alumni were asked to speak about Harvard from their pulpits on November 7, 1886, and four days of speeches and dinners marked the anniversary. Degrees, given in the vernacular for the first time, went to such non-Harvard men of public repute as L. Q. C. Lamar, Mark Hopkins, and John Wesley Powell. Although President Cleveland refused a degree, his attendance focused public attention on the occasion. In his brief speech, virtually apologizing for not being a college graduate, he called for scholars in politics. With the alumni in firm control of planning, academic antiquarianism abounded, but two promising new alumni associations—for the law school and the scientific school—grew out of the celebration.

The chief ornament, James Russell Lowell's oration, was not

designed to win public affection for Harvard. Learnedly, he assailed the "Spirit of the Age," its democracy, its materialism, its press, and its trades unions. In a speech of such tenor, it was a mixed compliment for Lowell to say of Eliot that he had "brought the University into closer and more telling relations with the national life," for in spite of the qualifying phrase, "in whatever that life has which is most distinctive and most hopeful," the implication remained that Eliot was of the business age and his program suspect. If one thought better of Harvard for what Lowell said, it was because it had preserved stern virtues of the Puritans, not because it had fitted itself to the needs of a new America.[49]

Such ceremonial anniversaries soon became standard features of university life in America. Princeton celebrated its one-hundred-fiftieth in 1896, Yale its two-hundredth in 1900, Johns Hopkins its twenty-fifth in 1902, and the University of Chicago its tenth the same year. The great university presidents of the era were brought into high relief by such affairs. In 1886, however, it was too early for Eliot to stand as a personification of the university.

Although in the early years he rarely refused speaking invitations, Eliot at first had few occasions to address audiences outside New York and New England. By the 1890s this had changed. His two Western tours of 1891 and 1892 may have begun as alumni relations junkets, but they expanded into swings around the circle to gain public support for the university idea in general and Harvard in particular. Some of the faculty felt he was "advertising the University too much." His address of 1891, "The Aims of Higher Education," identified the scholar with the American frontiersman and the university with progress. His statements on free silver (unsympathetic) and Mormons (sympathetic) brought attacks which sometimes had overtones of antagonism toward the university, but he succeeded on the whole in building prestige for American higher education. In the long run, the benefits of Eliot's tours and speeches came less from his comments on Harvard, or on universities in general, than from the impression that this wise and socially concerned gentleman exemplified university ideals. The day passed when a benighted San Bernardino newspaper could mention him as "Dr. Eliot of Dartmouth College, New Haven." In 1903 a Boston newspaper declared of Eliot, "His views on public matters appeal to a very wide range of people as sound sense, and this public appreciation goes to imputing that same sense and good judgment to the whole university." [50]

The university's displays at the Chicago Exposition in 1893 and at the Atlanta Exposition in 1895 served a purpose akin to that of Eliot's tours. Concern for popular acceptance of the university seems the most likely explanation of the effort Harvard devoted to these exhibitions, though a desire for more students also played a part. Assistant Professor Edward Cummings, in charge of the Chicago exhibit, reported praise from strangers and the distribution of many catalogues and pamphlets. After wondering at first if the printed material could be of much use to the indiscriminate throng, he was "startled when waiting for fire-works in the evening, to see an uncouth fellow slip out a 'Harvard University—' pamphlet and peruse it diligently by the flicker of an Electric light." Although there were an increasing number of "opportunities for useful propaganda," Cummings was not sanguine about any help the press might give. "As for serious or discriminating criticisms of educational exhibits, such reporters as I have chanced to see, seem to have neither time, patience, nor inclination for such work. . . . I should dread publicity at the hands of some of them almost more than neglect." By the time of the St. Louis Exposition of 1904, however, although large displays from the medical school and the observatory were sent, there was far less attention to the public's reaction. How to keep strangers out of the Harvard-Yale-Princeton Club on the exposition grounds was the main public concern of the local Harvard men. But the name Charles Eliot was impressed on the public by an elaborate monument (part of the "Civic Pride Monument") to Eliot's son and namesake, a landscape architect cut off in his prime.[51]

Another way in which the university could identify itself with the public was through the granting of honorary degrees. It

might thus "escape from the circle of University limitations, and
. . . take a lead in guiding popular impressions," as Henry Adams
indicated it would if it testified to its respect for Lincoln by
granting degrees to his biographers. This was no new idea. It had
surely not been for his scholarship that George Washington in
1776 received Harvard's first LL.D. On at least two occasions,
Eliot faced a problem when honorary degrees seemed the due of
political office-holders who were offensive to many Harvard men.
It had long been customary for the governor of Massachusetts
to attend Harvard commencements and for Harvard to award
each new governor the LL.D. When the election of 1882 put
into the governorship Benjamin F. Butler, who had charged
Harvard Medical School with misuse of bodies taken from the
almshouse and whom many Harvard alumni opposed an an un-
savory opportunist, Eliot and the Fellows still favored the traditional degree procedure. When Moorfield Storey raised opposition in the Overseers, Eliot argued that a snub would hurt the
university before the legislature, and he offered as a compromise
to drop all eulogy from the presentation. Storey condemned such
expediency as cowardly and carried a majority of the Overseers.
The next year, Governor George Dexter Robinson, an alumnus,
also received no degree, and Eliot announced that henceforth
Harvard degrees would not be political spoils. The policy shift
may have salved the feelings of Butler men, but it removed the
university further from democratic processes.[52]

Cleveland's modest refusal of a degree weakened the notion
that Presidents of the United States deserved degrees by virtue of
office. But when Senator George F. Hoar, president of the alumni
association, insisted on bringing President McKinley to commencement in 1901, the Fellows felt they could not avoid granting him an honorary degree. Again Storey raised opposition in
the Overseers. Although McKinley's tariff, Philippine, and civil
service policies were objectionable to many in the Harvard community, the twice-chosen of the people was voted the traditional
LL.D. Eliot, who judged McKinley "narrow-minded and com-
monplace," supported the decision, citing Hoar's claims on the

university and recalling that Andrew Jackson had doubtless been "a bitter dose to the College governors of that day." The matter was too controversial to be confined to the governing boards. Harvard men circulated petitions against the degree, and newspapers joined the argument. Shortly before the commencement, McKinley announced that his wife's health would not allow him to make the trip to Cambridge, and—though honorary degrees *in absentia* were not unprecedented at Harvard—he was considered to have forfeited the degree by his absence. Unabashed and taking the excuse at face value, Senator Hoar told those at the commencement dinner, "To-day all mankind know that the citizen of the republic foremost in honor, in power, in office, is also her foremost example of the family virtues." A year later, with a Harvard man in the White House, the university showed no hesitation in strengthening its tie to political leadership. After receiving his LL.D., Theodore Roosevelt spoke fittingly on the college graduate's duty in public service.[53]

Eliot's belief that "publicity" was a necessary institutional function developed largely during the latter half of his tenure. It grew out of a long period of sensitivity to newspaper criticism, some of it sensationalistic. As a young university president, Eliot spoke before a New York audience which he believed included no reporters, praising the freedom of Sheffield students from any chapel requirement. To his dismay he later found "two most scandalous [newspaper] reports, full of impertinences and gross mistakes." He drew the moral: "Either keep your mouth shut or write out what you say for the newspapers." [54] Later Eliot chided the supposed author of a New York *Tribune* article which repeated certain criticisms from an Overseers' committee report. Such reports, Eliot maintained, were meant to emphasize defects and therefore should not be shared with the general public.[55] But there was also danger in newspaper silence. For Harvard not to be mentioned at all left the public with the impression that academic achievement lay elsewhere.

In 1888 Eliot and a faculty member discussed the methods of publicity used by Johns Hopkins—presumably its *Circulars* and its readiness to be the subject of popular magazine articles. Probably as a result, an experimental *University Reporter* appeared in 1890. It did not survive a volley of faculty criticism, George Herbert Palmer, for example, fearing that its potential "brag and swagger" represented a tendency to "Johns-Hopkinize." But related efforts were made, chiefly under the guidance of Frank Bolles, Secretary of the University. He prepared and distributed reports and pamphlets (notably one on student expenses at Harvard), took part in founding the unofficial *Harvard Graduates' Magazine* in 1892, and wrote articles on the university for newspapers. The *Harvard Bulletin*, a weekly launched in 1898 by the alumni athletic association, included general news of interest to alumni in addition to reports of athletic affairs.[56]

Hoping to make Harvard better known, particularly in the West and South, Eliot in 1895 had Harvard publications sent to graduates who wrote for the press. A more distinctly commercial experiment came in 1900, when George V. T. Michaelis, a young Boston newspaperman who had just founded a business called "Publicity Bureau," approached Eliot, offering to write articles about Harvard to be sent as filler to newspapers throughout the country. Michaelis, described as "quick, fluent, indefatigable,—with a ready instinct for the commercial value of news,—and very adaptable," reached a trial agreement with Eliot to circulate articles for two hundred dollars a month.[57]

The agency prided itself on writing with such interest that newspapers which discarded official announcements would print its articles, yet it avoided the "mere puffs" of theatrical press agents. It sought to present Harvard as a national university and to play upon what one of its writers called "that curiously mingled feeling of loyalty which exists throughout the Upper Mississippi Valley toward New England and its intellectual institutions" while seeking to "disarm the feeling of envy with which that loyalty is mixed." Rather than directly attacking "the false idea of extravagance and dissipation" at Harvard, the agency sought to replace it with an image of industry. In spite of this incisive analysis of Harvard's strengths and weaknesses in the public mind and some financial support to the Germanic Museum for which the agency took credit, Eliot terminated payment after the first few months. But he allowed the Bureau to continue circulating articles on Harvard—"for the sake of the prestige which they think they obtain." The agency thus borrowed from Harvard the very quality it had promised to bestow upon the university.[58]

Many other articles on Harvard appeared without official effort, written by students earning their way and by professional newspapermen who made themselves at home in the *Crimson* office. Most such material was of course "positive." Under the editorship of Franklin D. Roosevelt, the *Crimson* threatened to exclude newsmen whose papers published erroneous or malicious reports. No formal news bureau was founded in the Eliot era, although the idea was considered. Jerome D. Greene, Secretary to the Corporation, made press relations one of his many functions. He sent the *Bulletin* (of which he had been the first editor) and the *Gazette* (an official weekly begun in 1905, containing announcements and listing faculty publications) to selected newspapers, and he placed articles on student achievements in hometown papers. Some success was indicated when President Harper of the University of Chicago, supposedly a master academic showman, turned to Harvard for guidance on press relations.[59]

Such public relations efforts brought satirical attack from several pens, including Thorstein Veblen's, and a recent scholar relates such ventures to an intellectually hollow institutional aggrandizement. In Eliot's case, however, such criticisms should be moderated. Upon leaving the presidency, he judged the most difficult problem in Harvard University to be the "task of affecting public opinion," but he pointed not to dollars or enrollment figures, but to the need for building public respect for intellectual achievement. He did not pretend that his various experiments with "publicity" had solved the problem.[60]

The university might celebrate its antiquity, send its president on cross-country junkets, pass pamphlets to tourists at world's fairs, vote honorary degrees to popular Presidents, and fill the

Western press with descriptions of its activities. But to win general support in a democratic nation the university needed to go beyond words and ceremonies. It needed to demonstrate concretely its concern for the people outside its walls.

VI

When the university extension movement had its first vogue in the early nineties, the Universities of Pennsylvania, Chicago, and Wisconsin took the lead. Harvard's refusal to send representatives to a conference of the American Society for the Extension of University Teaching was, Eliot reported, a faculty decision. They did not feel they had time for such work, he declared in 1892; fifteen years later, after the revival of the movement, the Harvard response was the same. Yet during the Eliot years Harvard offered many evening and Saturday courses for teachers and launched its summer school. When it was a question of aiding the lower schools, the effort appeared worthwhile. Albert B. Hart was defensive about the matter, suggesting that the "lustily blown trumpet" of university extension promoted only pseudo-university work and that Harvard's in-service teacher-training for Cambridge schools represented a superior "university participation." Various Harvard professors gave lectures for the Lowell Institute, but that unique product of Boston philanthropy seemed more closely allied with M.I.T. It was only after the Lowell Institute's single trustee succeeded Eliot in the presidency that Harvard entered a cooperative extension program with several neighboring colleges, under the aegis of the Institute.[61]

The creation of the Prospect Union indicated that some in the university cared about the education of more than an elite. The Union, a rather conservative manifestation of the settlement movement, opened in Cambridge in 1891, featuring evening classes for wage earners taught by Harvard students and instructors. Francis G. Peabody, a founder, counted it among the Union's merits that "Harvard students learned to understand and respect men bred in the hard school of labor, and wage earners discovered that a Harvard student might be neither a snob nor a prig." [62]

Eliot played scarcely any part in organizing the Union, but he was a member of its corporation, gave it books and money, and occasionally talked to the men. One of his topics was "A Healthy, Natural Life." The germ of the "Five-Foot Bookshelf" may lie in a statement Eliot drew up to aid the Union: "When education has been too brief or too limited in youth it is of the utmost importance that it be pursued in a systematic way in adult years."In spite of such support, Eliot joined with conservative faculty members in discouraging the use of the name "Harvard" in the titles of settlement projects. Barrett Wendell complained that the use of Harvard's name on a radical, ungrammatical publication implied "official sanction here of 'Extension' and 'Settlement'—matters from which as yet we are believed by ourselves to have kept prudently aloof." [63]

Harvard hesitated to undertake instruction of ambitious working men or culture-seeking dilettantes. For a university with newly dominant ideals of scholarship and professionalism such teaching seemed inappropriate. If such reluctance were branded undemocratic, at least some at Harvard were willing to bear the onus. But by the late 1890s Eliot had developed a rationale that fit the work of the professionalizing university into the life of a democratic nation. The new theory left questions for any thinking democrat, but it had a surface plausibility. The university would furnish democracy with its experts.

Universal suffrage would continue to settle those questions in which "just sentiments" were an adequate guide. But in other cases, where wise policy depended on "careful collection of facts, keen discrimination, sound reasoning, and sure foresight," the country must follow highly trained men—"experts in the matter in hand." In the midst of the free silver uproar, Eliot listed currency as a question which was too deep for popular sentiment to settle. He also counted education, long a bastion of popular control, among problems "which absolutely require for their satisfactory settlement the knowledge and trained judgment of experts." In an ever-increasing number of matters, Eliot predicted, the one proper decision for universal suffrage would be "to abide by expert opinion." Such experts would, of course, be products of the universities.[64]

In the concept of the expert Eliot sought to blend old and new values. "Now, the expert is always a highly individualistic product; but he is a product which an intelligent collectivism calls for, regulates, and supports." In keeping with his promotion of the expert as social servant, Eliot's picture of the withdrawn, impractical scholar gave way to a very different image. In 1905 he painted this portrait: "Nowadays a scholar is not a recluse, or a weakling incapable of the strenuous pursuits. He is not a bookworm, although he masters some books. He studies something thoroughly, learns all there is to know about it, and then pushes beyond. . . . He must use strenuously a tough and alert body, and possess a large vitality and a sober courage." Such scholars could take the long view and with their "constructive imagination" prepare to meet social needs. In one regard, however, Eliot's two portraits were alike. In both cases, the scholar was divorced from the people. "He is comparatively free," Eliot said in 1905, "from the pressure of public opinion, and from the hot gusts of public feeling. He has no occasion to discover and avail himself of the passing wishes or tastes of the multitude." This scholar-expert, like his predecessor the scholar-recluse, needed a mediator like Eliot to convince the public of his value.[65]

All this was an idea of the times, of course, and not Eliot's singular invention. The scholar-expert was a major element in "the Wisconsin Idea," which stressed the university's service to the state. This strand of Eliot's thought links him to the "social efficiency" movement of the early twentieth century, which emphasized social harmony and leadership by the competent. Yet Eliot's terminology was somewhat special, and he made quite individualistic use of the term "efficiency." For instance, he defined the "efficient nation" as one "made up, by aggregation, of individuals possessing [effective power for work and service]." If one accepts Edward Krug's division of the social efficiency ideal into social control and social service, Eliot's persisting individualism places him closer to the latter emphasis.[66]

Eliot's political philosophy had all along been marked by belief in the existence of a natural aristocracy and the propriety of social dominance by the "educated classes." The record of Harvard men in the Civil War had reassured him. Unable to serve in the war because of family responsibilities, Eliot had fulfilled his own sense of special obligation through service in an educational "reconstruction." Convinced of the inadequacy of ancestry and wealth as qualifications for a guiding elite, he had seized upon the professions, including the new "scientific" professions, as a better source of democratic leadership. No institution was more important in the selection and preparation of this elite than the university.

There is danger in any elitist theory of society that it will require a passive population, obedient and apolitical. Eliot did not want this any more than he wanted control given to "the fierce passions of the multitudes." He imagined a large working class, gradually rescued by technology from the most burdensome forms of labor, leading "a happy, natural life," ambitious for bright offspring, occasionally rising in political affairs to unseat rascality—but on the whole grateful for the trained skill of those in power and recognizing universities as the source of this social good. Meanwhile the university would protect itself from the leveling tendencies of equalitarianism. The university could serve the democratic society best by remaining somewhat separate and privileged. It was for the people, but not of them.

VI ❧

Who Should Have a College Education?

Here [at Harvard] the American and the foreigner, the Christian and the Jew, the Papist and the Protestant, the white man and the black man and the yellow man, can study side by side with equal right and learn alike whatever is worth learning.

JOSEPH H. CHOATE, *class of 1852, to alumni* (1894) [1]

I

It was far easier to use the elective system in celebrating liberty than in celebrating equality. In fact, Eliot spoke of the inequality which the elective system caused by making students "more and more unlike in their capacities and attainments" and used the system as a metaphor for social inequalities resulting under American liberty. But he found one defense for his educational liberalism which was squarely based on equalitarian values. He advanced it while discussing the lower schools, but its logic fit Harvard: "Democratic society cannot help seeking equality of condition for all men, though it is not so foolish as to believe in equality of natural faculties or powers. Now, the best chance of securing an approximate equality of condition lies precisely in this discovery, and development through education, of the peculiar endowments of each individual in the community." Had he felt strong equalitarian pressures against the elective system, he might have used this reasoning more widely, but he had little need to do so. The American in the street was not slow to judge the elective system to be "democratic." [2]

The sympathy that the public developed for the elective system was not easily transferred to Harvard College. Although universities were sometimes judged undemocratic because of what they taught—the trappings of esoteric culture rather than practical matters—this objection declined as the expansion of the elective system began to give the impression that they taught everything. The question of who went to college, on the other hand, could stir profound popular antagonism. Charges for tuition and tests for admission were particularly rigorous at Harvard. The university appeared in the popular imagination as the resort of a smug social class, a place dominated by "rich men's sons." This image, at least as old as Benjamin Franklin's satire of 1722 on blockheads sent to Harvard because their parents could afford it, had caused major political trouble for Harvard in the 1850s, at the time of the Boutwell committee and the Bowen appointment controversy.[3]

In his inaugural Eliot rejected the charge that Harvard was aristocratic, if aristocracy meant "a stupid and pretentious caste, founded on wealth, and birth, and an affectation of European manners." The college was "intensely American in affection, and intensely democratic in temper." It had always attracted "students in all conditions of life," and every year students entered "without any resources whatever." At this point the new president advanced the notion that the university recognized a natural aristocracy, with phrasing that revealed how restrictive this approach could be: "The community does not owe superior education to all children, but only to the élite—to those who, having the capacity, prove by hard work that they have also the necessary perseverance and endurance." The courage and martyrdom of Harvard men in the Civil War formed the theme of the inaugural's peroration. Their sacrifice answered recent doubts "whether culture were not selfish." But the example of these Harvard heroes appeared to support social inequality. What had been proved, Eliot said, was that "gentlemen" could be loyal to country and noble ideas, as once they had been to kings.[4]

Ironically, the very "democracy" of increasing numbers and liberalized curriculum undercut the internal democracy of intimacy with classmates. Social cleavages widened noticeably during the 1880s.[5] Criticism flared in the press after Collector Leverett Saltonstall, one of the Brahmin Democrats of the period, deplored the growing luxury and extravagance among Harvard students in an address of 1886. One member of the "fast set," queried about his associates' expenditures, claimed that though one or two might spend over ten thousand dollars a year, the average was a little below five thousand (at a time when the catalogue labeled annual expenditure of $1360 "very liberal"). As far away as Chicago an editorial warned of Harvard's "undoubted tendency . . . to become distinctively the rich man's college." From what could not be dismissed as an anti-intellectual standpoint, the editorial declared that Harvard was now the preferred college among the wealthy who were "more concerned that their sons shall acquire a certain dash of worldliness and social distinction than scholarly attainments." But a Boston newspaper, apparently using arguments furnished by Eliot, claimed that Harvard met a distinct duty to society in its attention to the sons of the rich, for it turned them from "mere luxury and animalism by cultivating the ideal, and particularly by encouraging intellectual ambition, aesthetic tastes and sound views of life," but that in any case not more than 10 per cent of the students in the college could properly be called rich. The point was still considered in need of proof in 1904, when the annual report presented statistics indicating that 12.6 per cent of Harvard College students were sons of "wage-earners." [6]

Tuition was raised just before Eliot took office, from $104 to $150. Thenceforth, Eliot resisted increases in tuition, and the basic rate remained the same throughout his administration. His most elaborate case against higher tuition emerged in 1904 in private correspondence with his persistent critic, Charles Francis Adams. To Adams he pointed out that students from public schools did better at Harvard than those from private schools and were "well-nigh sure to do better in after life"; a tuition increase would tend to reduce the 30 per cent of students currently coming from public schools. Eliot called for "a college of broad democratic resort" rather than one sharply divided between the well-to-do and those receiving scholarship aid.[7] At this juncture he presented his idea of a natural aristocracy more positively than he had in his inaugural. To a commencement audience in 1903 he said, "In our country it is to the last degree undesirable that the colleges should be accessible only to the well-to-do." Young people from poor families must be brought forward "to the service of the community." Such rhetoric suited the American mobilitarian tradition, and Eliot proved increasingly able to strike a democratic chord. When he defined "gentleman" in 1904, he avoided the exclusive aura he had once given the term. He distinguished "a real gentleman, who is also a democrat." Such a gentleman should be no "idler or mere pleasure-seeker," and Eliot rejected the view that his proper grade was "C." [8]

II

Admission policy revealed the tensions in one of the most sensitive areas where the university touched the rest of society, the determination of which of society's children would benefit from the institution's central function of teaching. During Eliot's administration the two major tendencies of admission reform had opposite effects on accessibility. The earlier phase brought higher requirements and additional required subjects. But increasingly, admission reform meant more options among entrance examination subjects.[9] The "higher standards" reforms suited Eliot's early ambition to elevate the college into a university. The movement for wider options accompanied the onward march of the elective system in the eighties and nineties. Although in part inspired by a desire to let small secondary schools with limited offerings prepare students for Harvard and thus broaden the base from which Harvard could draw students, admission options also reflected the belief that the benefits of liberty in course selection should not be denied to students at the secondary level who aspired to college entrance.

All nineteenth-century colleges were open to charges of exclusiveness, since only a small portion of the population attended.

But Harvard was particularly offensive to equalitarians. It did not issue the wide invitation to all neighboring youths which characterized the frontier college and the state university. The popular mind associated Harvard with Eastern wealth and New England cultural elitism. Its centuries of existence had given Harvard a greater backlog of vested family interest than any other college. In 1886, however, only one out of eight Harvard students was the son of a Harvard graduate.[10]

The year Eliot took office, 69 out of 155 entering freshmen at Harvard College came from private preparatory schools, 26 from other forms of private training, and 60 from public high schools and Latin schools.[11] But a student's secondary school origin was only a very rough index to his family background and financial status. There were few high schools in the country in 1870, and poor boys sometimes went to the academies without paying tuition. By 1890, when the number of high schools had greatly increased, only about 7 per cent of the population of both sexes between fourteen and seventeen years old were attending secondary school, and approximately one-third of these were in nonpublic schools.[12] Although in his annual reports Eliot would occasionally hail a rise or deplore a decline, the proportion of public school graduates entering Harvard College remained near 30 per cent throughout his administration.

Elevation of standards was paramount in Eliot's mind when he took up his presidential duties. His inaugural supported "rigorous examination for admission" as preventing "a waste of instruction upon incompetent persons" and pledged continuation of the recent increase in the "weight, range, and thoroughness" of these examinations. Before the seventies were out, Harvard had added physical geography, English composition, French or German, and physical science to its admission requirements. Because of such changes, Eliot freely admitted, "schools have been greatly incommoded, teachers annoyed, parents perplexed, and candidates alarmed." [13]

President McCosh of Princeton protested that the new Harvard standards barred young men from "smaller towns and country districts." Eliot himself suggested in 1877 that admission requirements had "probably been carried to as high a point as good judgment will allow." In the 1890s, when Charles Francis Adams launched a drive to expose the low quality of English composition among entering freshmen, he revived the theme of stricter requirements. His resolution, proposed for adoption by the Board of Overseers, was replaced, at Eliot's suggestion, by one which viewed with alarm, but did not in fact force a rise in admission standards. By then, the central motif was the "broader road," not the "higher standard." [14]

Analyzing the problem of college preparation in the United States in 1874, Eliot commented, characteristically, "The essence of freedom is in equality of opportunities, and the opportunity of education should be counted the most precious of all." The bar to college attendance that particularly galled him was the Greek admission requirement, the elimination of which he had favored even before his election to the presidency. He kept up his campaign against Greek with little encouragement from the faculty. In 1871 an awkward optional arrangement that lessened the Greek requirement for some students was adopted, but three years later Eliot could not even get the faculty to vote on a proposal to admit students who had studied no Greek. [15]

The struggle over Greek was an epoch battle of American education. Its significance is suggested by the role the persistence of Greek in university preparation played in keeping the German universities a mandarin preserve. By 1883 Eliot was so sure of the importance of the issue that he declared the question of options in entrance examinations "the gravest question of University policy which has arisen, or is likely to arise, in this generation." One faculty member complained that schools which did not insist on the classics lacked "tone," and Eliot's old teacher Francis Bowen read a pro-Greek address which lasted through two or three faculty meetings. But most voices from outside the university supported Eliot's position. A professor of language who held fast to the Greek admission requirement in 1875, declaring that to drop it would mean surrender to the nation's superficiality and materialism, ruefully admitted in 1883 that the faculty must "recognize the force of public opinion." [16]

By May 1886 the faculty settled on a compromise. There were now three roads for admission to Harvard College—the traditional one; a second, joining mastery of elementary Latin and Greek with advanced work in other fields; and a third, the most radical, allowing mathematics and physics to be substituted for all the Greek. With this third alternative, Eliot maintained, public high schools could more readily fit students for college. The greater openness of educational opportunity seemed obvious. Eliot read the potential effect in terms of social class. In 1874 he had emphasized the need to assure access to children of "professors, ministers, country physicians, [and] lawyers." A decade later, during the drive against Greek, he warned against cutting off potential students whose fathers were "farmers, mechanics, operatives, clerks, [and] tradesmen," in addition to those whose fathers were "professional men of small income." [17]

Contrary to Eliot's hopes, the reform of 1886 proved inefficacious. The Massachusetts Association of Classical and High School Teachers soon branded Harvard's Greek substitution proviso a "hollow mockery." As late as 1894, only 7 per cent of candidates for admission omitted Greek, and the percentage of students coming from public high schools continued to diminish.[18] The scarcity of Harvard students from high schools outside Massachusetts was particularly disturbing to those who, like Eliot, aspired to make Harvard a national institution.[19]

In 1894 a faculty committee was appointed to prepare new entrance requirements. The time was promising, for reformers could raise as their standard the Report of the Committee of Ten of the National Education Association, which suggested that school programs give greater opportunities for study of modern languages, science, and history, and that colleges accept such programs as preparation. Eliot, a power in the NEA, had shaped the report. He had, in effect, gone outside the university for leverage to use on his own faculty. Modern subjects had been given in the secondary schools long enough, he argued, that they were by then "taught with a skill and an amplitude which makes them substantial elements of a sound training." [20]

Harvard's new scheme began with redefinition of admission subjects by the various departments, generally raising the level required for entrance. Such renewed pressure for more advanced study in preparatory schools was less significant, however, than the expansion of options, which moved the college far beyond the purposely onerous alternative for Greek in the scheme of 1886. The vehicle of admission liberalization was a new point system (a point being equivalent to a half-year's work in a study, with four or five lessons a week). The student must take examinations showing his achievement in twenty-six "points," of which four must be "advanced subjects." The subjects for eighteen points were rather precisely prescribed: in addition to English, one ancient language (likely to be Latin in most cases) and one modern were required. This was a loss for Greek, even though it was slightly over-valued on the point scale. The faculty's range of options was resisted by the Overseers, who feared for the quality of Harvard freshmen and suspected unhealthy extension of the elective system into the lower schools. Although the Overseers allowed the dethroning of Greek, a conservative element successfully objected to the arrangement that let students omit algebra and history. After some resistance, the faculty yielded.[21]

Even as amended, however, the new scheme left enough choice "to enable a boy to make use of superior and extensive training in science, in modern languages, and in history, as well as in classics and mathematics." It was thus in keeping with the moderate revisionism of the Committee of Ten, and it lent support to secondary school curricular reform. Some Harvard men did not feel it was the college's business to concern itself with the state of the nation's secondary education. An alarming indication of this came in a resolution that was proposed, but not adopted, at a meeting of the Overseers. The resolution declared that Harvard was limited by charter to the collegiate instruction of young men, and that official actions should "be directed to the attainment of that end, and not primarily to the advancement of other objects, however laudable or useful." Professor Albert Bushnell Hart found himself subject to alumni criticism when he suggested that Harvard's admission reforms might help the lower schools.[22]

Eliot, though displeased by the Overseers' interference, still claimed a great deal for the new arrangement. "The new plan for admission," he prophesied, "will bring the College into closer connection with high schools throughout the country, and will tend to enlarge the election of studies in all secondary schools; in consequence it will tend to make secondary education less discursive for the individual pupil than it has been." Thus, for Eliot, Harvard's national influence, student liberty, and sound education were all gainers in this plan to make Harvard more accessible.[23]

Unlike earlier changes, the admission reforms of 1906 were administrative rather than substantive. At Eliot's behest, John Goddard Hart, Secretary of the Faculty and an administrator of the new breed, drew up a report that demonstrated the folly of having five separate committees admitting students to undergraduate work—committees manned by "weary professors." The faculty agreed to a single admission committee, with the majority of its members administrators. The committee, chaired by Hart, obtained a series of procedural changes from the faculty, including acceptance by Harvard of College Entrance Examination Board tests as substitutes for its own. This step made Harvard admission a possibility for students from a far greater area than previously, since CEEB examinations were offered in three times as many locations as the college's own. One cause of the reforms was the continuing drop in number of entrants from high schools amid a decline in total enrollment. After the changes, Dean Briggs happily cited an increase in inquiries from high schools outside metropolitan areas. The humanity of this bureaucratization was indicated by Briggs's report that the new committee took "infinite pains in doubtful cases" and strove both "to avoid the loose and accidental and to escape unintelligent entanglement in its own rules." Hart too had a distinctly Eliotesque sense of the goal of such rationalizations: "to bring out of the chaotic conditions of school and college work a simple order that makes for the greatest freedom of opportunity for individuals." [24]

Having won procedural reforms in 1906, Eliot returned his attention to the admission subjects. With data from the new Overseers' visiting committee on secondary school relations, he upbraided the Latin department for setting a requirement "at variance with the programmes of most American secondary schools." (The department shortly came into line.) Although noting with satisfaction the continuing decline of Greek, he protested its overvaluation on the point scale. He branded anomalous the practice of allowing such subjects as botany, government, and drawing for S.B. admission, but not for A.B. By the time he left office, the only such "anomaly" remaining was shopwork. [25]

Eliot, who had early used college admission policy as a way of elevating and standardizing American secondary education, had seen an array of other methods of secondary school development emerge during his years in office. In many new agencies he had taken a leading part. It was now up to the college to adapt to the secondary schools, especially if it cared to achieve wide class and regional representation. Eliot's annual report of 1907 put the matter succinctly: "Once the College could prescribe the programmes of neighboring high schools; but now the programmes of secondary schools, whether nearby or distant, are rightly settled by the needs of the communities in which the schools are situated. . . . [Harvard in its scheme of admission] must recognize a great variety of school programmes, and must not attempt to compel the use of any particular method of teaching any subject in secondary schools." [26]

An excellent example of Eliot's going outside to bring pressure on the faculty and boards of governors for what he wanted within the university was his part in the creation of the College Entrance Examination Board. His role here also indicated the advantage of presidential longevity: there was a span of thirty years between Eliot's first proposal of standardized examinations and Harvard's full participation in such a program.

Eliot is generally credited with the first public proposal for a standardizing examination board, in 1877. The idea led to a conference of New England colleges in 1879 which agreed to a common definition of the English requirement.[27] After the Committee of Ten had advanced the chances for standardization with its report, Eliot, speaking before the Association of Colleges in New England in 1894, proposed a cooperative board of examiners to function throughout the nation. The response was minimal, but in New York a group of schoolmasters and Columbia's Professor Nicholas Murray Butler began to press for a similar measure. An address by Eliot to this group advanced the slowly progressing cause.[28] When Butler decided that a meeting of the Association of Colleges and Secondary Schools of the Middle States and Maryland, to be held in December 1899, was the opportunity to bring such a board into being, he prevailed on Eliot to attend. A detailed plan for the new board was presented by Butler. In the debate, denigrators were squelched by Eliot, who managed to clarify, amuse, and convince at the same time. The plan was adopted unanimously.[29]

When the College Entrance Examination Board was formally organized in 1900, Eliot was unable to win his faculty's immediate support, perhaps because some of them expected a parallel New England board. But pressures to join were felt almost at once. The growing combination of other strong institutions put the university on notice, Harvard physicist Edwin H. Hall warned, that it could no longer afford idiosyncrasies which struck schoolmasters and pupils as arbitrary. Harvard joined the board in 1904, but for its first two years it accepted board examinations in only certain subjects and insisted on rereading those. At this juncture, Eliot, Dean Briggs, and Dean Hurlbut successfully brought out their heavy guns, praising the conservatism of the board and warning (in light of declining Harvard enrollments) that this narrow policy barred the way to Harvard for talented students in schools distant from the university's influence.[30]

For all his imaginative involvement in admission reforms, Eliot

failed to see the promise of the "certificate system." This plan, originated at the University of Michigan in 1870, stimulated the immense growth of high schools throughout the Midwest, keeping
them in helpful relation with the state university, yet not limiting
them to college preparation. The university granted to high
schools approved by an inspector (usually a university faculty
member) the right to send its graduates to the superior institution
without further examination, on the basis of a principal's "certificate" of their appropriate preparation. By 1899, 187 high schools,
some outside of Michigan, had entered this relationship. Other
state universities adopted the same practice.[31]

This system expanded greatly during the years that Eliot wres-
tled with admission questions at Harvard. He was never friendly
toward it. Though his criticisms may have improved it, he underestimated its contribution to the rapid advancement of secondary
education in the country. In 1874 Eliot told the Johns Hopkins
trustees that he regarded the system as "a very dangerous experiment," and later he took more public opportunities to offer detailed criticism. Admitting that the system worked well for
"rapid recruiting" and establishing friendly university–high
school relations, he argued that the quality of the inspection was
crucial and that the Michigan system failed that test. One faculty
member did not represent knowledge enough, once every three
years was not often enough, and one day was not long enough;
furthermore, the objectivity of the inspector was dubious, given
his university's interest in having more students. On one occasion
Eliot brashly declared the system absolutely without any power
to improve teaching or raise standards.[32] He expressed a strong
preference for the system in Minnesota, where a State High
School Board served as an independent inspecting authority.[33]

Eliot especially resented the spread of a more open version of
the certificate system into New England. By 1890 all New England colleges except Harvard, Yale, and Bowdoin accepted principals' or headmasters' certificates for admission—and this without any attempt to inspect the schools. Eliot's comments were

scathing. The system did not protect the college from incompetent students and offered no opportunities to improve the standards of the schools and publicize good ones.[34]

Advocates of the certificate system eventually directed a counterattack against the examination system. One Michigan professor condemned Harvard's relation to the schools as "feudal," and President Andrew S. Draper of the University of Illinois spoke of the achievement of Western states in making the road to college "smooth and continuous and practically free." A headmaster near Harvard described the difficulty which the examination system caused a teacher who hoped to interest his students in learning for its own sake: "In the eyes of parents and pupils the entrance examination is the goal of study and aspiration. It is the center of interest, and knowledge does not pay that has no relation to that crowning event." To this penetrating criticism Eliot had no satisfactory answer.[35]

Standardized admission procedures were inevitable, but in this regard the United States became two nations. In part the split was regional; in part it was between public and private colleges. After 1902 the North Central Association of Colleges and Secondary Schools, which had its own accreditation standards and its own board of inspectors, strengthened the certificate system. In the East the College Entrance Examination Board brought a group of secondary schools and private colleges into collaborative creation of examinations.[36] Eliot welcomed the regional associations, but held fast to his preference for admission by examination. Perhaps the individualization of that practice appealed to him. Whatever its limitations in improving the secondary schools, it offered a chance for the occasional "sport" from a non-accredited school to show his promise.

III

The problem of educational accessibility involved more than wealth and preparatory education. On matters of race, national background, and religion—those sources of peoplehood that in the American context are usefully categorized under the name

Charles W. Eliot as
a Harvard undergraduate,
c. 1853

Eliot as a member
of the Harvard faculty,
c. 1860

University Hall,
where Eliot pursued chemistry experiments in a basement laboratory,
and later occupied the president's office

James Walker,
president of Harvard, 1853-60,
Eliot's mentor

Thomas Hill,
president of Harvard, 1862-68,
Eliot's predecessor

Memorial Hall, built 1870-74

"In yonder old playground, fit spot whereon to commemorate the manliness
which there was nurtured, shall soon rise a noble monument. . . ."
—from Eliot's inaugural address, 1869

Eliot early in his Harvard presidency

Eliot with his grandson,
Charles W. Eliot II, 1904

Two of Eliot's collaborators in school reform
John Tetlow,
headmaster of Boston Girls' Latin School
and Girls' High School

Paul H. Hanus,
appointed at Harvard as
Assistant Professor of the History and
Art of Teaching, 1891

A student's room at Harvard, *c*. 1877

Students in Thayer Hall, *c*. 1885

Crew, a sport for which Eliot always had a good word
Boat race on the Charles River: Newell vs. Weld Senior Crews, May 29, 1900
(Photographer: Julian Burroughs).

Football, a sport persistently criticized by Eliot
Harvard Varsity at practice, 1900
(Photographer: Julian Burroughs).

Eliot with A. Lawrence Lowell,
at Lowell's inauguration as
president of Harvard, 1909

Eliot at ninety

President's House, Harvard, built in 1860,
replaced early in Lowell's administration

A Harvard parade down Massachusetts Avenue, Cambridge,
probably at the time of the 250th Anniversary Celebration, 1886

Leaders of American institutions at Harvard commencement, 1915
Left to right: George von L. Meyer, former ambassador and cabinet member;
Senator Henry Cabot Lodge; William Lawrence, Episcopal bishop of Massachusetts;
J. Pierpont Morgan; Eliot

One of the first advertisements for the Harvard Classics

"ethnicity"—Harvard also faced charges of exclusiveness. At the alumni commencement banquet of 1894, Joseph H. Choate, a leading New York lawyer who was highly respected by his fellow Harvard graduates, orated with democratic sweep: "All learning is here absolutely and forever free and open to all on equal terms, without regard to race, or creed, or color, or nationality. Here the American and the foreigner, the Christian and the Jew, the Papist and the Protestant, the white man and the black man and the yellow man, can study side by side with equal right and learn alike whatever is worth learning." Yet in the year he spoke, a handful of Harvard alumni were organizing the Immigration Restriction League of Boston. It was Choate's stance, not that of the IRL, that Eliot adopted. He saw self-defeating narrowness in the view that labeled some nationalities undesirable and sought to bar them from either the country or the university. "I am no kind of a restrictionist to anybody," he told the Economic Club of Boston in 1905. One scholarly investigator of nativism has used Eliot to exemplify the anti-nativist "minority with faith" during the years when restrictionism was on the rise.[37]

"The University recognizes among its officers and students neither class, caste, race, sect nor political party" wrote Eliot, well aware that this position exceeded the tolerance of the country at large. In its racial inclusiveness particularly, Harvard was too "democratic" for the nation. "Americans," Eliot observed, "taken by the million have never thought their ideals of public liberty applicable in the slightest degree to colored men—yellow, red, brown, or black." But at times he tried to mute the differences between the university's inclusiveness and the public's antipathy toward ethnic minorities. To do this, he stressed the distinction between political equality and social equality. Political equality did not necessarily lead to social intimacy, he repeatedly insisted, and neither, he implied, did ethnic inclusiveness do so at Harvard. When it suited the purpose of his argument, he could emphasize the similarity of the world inside Harvard to the imperfect world at large rather than the superiority of the university as a vanguard in the movement toward a better society. In the city-like atmosphere of his Harvard, relationships did indeed more often suggest the impersonality of the polling place than the intimacy of the dinner table. It inevitably followed from Harvard's inclusiveness, the editor of the *Harvard Graduates' Magazine* observed, that some students, notably "day scholars" and "New Americans," were "unclubable," but he doubted if they cared.[38]

"As a rule, I select my companions and guests, not by the color of skins, but by their social and personal quality," Eliot wrote a disturbed white Southerner after the outcry over Theodore Roosevelt's luncheon with Booker T. Washington. "It would never occur to me not to invite to my house an educated Chinaman or Japanese because their skin is yellow or brownish, or to avoid asking a negro to my table if he were an intelligent, refined and interesting person." Such superficially tolerant statements revealed standards to which "they" were expected to conform, standards raising a wall around both Eliot's dinner table and Harvard University.[39]

Eliot pictured American civilization as already established. It should be the goal of minorities to conform to "the common American ideals" rather than transform them. But Eliot raised obstructions in the path of immigrants who sought such acculturation. Decrying in 1875 the "heterogeneousness in the free schools," he favored an arrangement that became notorious ninety years later as the exclusionist "neighborhood school." If, as Eliot then maintained, "the pure child should not be thrown in with the impure, or the refined with the coarse," one of the principal sources of "improvement" would be denied to children in ghettoized schools. At times, perhaps unconsciously, Eliot equated ethnic background with mental ability. The need for classifying students by capacity, he said in 1890, "is much greater than it was earlier, since our population has become very much more heterogeneous than it was forty years ago." The heterogeneity he had in mind could scarcely have been other than ethnic. In 1894, when he spoke of grouping brighter children for a faster pace in school, it required discussion with his audience of schoolmasters to make it clear that the proposed division would not coincide "with lines of nationality or with the lines of division by parents' occupation." Eliot was on more defensible grounds and closer to his stated social philosophy when he spoke not of schooling by group but of "individualization." [40]

As a young man Eliot had, like most Americans of the day, expected eventual total assimilation of new ethnic groups. But he began to have doubts about this process. In 1902 he blamed "a good many troubles in the United States" (especially strikes) on "the difficulty of assimilating year after year large numbers of foreigners." As his view shifted, he came to favor preservation of different "races" (using the term in its loose, early twentieth-century sense). [41]

During a tour of the South in 1909, he supported the region's anti-miscegenation laws and declared his belief "that the Irish should not intermarry with the Americans of English descent; that the Germans should not marry the Italians; that the Jews should not marry the French. Each race should maintain its own individuality." Editors across the nation expressed disagreement, even the Charleston *News and Courier* contending that amalgamation of white "races" was beneficial. So great was the uproar in Massachusetts that Eliot sent back a clarifying telegram.

> It has been a common anticipation in the United States that the numerous races of which our population is made will blend into one race to be called American. This blending will be the effect not of rapid amalgamation but of the gradual diminution of differences through the effect of common education and common conditions in national industry and through governmental policies and practices. That kind of assimilation will preserve the best qualities of all races, some of which might easily be lost by a sudden blend. [42]

Eliot seemed to imagine that a shared culture would bring racial homogeneity without intermarriage, a sad confusion of inherited traits and learned behavior. He may, however, have been groping toward a concept of "primary" and "secondary" culture, seeing the first as learned at home and continuing to vary by ethnic group, and the second as an increasingly shared pattern of public life.

The most important "minority" in Massachusetts was the Irish Catholic. Although less strange than the new immigrants of the 1890s, the Irish were often looked on as representatives of a degraded race and a corrupt religion. At the very least, they seemed "muddy-booted and clannish." The rising political power of the Irish made it unlikely that Eliot, as Harvard's representative, would consciously exhibit prejudice against them. Indeed, in his politically active phase in the Democratic party, Eliot developed a hearty respect for the first two Irish mayors of Boston, Hugh O'Brien and Patrick Collins.[43]

Considering its Puritan origins, Harvard in the nineteenth century had developed remarkably good relations with the Roman Catholic community. To some degree this resulted from opposition to evangelical orthodoxy on the part of both Unitarians and Catholics. At least there the two groups had a common enemy. At the urging of Bishop John Carroll, Catholics from Baltimore had come to Harvard in the early 1800s, and special arrangements were made for their religious observances. In 1831, of the fourteen men on the teaching and administrative staff at Harvard, three were Catholics. In keeping with this tradition, Charles J. Bonaparte, a Baltimore Catholic with a background somewhat more aristocratic than most inhabitants of Beacon Hill, was elected to the Board of Overseers in 1891.[44]

Eliot was brought into early alliance with Catholic leaders by his efforts to protect Harvard from state fiscal policies. One of the first public roles in which he gained wide attention, in fact, was his opposition to the drive of 1874 to tax property used for religious and educational purposes. Eliot's letter to the special tax commission, circulated as a pamphlet, showed his cogency in argument. While Harvard alumni were noting with resignation that their business-oriented president was making his first mark as a public advocate on a money matter, Catholics were welcoming his breadth in defending all religious institutions against the threatened taxation. Since the attack was in part aroused by resentment against untaxed Catholic institutions, the debate gave Eliot a chance eloquently to resist anti-Catholic modifications of traditional state policies. In a contemporary address to the Young Men's Christian Union he sought to allay the fears of Catholicism felt by Protestants. No new taxes were placed on the university, and his position won the respect and gratitude of the Catholic hierarchy. Eliot's opposition to discrimination against Catholics was not simply expedient. He believed religious toleration to be one of America's "contributions to civilization." "To legislate, directly or indirectly," he argued, "either for or against any particular religious belief or worship would be utterly repugnant to all sound American opinion and practice." [45]

In the late 1880s, amid a national recrudescence of anti-Catholicism, the most serious outburst since the days of the Know-Nothings, Eliot maintained his earlier position. He testified against a bill that would have put parochial schools under public school committee supervision and sought to meet Catholic objections to secularized public schools with a plan which, though not accepted at the time, was a precursor of later released-time programs.[46]

At Harvard itself, Eliot needed all his wit to adapt the heritage of the Puritans to the religious diversity of nineteenth-century America. Particularly challenging were the four Dudleian lectures on Christianity, the third of which, according to the will of the donor, Chief Justice Paul Dudley, class of 1690, was to expose "the Idolatry of the Romish Church, Their Tyranny, Usurpations, damnable Heresies, fatal Errors, abominable Superstitions, and other crying Wickednesses in their high Places." Eliot sought both to preserve the college's reputation for keeping faith with benefactors and to avoid offense to Catholics. He secured Bishop John Joseph Keane, rector of the recently opened Catholic University of America, as lecturer on the second Dudleian topic, revealed religion, in 1890.[47] In spite of the implied understanding in Keane's willingness to participate, over fifty members of the Harvard faculty protested to the Corporation against holding the anti-Catholic third Dudleian lecture. But the Corporation, giving assurances that the subject would be treated "historically," let the lecture stand. The next year, Eliot strengthened the case for Harvard's religious impartiality by awarding Keane an LL.D. In 1903 he sought (unsuccessfully) to have a Catholic scholar give the third lecture, concentrating on the errors in Catholic "statesmanship" that had made the Reformation possible. Although he repeatedly proposed that the Corporation ask the legislature for relief from the prescribed third topic, his last year in office found him inviting another liberal Protestant theologian to give "this somewhat difficult lecture on an archaic subject." [48]

Catholic students at Harvard, whose understandable sensitivities worried faculty opponents of the Dudleian lecture, numbered about three hundred in 1894. In Eliotesque vein, the student president of the Catholic Club emphasized its desire to disprove charges of illiberality or irreligion at Harvard. In fact, according to this student, Harvard would "lead in the changing of the attitude of the American mind towards the Church." The Reverend Peter J. O'Callaghan, a Paulist, who was a Harvard graduate of 1888, conducted the college's Easter service in 1894. He reported that one of his classmates, a Catholic convert, had declared that "the best preparation a Protestant could have for entering the Catholic Church was a course of philosophy at Harvard." Doubtless neither this nor O'Callaghan's view that Harvard was the country's "most splendid and richest field for missionary effort" represented the pure Eliot view of the role of Catholics at Harvard.[49]

Yet having stood so strongly against anti-Catholic bigotry in the early nineties that he aroused charges of "papalizing" Harvard, Eliot found himself assailed as an enemy of the Church before the century was out. The trouble began with a list, first published in 1893, of colleges and universities whose graduates the law school agreed to admit without examination. A graduate from a college not on the list faced more than the inconvenience of an entrance examination. He was categorized as a "special student" and could graduate only if his grade average was fifteen percentage points above that required of regular students. The

list originally included no Catholic colleges, a fact which Eliot's
fellow Democrat, James Jeffrey Roche, editor of the *Pilot*, called
to his attention, observing that it would "naturally enough" be
interpreted as discrimination. Eliot answered with a letter published in the *Pilot*. Denying any calculated exclusion, he maintained that Catholic colleges usually did not give an education
equivalent to others because of their different historical development and their reliance on directors who had been trained chiefly
for the priesthood. Nevertheless, the list was extended to include
Georgetown, Holy Cross, and Boston College.[50] The application
of Fordham for inclusion, on grounds that all Jesuit colleges were
of the same grade, precipitated a re-examination of the entire
matter in the law school and the elimination of Boston College
and Holy Cross. Georgetown remained, a single token of nondis-
crimination. Soon the "cordial relations existing between the
Catholic educational system and Harvard," which President J.
Havens Richards of Georgetown had hoped would "never be disturbed," were awash with acrimony, including charges of black-
listing. Before the matter subsided, Eliot and the president of Boston College, W. G. Read Mullan, carried on an increasingly
chilly correspondence, which the Jesuit educator sent in its en-
tirety to the press. Aside from charges against Eliot's logical powers and good faith, his correspondent accused Harvard of seeking
"to discredit all Catholic education in order to fill its halls more
surely with Catholic students."[51]

A more general attack on Eliot and his educational program
accompanied the Boston College dispute. Ostensibly, the criticism
came in response to a casual statement by Eliot in the *Atlantic
Monthly* of October 1899, in the midst of an argument for election of studies in the secondary schools. Citing the Jesuit colleges
as an instance, comparable to that of Moslem schools, of uniformity and prescription, he claimed that the Jesuit curriculum had
"remained almost unchanged for four hundred years, disregarding
some trifling concessions made to natural science." The tone was
less brotherly than Eliot's admonition in the *Pilot* in 1893, but
once again, he doubtless felt that since Catholics were not the

only "ecclesiastical" group criticized, there was no anti-Catholic discrimination.[52]

A former president of Boston College, Timothy Brosnahan, a moderate reformer who had initiated some of the new work in science there, sought to answer Eliot in the *Atlantic Monthly*. Refused that opportunity, he argued his case in the *Sacred Heart Review*, later distributing his article as a pamphlet. Besides demonstrating the falseness of Eliot's chronology (the Jesuit order had not existed for four hundred years), Brosnahan observed that the free elective system at Harvard allowed choices of studies inferior to those required at Jesuit colleges. In a second pamphlet, taking the law school's exclusiveness as his point of departure, Brosnahan again directed his heaviest fire against the undergraduate course at Harvard, larding his arguments with anti-elective statements from Protestant college officials. Even the reader who noted his special pleading, and objected to *ad hominem* jabs at the "pathetically naïve" Eliot, was forced to grant much of his case. Given the openness of the Harvard elective system, some graduates of Boston College were surely better educated than some graduates of Harvard, yet the former suffered penalties both in entering the Harvard Law School and in graduating from it. Moreover, the dropping of Boston College and Holy Cross from the law school list was more damaging than simple non-inclusion since it subjected them to "the invidious distinction of being displaced." [53]

Eliot declined to offer the proofs or retractions that Brosnahan demanded, and he probably found the second pamphlet personally offensive. But he allowed himself one forthright statement of personal and institutional justification in his last letter to Father Mullan: "I have no quarrel whatever with the Jesuit Colleges, and no desire to diminish their influence, or their actual usefulness to the Catholic community—on the contrary, I should be glad to see that usefulness much augmented. As to the motives which have been or may be attributed to me, I feel no anxiety. Nobody will believe that I 'have determined to crush out Catholic education.' That truly would be a strenuous job, and one sure to fail." [54] Catholic students continued to attend Harvard in un-diminished numbers, and in 1904, without changing its admission policy, the law school stopped publishing its offensive list. Eliot urged Catholic educators who expressed sympathy with him in these disputes to make their case against inferior standards of Catholic colleges before Catholic audiences. The episode further diminished the Mugwump-style mutual respect between Harvard leaders and the Catholic community, which politically had broken down earlier. The weakness of such a relationship was indicated by Eliot's failure to give any credit to the Brosnahan–Mullan reforms at Boston College during the 1890s. Instead he relied on a stereotype of Jesuit education no different from one he had expressed in 1878. His often generous relations with Catholics and Catholic schools stood revealed as essentially paternalistic and lacking in true acquaintance. [55]

In 1903 trouble arose over the settlement work of Harvard students in East Cambridge, an area largely populated by working-class Catholics. The clergy of the local parish assailed "the superior, patronizing, see-me-do-you-a-favor style of the Christian young men of Harvard." The Catholic public now watched with hypersensitivity all statements by Eliot bearing on its faith. Even Eliot's supporters were shocked at remarks made on his Southern tour early in 1909. Besides opposing marriages that crossed ethnic lines, he said in a Memphis address, "In Protestant Massachusetts . . . the population today is mostly Catholic. There are Irish, Italian and Portuguese that present the same race problem to that part of the country that the negroes do to the South." In Montgomery a few days later, a newspaper interviewer quoted him as referring to the North and West as having, like the South, a "racial suffrage problem": "The alien races have been a disturbing factor in our politics ever since the Irish began to arrive in this country, sixty years ago." The Irish came with no experience in self-government, he said, and the same was true of the Italians. Back in Cambridge the Secretary to the Corporation, Jerome Greene, responded defensively to the strenuous reaction provoked by these comments. Eliot had probably not said what the press reported, he suggested, and besides, "The Irish Catholics of Massachusetts have no better friend among the descendants of the Puritans than President Eliot, and they ought to know it." Eliot himself sent a telegram of clarification, recalling his friendship with Mayor Collins and including this condescending praise: "The progress of Irish voters towards toleration of all religions, and towards honest and efficient government in towns and cities has been more remarkable and much more rapid during the last twenty years than that of men of the English blood who were the earlier comers." [56]

Partly through Eliot's own failings, Harvard probably stood lower in the opinion of Catholics at the end of his administration than it had at the beginning. The best hope for improved relations lay in the now numerous Catholic alumni of Harvard and their recollections of "a cordial welcome, and . . . fair play without the slightest interference with their religious beliefs and practices." [57]

The same liberty in regard to religious observances had been extended to the occasional Jewish student since the early nineteenth century. German Jews had little trouble fitting in. For them the right preparatory school could submerge ethnic difference. But East European Jews from Boston public schools found the social atmosphere frosty. When Charles Fleischer, the liberal Boston rabbi, suggested that Harvard make provision for the religious instruction of Jewish students, Eliot responded that the deep division between reform and orthodox Jews made it important for the administration to hold back and let students take the lead. In 1906 Jewish students organized a Menorah Society. Anti-Semitism was a problem that concerned Eliot far less than anti-Catholicism. But he vigorously countered the rumor which had reached a Jewish benefactor of the university that anti-Semitism had blocked his brother-in-law's nomination for the Board of Overseers.[58]

The severest trial of Eliot's ethnic views came in connection with black Americans. Like most Northerners Eliot agreed with the post-Reconstruction settlement that left white Southerners the controlling hand in Southern race relations. He approved the poll tax and the literacy test. Although he included the proviso that all tests should be applied equally to both races, he did not point out the numerous evasions in favor of whites. He approved also of segregating the races in Southern schools, an arrangement which he wanted the federal government to subsidize, and he even predicted that separate schools would be needed in the North if there were ever large numbers of blacks there. In short, he shared the belief of many who considered themselves men of good will: that there could be race distinction in law without race discrimination. Although Eliot's bluntness and question-asking at times offended white Southerners, those who met him on his Southern tours were understandably reminded of "the Southern gentleman of the old school." [59]

Better than most men of his day Eliot grasped the cultural sources of so-called "racial" differences, and he avoided most of the pseudo-science on the subject. When Charles Francis Adams published an article which claimed that an African trip had opened his eyes to the inapplicability of American equalitarianism to black men, Eliot judged it "very silly." Although Eliot could assert that the black masses had yet to learn "that civilization is built on willingness to work hard six days in the week, and to be frugal all the time," he attributed this failure to the recency of the slave experience, since for slaves "labor is a curse and frugality an absurdity." But the slowness with which he expected American culture to work its transformation was so great that the "inferiority" might almost as well have been genetic. In 1909 he prescribed "four of five generations more" for American culture to do its elevating work on Negroes, whom he described as only recently removed from "savagery." He was willing to leave it for the twenty-first century to make the necessary readjustment after these results were in. A season spent in Bermuda did not encourage him, for he found blacks there, seventy years out of slavery, still "very inferior to the whites, physically, mentally, and morally." [60]

Yet the gravest problem in American race relations, Eliot assured one correspondent, was not the condition of the blacks, but the barbarism of the whites, on whom slavery seemed to have had the worse effect. One source of his generation's support for segregation was indicated in Eliot's statement that "contact with a colored race has always demoralized in certain respects the [white] Americans themselves." The sexual aspect of black-white relations was the worst, since it "leads to constant sin." [61]

This notion of white demoralization helps explain Eliot's stand in 1907 on the Berea College case, which required a private college in Kentucky to end its racial integration. During the period when the case was under appeal, Eliot spoke before the Twentieth Century Club at a meeting to raise funds for Berea. He again expressed his view that if the proportions of blacks and whites were more nearly equal in the North, sentiment there might properly favor segregated education. Since as much good might be done for the black students in a separate branch, the division at Berea "is not really an abandonment of the principle, although it may be a departure from the original purpose." He then turned to the situation at his own institution: "At present Harvard has about five thousand white students and about thirty of the colored race. The latter are hidden in the great mass and are not noticeable. If they were in equal numbers or in a majority, we might deem a separation necessary." [62]

It is easy to believe the comment of a Harvard-trained Southerner that these words "struck consternation to the radicals of both the white and colored races in the North and East, and gladdened the hearts of many of the South and West." Later, Jerome Greene was at pains not to assuage the insult to blacks, but to make sure that Eliot's words were not misunderstood as suggesting that the proportion of black students at Harvard was in fact on the increase. This concern suggested that among Eliot's motivations was a wish to counteract the impression in the South that Harvard's racial policy would be offensive to white Southern students. He had earlier expressed the fear that white Southerners thought Harvard "too hospitable" to Negroes. Negroes were not, he informed one inquirer, admitted to small social clubs, though some were in athletic clubs.[63]

Though he could condone such internal discrimination, Eliot would not have tolerated barring blacks from Harvard. His pluralistic, permissive view of student life at the university left Harvard's door open. Once inside, students could make whatever "social" arrangements they liked, including racially restricted clubs. But when President Lowell defended the barring of black students from the new freshman dormitories in 1923, Eliot strongly disapproved.[64]

Eliot's public stance on "the Negro question" resembled the accommodationism of Booker T. Washington. Shortly after his famous Atlanta Exposition address, Washington received an honorary A.M. from Harvard. Although Eliot's citation when conferring the degree was in general terms ("teacher, wise helper of his race"), he used blunter language four years later when honoring Hollis Burke Frissell, the white principal of Hampton Institute, Washington's alma mater. Eliot praised Frissell for "teaching the Negro and the Indian that the prime means of civilization are faithful family life, habits of forethought and thrift, and steady manual labor." In 1903 Washington returned to Harvard and was introduced at the alumni dinner as "one of the whitest souls in our country."[65] The black leader responded with his wonted equanimity. After Eliot visited Tuskegee in 1906, he wrote to Washington, criticizing the school's tolerance of intellectual mediocrity. His recommendations for higher academic standards at Tuskegee and a turn away from its unrelieved emphasis on industrial training were evidence that Eliot's humanistic individualism could transcend his racial bias.[66]

IV

Unlike complaints of class and ethnic exclusiveness at Harvard, objections to the barrier against women came from a group with whom leaders at Harvard were in intimate daily relations. Wives, sisters, and daughters of Harvard alumni and faculty were among those who demanded equal education for women, as were Brahmin reformers like Thomas Wentworth Higginson and Wendell Phillips. These agitators found scant comfort in Eliot's inaugural, even though it promisingly hailed the sexual equalitarianism of American homes and American hatred of all disabilities. The Corporation would not receive women into any part of the university requiring residence near by, Eliot said, but he hinted that professional education for women at Harvard might be allowed. He referred to women's admission to the University Courses as a "cautious and well-considered experiment," which would "contribute to the intellectual emancipation of women." Sexual equalitarians were unimpressed. Their reactions ranged from a suggestion that Eliot consider the success of coeducation in the West to a conclusion that he was a "Satan." [67]

When Eliot did see women in coeducational classes in the West, he reported them "worn, frail and bloodless." He shared a public platform with Wendell Phillips to answer Phillips's case for the admission of women to Harvard College. He distressed the audience at the first Smith College commencement in 1879 by dwelling on dangers in higher education for women, and twenty years later he complimented the new president of Wellesley on her chance for pioneering, since "society as a whole has not yet made up its mind in what intellectual fields women may be safely and profitably employed on a large scale." [68]

In keeping with the hopes expressed in his inaugural, however, Eliot winked at attendance by women at divinity school lectures and urged that the Corporation accept a gift to the medical school conditioned on its equal admission of women. Yet it was not professional education that first brought women a Harvard education, but rather an arrangement by which Harvard professors repeated their undergraduate lectures in Cambridge for "The Society for the Collegiate Instruction of Women," familiarly known as the "Harvard Annex." This program was initiated in 1878 by Mr. and Mrs. Arthur Gilman, residents of Cambridge who had a daughter nearing college age, and certain socially prominent women with Harvard connections, notably Elizabeth

Cary Agassiz, widow of the great zoologist. Eliot, frustrated in his hopes that Harvard's professional schools might include women, lent his support to the Annex experiment from the beginning, though he carefully guarded the prerogatives of the Corporation and occasionally assured suspicious conservatives that Harvard had not embarked on coeducation. As in the case of certain ethnic minorities, inclusion of women at Harvard was regarded by portions of its constituency as a sign of institutional decay.[69]

Harvard students accepted with little complaint the nearness of the Annex and the attendance of an occasional woman at a graduate course in the Yard. "The young women go and come to their exercises as they might to church," the alumni were assured, "and there is little or no class-room acquaintance between the students of the two sexes." By 1893 Eliot and the Fellows supported the chartering of their neighbor, agreeing that the Harvard Corporation would serve as "Visitors" for the Annex (a function which meant approving all faculty nominations) and that the women's diplomas would bear the Harvard seal and be countersigned by the president of Harvard. Through a happy rediscovery of the identity of the first benefactress of Harvard, her family name, Radcliffe, was given to the new college, and Harvard men could savor a new display of their college's antiquity.[70]

The ending of sexual exclusiveness was more cautious than most reforms of the Eliot era. Others had the original ideas and did the spadework, but when they called on Eliot for support, they were not disappointed. Mrs. Agassiz, herself an imposing personage, stood rather in awe of Eliot. Both of them testified before the legislature's Committee on Education in 1894, seeking a charter for Radcliffe. Later each credited the other with winning over a potentially hostile committee. Few public occasions at Radcliffe lacked a brief address by Eliot. One of his persistent themes was that Radcliffe should grant the Ph.D., as it did beginning in 1902.[71]

It was in keeping for Eliot, an avowed enemy of uniformity, to seek development of differences between the sexes. He thought it incumbent on women's colleges not simply to duplicate the programs at men's colleges, but to find special fields suitable to women's interests in the home, the young, and art. He had faint praise for the woman who simply performed as a man in a largely male occupation. Yet he was not narrowly prescriptive in his statements of what this differentiated education for women should be. He told one Radcliffe audience, "I do not believe that we have yet discovered what is the wholesome and altogether desirable training for civilized women. We have it all to learn; and what prospect could be more delightful than that?" Education of men and women was identical in one important aim, Eliot believed —"emancipation from the intellectual inertia of the human race." [72]

Eliot's repeated references to the need for differentiated women's education helped launch a running dispute with President M. Carey Thomas of Bryn Mawr, who concluded that his view on women's education was the "dark spot of mediaevalism" in his "otherwise luminous intelligence." Refusing the label of pessimist, Eliot responded that it was President Thomas's views which included the "gloomy prophecy," since she imagined a large role for leisure in the later lives of educated women. "Nothing," Eliot instructed, "but lives of strenuous activity and earnest service justify the higher education either for men or for women." [73]

By 1908 Eliot readily admitted the removal of his fears of thirty-five years before, fears that women lacked the intellectual capacity for higher education, that it would damage their health, and that it would defeminize them. But he clung to his view that women's education should not be identical with men's. The Harvard compromise, coordinate education, set the pattern which opened to women the resources of older Eastern institutions. Eliot could firmly deny both that Harvard deprived women of their intellectual rights and that it had embarked on so perilous a course as "what is called co-education." [74]

To the end Eliot maintained that not everyone should have a college education, but only a natural aristocracy. Under his direction, however, wealth, secondary school background, ethnicity, and sex often lost their importance in determining who studied at Harvard. Well before his retirement the students there more closely resembled the inclusive population of a Western state university than the homogeneous New England college where Eliot had pursued his studies in the 1850s.

VII ❦

Utility and Its Limits

Poetry and philosophy and science do indeed conspire to promote the material welfare of mankind; but science no more than poetry finds its best warrant in its utility.

CHARLES W. ELIOT, *in his
inaugural* [1]

I

The idea that higher education should meet the practical needs of society had vigorous representatives in America at least as early as the 1750s, when Provost William Smith sought to establish a mechanic arts course at the College of Philadelphia. After the Revolution, Benjamin Rush proposed a federal university that would eschew the European infatuation with antiquity and would instead direct American youth to "those branches of knowledge which increase the conveniences of life, lessen human misery, improve our country, promote population, exalt the human understanding, and establish domestic, social and political happiness." But such utilitarian demands clashed with other ideals for higher education. It should preserve a cultural heritage unimpeded by concerns of the workaday world, some claimed. Others argued that, since truth was good in itself, to discover and impart it provided full justification for colleges and universities. [2]

The Yale Report of 1828 had been designed to answer complaints that the college did nothing for the merchant or manufacturer. In spite of Yale's sturdy defense of the liberal arts, colleges dropped in public esteem while increasing in number. In Jacksonian America they lost ground even as necessary training for ministers, doctors, and lawyers, for, after all, one could save souls and bodies without using Latin or Greek. By the 1850s persistent spokesmen were assailing the colleges for their failure to help farmers. The attention to agricultural chemistry at Sheffield had been a gentlemanly gesture toward meeting such complaints. Elsewhere states began to establish colleges that gave agricultural training, even before passage of the Morrill Act.[3] For decades West Point and Rensselaer had been the only American sources of formal training for engineers; then, between 1859 and 1871, at least five new educational institutions opened with a declared primary concern for industrial utility. Significantly, they usually did not call themselves colleges or universities.[4]

Where more than in America were people's minds so fixed on physical development? Frontiers beckoned to many besides farmers. New resources were waiting to be discovered, new industries to be founded. The frenetic pace of the 1850s was taken up again after 1865, with the nation's energies seemingly increased by the war experience. The iconography of victory displayed westward-moving wagons, sheaves of grain, and smoking factory chimneys. In 1870 President Barnard of Columbia, adopting an earlier tactic of President Wayland, presented statistics that seemed to indicate a declining proportion of the nation's young men in college. Worse for the colleges than being pressed to be useful was the possibility of being ignored and starved to death for want of students. Although some college leaders continued to take pride in their institutions' isolation from society, seeing them as havens from materialism and philistinism, others tried to share in national development, whatever the dangers of contamination. The public saw such change of direction in the new Cornell University, with its down-to-earth founder and its politically astute president.[5]

Understandably, many imagined Eliot to share the values of Cornell University, and there was suspicion among the Harvard faculty of his association with a technological institute. Eliot knew of this anxiety and offered reassurance in his inaugural. "A university is not closely concerned with the applications of knowledge, until its general education branches into professional. Poetry and philosophy and science do indeed conspire to promote the material welfare of mankind; but science no more than poetry finds its best warrant in its utility. Truth and right are above utility in all realms of thought and action." This statement, which subordinated but did not disclaim utilitarian goals for the university, remained Eliot's credo. His later contradictory statements on the subject, when brought back to this point of departure, usually gain coherence and consistency. It was his continuing belief that truth and use were not antagonistic which attracted him to Matthew Arnold's assertion that two passions governed educated men, the passion for pure knowledge and the passion for doing good.[6]

Eliot's statements to the public were sometimes distinctly practicalist. In fighting the imposition of tariffs on research instruments he stressed the applications of results of scientific research. Devotees of liberal culture may well have bridled at his statement of 1896: "Universities are no longer merely students of the past, meditative observers of the present, or critics at safe distance of the actual struggles and strifes of the working world." When he cited inventions or commercial developments based on apparently useless discoveries by investigators profoundly indifferent to such application, as he did on his Western tours, Eliot revealed his belief that much of the public would not accept a purely intellectual or cultural rationale for universities. Not surprisingly, a high school principal seeking to praise Eliot could say that his aim was "to democratize the upper education, to deprive it of its old shibboleths, to strip off its academic robes and make it go to work to earn its living and serve its generation." [7]

Although he cited direct or indirect practical advantages from the work of universities, Eliot warned against too avidly seeking such benefits. In 1883, following a paean to the machine age by Governor Benjamin Butler, Eliot pointedly asserted from the same platform: "Above all material things, is man—the thoughtful, passionate and emotional being, the intellectual, and religious man." He derided the notion that a child was taught to read "that he may be able to read a way bill, a promissory note, or an invoice." In 1897 he urged a journalist to drop his plans for an article on the usefulness of universities. His approach, Eliot told him, ignored

> the principal service which every university renders,—namely, the service which its graduates render to the community. What you call the extra-pedagogical activities of American universities are of course important; but their pedagogical activities are infinitely more important to the industrial and political life of the community. With regard to the contributions to science which universities make, it is a grave error to suppose that only those which contribute *immediately* to industrial progress are important from that point of view. The plain fact is that nobody can tell which of the contributions of to-day are to be most important for industrial or social progress fifty or one hundred years hence.

A utilitarian Eliot may have been—he once so labeled himself, and he showed many marks of the Benthamite. But he rejected a simplistic practicalism that ignored humane and scientific values.[8]

No one denied the appropriateness in the professional schools of applied studies and direct preparation for social utility. But Eliot's critics charged that he let such aims into the liberal arts college, where attention should be concentrated on the personal development and the mental training of the student, and the broadening of his sympathies and interests. The concern in the college should not be how a student was to earn a living, or even, except in the most adventitious sense, how he might "serve society."

When Eliot argued for the elective system on the ground that it allowed a young man to follow his bent, did that not imply his bent toward a vocation? Recall the lyrical advice in his inaugural that a youth should welcome discovery of his special taste and capacity, since it put him on the road "to happy, enthusiastic work, and, God willing, to usefulness and success." Eliot believed, for instance, that if a student at eighteen decided to become a physician, he should ask for courses to prepare him for medical school and take part of his work in biology, physics, chemistry, and modern languages. If the youth had no precise idea of his life work, but took courses in English and government simply because he enjoyed them, he was unconsciously preparing himself for his vocation, perhaps journalism.[9] Underlying this, of course, was Eliot's unquestioned conviction that each man had a life work awaiting him. He would have been horrified at the thought of a student saying, "I am at Harvard because I enjoy it, and in the life I plan to lead—spending my inherited fortune in living abroad, collecting art and mistresses—it gives me some helpful qualities." [10] Yet in retrospect Harvard's free elective system was more often associated with dilettantism than with a narrowing pre-professional concern. This, though no pleasure to Eliot, indicated that the college had not been vocationalized to any marked degree.[11]

By campaigning for the bachelor's degree as a requirement for admission to professional schools, Eliot strengthened the liberal arts college. His proposal for a three-year A.B. countered a plan that would have allowed liberal arts credit for the first year of professional studies. His scheme helped preserve a nonprofessional ethos among baccalaureate candidates, even though it worked against leisured cultural development in favor of more rapid movement toward a vocation. In the later years of his administration, Eliot referred rather clumsily to "culture courses," meaning apparently courses far divorced from any conceivable utility. He favored them—but as an attractive appendage. Music was his ideal culture course, and he proudly recalled that during the 1870s, when an economy drive was on, he alone of the Corporation insisted on retaining it in the curriculum.[12]

But it was not true, as Eliot sometimes asserted, that no professional or technical subjects counted toward the Harvard A.B. By 1886, all the engineering courses offered in Lawrence were also electives for A.B. candidates. In fact, a student who passed the admission examinations of the college could take a full program in engineering and graduate A.B. The establishment of the Graduate School of Applied Science in 1906, however, revealed Eliot's hope that engineering would join those professions which required postgraduate training.[13] Similarly, although Eliot at times spoke of the A.B. course as direct preparation for a business career, the opening of the Graduate School of Business Administration in 1908 enhanced the nonprofessional status of the undergraduate program.

Eliot once predicted that the distinction between liberal and professional education would endure. But what precisely was liberal education? That which broadened the sympathies and opened the mind, he sometimes said.[14] Yet he must have bewildered the audience that heard him say, in one address, "Everything which the universities now teach is quick with life, and capable of direct application to modern uses," and, "Liberal education is an end in itself apart from all its utilities and applications."[15] Eliot could be vague and contradictory about liberal education because for him the main function of the college was mental training. He often referred to power, or power in action, as the leading achievement of collegiate education. He showed the relative importance of this goal in an address of 1891.

> In this comparative seclusion [of the college] the young man learns something of what has been done and thought in the world [so much for Matthew Arnold and his followers!], before he takes active part in its work. He puts himself in some one subject abreast of the accumulated wisdom of the past; he develops and increases his own powers, and gains command of those powers. He gets knowledge, to be sure, but, better than that, he gets power. . . . The powers of exposition and application are more important than the power of acquisition. . . . The student who cannot apply the principles of geometry to new problems may have gained knowledge through his study of that subject, but he has not gained available power.[16]

Eliot never doubted that the future would see college-trained men at work in the world, and that colleges should be designed with that future in mind. In this sense he was indeed an educational utilitarian.

On the other hand, he often sought to ward off public demands for practicality. "Our times," he observed in 1873, "are enterprising, laborious and stirring, but our energies are given to subduing the earth. Railroads, mines, telegraphs, ships, mills, banks—these are the things which engross us. Men of force escape with difficulty from being absorbed in these pursuits." The university must provide a haven where a few determined men could pursue "a life of study and research," in spite of public indifference to "profound scholarship of any kind." [17] It was still in the interests of research that Eliot posited a far different set of public attitudes in 1896. Urging thoroughness in medical education, he asserted that "public confidence is given to men who are believed to seek truth for truth's sake, holding themselves free from the influence of inherited dogmas, consecrated phrases, and preconceived opinions concerning the desirable results of current inquiries." Doubtless Eliot exaggerated public concern for objective truth. Nevertheless, the bureaucratic system of values emerging at the turn of the century owed much to the research ideal of suspended judgment, and academic leaders like Eliot communicated this standard to the society outside the university.[18]

The frequency with which Eliot asked the public not to demand immediate usefulness from universities raises questions about accusations against him of "pork-chopism" and the usual categorization of him as a utilitarian.[19] In the case of the professions, Eliot opposed two opposite attitudes—a supercilious "learnedness" which claimed through classical education a status unrelated to professional function, and a shallow pragmatism that stressed ability to perform while ignoring the abstract learning that underlay practice. His ideal profession, rather than being "learned" or "practical," was "scientific." Reforms during Eliot's administration moved the professional faculties away from practical preparation for a craft and toward theory and research. Part of the motive, of course, was the professionals' own growing awareness that scientific grounding set them importantly apart from other occupations.

The case method with which Dean C. C. Langdell revolutionized the law school after 1870 was undeniably a product of the positivistic temper. But some of Langdell's contemporaries looked on his reforms as a dangerous deviation from the practical and factual. Eliot's closest adviser, Gurney, warned him of Langdell's "too academic treatment of a great practical profession." Langdell's ideal of breeding professors of law rather than practitioners, Gurney claimed, over-corrected a past fault of law schools; also, Langdell seemed immodestly eager to hire his own students rather than established practitioners.[20] John Chipman Gray, an active member of a distinguished law firm as well as a professor in the law school, confided a similar unhappiness with the tendency of Langdell's reforms. A law school "where the majority of the professors shuns and despises the contact with actual facts," Gray said, "has got the seeds of ruin in it and will go and ought to go to the devil." In spite of such advice Eliot supported the idea of a separate profession of legal scholars and teachers. His annual report of 1874 warned against hasty inferences "that practitioners would make the best teachers of law," and by 1895 he could call the shift in the source of law professors a success, one working far-reaching changes in the legal profession.[21]

In the case of the medical school, Eliot opposed the approach of Henry J. Bigelow, who warned that pure science might distract medical students from the practical and useful. Although the president was more agreeable to the practitioner-teacher in medicine than in law, the proportion of medical professors who did not practice gradually increased. The appointment of the physiologist Henry P. Bowditch as dean of the school in 1883 marked it as "an institution for the teaching of medical science instead of one which an association of practitioners conducted." Endowments were slow in coming to the medical school. Perhaps the idea of the school as a proprietary enterprise persisted in spite of Eliot's early abolition of the fee system. He felt obliged to urge gifts for the medical school on those who favored the humanities and theology, noting that it was "impossible to separate physical from mental and moral well-being." On behalf of the dental school also, Eliot's re-

peated pleas for endowment stressed the humane, even the philosophical, aspects of the profession.[22]

The Bussey Institution (for the study of agriculture and horti-
culture) and the veterinary school both opened during Eliot's
administration. Ignoring the obviously superior possibilities of
various land-grant institutions in predominantly agricultural regions, Eliot repeatedly justified these programs in applied biology. By their sheer inadequacy they probably lessened any public
impression of Harvard as a "practical" institution. Both suffered
from lack of funds and students, and both were given to unedify-
ing squabbles. The veterinary school closed in 1901, and in 1908
the Bussey was absorbed into the new Graduate School of Applied Science.[23] Harvard's School of Mining and Practical Geology had few students during its decade of existence under a separate corporation. Its work was formally absorbed into Lawrence
in 1875, but for thirty years thereafter no one took the degree of
Mining Engineer.[24]

Eliot's resistance to the idea of practitioner-teachers and his
pressure for longer courses that allowed attention to supporting
disciplines helped free professional schools from the reputation of
offering principally "tricks of the trade." But there was no question that he wanted these schools to prove themselves practically
useful. The credo of his inaugural had specified that at the professional level the university should concern itself closely with application of knowledge. He wanted the medical school to produce doctors who cured their patients, and for the law school he
once raised "two practical tests": "1. The test of immediate avail-
ability. Can its fresh graduates at once make themselves useful to
a lawyer in active practice and can those among them who have
no resources earn a living immediately? 2. the test of ultimate
success in the front ranks of the American bar." In fact, Eliot
imagined far-ranging social effectiveness for the graduates of the
improved professional schools. He increasingly saw the professions as centers of improvement for the entire society, greater in
influence than political bodies.[25]

II

The problem of applied knowledge in a university arose most sharply for Eliot in relation to Lawrence Scientific School. He took office with definite reform ideas for this school, akin to those he had urged in the early 1860s. In his article of 1869, "The New Education," he admitted that the school had served certain advanced students well, but he criticized its low standards for admission and complained that in many cases its students narrowly pursued a single science. In the same article he described the disadvantages in offering technical and classical courses in the same institution:

> In the polytechnic school should be found a mental training inferior to none in breadth and vigor, a thirst for knowledge, a genuine enthusiasm in scientific research, and a true love of nature; but underneath all these things is a temper or leading motive unlike that of a college. The student in a polytechnic school has a practical end constantly in view. . . . The practical spirit and the literary or scholastic spirit are both good, but they are incompatible. If commingled, they are both spoiled.

This educational separatism, too radical for Eliot to sustain, sprang from his knowledge of the stepchild treatment given scientific schools and his loyalty to the conception of M.I.T.[26]

Eliot did not fret about consistency. He was scarcely settled in the Harvard presidency before he proposed that M.I.T. unite with Harvard's scientific school. It is hard to interpret this effort as anything other than institutional aggrandizement. The author of "The New Education" was perhaps the least appropriate educator in America to lead a merger between a promising polytechnical institution and a university. Eliot's own earlier arguments were used against him, along with widespread public support for M.I.T.'s independence, and (as was the case in Eliot's three later M.I.T.-Harvard merger attempts) the plan failed. Undaunted, he declared his intention to "build up a thoroughly good Department of Applied Science at Cambridge." [27]

The debate over applied scientific education at Harvard after the failure of the merger plan evoked one of the most revealing conflicts of Eliot's presidency. Two broad schemes can be distinguished. One was the old Lazzaroni plan to unite the various scientific branches and establish professorships for advanced scholars whose investigation and teaching would make Harvard a "true university." Advocating this plan, but failing to act in concert, apparently because of their strained personal relations, were Josiah P. Cooke, Eliot's former mentor, and Wolcott Gibbs, who had resented in print Eliot's recent aspersions on Lawrence. Harvard already had in its various scientific appendages, Cooke maintained, "a nucleus for the New University, of which any European University would be proud." Rather than exerting itself in the "preoccupied" area of technological education, Harvard should emulate Heidelberg and Bonn and become "the first true American University." Cooke asked Eliot to be true to the ideal of separation expressed in "The New Education," not to prevent contamination but to allow concentration of resources in building an institution of advanced learning.[28]

The other plan, whose chief spokesman was Henry L. Eustis, professor of engineering at Lawrence since its opening, called for Harvard to develop Lawrence as a college of engineering and applied science, with standards of admission and graduation somewhat higher than those of existing American technological schools. As the sole professor of engineering in the school, he had been doing the work of several men, Eustis claimed, and he urged that Harvard enlarge its engineering staff in order to institute a four-year course at least equal to those of M.I.T. and Rensselaer. On the plan supported by Cooke and Gibbs, Eustis heaped democratic and utilitarian scorn:

> Is not this a scheme for building a grand temple of science, placed on such an elevation that very few could ever scale its heights, and fewer still could decipher the inscriptions on its walls? . . . I presume the advocates of this scheme would say that such should be the first object of an university. If this be so, if this be the special function of an university, then we doubt if

the American people are yet ready to see our College transformed into an University. Harvard College is primarily an educational institution, and the advancement of science comes in
only as a necessary incident.[29]

Between these two plans for the scientific school—the "university" and the "polytechnical"—Eliot had the power to
choose, and the young president had no timidity about exercising
his authority. He sharply rejected the recommendation in the
university plan that Harvard abjure the teaching of applied science. The practical appeal of the polytechnical plan, he hoped,
would bring immediate financial support and elevate Lawrence's
prestige. He sketched figures in the margin of Eustis's draft, esti-
mating the cost of the new engineering professorships. In March
1871, he sent a letter to the children of Abbott Lawrence: the
school that bore their father's name was dying, and the reason
was "simply this—The Sheffield Scientific School at Yale and
the Institute of Technology at Boston have many more teachers,
a better equipment, and a vastly greater variety of instruction."
As little as $90,000 would allow saving measures to be taken.[30]

The response was a much smaller gift for the renovation of
Lawrence Hall. Nevertheless, with Eustis replacing Gibbs as dean
of Lawrence, Eliot found ways to increase the engineering offering, to systematize the teaching in the school, and to strengthen
its ties to the rest of Harvard. In June 1871, the school announced a four-year course leading to the degree of Civil Engineer. Courses for the S.B. degree, in such fields as chemistry and
natural history, were to be three years (by 1876 all S.B. courses
were four years). Undoubtedly the changes made Lawrence a
sounder institution, but its failure to attract many students suggested that its purposes were better fulfilled elsewhere. If Eliot
had hoped for a conspicuous demonstration of Harvard's practical usefulness, he was disappointed.[31]

These reforms at Lawrence involved an action by Eliot which
has lived in tradition to brand him as vindictive.[32] Citing economy and gains in the teaching of physics, Eliot transferred all
Gibbs's courses in chemistry to Cooke and his assistants in the

newly enlarged college chemistry laboratory, leaving Gibbs only the subjects of light and heat and their applications. As if it justified the change, Eliot pointed out that the title of the Rumford Professorship was "of the Application of Science to the Useful Arts" and that light and heat had been Count Rumford's chief scientific interests.

Besides economy, Eliot was motivated by a desire to integrate the work in pure and applied science and to bring Lawrence students closer to the life of the college. The change put Lawrence students side by side with college students, in chemistry under Cooke and in physics under Gibbs. The simultaneous admission of Lawrence students to college dormitories and the increasing freedom of cross-enrollment given college and scientific school students bespeak the same integrative purpose. By 1886 all faculty members of Lawrence were also members of the faculty of Harvard College.[33]

Was Eliot guilty of spite against the man who had bested him in academic competition? This was the version Gibbs and his friends presented. As soon as Eliot's election as president appeared likely, Gibbs had a premonition that his life would become uncomfortable. Noting at the time that he was accused of a "mean intention," Eliot denied it, but he had not been scrupulous about avoiding the appearance of evil.[34] It is insensitivity to possible effects on Gibbs's research, not personal vindictiveness, for which Eliot bears legitimate blame. Although Gibbs was given a small private chemistry laboratory, he was deprived of advanced chemistry students.[35] After his retirement in 1887, Gibbs was elected emeritus professor, a distinct honor in that period. In informing him of the action, Eliot referred to the 1871 shift of Gibbs's teaching responsibilities, expressing his later doubts about its effect on Gibbs and conveying an implicit apology.[36]

Institutionally more significant than any injury to Gibbs is the possibility that Eliot thwarted a promising plan for university development by emphasizing applied programs in Lawrence and putting systematic teaching ahead of scholarship. But it is by no means clear that this was the case. Although he did not adopt the approach urged by Cooke and Gibbs, Eliot also wanted Harvard to become a "true university." Rather than have a group of scientists set apart to serve the ideal of research and advanced teaching (he remembered the irascibility of Louis Agassiz and the cultishness of his entourage), Eliot preferred that advanced work grow out of the college by means of the elective system. This proved a successful strategy, and it suited Eliot's gradualist view of university development.

Eliot expected the scientific school to contribute to the elevation of Harvard into a great university. Lawrence, he boasted, had "means of giving advanced instruction in natural history, chemistry, and physics, which, in some departments, are unequalled in this country, and in all departments are unsurpassed." [37] One of the new advanced degrees announced in 1872 was the Doctorate of Science, designed to assure admission to a doctoral program for holders of the S.B. The requirements for the S.D. were made more stringent than for the Ph.D. Although the standards for the S.B. were lower than those for the A.B., the two doctoral degrees (both granted by the Academic Council) were thus made equivalent. However, only twelve S.D.'s were given before 1890.

Despite Eliot's hopes (and some maintained because of his interference), the 1870s and 1880s were a lean epoch for Lawrence. Gibbs branded the reorganization "a ridiculous fizzle." The engineering staff did not continue to grow. The number of students hovered near thirty. Though standards were raised, the one-year teachers' course and the frequent admissions of special students kept the school academically suspect. Eliot's suggestion that Lawrence give up its separate identity was resisted by its graduates, who in 1886 organized an alumni association in hopes of reviving the school. Under the reorganization of 1890 the Lawrence faculty merged into the Faculty of Arts and Sciences, but the school kept a separate administrative board and separate degree programs. The dean of Lawrence, Winfield Scott Chaplin, had managed to start enrollments climbing before he departed to the chancellorship of Washington University in 1891. [38]

Any disappointment over Chaplin's departure was counteracted by two happy developments of the same year. The administratively gifted Nathaniel S. Shaler became the new dean of Lawrence, and the mining tycoon Gordon McKay, his friend, confided that he would leave his fortune for work in applied sciences at Harvard with the provision that instruction be kept accessible to graduates of free public schools. In the same spirit, Lawrence had already dropped Latin as an entrance requirement in 1888, but in other ways admission standards were raised. The school began to escape what Shaler called "its ancient and unhappy reputation." As the prestige of the S.B. rose, the number of candidates increased.[39]

Eliot began to think boldly of new programs of patent social usefulness, such as highway, sanitary, and mechanical engineering, thus completely reversing his separation theory of 1869. The modern university gave students of applied science "advantages not otherwise to be obtained," and these students contributed to the university their "earnest spirit and . . . urgent motive." In 1897, in the midst of another abortive negotiation for union of Harvard and M.I.T., Eliot wrote to one of the Fellows that however the matter turned out, Harvard must have its school of applied science. "It seems to me that the next twenty-five years will demonstrate beyond question that a university cannot disregard, much less abandon, the so-called technical subjects of instruction. I believe that we are only beginning to get the industrial and social effects of the manufacture and distribution of power, and that within a generation a university without an engineering department will seem much more absurd than a university without a Greek department." That which had social effects, he implicitly argued, was the proper concern of the university.[40]

Eliot's efforts to promote applied science brought accusations of betrayal of the university ideal. Alexander Agassiz, director of the zoological museum and former member of the Corporation, insisted in 1902, with a conviction that his father would have shared, that technical instruction did not belong in a university.[41] But this view invoked a Platonic, or at least a European, "university." Harvard's acceptance of Abbott Lawrence's gift in 1847 had forecast what kind of university would grow from American soil. Its functions would be plural, and it would attend to matters of social utility.

In 1906, with money from the McKay bequest soon to become available and yet another drive for union with M.I.T. foiled, Lawrence gave way to the Graduate School of Applied Science. Harvard College thenceforth awarded the S.B., differentiated from the A.B. only by the lack of training in a classical language.[42] Harvard could now train engineers more thoroughly than Eustis had dared hope, and yet it supported the high scholarship that Gibbs had pleaded for. Eliot's policy had been to unite and conquer, but it had taken time.

With evident satisfaction Eliot assured a faculty member that part of the McKay funds would be used for applied chemistry. "[My] memory goes back . . . to a period when the Chemical Department really had very little interest indeed in Applied Chemistry. I recall distinctly some strong statements on this subject made by Professor [Charles Loring] Jackson which would not now be made." Jackson may have changed his ideas, but so had Eliot, for he had learned in the late eighties—from Jackson as much as anyone—of his faculty's allegiance to the research ideal. Although favorable references to research appeared in his earlier addresses, Eliot's strongest statements—those of a convinced man—came after 1890. He pointed out the error of those who thought of "students of science as seeking practical or utilitarian ends." It was "certainly . . . not discreditable to men of science that they are apt to value discoveries which have no popular quality or commercial utility more highly than those which immediately attract the favor of the multitude by their industrial effects, or by their striking novelty combined with intelligibility." Shortly after the organization of the graduate school, Eliot could say without apology that most of its students had only a secondary interest in the applications of knowledge. The credo of his inaugural, with its distinction between nonutilitarian general education and utilitarian professional education, had lacked this element—recognition of advanced, non-applied studies.[43]

Eliot's full enlightenment on this matter had come rather slowly despite the spirit of the Harvard laboratories, which strongly resisted any commercial connections. Gibbs refused to serve as consultant to industrial firms, and Cooke regarded faculty status in an institution of higher learning as a position of trust "to be administered for the diffusion and advancement of knowledge." No one holding such a trust should perform commercial work for gain, he contended, since in America "it is very hard to maintain the higher life even in our institutions of learning and the commercial spirit is fatal to it." [44]

Against this ideal of truth for its own sake, Eliot had to weigh pleas for practicality from outside the university. Calvin M. Woodward, founder of the St. Louis Manual Training High School and president of the governing board of the University of Missouri, was suspicious of a candidate from Harvard for a chair of electrical engineering at Missouri. "We all have great faith in Harvard's teaching of *theoretical* electricity, but we want evidence of familiarity with the *apparatus* and *machinery* of electricity which is equally essential to the engineer. Cornell is strong on the latter side." The same year, 1896, Assistant Secretary of the Treasury Charles S. Hamlin, like Woodward a Harvard alumnus, felt humiliated when he was told by Washington scientists that no Harvard zoologist was qualified to investigate the Bering Sea fur seal herds, then a subject of international dispute. The Harvard zoologists were criticized as working "along very narrow lines," tending toward "German thought." Hamlin had been forced to invite first a Yale and then a Stanford man.[45]

Although he defended the university-based scientist's right to be indifferent to "popular quality or commercial utility," Eliot did not share Cooke's belief that such indifference was a duty. The official stand of the Corporation permitted faculty services to commercial firms. In 1881 Eliot accompanied requests to the American Bell Telephone Company for contributions toward the new physics laboratory with assurances that professors could use university laboratories in work for private companies. He did not question Professor Shaler's right to assume management of the aging Gordon McKay's mining companies. He knew that the profits were destined for the university.[46]

III

Mutual aid between university and industry, as in the cases of Bell Telephone and the McKay mines, was not the principal avenue by which Harvard received gifts. Nor was payment for services to be rendered the only theme in Eliot's frequent calls for support. The largest endowments of science in the mid-nineteenth century went, after all, to astronomy and astrophysics, presumably fields with minimal economic consequences. Donors as well as scientists could value the human curiosity that seeks knowledge apart from practical concerns; then too, the less practical the branch of the university aided, the more prestige the gift acquired as "conspicuous waste." There is, moreover, no need to discredit fellow-feeling as a motive. Harvard's benefactors often showed simply a humanitarian wish to help youth and a belief that it was good for young men to attend Harvard. In such a spirit Price Greenleaf, not an alumnus, left the college over half a million dollars in 1887 to aid impecunious undergraduates.[47]

Most gifts to Harvard came without direct solicitation, although Eliot's broad pleas for support and his reputation for financial astuteness may have evoked them. If a newspaper interviewer of 1891 can be believed, Eliot recalled the first aim of his regime had been to give "the institution the benefit of a business administration, attempting to extend business principles like a system of telegraph wires throughout the various departments" and he claimed that the resulting orderliness had brought Harvard "close to the hearts of our business men." [48] Eliot accepted in good faith the endowment in 1898 of the William Belden Noble Lectures, whose object was "to extend the influence of Jesus as 'the Way, the Truth, and the Life.'" He preferred, however, contributions to more secular and newer fields, less likely to have benefited in earlier generations. In 1902 he judged it an improvement that Harvard benefactors had recently turned from divinity, the classics, and belles-lettres to medicine, architecture, and the social sciences.[49]

The proportions of Harvard income from both tuition payments and cooperative alumni giving rose during Eliot's administration. Aid to the professional schools came, predictably, from members of the respective professions. There was thus little pressure on Eliot to flaunt the needs of the university before wealthy outsiders. Nevertheless, early in the 1900s, when great gifts to build a new medical school came from John D. Rockefeller, J. Pierpont Morgan, and Mrs. Collis P. Huntington, they accorded with Eliot's sense of the appropriate relationship between capitalism and higher education. Charles J. Bonaparte, president of the alumni association, made light of charges that the university was accepting "tainted money," and though Eliot had taken such objections seriously enough to inquire into the details of Rockefeller's early business practices, his doubts had been rather easily dispelled.[50] The fund-raising for the medical school enraged John Jay Chapman, who wrote to a friend, "Pierpont Morgan is the actual apex as well as the type, of the commercial perversions of the era. . . . Now then, at the dedication of the New Medical School, Eliot goes about in a cab with Pierpont, hangs laurel wreaths on his nose, and gives him his papal kiss. Now . . . what has Eliot got to say to the young man entering business or politics who is about to be corrupted by Morgan and his class?"[50]

Eliot would have responded to Chapman with his entire social philosophy, which embraced a mild form of the Gospel of Wealth. Darwinian imagery was rare in his writings on the problems of wealth, and he disavowed the notion of extinction for the unfit. But he held firmly to the Franklinian ethic that material prosperity was "a fruit of character; for it is energetic, honest, and sensible men that make prosperous business." He could echo Andrew Carnegie in hopeful prognostications that private wealth in America would be converted to public ends.[51]

Shortly before Eliot entered the presidency, the Overseers, complaining that teaching at Harvard was divorced from the experience of practical businessmen, urged lecture series to fill the need. The concern was not merely for informing students of business techniques, but also for showing the "mutual interests" of capital and labor and "the true principles which govern national obligations and national integrity." [52] The well-being of the Boston moneyed classes was involved, as well as practicalist criticism of the academic status quo. In such circumstances, Eliot joined the attack on Francis Bowen's textbook because of its mild financial heresy and obtained the appointment of the orthodox Dunbar as professor of political economy. Eliot continued to preach resumption of specie payment and the sanctity of the national debt, views that he and most Harvard alumni regarded as resting on moral law as well as on economic prudence. [53]

When Eliot visited Missouri in 1891, he professed his inability to understand the agitation against the railroads, the very "means of developing the west," or the support for free silver coinage, when "the interest of our country is to be found in a stable and unfluctuating currency." He urged Western bankers and businessmen to educate the public which, he asserted, was swamping the ballot box with uninformed opinions. For his pains, he was abused in editorials as an impractical intellectual blinded by regional and class bias. [54]

As the silver controversy mounted during the nineties, however, Eliot showed that he had moved far toward the professorial ideal of academic freedom. After Edward A. Ross was forced out at Stanford, in part because of his expressed support for free silver, Eliot could still say that Ross's widely offending pamphlet of 1896, *Honest Dollars*, was "a very clear and vigorous presentation of the silver side of the controversy." In private correspondence, he was sharp with President David Starr Jordan of Stanford, calling that University's situation "in the highest degree exceptional" since Mrs. Stanford's reserved powers placed it "completely in the hands of one aged woman." Against the wishes of Jordan, Eliot agreed to a series of lectures by Ross at Harvard the year after he left Stanford. Eliot's record here is mixed, however. He noted that the lectures were on "a safe subject," and when Ross's associates in the American Economic Association sought to investigate Ross's ouster from Stanford, Eliot judged the undertaking ill-advised.[55]

Eliot's defense was more vigorous when members of his own economics department were charged with slanted teaching. When the father of a student attacked Harvard's instruction on the tariff issue, Eliot responded with a statement that linked the freedom of teachers to the freedom of students. "We leave [our teachers] free, as we leave our students free to form their own opinions. You would not have us do otherwise, I am sure. As to what Harvard can 'afford' to be or do, I believe she can afford to be open-eyed impartial and free, and that she could not afford to be anything else." When the majority of an Overseers' committee in 1889 accused the economists of one-sided teaching on behalf of free trade and hinted that since protectionists were college benefactors, protectionism deserved a hearing, Eliot again resisted. He was aided by the trenchant minority report of Henry Ware Putnam, which argued for "free and disinterested pursuit of truth in a purely scientific spirit" and rejected the idea that the college accept doctrinal conditions set by donors. In an address, "Why the College Professors are Tariff-reformers," Eliot declared, "This allegation—that the influence of the colleges is in general adverse to the existing tariff—is true in the main, and the fact is rather an ominous one for the tariff." Professors, he claimed, did not suffer from the common delusion that wages could be kept up by taxing things which a few produced and the many consumed.[56]

The economic interests of Boston, a seaport and railway center in a region of matured industries, were generally served by lower tariffs; thus Eliot and Harvard economists were not challenging their immediate constituency by supporting tariff reduction. In any case, Eliot's most immediate connection with "businessmen" was with members of the Corporation, who represented the old mercantile and manufacturing fortunes of Boston, then rapidly shifting into investment banking. They were secure enough in wealth and family tradition to take a disinterested stand on most university matters. They disapproved of what they regarded as current business tendencies toward selfishness, duplicity, and vulgarity. For example, although Eliot was accused of "throwing the college into the office of Lee Higginson," presumably by welcoming members of this investment banking firm as Fellows, it was Henry Lee Higginson himself who took the strongest stand on the Corporation against instituting at Harvard programs in railroad management or in investment banking.[57]

There are other grounds for resisting the categorization of businessmen as practicalists in university affairs. When interest in college training for those planning business careers began to rise in the 1890s, it often reflected a search for gentility. Even publications by businessmen that assailed college training as breeding impracticality and ineffectiveness, as well as wasting time, included an occasional defensive admission of benefits for college graduates in "social standing." Increasingly, social polish and gregariousness seemed valuable traits in the business world. Discussing the education of his sons, the industrialist Edward Atkinson declared that Harvard was proving itself better suited than M.I.T. "to qualify men for the highest positions in manufactures and commerce." "I think," he observed in a passage indicative of the rise of the marketing personality, "the exclusive devotion of students at the Institute to the very hard work which is required of them and the very narrow lives which they are compelled to lead for lack of the Clubs, Societies, etc., such as may be enjoyed in the University, tends to develop a narrow type." Such arguments could scarcely have pleased Eliot, who preferred to ignore the easiness of courses at Harvard and the emphasis on social life. For him its ideal product was a hard-working man with a specific vocational goal.[58]

For Eliot the best argument on behalf of college education as preparatory to business lay in mental discipline. "It stands to reason," he argued, "that thorough mental training must give a man an advantage in any business which requires strong mental work." When Joseph Wharton, Andrew Carnegie, and others declared that most successful businessmen were not college-educated, Eliot sought contrary evidence, dwelling on examples from his own college class. In 1902 his annual letter to the Associated Harvard Clubs urged alumni to correct the erroneous impression that a college education did not aid practical businessmen, and he praised a book by a fellow university president written to achieve the same end. As if in reward for Eliot's efforts, the portion of the Harvard graduating class that planned to enter business rose from one-fifth in 1897 to one-half in 1904.[59]

Since Eliot argued that mental training was an adequate educational basis for achievement in business, courses designed for practical application by future businessmen found little place at Harvard. Eliot's principle of counting only liberal studies for the A.B., though not rigidly adhered to, impeded any response to those businessmen who favored direct vocational training. Jerome Greene had to stretch the truth in order to tell an inquirer of 1901 that the economics department offered "a number of courses relating to practical business affairs . . . courses in the financial management, accounting, and organization of railroads and industrial corporations; in the history of the tariff; in banking and in the history of financial legislation." Most of the faculty resisted pressures for courses preparatory to business. A professor of economics, Thomas N. Carver, far from mollifying business critics, declared that it was "not the function of a university to teach *business*." [60]

Another rationale besides social polish, mental training, or practical training was available to justify higher education for aspiring businessmen. If business could be viewed as a profession, then training for it fit the pattern of postgraduate specialization that Eliot had done so much to establish. Eliot himself, as early as 1884, had classed "industrial leadership" among the "intellectual professions" whose members should be liberally educated. Yet, rather inconsistently, he imagined its preparation as limited to the undergraduate level.[61]

Beginning in 1895, the idea of postgraduate professional training for railroad managers was promoted by George B. Leighton, a Harvard A.B. of 1888 and president of the Los Angeles Terminal Railway. He wanted Harvard to fit men for "new and important work in this busy and highly organized life." Stressing the analogy with other professional schools, he dismissed resistance to his program as "probably just the doubts that were met when the first medical and law schools were established." Leighton pressed his case with letters and interviews, and he won the support of William H. Baldwin, Jr., vice president of the Southern Railway, and Robert Bacon, Harvard Overseer and partner of J. P. Morgan. Although Fellow Henry L. Higginson argued strongly against Leighton's plan as contradicting Harvard's institutional purpose, the objections officially raised by the Corporation concerned expense. Nothing significant came of Leighton's proposal. In fact, the economics department's half-course on railway transportation was generalized into a course on monopolistic industries.[62]

The idea of business training as appropriate for a professional school stayed with Eliot. He linked the idea to development of foreign trade, a frequent prescription for the depression of the nineties. Recent diplomatic crises also concerned him, and he was attracted by Professor Archibald C. Coolidge's proposal for a school like the École des Sciences Politiques to train men for diplomatic and consular posts. By the time a firm plan emerged, the diplomatic aspect had dropped out, largely at the urging of Professor A. Lawrence Lowell and Francis Cabot Lowell of the Corporation. Eliot, believing that businessmen's interest promised funds for the alternate plan, rationalized that the school would still furnish "an excellent training for government service and public life in general." Later generations have to remind themselves that "administration" was once a word with positive connotations. The name "Graduate School of Business Administration" made the school more acceptable.[63]

The school, which opened in 1908, found itself caught between the disdain of the academy and the skepticism of the business world. Eliot's argument that business leadership had become a highly intellectual occupation with special ethical standards failed to convince anti-utilitarians. Doubtless there were expressions among the Harvard faculty of John Jay Chapman's view: "Business is not a profession; and no amount of rhetoric and no expenditure in circulars can make it into a profession." The major contributor of funds to launch the school was not a businessman, but a foundation, the General Education Board. To win business support Eliot came close to defining the university as baldly utilitarian. In a letter to one doubting businessman he wrote, "We quite agree with you that a theoretical education without numerous practical applications is of no use in any field of human activity. We therefore, throughout this University, make constant and numerous applications of all our teaching." Eliot would probably not have made so sweeping a claim in a careful public statement. But it revealed him in a position that undercut his praise for scientific indifference to practical application. Nor was there any need for so blatantly practical a rationale. The business school fit the pattern of specialization and professionalism, which made the university both a home for theory and a central participant in the new complexities of industrial America.[64]

IV

It is the nature of the mediator to be inconsistent, to share as fully as possible the perspective of both sides. Only thus can he carry back to each party in the mediation what is good or tolerable or inescapable in the position of the other. When a university president mediated between the cluster of ideas which can be called "practicalism" and that which can be called "truth for its own sake," inconsistency was virtually unavoidable. To some, inconsistency seemed too kind a word. University presidents were reputed to be mendacious.

The four decades between Eliot's "The New Education" and the founding of the Graduate School of Business Administration saw important changes in the rationale of the university and in American social thought. Yet both the strain of American practicalism and the desire for university autonomy persisted, pulling in opposite directions. Attempts at accommodation recurred throughout Eliot's administration. When it came to being useful in the economic projects of businessmen, Eliot sought to tread carefully. At worst, he offered a greater compromise of the university's cultural and scientific ideals than was asked. At best, he won a fuller appreciation by outsiders of the special allegiance the university owed to truth.

The reference in Eliot's inaugural to poetry, philosophy, and science as not principally warranted by their utility linked the ideals of Charles Eliot Norton and Asa Gray. It was Eliot's achievement to see that poetry and science, with their different views of the world, were alike in being human constructions whose worth did not rest on claims of usefulness. In his 1891 address in Chicago, Eliot stressed the same three aspects of the life of the mind. "A university," he said, "keeps alive philosophy, poetry and science, and maintains ideal standards." [65] It did this in a social environment where material production often appeared to be the dominant concern.

In designing a modus vivendi for the university in an equalitarian society, Eliot insisted that the university must remain somewhat apart. In facing the problems which American practicalism brought the university, Eliot also sought to keep the university to one side of the utilitarian mainstream. As he made clear in his letter to the utility-praising journalist in 1897, if Eliot had to defend the university as useful, he would choose the ground of its usefulness as an educator of men.[66]

VIII ஒ

Reform in the Lower Schools

> My main efforts for forty years have been given to increasing
> the amount of liberty and variety in education, in place of
> compulsion and uniformity.
>
> CHARLES W. ELIOT (1908) [1]

I

American public high schools were the "people's colleges,"
orators rhapsodized; they prepared students "for life and not for
college." It was true that high schools, small though their enrollment was in the nineteenth century, shared the common school
ethos of educational accessibility and direct social utility. But
they also offered the programs students needed for college entrance, thus serving as the middle rungs of an educational ladder.
Bearing this dual responsibility, high schools could not easily
equal the quality of preparatory courses in endowed academies or
private schools, but they were usually free and their development
in cities accommodated growing numbers of urban Americans
who sought education beyond the elementary. In the West especially, the college-preparatory function gained in importance.
During the 1880s the high school became the major form of secondary education in the United States.[2]

In Boston, the home of the first American high school, the situation was atypical. That city boasted, in addition to numerous
private schools that "fitted for college," Boston Public Latin
School, a tax-supported secondary institution founded to prepare

students for the traditional higher education. Boston English High School, in contrast, had been established in 1821 for those who would enter "mercantile or mechanical" pursuits. Accordingly, its curriculum omitted both Latin and Greek, without which no student could enter Harvard. Yet even this high school had taken on preparatory functions, and some of its graduates entered Lawrence Scientific School.[3]

The low admission standards of Lawrence had troubled Eliot long before he became president of Harvard. Within a few months of taking office, in hopes of elevating Lawrence's standards, he suggested to Boston's superintendent of schools that preparation for both classical and scientific higher education be offered in the Latin School and that the English High School be confined "to its proper function," that is, the training of students who had no plans for higher education.[4]

In 1873 Eliot chose a broader forum to express his lack of sympathy with the preparatory efforts of high schools. At a meeting of the National Education Association, he spoke in response to President McCosh's advocacy of federal aid to high schools. He challenged both McCosh's figures and his political theory, generalizing from the case of Harvard that not many in high schools were preparing for college and declaring that the federal aid, though "only a drop in the bucket," would be a demoralizing drop of poison for "self-reliant freemen." In any case, he preferred academies as college-preparatory institutions:

> We in Massachusetts . . . are endowing academies, not to take the place of high schools, but to supplement them. The first work of public schools, supported by local taxation, is not now to fit for college, though that was the intention when they were established [i.e. the Latin grammar schools]. Their work is to train their pupils in English, in mathematics, in classics a little, up to their seventeenth year. A small per cent go to college. From academies almost all go to college.
>
> There is a scepticism of the masses in Massachusetts, as to the justice of every body paying for the advanced education of some body's child. The mechanic, the blacksmith, the weaver, say: Why

should I pay for the professional education of the lawyer's son, the minister's son? Community does not provide *my* son his forge or loom. . . . I speak not of the reasonableness, but of the fact,—a fact which contributes to make public schools less adapted to fit young men for college. Because of this lack, denominations establish schools.[5]

After Michael Katz's studies of working class resistance to the high school movement in Massachusetts—notably the 1860 abolition of Beverly High School by working class voters—there can be no doubt that Eliot was pointing to a social reality. But the factuality on which he prided himself turned toward the past, toward those public antagonisms that had led Harvard to break loose from the state. In contrast, McCosh touched the growing hope for the future. He countered Eliot's comments with the assertion, "We want schools such that there shall be no poor boy in the country who shall not have within a few miles of him such a school as will enable him to go on to the highest place." [6]

In the landmark Kalamazoo case of 1874, the Supreme Court of Michigan firmly rejected the argument that since most students did not attend school beyond the elementary years, taxation for free high schools was illegal. By stating that the principle of tax-supported common schools could properly be pushed upward, the decision blocked a movement to hobble the high schools. The case had no immediate effect on Eliot's thought. He insisted that whereas elementary education was of "direct and universal benefit" and therefore legitimately a public charge, tuition-free high schools were different, requiring an unwarranted public support for a small class. Nor, according to Eliot, was that class likely to grow large.[7] He argued in 1875 that parents should be required to pay part of their children's educational expenses, perhaps as soon as the children reached age twelve, thus stimulating the family's labor and frugality. For very poor but bright boys he recommended scholarships from either public funds or private endowments. As for those who were both poor and dull, society lost nothing when they pursued only the compulsory minimum of schooling.[8]

Eliot spoke in 1876 on the need for radical bifurcation of secondary school programs. His audience, the Massachusetts Classical and High School Teachers Association, was scarcely appropriate, inasmuch as the two groups of teachers had found enough in common to have formed a single organization. Eliot sharply differentiated preparatory study from nonpreparatory, seeing only the latter as appropriate to the high school. Admitting the union of the two curriculums in Massachusetts high schools, he deprecated it. Those not bound for college needed only one foreign language and should study chemistry and physics. To place together in a French class students who had taken Latin and students who had not was "monstrous." "There is a different temper or spirit in a High School proper," he declared, "from that which characterizes a classical school, and the two spirits do not mix well. . . . These two courses both good appeal to different classes of the community and each should be supported by the undistracted interest of its own constituency." [9]

Eliot had the biases of a Boston Brahmin reinforced by personal struggles somewhat akin to those of the self-made man: his triumph over reactions to his facial birthmark and his recovery after being forced out of Harvard in 1863. It was little wonder that he preached his self-reliance straight. But a look at the man in his institutional role recalls that these comments came from a college president who was trying to build a "true university," a new thing in the United States. In these early years Eliot's strategy was one of elevating the college, as revealed in his inaugural: "When the gradual improvement of American schools has lifted them to a level with the German gymnasia, we may expect to see the American college bearing a nearer resemblance to the German faculties of philosophy than it now does." [10]

This "Gymnasium syndrome" dominated Eliot's early thought about secondary education. Even his dramatic reference to the "scepticism of the masses" toward free public education for the profession-bound minority was used as part of a special argument—as "a fact which contributes to make public schools less adapted to fit young men for college." It was because endowed schools promised better-prepared college freshmen that he sympathized with their increase. Appropriately, his most important restatement of "anti-high school" ideas came before an audience at Phillips Exeter Academy, where he urged those who hoped for "a few real universities" to "take the keenest interest in the welfare of good secondary schools whose future is secured by endowment." [11] It was not that Eliot expected American secondary schools precisely to duplicate the Gymnasium, but he did expect them to push their work upward, allowing "university" studies in American colleges. Public high schools, faced with problems of extracting tax support and saddled with a dual function, would be slow to raise standards. Thus he was less concerned with them than with endowed academies and a few public secondary schools with special college-oriented traditions. His central motive was to obtain students for a new university-minded Harvard. Such a desire was understandable, but it was too narrow a ground for one who chose to play educational statesman at the NEA and to pontificate about the safety of the republic.

Eliot's interest in students for Harvard also helps explain his shift of position in the mid-eighties. There simply were not enough endowed schools, nor enough students from them choosing Harvard, to provide the numbers that he believed an aspiring university needed. The increase in the number of high schools and their ambitions to serve college-bound students as well as those who have received the hideous label "terminal," ultimately suggested to Eliot the folly of advocating a separate category of institutions to prepare students for higher education. His annual reports revealed close attention to the sources of students, and in the early eighties entrants from high schools were dropping proportionally and absolutely.[12] Besides, he was growing increasingly skeptical about a single form of preparation for college. Even if high schools taught classics inadequately, some of their other subjects might prepare students as well.

But beyond such institutional motivation for his changed view lay Eliot's broadening concern for lower schools, and especially for the public schools. He had loyally attended meetings of the Massachusetts Classical and High School Teachers Association, where he listened as well as talked. He had grown to appreciate such leaders as John Tetlow, the able headmaster of Boston Girls' Latin School and Girls' High School. Eliot had brought secondary school teachers together with his faculty in an unprecedented meeting at Harvard in 1876, and throughout the 1870s he had strongly favored tenure for public school teachers. At least twice he submitted complete curriculums (notable for their stress on sciences) to near by public secondary schools undergoing reform.[13]

Eliot began to show the effect of such concerns when he wrote a highly ambivalent article, "The Relation of Government to Education in the United States down to 1882." It showed a mind seeking the "facts," but still entangled in laissez-faire dogma. Working out a detailed historical account of educational efforts by the federal and Massachusetts governments, Eliot argued that the nation had traditionally favored municipal, corporate, and private educational institutions. State and federal governments, he insisted, had generally limited themselves to founding such institutions or giving them temporary grants not drawn from taxation. But he seemed impressed by how much governmental involvement there had been and by evidence of heightened pressures for government activity. The problems of poor Massachusetts towns, caught between a shrinking tax base and rising educational costs and burdened by "bad methods of instruction and wasteful methods of administration," aroused his concern, as did the fact that the educational laws of Massachusetts were often disobeyed with impunity. Tentatively and painfully, he recorded what a growing part of him wanted to see happen: "It would be quite practicable to contrive governmental machinery, national or state, which with the public treasury to draw from, would give the people of Massachusetts on the average much better free schools than they now have, and bring into proper relation the successive parts of the educational system, so as to create for the intelligent and industrious pupil an easy and uninterrupted ascent from the bottom to the top of the school and college organization." Such, he said, was the achievement of Europe. He stopped short of advocating it for America, however, for in America men cared most for protecting the "roots of liberty." A bit forlornly, he again sought a hopeful sign in the increase of endowed and private schools.[14]

Two years later, Eliot made his changed position unmistakably clear in his address, "Present Relations of Massachusetts High Schools to Massachusetts Colleges." [15] Abandoning the stance of historian, he cast himself as advocate. Gone were the baldly factual references to how few high school students go on to college. Gone was any expectation that endowed academies and private schools could suffice as college feeders. The ideas of an uninterrupted educational ladder and of equal educational opportunity across class lines now lent a strong evaluative tone to Eliot's reported observations:

> Since the High School supplies the only means by which parents who cannot meet the charges of private schools or academies can get their children prepared for college, it is much to be regreted that the number of students who make their way to College from High Schools is so small. . . . Broken or obstructed connection between the public secondary schools and the colleges is an evil which every friend of education must wish to remedy.

He had concrete suggestions. Weak high schools should combine, and colleges should widen their admission options. A dozen years later, in an effort to convert other college presidents, Eliot expressed the same notions even more emphatically, calling the academies and private schools "a feeble minority," announcing, "The public high school has come to stay," and warning that if colleges wanted more students they must "make connections" with public schools. Less than a year after his 1884 address, he joined John Tetlow of the Massachusetts Classical and High School Teachers Association in forming the New England Association of Colleges and Preparatory Schools, its principal concern to be admission reform.[16] In 1886 he claimed that Harvard's recent admission liberalization would encourage "a new kind of school—a kind into which the public high school may advantageously be developed." The program of such a school would both provide college preparation and train "boys who at eighteen are to go into business or technical pursuits." No longer would boys have to make the decision for or against college at fourteen years of age. The prediction was over-sanguine, but the admission change was not without influence. Boston English High School became for the first time an acceptable preparatory school for Harvard College.[17]

In the late eighties, with major institutional changes at Harvard safely established, Eliot's interest in the lower schools blossomed. An address to the Department of Superintendence of the NEA in 1888, "Can School Programmes be Shortened and Enriched?" indicated his eagerness for a national platform and sounded a new theme. Education was taking too long. A man trained in the professions could "hardly begin to support himself before he is twenty-seven years old." Partly because of this, Eliot alleged, college enrollments were declining relative to total population.[18] His objections against slow-paced programs centered increasingly on the grammar school (upper elementary) years. In addition to urging better teaching and longer school days, he recommended pushing into these years some of the work in foreign languages, algebra, geometry, and physics currently reserved for high schools. His address of 1890, "The Gap between Common Schools and Colleges," offered an ambitious list of proposals for increasing the number of high schools, introducing college preparatory courses where they were lacking, and standardizing programs through state inspection and cooperative college admission examinations. At first Eliot self-effacingly referred to himself as an outsider, but he soon lost such reserve. Undaunted by criticism from exasperated teachers and newspaper charges that he was neglecting his proper sphere for a campaign against the public schools, he generalized boldly about education, asserting the commonness of problems from kindergarten to graduate seminar.[19]

The high schools of 1890 needed the reforming attention that Eliot, among others, offered. It was often hard to distinguish the high school of that day from the college or the elementary school. Most high schools did not have separate buildings, and in some rural areas children advanced into high school textbooks without leaving a one-room school. In many New England towns, on the other hand, only after nine or ten elementary years was a student considered ready for high school. Six-year academies and secondary schools that called themselves colleges added to the confusion, and most colleges still included preparatory departments. It was little wonder that both high schools and colleges used admission examinations as a way to define themselves. To a man like Eliot, who had just supervised a major reorganization at his own university, all this was intolerable. "The system of American education—if we may call it system—is very confused," he told an audience in 1891. "It needs arrangement, order." [20]

When representatives of colleges and secondary schools met under the auspices of the NEA early in July 1892, Eliot was ready to seize the opportunity. The informal conference grew out of a rather vague assessment of problems in college-school relations which had been made by President James H. Baker of the University of Colorado and a committee he headed. Finding the representatives on the brink of forming another association, Eliot suggested an alternative—that they should set up a committee representing colleges and schools which would arrange conferences on the basis of subjects and then draw on these conferences for a report. The plan, influenced by the New England Association's efforts to standardize college entrance examinations in English, was accepted by the conference, and the National Council of Education, the elite of the NEA, agreed to set up a "Committee on Secondary School Studies," generally known as the "Committee of Ten." By naming Eliot chairman, the Council guaranteed a hard-working, promptly reporting committee. The parental interest of Nicholas Murray Butler, a young professor of philosophy at Columbia and editor of the *Educational Review*, who later recalled himself as the originator of the committee, assured wide publicity for its recommendations. Within a week Eliot formally announced his hope that "desirable uniformity" in secondary school subjects could now be established "through recommendations as to selection, definition, time-allotment, and method, which proceed from judicious experts acting under the sanction of a national association like this, to be soon adopted provisionally by a few leading cities and institutions, and to be constantly improved by cooperative experimentation." [21] The presence of John Tetlow on the committee gave Eliot a gifted collaborator close at hand.

The committee's report was not revolutionary. Most of its recommendations were already the practice in large school systems. But it deserves a place in educational annals both for the content of its recommendations, notably the elevation of what Eliot called "the newer subjects" in the secondary school curriculum, and for its form, a committee drawing leaders from both universities and lower schools and claiming national applicability for its recommendations. It was a typically American response to problems that central governments were dealing with in Europe. The committee gained prestige from the leadership of a man who had recently been acclaimed before a New England audience as "by all odds the leader in American education to-day." Reciprocally, the committee gave Eliot the national platform he sought and established his reputation as an educational leader for lower schools as well as universities and for public as well as private education.[22]

II

Eliot should not be counted among the founding fathers of that unique American institution, the comprehensive high school. It is true that he urged inclusion in the high school of youths of diverse educational and occupational futures, but his proposals had distinct class limitations. He continued to see a place for endowed, tuition-charging boarding schools away from cities for children of the wealthy; in fact, he praised such parents for recognizing the progressiveness of these schools.[23] He did not imagine the high school as including those young people whose families needed their wages, and he expected the majority to find themselves thus excluded.

In keeping with the gradual upward thrust of the American ideal of universal education, Eliot spoke out for a broadly inclusive grammar school before he applied such notions to the high school. Among the sources of Eliot's eagerness to have some traditional secondary school subjects begun in the grammar schools were his wish to keep students from upper class families from leaving these public schools for endowed academies and his expectation that new interests aroused by these subjects might hold a student who otherwise would leave out of boredom. Thus Eliot could claim in 1893 that his proposed changes would make the grammar school "a good school for pupils of all destinations, and not, as now, only a school for pupils whose destination is of the humblest." But he did not imagine a "comprehensive" school, for in 1892 he mentioned offhandedly the probability that students might in time select among grammar schools differentiated by subjects offered. More important than any idea of mingling students of diverse social groups or subject interests were his concern for saving time and his belief that the subjects whose inclusion he sought allowed better mental training.[24]

A theme sounded by Eliot in 1873 found conspicuous expression in the *Report* of the Committee of Ten: the chief aim of American secondary schools was not the training of college-preparatory students. This declaration seemed to forecast a comprehensive school that would prepare students for a wide variety of futures and that would include an ever-larger portion of the nation's youth. But what the committee gave to democratic education with one hand it took away with the other. The main function of the nation's secondary schools, said the *Report*, "is to prepare for the duties of life that small proportion of all the children in the country . . . who show themselves able to profit by an education prolonged to the eighteenth year, and whose parents are able to support them while they remain so long at school." [25] The words "prolonged" and "so long" suggested unusualness and difficulty. The high school seen this way was an elitist institution, its selectivity based on both intellectual ability and economic class. The *Report*'s stress on more accessible college education was not paralleled by plans for more accessible secondary education. Its inherent class dynamics would facilitate the mobility of lower middle class youth into the professions, but leave most lower class youth at the occupational level of their parents.[26]

Eliot did not propose a single high school for students of all social classes, abilities, and educational ambitions. After Cambridge, Somerville, and Worcester decided to imitate the Boston pattern of separate Latin and English high schools, he cited the change without negative comment. He welcomed the appearance of mechanic arts high schools in Boston and Cambridge and of trade-oriented evening schools. On the other hand, he passionately opposed dividing college-bound from "terminal" students if in a given school they were taking the same subject. Here he held to a position formulated by the Committee of Ten.[27]

The committee sent a list of questions to the subject conferences in order to gauge opinion on curricular issues. Particularly significant was Question 7: "Should the subject be treated differently for pupils who are going to college, for those who are going to a scientific school, and for those who, presumably, are going to neither?" [28] The question was genuinely open, but all the conferences favored keeping preparatory and nonpreparatory students in the same classes. The *Report* put the recommendation emphatically: "Ninety-eight teachers . . . unanimously declare that every subject which is taught at all in a secondary school should be taught in the same way and to the same extent to every pupil so long as he pursues it, no matter what the probable destination of the pupil may be, or at what point his education is to cease." The response to Question 7, interpreted this way, was dubious pedagogy. A good teacher might very well not want to teach first year French "in the same way" to students who were going to pursue it a second year and those who were not (such matters as the thoroughness of treating the subjunctive and the amount and choice of literature come to mind). As to pursuing the subject "to the same extent," the *Report* itself in its model programs allowed certain "trifling exceptions." But the new "principle" was convenient for a high school since it promised simplification and economy, as Eliot noted. Both critics and supporters, however, often overlooked the fact that the *Report* limited the principle's application to "pupils of like intelligence and maturity." [29]

As Eliot was later at pains to point out, the *Report* did not say that all students should take the same subjects or take them for the same length of time. But as he advanced the argument, he revealed his own belief that the vast majority of high school classes should include both finishing and college-preparatory students, a concept that can conveniently be called "commonness." The college-bound might need some special subjects, Eliot agreed, but he implied that this was largely the result of illiberal college entrance examinations. Similarly, during the 1890s he only grudgingly admitted that nonpreparatory students might take subjects that were directly vocational. He wanted any "bifurcation" delayed as long as possible. It was not likely, he argued, for a student to know his educational future until he tried a wide variety of subjects, any one of which might be peculiarly fitted to stir his "powers." The high school, moreover, needed time to discover unrecognized potential in students from uneducated families. It followed that any early division of pre-professional students from those whose future occupations needed less formal training was objectionable. But this reasoning, it must be remembered, applied to an institution which Eliot saw as highly selective.[30]

Eliot's advocacy of commonness is better understood by recalling his belief that mental training was the central aim of education. Observing that non-college-bound students were often diverted to the "information" courses, he insisted that this was unfair: mental power should be the aim for this group too. In 1892 he cited as the central flaw of high schools—in fact, as the way in which "public education has failed"—the neglect of "training of the reasoning faculty," or, as he also expressed it, "solid mental training." His concern for mental training was at a peak in the early nineties, the era of the *Report*. Earlier he had allowed information as an object "not inconsistent" with training, though less important, and he spoke similarly in 1896.[31] But usually, even when he defended particular subjects in language that marked them as informational, he did not admit that he had thereby embraced this aim of learning.[32] His generalized comments returned to observation, reasoning, or some other mental function. In 1899 he put on the level of mental training a second goal, the implanting of "intellectual longing." "Secondary schools," he urged, "need no longer feel that now or never is the time for their pupils to acquire useful information. It will be enough if they teach them how to get trustworthy information, and to desire it." [33]

But the *Report* had barely mentioned any justification for school subjects besides mental training. Charles De Garmo, grounded in the Herbartian doctrine of apperception, observed that whereas the recommendations of the conferences agreed that "intellectual power is inseparably connected with ideas—with real knowledge," the main *Report* scarcely mentioned knowledge. The language of mental discipline dominated passages on educational values. In an article justifying the committee's course of study, one of its members used terms that pointed to information—"acquaintance," "suggestions of thought and experience," "more intelligent comprehension," but scarcely a hint of this rationale appears in the *Report* of the Ten. Eliot did more than disparage "scrappy information studies"; for him the mere term "informational" was meant to denigrate.[34]

Even if Eliot had been less sure of its primacy, there was an important tactical reason for his excessive attention to mental training at the time he wrote the *Report*. With his theme of "commonness," he hoped both to convince public school leaders that what was good preparation for college was good education in itself and to convince college faculties that any education that was good in itself was good preparation for college. Training fitted this dual argument far better than information. Both parties were to yield something, and they could do so most gracefully in the name of mental training. College faculties would give up the traditional list of admission subjects. Schoolmen would give up subjects that bore little relation to further intellectual pursuits.

Accordingly, although the *Report* widened the concept of what subjects were good mental training (further than most classics professors wished), it still applied the criterion somewhat narrowly (in comparison with what principals with an eye to local businessmen wished). After Principal Oscar Robinson of Albany High School, a committee member, protested Eliot's exclusion of vocational subjects in a draft report, the final version suggested optional substitution of commercial arithmetic or bookkeeping (a time-honored secondary school subject) for half of both the second and third years of mathematics. The *Report* also raised the possibility that a high school could "provide more amply for subjects thought to have practical importance in trade or the useful arts" by permitting options for the third and fourth years of science in the "English" curriculum. At most, these alternatives allowed only three-twentieths of the student's program for such vocational preparation.[35]

Perhaps the moderate revisionism that was accomplished— the promotion of modern languages, science, and history to the status of the classics and mathematics—was venture enough for so new an undertaking as national recommendations for secondary education. But this advance could have been made without projecting the high school as an elitist institution. When Eliot masterminded the *Report*, his belief in mental discipline as the essential purpose of education was, unfortunately, at its height. Unfortunately, too, he still bore traces of the views which had let him imply that weavers' sons would be weavers.

The *Report* of the Ten did not quiet charges of "college domination" and demands for high school "autonomy." In the 1880s such criticism had struck at college insistence on Greek and mathematics for entrance, but now it was addressed to the Ten's enlarged canon of secondary subjects, which omitted most "practical" subjects as inadequately disciplinary. After all, the high school was a tax-supported enterprise. "If the public gives to one girl her Latin," asked a principal, "why shall the public not give to another girl her type-writing?" [36] Eliot's proposal that bifurcation take place as late as possible was not seen in such quarters as a democratic opening of careers, but as a narrowing of the curriculum by the ideal of intellectual preparation for college. As evidence, critics could cite the growth of the percentage of students enrolled in Latin, from 34.7 per cent in 1890 to 50.6 per cent in 1900. Their argument envisioned high school officers assuring the unwary student that Latin would develop his mind, when in fact they were seeking to please college admission committees. The increase in Latin struck G. Stanley Hall, president of Clark University, as especially revealing of continuing unhealthy college influence. He wanted high schools to tell colleges, "You must no longer prescribe our work or define our field." [37]

III

Since Eliot's widest fame had come as a proponent of the free elective system for colleges, observers were alert for indications that he sought a similar electivism in the lower schools. If one granted Eliot mental training as the chief goal of education, they wondered, would he argue further that it did not matter in what subject such training was given? Without reaching this extreme position, Eliot tended increasingly to urge free subject election below the college level.

His hesitancy to declare all school subjects educationally equivalent was indicated in the years before the Ten's *Report* by his advocacy of what would later be called "distribution." In fact, his early rationale for the college elective system was based on the understanding that students would experience a wide range of subjects in the lower schools. As he put the matter in his inaugural, "through all the period of boyhood the school studies should be representative; all the main fields of knowledge should be entered upon." He usually avoided naming the "main fields," probably hoping that the canon was changing. He admitted in

1869, for instance, that there were good arguments on both sides regarding the essentiality of history. But by 1885, he had settled on "four great subdivisions of elementary knowledge"— language, history, mathematics, and natural science. At this point, arguing hard against McCosh, he emphasized the likelihood that college-bound youth would pursue these generally recognized indispensable fields before college and free election. Soon afterwards, he recommended that nonpreparatory high school students also study the four main fields.[38]

When the Committee of Ten recommended a basic core, it was made up of the same four "main lines." This required core was defended as letting the student test his capacity in various fields and guaranteeing breadth for students who left high school after two years. When a similar recommendation was made by the Committee on College-Entrance Requirements in 1899, however, with the more emphatic label of "constants," Eliot appears not to have embraced the idea. It became increasingly clear that he wanted the free elective system in the high schools. The necessary exposure to the four main lines he began to envision as taking place before the student was fourteen years old.[39]

At one stage of his thought, Eliot exempted both ends of formal schooling from the elective system—the "first three or four years" being needed for necessary elements and the upper years for "strictly professional information and practice." But his public remarks suggested an ever earlier point as the ideal time for electives to begin—age thirteen, age nine, and (by 1903) kindergarten. The other members of the Committee of Ten probably extracted from Eliot more support for requirement of essentials at the secondary level than he was ever again willing to give. When in 1898 the Harvard faculty tried to drop one of the main lines, history, from admission requirements and greatly to lessen the amount of another, mathematics, it was the Overseers, not Eliot, who protested. Eliot, increasingly willing to have the main lines themselves considered equivalent in college admission, described with apparent sympathy such a system at Stanford. This constant pushing back of the appropriate age for student choice of subject undercut Eliot's earlier argument that pre-college training guaranteed breadth. Hugo Münsterberg noted this effect when he compared the older and newer addresses after Eliot's *Educational Reform* was published in 1898. Now, Münsterberg protested, even his seven-year-old daughter had her "electives"! [40]

Student choice of studies in secondary school was not new. The practice had existed in the antebellum academies, and it was adopted in the larger urban high schools well before Eliot began his public school campaign. Often electivism was practiced at the secondary level without being so named. But Eliot dramatized the issue. Certain public school men made good use of his prestige in their advocacy of the elective principle. Among them was Samuel Thurber, who believed that in "the people's college" the people should say what they wanted to study. Chicago's Superintendent Augustus F. Nightingale, fighting the conservatives in the North Central Association who demanded mathematics and foreign language throughout the four years of high school and the first two years of college, solicited a letter from Eliot. Nightingale quoted Eliot as declaring, "English, the modern languages, history, and the sciences can be made in the secondary schools the vehicle of just as substantial training for the human mind as Latin, Greek, and mathematics." The most thorough-going application of the elective system in public schools was made in Boston under the leadership of Superintendent Edwin P. Seaver, an ally of Eliot's. So radical was Seaver's program, in fact, that Eliot at first suggested compromise, fearing the community was not ready for a wholly elective system. [41]

Free election of subjects was probably never more than a minority view among high school leaders of Eliot's day, but from 1900 to 1905 that minority was riding high and Eliot was its hero. In 1901 President Baker of the University of Colorado returned to the battle against "equivalence" that had inspired his minority statement in the Ten's *Report*. He branded free subject election "pursuit of inclination"—a corrupting romanticism. What Eliot's opponents usually wanted, as Baker did, was election of "courses" (curriculums, sometimes called "groups," worked out in detail and given such labels as "classical," "English," or "Latin-scientific"). Shortly before the creation of the Committee of Ten, Eliot had welcomed the presence of parallel courses in high schools as a tendency toward freedom and variety, but he was soon seeking to counteract any impression that the four courses worked out by the Ten meant advocacy of the course system. He attacked the practice as an "imperfect application of the elective principle." In 1902 he hailed progress on this front, listing first among recent improvements in education the extension of election by subject in secondary schools. The high school group system, he declared, gave the illusion of wide choice and was cheaper than a thorough-going elective system, but in fact its arrangements were arbitrary and it committed fourteen-year-olds to a particular set of studies.[42]

Eliot tended increasingly to make his arguments without distinguishing between schools and colleges. The elective system, he pronounced in 1897, added to the merit of "any academic school," by letting it serve "a greater variety of minds and characters." He spoke less and less of the secondary schools' guaranteeing student exposure to the main branches of learning. But although he grew vague about breadth, Eliot continued to call for depth in pursuit of secondary school subjects. The Harvard admission examinations rather awkwardly sought this goal, but Eliot suggested no device by which high schools themselves could assure concentration, other than refusing to offer brief subjects. The course system did guarantee depth, but he wanted it abandoned.[43]

IV

In his campaign for better schools Eliot made teaching method at least as important as curricular design. "Effective training of the reasoning powers cannot be secured simply by choosing this subject or that for study," he wrote. "The method of study and the aim in studying are the all-important things." As a means for colleges to help improve school methods, Eliot had turned optimistically to admission examinations, where he claimed the shift to sight-translation, for example, would liberate preparatory school teachers from routine, exalt practical mastery, impart interest, and improve teacher-pupil relations. He also encouraged his faculty to create textbooks and course guides, following the pattern of his own early efforts to advance laboratory instruction in chemistry. The chief value of the Committee of Ten's *Report*, he suggested, lay in the conclusions of the conferences, where college and secondary school teachers agreed on how best to pursue a subject in the schools.[44]

In his early pronouncements on public schools Eliot called for individualized instruction to replace the "inevitable uniformity of method and pace"—the "machine methods"—that were the bane of large classes. To support this goal, he proposed a program of assistant teachers, reduction of the number of pupils per teacher to twenty-five or fewer, and laboratory courses. But in time he sounded a note of bureaucratic "realism," remarking in 1905, "It is well to talk much and strongly . . . about individualizing instruction . . . but every superintendent and principal of the least experience knows that every secondary school must have a program or programs, and that most of the instruction must be addressed to classes and not to individual pupils." On these grounds, he increasingly prescribed grouping by proficiency and capacity.[45] In the 1890s a number of techniques were practiced to achieve such grouping, including, in the Cambridge grammar schools, a two-division system which let students finish in four, five, or six years. By 1897 Eliot was calling for secondary schools to practice "division of each class by subject into sections according to proficiency." The Ten's *Report* had specifically allowed for this division, and such grouping suggested the narrowness of the committee's recommendation of "commonness." In fact, as it became clear to Eliot that he had been underestimating the percentage of youth who would choose to enter high school, commonness seemed less sensible to him. By 1901 he could declare his willingness to allow a "sink" for incompetents in the high schools which would set them apart from all programs that led to post-secondary education.[46] Grouping by ability was perhaps more easily attainable than "individualized instruction," but it sacrificed the chance that an apparently unpromising individual might flourish in a classroom with students of varied abilities, backgrounds, and aspirations.

Part of what Eliot meant by "individualized instruction" was avoidance of a forced average pace. Occasionally he pleaded for the over-hurried dull student, but closer to his heart was the needlessly delayed bright child. When he spoke nostalgically of the one-room school, it was because it let an able student pass rapidly through the grades. Eliot is properly considered the father of the "Economy of Time" movement, and his address of 1888, "Can School Programmes Be Shortened and Enriched?" its opening pronouncement. But he never carried the idea of more rapid education to the lengths of educators who, after 1912, felt themselves the voice of scientific management in the schools.[47] It was not expense that brought the length of education to Eliot's attention, nor any belief that education could be narrowed to concrete predicted life activities. He was troubled by the social loss when young men entered their professions at twenty-six or later and by the boredom and false discipline students experienced when they were forced to undergo redundant instruction. As a college president with an eye to enrollment, he noted that parents hesitated to launch their sons into higher education if they were too close to their majority. He wanted elementary schooling shortened to eight years from the nine—sometimes ten—that it lasted in New England. Although he never attacked the four-year high school directly, at this level too he hoped for individual acceleration by able students.[48]

The Ten's *Report* included some provocative sentences linking "educational value" to time, notably: "If twice as much time is given in a school to Latin as is given to mathematics, the attainments of the pupils in Latin ought to be twice as great as they are in mathematics, provided that equally good work is done in the two subjects; and Latin will have twice the educational value of mathematics." This ill-considered sentence, justifiably criticized by Baker, came close to equating time spent with learning achieved. But the phrase "equally good work" brought the quality of learning into the supposed equation. In context the statement was not so unrelievedly time-minded, since the same paragraph denied time-equivalence in the name of depth. (Several briefly studied subjects were said not to attain the effect of a single subject pursued for the same length of time.) [49] Eliot often sidestepped the question of disciplinary equivalence by stressing bureaucratic convenience. A college, once it admitted a field to its list of admission subjects, should not fret about its exact educational contribution, but weight it according to the time devoted to it in the secondary school. In answer to President Hall's allegation that the *Report* declared all subjects "of equal educational value if taught equally well," Eliot stressed the "intensely practical bearing" of the committee's opinions on equivalence of studies. "They were not educational dogmas, but practical suggestions to produce smooth action in a complicated educational machine, which has to be mended and improved while incessantly running." [50]

A later NEA committee and the regional associations of colleges and secondary schools consummated the idea of time-equivalence with a plan for "units." The time-allotment unit ultimately liberated pre-college students from the necessity of having to prepare in a particular way for a particular college and promoted election by subject for all secondary students. The process exemplified the truth that bureaucratic inventions can be liberating for individuals. Eliot saw this more clearly than his critics did. He properly found no inconsistency in calling for individualized instruction while insisting that "some amount of standardizing, qualifying, calibrating, or schematizing of the subjects to be taught, to use . . . rather contemptuous words, is absolutely indispensable in every school." [51]

V

As president of Harvard, with its long history of controlling feeder schools, and as chief architect of the Ten's *Report*, with its unsympathetic treatment of "practical" subjects, Eliot was a handy symbol of secondary school exclusiveness. He had neither foreseen nor advocated the revolutionary expansion of high schools that set in just as he turned his attention to their affairs. The number of students in high school rose from 203,000 in 1890 to 519,000 in 1900, and to over a million by 1912. When he did recognize this growth, Eliot called vocational motivation a leading cause and associated the increase with his campaigns against informational courses. He argued that employers wanted the "trained" product of high schools that emphasized mental discipline. Scorning more specifically vocational aims, he insisted that the high school commercial course remained "hopelessly inferior." It existed only because its practical sound attracted school boards and parents. "For the purposes of mental training, or of mental power-getting, this course is never to be recommended; and it is rare that the slight knowledge of these arts acquired by pupils in the public schools proves to be of much use to them in winning a livelihood." [52]

Drawing and manual training won Eliot's approval—not as direct preparation for a craft, but as "individualized" instruction akin to laboratory work and as "sense-training," a necessary part of the training of observation. Although in his support for evening schools he admitted that manual training could also serve a vocational aim, he hoped such training would be far broader than mere apprenticeship, helping the young worker "to understand principles as well as practice; and to escape from the contracting influence of automatic repetition." As late as 1905, aroused by Hall's attack on the Ten's theme of commonness, Eliot called the American high school "emphatically a school in which training for power and general cultivation are the fundamental ideas, as distinguished from training in special means of obtaining a predestined sort of livelihood." He declared the differentiated secondary schools of England and Germany unsuited to a democratic society.[53]

But the same year saw the appointment in Massachusetts of the Douglas Commission, whose report in 1906 launched an evangelistic drive for vocational education. In this environment

Eliot faltered in his support of general training common to all secondary students. Carroll D. Wright, chairman of the Douglas Commission, was admired by Eliot, and Paul Hanus, Eliot's protégé, became head of the new Massachusetts Commission on Industrial Education, which promoted separate vocational schools. The National Society for the Promotion of Industrial Education (NSPIE) was formed in 1906, and in December 1907 President Roosevelt embraced the cause in his annual message to Congress.[54]

Since about 1905, Eliot had been stiffening his criticisms of lower schools, returning to old complaints and adding new ones: school days and terms were too short; extracurricular activities, especially athletics, received exaggerated attention; the schools neglected to instill the will to work. Perhaps he blamed lower schools for the undergraduate lassitude that others ascribed to his elective system. Apostle of liberty though he was, Eliot began to speak of things students "must" do. Like many others, he was struck by the conclusion of Susan Kingsbury, a researcher for the Douglas Commission, that students often withdrew from school by their own choice, against parental wishes and without hope of getting good jobs. A rise in the minimum school-leaving age seemed a reasonable corrective. The drift in Eliot's social philosophy that let him decide during the 1880s that taxpayers must support tuition-free high schools carried the implication that society could require students to stay in school till late adolescence. Both restrictions on liberty rested on his observation that industrial society's problems, especially density of population, rendered certain liberal values obsolete. He began to speak of the need for control and the limits of "the individualistic principle." He became a supporter of "no-license" (local exclusion of liquor sale) and called for state mounted police.[55] Yet in regard to one social realm, labor, Eliot generally opposed "control." His objections to unions increasingly stressed their monopolization of apprenticeship and, therefore, craft-entry.[56] All these tendencies in his thought came startlingly into public view when he addressed the first national meeting of the NSPIE in January 1908.[57]

Eliot began by reducing the slogan "industrial education" to the idea of trade schools modeled on those in Munich, which Hanus had publicized in America. These would be distinct from other public schools and would permit attendance to be either full-time or, for employed adolescents, part-time. In these "trade schools in a very strict sense," where even arithmetic examples would be drawn from the craft the student had chosen, courses would differ from existing manual training, which was "for culture not skill." Presented as a new way of encouraging students to stay in school, the plan would have accorded with Eliot's long-standing advocacy of student liberty. But, with surprisingly emphatic language, he linked the proposal to a rise in the legal age for leaving school. Children should remain "under the observation of the community up to the seventeenth or eighteenth year, and be absolutely required to attend a continuation school, for part time at least if attending no other."

Eliot's support for separate trade schools doubtless startled those who associated him with the theme of commonness or recalled his disdain for the high school commercial course and European differentiation of secondary schools. But Eliot had a long record of urging separation of groups of schoolchildren. One needed only to recall his eagerness to keep the high school and Latin school separate in 1869, his emphasis on neighborhood schools in 1875, his insistence on ability grouping within subjects, and his support for mechanic arts high schools and evening schools. In arguing against bifurcation in high schools in the nineties, he had assumed that only a small minority of students would continue their education beyond age fourteen. If all students were to be required to stay in school till seventeen or eighteen, then the floor set by ability and family income would be removed. This greater inclusiveness would make it harder to defend Eliot's vision of the high school dedicated to mental training with students in the same classes whatever their intentions about college.

An astute follower of Eliot's thought might have predicted his embracing of trade schools. But when he took up the question of selecting students for these schools, he spoke in language that seemed totally inappropriate for an advocate of the free elective system. "The teachers of the elementary school ought to sort the pupils and sort them by their evident or probable destinies," he said, denying that such sorting was undemocratic, since democracy meant not equality but (in Pasteur's phrase) letting "each individual put forth his utmost effort." When he cited the work of such schools in Germany and Switzerland, however, Eliot indicated limits to the teacher's powers. In those countries, he noted, the sorting was done "by the teachers and parents in combination, with the help of the children." The link between such Old World "streaming" and Eliot's advocacy of the elective system was the idea of specialization. Significantly, he reverted to one of the arguments of his inaugural, the falsity of the notion that a Yankee could turn his hand to anything. The teachers, he maintained, would tell the child "in what line he or she can have the most successful and the happiest life."

Eliot expressed alarm at the fate to which industrial society condemned students who left school by the end of the eighth grade. They could enter only occupations that were "trivial, unskilled, and uninforming, preparing them for nothing better as they grow older." But how could trade schools guarantee to an entire generation work that was itself educative? He gave no hint that those jobs which created "automatic" workers could be abolished.[58] It followed that though his trade schools might let some escape into skilled occupations, the troubling mass of factory workers would remain. But the individual's joy in self-improving work was not Eliot's only concern. He had often suggested that because of America's great liberty the schools must implant moral restraints. Now he argued that longer schooling, required by law, would elevate "the moral tone of our population," implying that "automatic" workers, however blighted, would at least behave themselves.

The address evoked negative editorial comments, based on Chicago newspaper accounts which inaccurately, though understandably, applied Eliot's call for compulsion not only to raising the school-leaving age but also to his proposal that teachers sort their pupils (where he had left the matter of compulsion ambiguous). Louis Post's pro-labor journal, *The Public*, cited a trend in Eliot's speeches indicative of "a warping of his democracy" and denounced this latest proposal as a call for an individual-crushing bureaucracy designed to cheapen labor and weaken unions. Unwilling to admit inconsistency, an outraged Eliot demanded retraction:

> My main efforts for forty years have been given to increasing the amount of liberty and variety in education, in place of compulsion and uniformity. None but a stranger to me, and to all my educational activities, could believe that I could make the monstrous proposition which you attribute to me. What I really believe is that the teachers in the public schools could help the parents and the children to voluntarily aim at callings in which they (the children) are fitted to succeed, and therefore to be useful and happy.[59]

Eliot soon took new occasions to speak on industrial education, and he now changed several aspects of his NSPIE message.[60] No longer insisting on separate institutions to train for trades, he moved away from the sharp distinction between "culture" and "skill" and back toward the position he had taken in 1902, when he had admitted that manual training could serve both general education and vocational preparation.[61] Although he still saw teachers as professional experts and therefore as guides in children's choice of trade courses, he now applied the term "election" to the process. Picturing an industrial training which stressed "the theoretic part of a trade," Eliot insisted that liberal education ("any process capable of developing a liberal mind") should be the goal of the public schools for all students, including those intending to enter trades or mechanical pursuits.

At the time of these addresses, Eliot grew more specific about the American class structure. He had long suggested a fluidity in society by emphasizing the school's duty to select gifted youths for extended training. Now he distinguished four classes—managerial, commercial, mechanical, and "rough workers" (in agriculture and extractive industries). This stratification he called "indispensable to society." He insisted that although the borders of classes blended and their limits were easily passed by individuals, each class had "distinct educational needs," a fact which "democrats decline to see." [62] One could readily imagine the democratic objection, for inevitably if the school was to meet such differing class needs, it must declare to which class a student belonged. The temptation to make it that of his parents would probably control most cases. Would class limits then be passed so easily by individuals? This problem Eliot ignored. Equally troublesome was his recommendation that schools prepare for diverse occupational levels and yet give all students a liberal education. This goal required a more elaborate prescription than he offered.

In fact few trade schools were founded.[63] Eliot's involvement in the movement on their behalf had exposed anew his willingness to separate groups of students and had threatened to compromise his campaign for free election by subject. But his attempt to forward industrial education had at least helped him move away from his elitist view of the high school. He now saw ways for more than a small proportion of youth to stay in school beyond the elementary years. His new position, tinged with antiunionism and the urge for tighter social control, and irritatingly vague in its assumption of class mobility and its call for universal liberal education, was nevertheless more inclusive than his position of the nineties. It envisioned new routes by which a school could encourage "happy and productive lives."

VI

Judgment of a university president's relationship to his nation's educational system cannot be adequately based on his public statements, his clarifications of institutional identity and sequence, or his effectiveness in changing other schools. A central question remains. Has he institutionalized within his own university constructive links to lower schools?

The most casual form of mutual service between the nation's higher and lower schools was perhaps the long winter vacation that let college students earn money by teaching, thus helping rural schools and lowering college fuel bills. It was a far cry from this practice, which Eliot helped abolish, to considering teaching in the lower schools as a profession for which universities should provide elaborate training. Meanwhile, an educational bureaucracy was growing up that included school superintendents and other claimants for advanced training, and the call for university research into social problems seemed fully applicable to problems of the schools. In addition to its admission recommendations, the Committee of Ten had sermonized the colleges on just such duties.[64]

Harvard made gestures of support toward the lower schools throughout the early years of Eliot's administration. The summer courses of Gray and Agassiz brought secondary school science teachers under the guidance of those renowned biologists. A one-year teachers' course in the scientific school had been established in 1871, for which the Corporation offered a scholarship to male normal school graduates. From 1881 to 1883 Eliot hired G. Stanley Hall to give pedagogical lectures to teachers in Boston. But until the nineties the summer programs remained an insignificant enterprise conducted by a few departments, only a handful of students enrolled in the special Lawrence course, and Hall's suggestions for moving his work to Cambridge and founding a pedagogical library came to nothing.[65]

A flurry of concern for teacher education in the early nineties suggested that Harvard might take more decisive measures. When certain high school principals suggested in 1889 that Harvard establish "normal" work for secondary school teachers, Eliot bluntly put them down, expressing doubt that there was any work in methods, educational philosophy, or educational history that Harvard could beneficially offer. He declared offhandedly that his university would welcome the elevation of normal schools so that they could train secondary school teachers.

Eliot's expression of faith in the normal schools was highly uncharacteristic, and when the leaders of the principals' movement pressed the state legislature to establish a one-year "Normal College" in Boston for students holding the bachelor's degree, he quickly changed his mind. He undermined the bill before the legislature by implying that Harvard would after all establish such pedagogical training. He asked his faculty to consider a one-year normal course, and a committee headed by Josiah Royce dutifully supported the plan. A more resistant faculty struck out the term "normal" and blocked admission of women to the new courses. But it agreed to the crucial change—a new faculty appointment in "the history and art of teaching." [66]

This new effort by Harvard in pedagogical training was followed in 1894 by the elevation of all Massachusetts normal schools to post-secondary status, opening new possibilities for institutional rivalry. Eliot could not ignore the continued inferiority of these schools, and he drew attention to their weak entrance requirements. During the nineties, he spoke as if the normal schools, even though now on a "collegiate" level, should still restrict themselves to preparation of elementary teachers. The suggestion that Harvard and other colleges would adequately meet the need for secondary school faculties rested on Eliot's continuing underestimation of the numbers seeking secondary education.[67]

The limits of the normal schools were also suggested when Harvard interested itself in the reform of the Cambridge schools. Elected to the local school committee, Professor Albert B. Hart joined in a move to "shorten and enrich" the grammar school years. He gave wide notice of the in-service teacher training which was Harvard's rather modest contribution. It would be healthy for the normal schools, he implied, if their graduates' limitations were exposed by the superior performance of those who took the Harvard work.[68]

It was from a normal school, however, that Eliot drew Harvard's new instructor in the history and art of teaching—Paul H. Hanus, who had just become professor of pedagogy at the Colorado State Normal School. Formerly a mathematics teacher at the state university and principal of a Denver high school, he probably appealed to Eliot as a practical schoolman without formal training in pedagogy and without allegiance to any pedagogical system. As a principal he had developed excellent public relations, and this skill suited the new position, which Eliot saw partly as an ambassadorship from Harvard to the lower schools. Since he was only thirty-six, Hanus could be shaped by institutional needs. If Eliot's choice did not produce another Langdell, it was far from arbitrary.[69]

Hanus responded creatively to the public pressures that had opened the way for an educationist at Harvard. As a frequent lecturer to educational associations, a member of the NEA's Committee on College-Entrance Requirements, and chairman of the Massachusetts Commission on Industrial Education, Hanus gained recognition and moved beyond the good relations with feeder schools that Eliot had imagined for him. Quietly accruing power as the faculty lost interest in the new venture, he raised himself from teacher of three non-credit courses, guarded by a faculty committee, to head of an independent Division of Education (in 1906). Yet in spite of all this, there were only two regular faculty members in education at Harvard until 1907. Hanus's program was far outstripped by that of the University of Chicago, with its famous laboratory school, and by Columbia's Teachers College. When Hanus tried to use the latter as a challenge for Harvard, Eliot warned that the university's constituency would regard it as an "exaggerated and undesirable standard." Considering Eliot's concern for the schools, the modesty of Harvard's program is puzzling.[70]

Part of the explanation lies in the limits set for Eliot by faculty and Corporation opinions. Not many in the faculty shared Eliot's view that education was an emerging "science." Hugo Münsterberg not only blocked the enrollment of graduate students in Hanus's courses, he also predicted the demise of so unworthy a department. Barrett Wendell scoffed at such courses and implied that Eliot was uncritically willing to welcome school teachers into Harvard programs. "Some of our very best scholars in the Faculty," Eliot recognized, "manifest profound distrust in instruction in methods of teaching." But he did not share this view:

"They think if a man knows his subject he will find some way of imparting it. He may, by practicing for years on his classes—to their great disadvantage." Yet Eliot could not ignore faculty sentiment, and he hesitated to connect his public pleas for teacher professionalism and expert supervision with the internal development of Hanus's department.[71]

One would also have expected Eliot to give support to education as a field for research, especially since he called for empirical tests of educational theories. "Theoretical or a priori determinations of educational values have for me very little significance," Eliot wrote a critic. "A practical determination by experiment is the only one which will convince me." But did he actually have in mind anything more controlled than the everyday experience of schoolmen and students? An exposer of educational clichés, he probably liked to believe that his positions were as scientific as any of his day. He relied on direct observation and data-gathering, as in his "examination of the actual work done" in a "tolerably representative" Massachusetts grammar school. The *Report* of the Committee of Ten, he proudly declared, was "the first educational research ever undertaken" by the NEA. According to Eliot's increasingly firm contention, creation of scientific knowledge was a defining characteristic of a university, and social service was essential to American universities. He might consistently have seen an obligation for Harvard to unite these purposes in the field of education. Yet apparently Eliot never made research a standard for judging Hanus.[72]

When, in 1903, an emboldened Hanus suggested that the university establish a School of Education, parallel to the professional schools, he exposed the narrowness of Eliot's expectations. The current view of the Corporation concerning professional schools made Hanus's proposal unwelcome. Harvard had seen separate schools of agriculture, mining, and veterinary science limp along toward collapse. With the receipt of the McKay bequest a general tidying up seemed at hand. It was no time to spawn another professional school. Yet, given Harvard's location and clientele, those schools had been ill-conceived. The stature of the university's president among schoolmen and the model of other urban universities suggested greater potential for a school of education.

In this context Eliot advised Hanus to "neither talk nor think" about such a new school. The established degrees of A.B., A.M., and Ph.D., Eliot argued, would be more valuable for teachers than special degrees (indeed, the disappearance of the S.D. indicated as much), and teachers did not need as much technical information and skill as aspirants to the three traditional professions. Hanus believed that such comments ignored the possibility for professional training of educational leaders and betrayed an unimaginative concentration on future classroom teachers. He gamely resisted Eliot's advice not to press the issue and elicited an admission from him that if a single donor should offer a large sum for a school, it would probably be accepted. When the Graduate School of Education opened in 1920 with a major gift from the General Education Board, Eliot gave it his blessing as a "pioneering" venture. But in this field other universities had already left Harvard far behind.[73]

Eliot withheld from the program in education the creative guidance he had given the medical school. Nor did he say anything on behalf of education to equal his eloquent pleas for philanthropic support for the dental and veterinary schools. As a result, Hanus, a man of modest abilities, became the guiding force in the study of education at Harvard. Often he echoed the values Eliot expressed in public addresses, but without Eliot's support he found it difficult to embody them in the curriculum or structure of the university.[74]

Eliot did not think of himself as relying solely on the education department to make Harvard's contribution to school betterment. He pointed to the growth of Radcliffe as another means by which Harvard was elevating teaching in the schools, and his homilies to the women students emphasized teaching above any other career. Hopeful that local alumni associations would effectively influence public education, he counted on the Harvard Clubs in various cities to spread his gospel of school reform. Sev-

eral of them obediently constituted themselves upper class reformers of public schools. The Buffalo Harvard Club got exactly
what it requested in new "flexibility" for the course of study at
the local high school and, after investigating its athletic rules,
successfully insisted on the adoption of eligibility standards like
those at Harvard. At the meeting of the Associated Harvard
Clubs in 1908, ten clubs reported on public education in their cities, and Eliot spurred them on with a check-list for judging and
reforming a city school system.[75]

The Harvard Teachers' Association was founded in 1891. It
was open to all teachers who had studied at Harvard, including
summer students. Engineered by Shaler and Hanus, the organization held annual meetings (with Eliot regularly present), printed
proceedings in the *Educational Review*, and issued a series of
leaflets. Topics for debate included the Committee of Ten *Report*, the elective system, and the financing of education. Teachers reported to each other on how their Harvard-learned ideas
had fared in the hard world of the lower schools.[76]

These associations shared the organizational spirit of the times.
Eliot's administration coincided with a period when business corporations and labor unions were discovering in the pressures of
industrial life reasons to turn away from older traditions of individual, local, or small group operation and to form great new organizations. In spite of his individualistic credo and his belief in
Harvard's unique qualities, Eliot encouraged a similar tendency
among educators and schools.

Like Tocqueville, he believed that free association was a pattern suitable to America's governmental weakness and physical
expanse, but observing that technology was shrinking the country and creating problems of great complexity, he came to consider the old localism obsolete and the old voluntarism amateur-
ish. "Unlike Germany, England and France," he commented in
1894, "we have no educational authority in the United States to
impose just restrictions and set high standards. This authority
must be replaced by the weight of public opinion, informed
through the discussions and final agreements of bodies of educa-

tional experts." To give such experts visibility so that they could influence the public was part of his motive for supporting educational organizations. After aiding in the formation of the New England Association of Colleges and Preparatory Schools, he praised the emergence of comparable regional associations, the future authorities for accreditation. With his concern for institutional articulation, he especially valued organizations like these which included both colleges and schools, but he was also a founder of the exclusive Association of American Universities, whose initial object was to guard the quality of American graduate degrees.[77]

Government had remarkably little to do with the educational standardization of Eliot's day. Through the new associations schools and colleges kept each other in step. A widespread desire for definition and predictability brought allegiance to the new educational bureaucracies. After the labors of Eliot and his generation, one could know with considerable precision the meaning of "university," "Ph.D.," and "medical school."

Eliot's increasing concern with educational associations can be exemplified by his involvement in the National Education Association. This body, founded in 1857 as the National Teachers Association, met in Boston in 1872, but it was then so insignificant that Eliot later could not recall whether he had bothered to attend. His maiden address at an NEA meeting, given in 1873, was his assault on the national university idea. Intemperate though it was, it benefited the organization by attacking a somnolent committee and bringing sharp controversy into the meetings. Although he sent a letter of clarification to the next convention, he branded the group's journal of proceedings "a stupid volume of small circulation" and apparently did not attend again for fifteen years. Then, beginning with his address in 1888 on shortening and enriching school programs, he quickly became a power within the organization. "It is always a successful meeting when you are present," William Torrey Harris wrote him in 1896.[78]

When he headed the Committee of Ten, Eliot used the NEA as a vehicle for reforms he wanted in schools and colleges. In

1903, as president of the association, he turned his attention to some of its own inadequacies. Though nearly seventy years old, he was anything but a figurehead president. The convention took place in Boston, and Eliot performed many of the functions of a program chairman. He instituted a series of reforms—a preliminary meeting of department presidents (comparable to later session chairmen), submission of papers before the meeting, strict time limits on papers, elimination of prayers and music, and reports by department presidents from which he extracted recommendations for further improvements. During his presidency Eliot also helped shape an influential successor to the Committee of Ten, the Committee on Economy of Time in Education, steering it away from Baker's interest in subject values and toward his own special concern. Under a wave of feminist protest, he lost in his effort to keep appointments to the nominating committee largely in the hands of the organization's president, a failure that hurt what he regarded as responsible centralization. But on the whole, his was a reforming administration.[79]

NEA meetings partly deserved the satirical label of "grand educational picnics": the bargain railroad fares and excursion psychology doubtless played a large role in building up attendance. More than thirty thousand appeared at the Boston meetings. Never averse to breaking numerical records, Eliot boasted, "The like of it was never seen before in any country." At his behest, Harvard seized the opportunity to ingratiate itself with the throngs of teachers, providing guides, teas, departmental displays, lectures, and excursions. The visitors reciprocated by boosting the enrollment at Harvard's summer school to a new high.[80]

But an era was drawing to a close. The NEA soon turned toward concerns of teacher welfare, and it lost relevance for college presidents and professors. Newer organizations brought college men and schoolmen together for such specific objects as designing admission examinations and accrediting schools, and new philanthropic foundations gave Eliot and others the leverage of money in reforming schools and colleges. After 1910 the participation by college representatives in the NEA declined sharply.

Eliot was consulted in some later crises, but only as an elder statesman who was gradually becoming an outsider.[81]

VII

Eliot believed himself the first in America to use the phrase "the New Education." As he admitted, his reference in 1869 had been only to higher education, but by the 1890s, when the phrase was widely used to identify the ferment transforming the schools, it was still appropriate to count Eliot a leader.[82] No one man launched the Progressive Era in American education, but among the notable events in the watershed years of the late eighties and early nineties were Eliot's addresses on the schools and such articles as his "Wherein Popular Education Has Failed," which appeared in the *Forum* in 1892, alongside Joseph Mayer Rice's muckraking series on the schools.[83]

Eliot had preferences, of course, among Progressive tendencies. Although he called for experimentation and recognized the innovative possibilities of private schools, he stood principally for organization, professionalism, and the freedoms of rational order. Although he tried, clumsily, to plead for the arts, he remained a scientist who saw the laboratory as the ideal learning situation. He was eloquent in denouncing rote-learning and urging that children's individuality be a primary concern of the school, but he justified such attention as preparation for productive lives, which he too readily equated with happiness. Although he extended the period of education which he believed society should guarantee to all children, he asked the schools to prefer achievement to equality.

In spite of such partialities, as Eliot continued to involve himself in the shaping of the lower schools, schoolmen grew less likely to view his efforts as unwanted interference from "the East" or as an assault by an uninformed meddler from the upper class. Increasingly superintendents and profession-minded teachers prided themselves on being engaged in a common enterprise with a renowned leader of higher education, a creator of the American university.[84] To students in the public schools, this erect, confident visitor from "Boston" conveyed the message that education should be adventure, not drudgery, and that it should not end when one left the local school, whether he went on to college or not.[85]

"Catalyst," a more modest claim for Eliot than his contemporaries' extravagances, is perhaps the word that best indicates his function in American public education. He failed to obtain many of his most strongly urged reforms. Superintendents who tried to provide the enrichment of grammar schools that he called for were often blocked by lay opposition against such "hard" or "impractical" subjects. Most high schools resisted his pleas for liberating students from the course system and for keeping preparatory and nonpreparatory students together. The secondary modern subjects gained status as he wished, but so did commercial studies that he considered of dubious merit.[86]

Changes were not always the ones Eliot favored. But the era would have been less effectively reform-minded without him. At meetings of educational associations, his presence added authority, optimism, and argumentative bite. The president of the Massachusetts Classical and High School Teachers Association spoke of him in 1892 as "almost constantly with us, a most original, stimulating, inspiring, and I may almost say, provoking, force."[87] A quoted, or misquoted, Eliot aphorism enlivened many a public address on education. Although he unrelentingly repeated favorite arguments, he also took up such new causes as kindergartens, schools as community centers, and park settings for city schools. His presidential address to the NEA, given at the climax of his influence on schoolmen, sounded the theme that underlay most of his recommendations. Culture must be redefined beyond exclusively literary acquirements—this in the name of expanded human knowledge, new awareness of human diversity, and new needs of industrial society.[88]

After he left the presidency of Harvard, Eliot's influence continued, through the General Education Board and through his personal command of public attention. Other good causes pushed the public schools from the center of his reform concerns. But he shared in the initial plans for the Lincoln School in 1915, and in 1917 he struck a hard blow at compulsory Latin. In 1919 he was the appropriate honorary president of a new organization that named itself for Progressive Education.[89]

The Resurgence of Collegiate Concerns

Look to it, gentlemen, that there be no reaction.

CHARLES W. ELIOT,
to alumni (1894) [1]

I

To the great benefit of Harvard and American education, Eliot was not followed in the presidency by an uncritical admirer. Harvard thus escaped the widespread institutional tendency to choose a weak leader after a strong one. This course was possible largely because within the Harvard community a body of thought had developed which was critical of what Eliot had wrought. There was no conspiracy or concealment in this. From the high-minded, objective, liberal Eliot one did not need to hide criticisms and doubts. Yet because Eliot failed to comprehend much of the criticism, the movement for counterreform gained power and coherence, and it produced in Abbott Lawrence Lowell a leader who by 1909 appeared to be the "obvious" successor to Eliot.

It would be wrong to identify Eliot's critics of his last decade in office with those of his first. The conservative members of his original faculty who had objected to new liberties for students, broader admission standards, and importation of recognized scholars at high rank, and who had put a special value on Greek as a disciplinary subject—few of these remained after the 1890s.

263

The later critics were often products of Eliot's Harvard, who had observed its weaknesses from the students' side. They welcomed much of his achievement and were, in many cases, personally devoted to him. Yet there were links between the faculty members who brought in critical committee reports from 1903 on and the element that had slowed Eliot's initial reforms in the 1870s. The counterreformers sometimes looked to the values of the pre-Eliot, collegiate past.

Defense of Greek as a peculiarly disciplinary subject was out of place at Harvard by the turn of the century. But there had long been another rationale for teaching ancient languages, a view of collegiate purpose which seemed to gain point with the years. Evidence of this view had been recognized, though scorned, in 1867 by E. L. Youmans. "The classicists," he wrote, "are fond of presenting the issue as between liberal culture and money-making, and triumphantly contrast the refined and generous feelings which cluster around the former, with the vulgar and sordid motives which characterize the latter." Irving Babbitt of Harvard's French department drew on this earlier tradition when he complained of the prevalence of "hustling scholars" as evidence that the college neglected "all that the Greek summed up in his idea of leisure." [2]

Liberal culture as an institutional aim, contrasting with social service, vocationalism, or research for the sake of new knowledge, continued with men like James Russell Lowell and Charles Eliot Norton as a muted strain in Harvard life throughout the Eliot years. This vision of collegiate purpose rallied critics of the academic style created by the university builders. Advocates of liberal culture drew inspiration from Matthew Arnold, and they generally accepted his definition of culture, "a wide vision of the best things which man has done or aspired after"—a phrase which succinctly presented their aspirations toward breadth, taste, heritage, and idealism. Collegiate aims which they embraced included also "character" and "gentlemanliness." They stressed standards and felt threatened by numbers. Few of their formulations attended to democratic values. In many ways they resembled the orthodox German university professors who sought to revive philosophical Idealism as a protection against industrialism, with its mass culture, interest politics, and technological emphases.[3]

No single figure at Harvard fully represented this resurgence of collegiate concerns. Charles Francis Adams, who could assail required Greek as "a college fetich" in 1883 and thus be mistaken for an ally of Eliot, was even more virulent in his attack on the elective system in 1906. Yet his plea then was not for culture, but rather for a return to the disciplining of mental faculties. Francis Cabot Lowell, who became a Fellow in 1895, had originally won election as an Overseer in 1886 after admitting his fears about the high degree of specialization allowed in the college. Linking advocacy of liberal culture to particular disciplines can only be approximate. An outside observer at the end of the Eliot regime generalized that Harvard's men of science were "in the thick of the fight, inventive, productive, progressive," while its men of letters stood aloof, "commenting and criticizing, and more concerned with the past than with the present and future." Yet an assistant professor of Greek who resigned in 1891, feeling that he was battling in "the strife between scientific method and the Ideal spirit, on the unpopular side," had found the "scientific" enemy ensconced within the Greek department itself. Hugo Münsterberg, the German-bred experimental psychologist, proudly identified himself with the rising counterwave of Idealism, the new interest in knowledge's "absolute meaning and its relation to all other human values,—those of morality, beauty, and religion." [4]

Among those who stood in opposition to Eliot's policies, Barrett Wendell was particularly self-revealing. A member of the English department who cultivated his eccentricities, Wendell was grateful to Eliot for gambling on him as a teacher in 1880. During his early years on the faculty, he disapproved of those who hoped to "smash" Eliot, for he was inspired by the president's fairness and dedication. In early letters to Eliot, expressing fears of his unworthiness to be a professor, Wendell begged to be allowed to resign like a gentleman. But in the midst of his insecurity he did not hesitate to explain to Eliot why as president he tended to think of human beings "too statistically." Eliot was well aware that Wendell had become one of Harvard's best teachers. His students were fascinated by his mannerisms, which, rather than distracting their attention, seemed to focus it on his teaching. In 1898 Wendell became a professor. That achievement, in combination with the arrival on the faculty of his friend Lawrence Lowell, strengthened Wendell's faith in his own educational judgment.[5]

In educational ideas, Wendell shared a good deal with Eliot. He too emphasized disciplinary values while admitting the element of mystery in teaching and learning. But his differences from Eliot were sharp and eventually seemed to him almost absolute. He rather looked down on scholarship as a profession, writing a friend somewhat apologetically about Lowell's concern for research, "If scholarship and that kind of thing tend only towards scholarship in perpetuity, then [your criticisms] are right. Of course, few able youths nowadays wish to be professional scholars. If scholarship, on the other hand, has such gymnastic value that a good classical man, for example, has a positive advantage in legal or political argument, or in practical conduct of affairs, over a man of equal natural ability who has less training, then you are a bit off." Eliot's definition of education, he believed, reduced it to "specialized training for a specific end." With his friend Lowell safely in the presidency, Wendell helped arrange a "classical dinner" in celebration. The bill of fare was such as only consultation of the Latin classics certified as authentically ancient. To one who had objected to the elective system as wasteful, disorderly, "à la carte" education, the symbolism was rich indeed.[6]

Personal idiosyncrasies kept Barrett Wendell from becoming a leader of the counterreformers. Perhaps he was not an able committeeman. But in letters and essays he brilliantly articulated the views of Eliot's latter-day critics. Wendell's links to other doubters were many. James Russell Lowell's small classes in Dante affected the whole course of Wendell's thought and teaching. He had been an intimate of Lawrence Lowell since boyhood.

Like him, Wendell had tried law but had not thrived in it (he failed to pass his bar examination and never retook it). He was attached to Charles Francis Adams, and he held Henry Cabot Lodge up as a model to students. His colleague LeBaron Russell Briggs and he, though of radically different personalities, developed a warm and effective collaboration as teachers of English composition, virtually creating that subject in its twentieth-century form.[7]

Wendell, who liked to think of himself as a man of letters, feared contamination by philistinism. Especially after the shock of Bryan's candidacy in 1896, which made him regret that he had voted for Cleveland in 1884, he emphasized his doubts of democracy. His social theory was strongly class-oriented. He described the good society as "each in his place, none unworthily secure, . . . none undeservedly oppressed." [8] Those "socially of the better sort" had special obligations, among which was the relief of the worthy poor. His attention to his ancestry in colonial New York included an elaborate effort to reconstruct its heraldry. He carried his cane on his little finger, spoke in a pseudo-English voice, and sported a goatee. In spite of all this, Wendell was too much given to self-mockery and the effort to be "deliberately startling," to qualify fully as a snob.[9]

On Lowell's initiative, Wendell composed the Phi Beta Kappa poem in the spring of Eliot's retirement. There could be but one theme, and Wendell determined that while he would give a seeming laudation, he would edge the poetry with satire and express his truest judgment of Eliot the man. In witty couplets he managed to criticize Eliot for, among other things, not showing warm interest in a faculty member's best efforts, being too susceptible to experimental proposals, loving statistics, not worrying about the caliber of freshmen, being soft on public school teachers and hard on clergymen, and trying to equate veterinarians with physicians. In short, Eliot "was not quite free from lingering foibles of humanity." After all that, it was scant praise to hail a man's "incarnate magnanimity." An ingenious passage described Eliot's optimism about humanity as both his central virtue and

268 · Between Harvard and America

central failing. Just as Jonathan Edwards had kept Calvinism alive past its day, the poem analogized, Eliot had preserved the Unitarian faith of Channing even though wiser men had noted its limits. They had seen the persistence of what Wendell enjoyed calling "envy, malice, and all uncharitableness." His criticisms were of more than the man, however, for Eliot had come to symbolize the new university order.[10]

L. B. R. Briggs was as inconspicuous in appearance as Wendell was dramatic. But Eliot saw beneath exteriors, and in one of his most inspired appointments he made Briggs dean of the college. In the words of Briggs's successor, he was "a just man, tender yet clear-sighted, who in protecting the College never once forgot the individual. No one of all this army [the undergraduates] has ever felt himself neglected or without a friend." Whatever the divisions among Harvard students, one thing they could agree on and one memory they shared—the friendliness of Dean Briggs. His elevation in 1902 to the deanship of the Faculty of Arts and Sciences, rather than limiting his concern for the college, seemed to increase it. In his first report in the new office he expressed fear that Harvard shared the tendency of universities that were "pushing blindly out from under them the college props on which they stand." In the counterreforming camp of liberal culture, Briggs displayed neither the superciliousness of Wendell nor the hard-driving personal scholarship of Lawrence Lowell. He could refer to "crude specialists that one shudders to think of as educated men (learned men doubtless, but not educated men)." He had doubts about the elective system and leaned toward a required freshman year. He criticized certain effects of graduate training, observing that preparation of a "Germanized" thesis might make the graduate student a worse teacher rather than a better one. Regretfully he concluded that athletics were providing better discipline than study was. Briggs's peculiar sweetness of character and his popularity with students and recent alumni gave him leverage for shifting the college toward his version of liberal culture.[11]

Yet Briggs and Eliot liked each other, and Briggs combined his objections to Eliot's Harvard with an intense personal loyalty to the man. At times he echoed Eliot's rationale for certain aspects of the new Harvard. Briggs did not have a particularly original mind, and his opinion that something was wrong in the college is all the more convincing because he was not given to theorizing. Briggs could regret the loss of "the old-school culture and repose, the old-school dignity and poise." He could brand the elective system as "the theory that all studies are born free and equal, but that the new studies are freer and more equal than the old." Yet he called Eliot the man "in whom, always and with our whole hearts, we must believe." [12]

Like Eliot, Abbott Lawrence Lowell represented a Harvard dynasty. His grandfather had been senior Fellow on the Corporation that elected Eliot, and his brother-in-law, who was also his cousin, had been on the Corporation since 1895. Lowell was the third in direct descent to be sole trustee of the Lowell Institute, and, like his father and grandfather, he served on the Corporation of the Massachusetts Institute of Technology. A member of the class of 1877, Lowell had earned a degree in the law school. His career at the bar was undistinguished, but he supplemented it with a series of books on government that won him increasing recognition among intellectuals. Invited to Harvard in 1897 as a part-time lecturer, he proved an effective and popular teacher. He accepted a professorship of government in 1900, but chose to teach only half-time so that he could continue his writing.

Lowell was delighted to move from the legal to the academic world. He had resigned from his law firm upon receiving his first, part-time Harvard appointment. Emerging as a major spokesman on college policy, he was a member of the most important special faculty committees from 1902 to 1909. His efforts on these committees and his addresses to alumni revealed his ambition to influence Harvard affairs. He had, in fact, set his cap for the Harvard presidency. He needed to prove himself and win support, since, as he knew, he would not be Eliot's nominee.[13]

Three central themes—scholarship, culture, and community —shaped Lowell's educational thought. By 1904 they were clearly delineated, and they changed little thereafter. He applied them with continuing fruitfulness to institutional design throughout his presidency.

In his idea of scholarship, Lowell displayed an unusual combination of old-fashioned belief in mental discipline and newer ideas about student motivation. At times he came close to recommending exercise of mental faculties; he advocated "practice" and spoke of mental forces which could be "freed by use." He strongly resented "the very habit, which has come over the whole educational world, of making the acquisition of knowledge easy." Students, he believed, were not studying enough. But Lowell did not want drill or unpleasant tasks assigned chiefly for their unpleasantness. There must be inspiration for the students, but not through the social or vocational utility of what they were studying. The worst thing the college could do would be to make the student look on thinking "as a means of earning bread." Little wonder that he differed from Eliot, who, according to Lowell, "regarded the College chiefly as a place for learning the subjects that would practically best fit a man for his subsequent career." Lowell made remarkable analogic use of the enthusiasm for athletics. The drive of the athlete, he believed, was partly for personal fame and partly for the institution. Judging these motives worthy, he hoped to attach them to scholarship. The loss of competition in the college disturbed him. Nobody knew who the first scholar was any longer, and nobody cared—he was probably some "long-haired grind." [14]

Much of the "university" vision of scholarship which had helped create the graduate school was applied by Lowell to students in the college. They too should aspire to high scholarship; in fact, only in the college could they be made so to aspire. The graduate school had turned out to be merely another professional school, whose students docilely followed their specialties. "No one goes into a graduate school in order to acquire a love of learning," Lowell observed. He had no desire to discard the research ideal. He once spoke of contributing new human knowledge as "perhaps, the most essential function of a university." He had himself become a scholar without graduate school attendance, however, and he refused to make ideals of scholarship something post-collegiate.[15]

Lowell showed himself part of the liberal culture movement by his insistence that achievement in a special field was not an adequate outcome of a college education. He spoke in favor of the "well-rounded man," using a phrase repugnant to Eliot, and favored general courses that could acquaint a student with a field without the assumption that he was a future specialist. The college would give the student standards to judge by, and it would develop his mental power so that he could continue to grow intellectually. These standards and this power could not come from "the pursuit of purely utilitarian things." Perhaps Lowell was never closer to the idealist wing of liberal culture than in his peroration to New York alumni in 1904. "I shall be told that I am struggling against the spirit of the age, which is materialistic and plutocratic. But while it is true that every institution—and a university no less than any other—must recognize and adapt itself to the spirit of the times, it is also true that the very object of a university is to keep before men's minds those things that lie beyond the spirit of the age, the deeper things whose value is eternal." A similar passage in his inaugural of 1909 omitted the reference to the eternal and elevated the theme of service.[16]

In his distress at loss of community, Lowell was very much a man of his era. Calling for "an intellectual and social cohesion," he linked this value to others. Without a community in which he could measure himself and compete, the individual would have no valid standards, no recognition for his achievement, no satisfaction in the achievement of others. Nor would he attain breadth unless he could associate with those whose special interests differed from his own. But the academic community Lowell valued was more than an intellectual matter. The development of character in college youths depended "not merely on their being instructed, but mostly on their living together in an atmosphere of good fellowship." He depicted the poverty among Harvard students more compellingly than Eliot did, and denounced the division between rich and poor students, which Eliot tolerated. Arguing that students should be consulted and their proposals given a trial, he helped win faculty approval of the new Student Council, which was set up in 1908 in an attempt to limit the distraction of winter sports, then threatened with a faculty ban. But beyond these gains, Lowell saw community as good in itself. What had been lost in the disappearance of the old-time college, he believed, was partly the striving for intellectual pre-eminence, partly cultural breadth, but more than anything else fellow-feeling and unity among the students. These qualities he was determined to restore.[17]

II

In 1899, when Harvard ended the last required courses except the English and foreign language of the freshman year and established a newly permissive set of admission requirements, Eliot's reform of the college had reached its culmination. From then on, the thrust of reform came from other sources within his faculty.

In the spring of 1901 the faculty by a narrow margin failed to pass a regulation favored by Eliot and the professional schools that would have strongly encouraged the three-year A.B. During the 1901–2 term, in response to prodding from the Overseers for clarification, the faculty continued to wrestle with the three-year-degree question. The faculty declined to stimulate the speedier degree by cutting the number of courses required from seventeen (or seventeen and one-half if one made below C in freshman English) to fifteen, a plan probably favored by Eliot. Instead they turned their attention to an existing regulation that somewhat discouraged the three-year degree and appeared unnecessarily idiosyncratic. This was the rule that only a student who was graduating *cum laude* (defined as attaining A or B in at least nine courses) or above could at the end of his third year actually receive the degree. A student without reaching the *cum laude* level could take a "leave of absence" and without doing any additional work receive the degree at the end of what would have been his fourth year. Since students were fond of remaining with the class in which they had entered—for the sake of reunions and class reports—many three-year men chose to wait a year for the degree in any case. Thus the special requirement of quality was a rather hollow affair.

Faculty members dissatisfied with the standards of the college took consideration of this rule as their opportunity to suggest a higher minimum quality for all A.B. candidates. After lively debate between those who wanted the required average raised "somewhat" and those who wanted it raised "distinctly," the faculty settled for a very moderate increase. The student must pass two-thirds rather than one-half of his courses with grades above D.

Small though the increase was, it had immense significance as the beginning of a persistent and vigorous concern for the intellectual quality of college work. Dean Briggs summarized the debate. "The Faculty raised the question whether it could fairly demand better grades without better teaching. This question led to discussion of the lecture system in large elective courses and further, led to the appointment of a committee which should consider ways of making college instruction more efficient." Briggs, who had worked for the creation of this "Committee on Improving Instruction in Harvard College," became its chairman, but Lowell soon emerged as its leading inventor of investigative techniques and reform suggestions.[18]

In a procedure so new as to be revolutionary, the committee sent questionnaires to a cross-section of students (representing all grades given in all courses), asking, among other things, how much they studied. "These replies from students," wrote the chairman, "confirmed the Committee in its conviction that acquaintance with methods of instruction involves acquaintance with those methods as seen and felt by the persons to whom they are applied." [19] Questionnaires also went to the faculty, asking how much they believed students studied. The initial finding—that students were largely satisfied with their choice of electives—was a predictable student vote of confidence in free election and the quality of teaching. The rest of the report was full of unpleasant conclusions, expressed with unusual cogency.

Bluntly the committee announced that most of the faculty "deceive themselves as to the amount of work which their courses require." In fact, the one widespread general criticism from students was "that they feel the need of being kept up to their work more regularly." Whereas faculty imagined six hours a week of out-of-class work done for a three-hour course, the committee figures purported to show that the average was in fact less than three and one-half hours. Setting the criteria of "intellectual vigor and self-sufficiency," the committee declared it found in the college "too much teaching and too little studying." [20]

Although the committee did not oppose the large lecture courses which had grown up under the elective system, it found that here the question of standards was "peculiarly pressing." Admitting that the assistants in such courses were "necessarily young men, and therefore without experience in teaching," the committee nevertheless felt that a greater effort could be made to provide "the very best available men," in part by higher salaries. The assistants, furthermore, should have smaller sections. Nor did the heads of such large courses escape censure. They could contribute to course morale, the committee observed, by teaching a section or otherwise making themselves more directly available to students. Certain lecturers failed to interest, some were inaudible, and some wasted time dictating data or having it copied from the blackboard. The committee suggested that chairmen look at the anonymous student comments on courses in their departments.

Both students and faculty, it appeared, had come to look on certain subjects "as designed peculiarly for general culture, and certain others as designed for the scholastic training of specialists." The committee traced this division in part to the practice in some departments of offering only courses suited to the aspiring specialist. Hence the suggestion that "every Department ought to provide courses for students who are not to be specialists in it," which would "familiarize the student with the conceptions of principles on which the subject is based, with the methods of thought of those who pursue it, and with the tests of truth that are used in it."

In further defense of general culture, the committee opposed the exclusive linking of honors at graduation to the ideal of the young specialist. It believed that "students in pursuit of general culture should be encouraged in a thorough and somewhat advanced study of subjects to which they do not intend to devote their lives." This could be done in part by making honors requirements "less professional and of wider human interest" and by securing wide recognition for honors winners. Two sorts of specialization were distinguished by the committee—the disciplinary or cultural and the professional or vocational—and its report implied that even advanced courses in the college should be shifted to serve non-vocational ends.

Two themes characterized the eleven conclusions with which the committee summarized its report. (It proposed no formal faculty votes.) The first, the threat of specialism and professionalism to general culture, could be seen in the recommendation that the respective amounts of study required for all courses be made "as nearly equivalent as possible" (thus a student could not give great effort to his specialty while coasting in other courses), in the recommendation that introductory courses should not be required as preliminary to other courses in a department (this restriction, it was felt, prevented introductory courses from serving general culture), and in this pronouncement: "Every subject in the College should be taught on the principle that a thorough knowledge of it is a valuable part of a liberal education."

The second major theme was the importance of intellectual effort by students. The committee labeled the average amount of study "discreditably small," frowned on the taking of six courses at a time, singled out large lecture courses as needing stiffening up (with an increase in the number of assistants suggested as a means), and recommended the taking of honors in some subject by "every serious man with health and ability." This last was, of course, a call not for professional specialization, but for intellectual achievement irrespective of vocational intentions.

This report was a turning point for Harvard, but Eliot revealed no suspicion of the fact. He saw it as a side excursion on the journey to the standard three-year degree. In his report of 1902, he emphasized the regularizing of the three-year degree by dropping the *cum laude* requirement rather than the raising of the minimum grade average for all A.B.'s. The elective system, Eliot said, had already so raised the quality of instruction that the scholarship demanded for an A.B. was higher than in any former generation.[21]

Eliot agreed that the large lecture courses, in which four-ninths of undergraduate work was done, deserved the committee's inspection. But for his part he spoke of them supportively. "The student [in such courses] is, by no means a mere listener to lectures; he must be a reader also, and must give frequent account of the work he does." Even the notorious Geology 4, where Eliot admitted "there is less attempt to keep informed concerning the weekly progress of each student," he called "a profitable course of instruction for large numbers of students." Eliot was much more interested in the liberty of the students and the variety of courses open to them under "a wide elective system." He dwelt on the intermixture of graduate and undergraduate students in almost every course and said with satisfaction, "There is no telling where the College ends and the Graduate School begins; they are interfused or commingled," a sentence which no doubt hardened the grim set of the jaw on some of his college-idealizing critics.[22]

But although Eliot missed much of the argument in the new wave of criticism, there was a sense in which the critics failed to grasp his reasoning. The committee's report did not treat courses requiring laboratory work or theses, the very courses which partook of the advanced, investigative, independent quality of graduate study. Eliot saw student involvement in such courses as one of the wellsprings of intellectual striving and the main source of acquaintance with scholarly standards. In fact, his disciple George Herbert Palmer had once justified in print the selection of an "easy" course by a student who wanted to do extra work in other courses.[23] The possibility that things might indeed be working out this way in the college was not really tested because of the selective emphasis of the committee on large introductory lecture courses.

The report's antagonism toward specialists and professionalism was a counterreforming thrust against Eliot's "Germanized" college. But its second theme, the increase of intellectual effort, was an extension of one of his major objectives. The committee's ideal workday was three hours shorter than Eliot's, but both were longer than students considered realistic. "Nobody I know works seven hours a day," a freshman blurted out to a dean.[24] Although he still hoped to establish a standard three-year A.B., Eliot concluded that in general he could assent to these new collegiate reformers. Since he would be unlikely to outlast this generation of critics, he chose an optimistic angle of vision which viewed them as furthering his cause.

He spoke in 1904 of "encouraging progress" in giving form to the committee's proposals for "improving the College instruction, stimulating scholarly ambition [an ambiguous phrase that both he and his critics could agree on], and preventing shirks and malingerers from obtaining the A.B." Geology 4, he announced without comment, was no longer a course that could be counted toward the A.B.[25]

The report of the Briggs committee was accepted by the faculty on December 1, 1903. After the work of a series of relatively ineffectual committees dealing with honors degrees, a second major committee, with Lowell as chairman and its membership handpicked by him, was appointed in the spring of 1908. Its mandate from the faculty was "to consider how the tests for rank and scholarly distinction in Harvard College can be made a more generally recognized measure of intellectual power." Lowell could be counted on to interpret this broadly.[26]

The Lowell committee obtained views of faculty, students, and recent alumni and made telling comparisons between attitudes toward study in college and in law school. Alumni recalled an atmosphere of intellectual indifference in the college and regretted neglected opportunities for learning. In fact, the committee concluded, contentment with inactivity and mediocrity had spread from the classroom to extracurricular activities. It reiterated suggestions of the Briggs committee, but went further, directly

indicting the free elective system. There was no "spirit of emulation" since men were "out of sight of one another." The question
of community was thus brought into vital relation with the question of intellectual effort and achievement.

The free elective system assured no systematic education for
the individual, the report charged. To correct this fault, "students
should be encouraged by all possible means to take a group of
courses leading to a degree with distinction [whether they ultimately won it or not], while scattering the rest of their electives
so as to include something in each of the fields in which an educated man ought not to be wholly ignorant." This combination,
later called concentration and distribution, had been advocated
by such academic leaders as David Starr Jordan of Stanford and
William DeWitt Hyde of Bowdoin. But at Harvard it had for
some time been associated with Lowell. Dean Hurlbut's report of
1906 had pointed to Lowell's ideal for Harvard education—
"mastery, so far as that may be implied in a degree of Bachelor
of Arts, in some one field of learning, and such an understanding
of other fields as will enable one to listen intelligently to those
who are masters in those fields." [27]

All departments, according to the Lowell committee, should
offer "a general, as distinguished from a purely introductory,
course" to enhance the scattering of courses. Further, there
should be more advisers, departments should prepare model,
though not compulsory, programs, and theses submitted for degrees with distinction might well relate to more than one course.
These recommendations, including the requirement of concentration and distribution that brought an end to the free elective system at Harvard, were passed in the fall of 1909, with only a
handful in opposition. By then Abbott Lawrence Lowell was
president of the university. [28]

III

In 1900, perhaps in part misled by the advances of the elective
principle at Yale, Eliot had rejoiced in the inevitable triumph of
the "system of liberty." But what Yale was adopting was not the

free elective system, for it retained close limits on the subjects of the freshman year and demanded that work in two majors and three minors be taken at three increasingly difficult levels, thus preventing wide scattering among elementary courses. As president of Princeton after 1902, Woodrow Wilson not only introduced the preceptorial method to encourage closer intellectual relations between faculty and undergraduates, but also increased the amount of course prescription. In fact, the curricular pendulum in American higher education was on the point of swinging back toward prescription and control. Such was the case even at Harvard, though of this Eliot for some time had no inkling.[29]

There were signs, including statistical signs, that all was not well. In 1901 there was a small drop in the total student enrollment at Harvard, notably in the college. The *Harvard Graduates' Magazine*, which, during the university's spectacular growth in the 1890s, had placed great emphasis on comparative enrollment statistics, noted that Yale, embarrassingly, had made a sharp gain at the moment Harvard was shrinking. By 1905 the "disagreeable nature of the facts" was even plainer, total enrollment having dropped by 205 in 1904 and by 169 in 1905. As a leader who had stated the university's obligation to be sensitive to the opinions of the educated classes, Eliot could not for long ignore such evidence. The loss of New Englanders, especially of western Massachusetts students, was startling. Where were they going? In part, to the smaller New England colleges, particularly Dartmouth. The rise of the three-year degree, which shortened the time some students spent at Harvard, explained part of the decline, but it did not explain the drop in the number of entering freshmen. Increasingly, hard feelings between wealthy students of the Gold Coast and the social "outs" of the Yard made Harvard seem forbidding. All this was bluntly admitted in the pages of the *Harvard Graduates' Magazine*, and the press commented extensively on the matter.[30]

The percentage of Harvard income from tuition was so high (over 60 per cent in 1903–4) that lower enrollments forced economy measures, including the dropping of some graduate courses.[31] A "Teachers' Endowment" presented by alumni in 1905 provided only temporary relief, and some valued faculty members were lost to other universities. Deficits plagued the university through the decade.[32]

"The sharpest criticism of Harvard, as well as of the rest of the universe, has come from Harvard men," observed a Midwestern commentator. Harvard under Eliot had always been exceptionally free with self-criticism, and his tolerance of opposition was almost inhumanly high. But in 1904–5 he experienced a "wave of criticism." There were faculty complaints of overwork, the erection of too many buildings, and undue emphasis on the scientific school and the medical school. The deficit was ascribed to Eliot's encouragement of three-year A.B.'s.[33] Charles Francis Adams took the opportunity of his 1906 Phi Beta Kappa address at Columbia to attack the elective system as a mischievous educational fad which failed to develop symmetrical minds, and he urged the subdivision of the university into residential colleges. Adams might be discounted as melodramatic and inconsistent, but it was not easy to dismiss suggestions by articulate undergraduates that the elective system encouraged triviality. One morning in 1876–77 the Harvard community had awakened to find University Hall emblazoned with a painted warning, "The University is going to Hell." Could the prediction finally be coming true? [34]

It is puzzling that Eliot, whose success as a university president had come in large part from his ability to listen to others and win adoption for their best ideas, failed to become the champion of proposals for the reformation of the college in the twentieth century. After all, he had changed from one who objected to the "exaggerated elective system" to an advocate of free election. Why could he not also come to see the need of "ballasting"? He had once minimized the significance to a university of research. Faculty members had set him right in the late eighties and made him a champion of advanced scholarship. Perhaps because of this shift of interest to faculty-scholars, the renewed stress on undergraduate general education struck him as reactionary. It is puzzling, too, that after recognizing some of the limitations of individualism in social policy, he did not question its dominance in the undergraduate curriculum. Eliot did not remain oblivious to the movements for collegiate counterreformation, but he neither selected out for support their most promising ideas nor grasped much of their rationale.

As if to prove himself still a friend of the college, Eliot in 1904 expressed worry that so large a proportion of new endowment was going to the professional schools. It was easy enough to echo this complaint of Dean Briggs, a trusted associate. But the strident objections of Charles Francis Adams and the intricate anti-naturalism of Irving Babbitt were not designed to convert the president. After Adams's Columbia address Eliot launched a counterattack. Significantly, he presented one of his most forthright rebuttals to students. Surely they could be counted on to support the ideology that had liberated them. "Now just in the last few years," he told new students in 1906, "we have had a striking illustration of strong reaction against prevailing educational policies. There has come upon us right here on these grounds and among Harvard's constituents, and widespread over the country as well, a distrust of freedom for students, of freedom for citizens, of freedom for backward races of men. That is one of the striking phenomena of our day, a distrust of freedom." The linking of liberalism in education to other human freedoms revealed a man who felt himself part of a universal struggle. In the name of freedom Eliot kept his distance from the college counterreformers, and in private correspondence he accused some of his critics of educational obscurantism.[35]

In the drive for higher undergraduate standards Eliot was sympathetic, though not creative. He described the honors programs rather mildly, as "guidance for students who desire to make a judicious specialization in their studies." An Overseers' plan for more public marks of approval for the best students got a cold reception from Eliot. "High scholarship in college must . . . be its own reward through the acquisition of the habits and powers of the scholar, and this reward cannot be enhanced by efforts after publicity through public meetings, special garments, or decorations which only high scholars can wear." [36]

Eliot's responses to charges of atomism and loneliness at Harvard included appealing to "university spirit" and listing various scholarly clubs, summer engineering programs, and debating teams as "opportunity for beginning congenial companionships." He was troubled by the growing preference for small colleges. "If, as time goes on," he said, "it shall appear that Harvard College has outgrown its organization, the thing to do is to enlarge the organization." But if as his critics suggested, growth had killed collegiate virtues, then not organizational enlargement (presumably more deans), but decentralization was called for. The pattern of English residential colleges was repeatedly suggested for Harvard, but Eliot never warmed to it. He believed that human relations must have intensity; thus, though he failed to solve the problem of personal isolation at Harvard, he refused to settle for counterfeit fellowship. "To know by name and pat on the back two hundred men is not much of an object; but to know a few men body and soul, and to have sympathetic intercourse with these few, is a large part of what a university can do for youth." [37]

Toward the end of his forty-year tenure the original iconoclast could scarcely avoid appearing as something of an icon. When Charles T. Copeland observed the stuffed head of a deer in the New York Harvard Club, he claimed to be reminded of Eliot, suggesting the slightly inhuman nimbus that had gathered with the years. Puzzled by the driving dissatisfaction of Lawrence Lowell, Eliot asked a younger faculty member, "What is it this man wants?" He never fully found out, nor did he foresee much help from that quarter for Harvard's new time of troubles. His last annual report did not make cheerful reading. "The University finds itself in a position of extreme isolation, which has checked its growth as regards numbers, and checked the expenditure of the Corporation for intellectual objects." The only corrective he suggested was a frank adoption of the three-year degree.[38]

Lowell was not magnanimous in his inaugural address. He

named the presidents of Dartmouth, Princeton, Yale, and M.I.T. as prominently as he did the outgoing president of Harvard. In aphorisms almost as trenchant as those in Eliot's inaugural of 1869 he emphasized the division between his ideals and Eliot's. "May we not feel that the most vital measure for saving the college is not to shorten its duration, but to ensure that it shall be worth saving? . . . It is [in the college] that character ought to be shaped, that aspirations ought to be formed, that citizens ought to be trained, and scholarly tastes implanted. . . . We must go forward and develop the elective system, making it really systematic. . . . Taken gradually, liberty is a powerful stimulant; but taken suddenly in large doses, it is liable to act as an intoxicant or an opiate." [39]

Pointedly, Lowell obtained Woodrow Wilson for Phi Beta Kappa speaker and Wendell for Phi Beta Kappa poet in the spring of 1909. They were selected to mark the sharpness of the change from Eliot's regime, and they performed their task adroitly, Wilson prescribing for the college "a new synthesis, a definite aim, and new processes of authoritative direction" and Wendell presenting his satirical poem, "De Pracside Magnifico." [40]

The day of Lowell's inauguration, October 6, 1909, was, of course, a day for Eliot to take second place. He was all generosity and optimism. But there was a shade of incomprehension still, even with the counterreform victoriously under way. He chose to emphasize Lowell's attainments as a scholar, with the comforting implication that the whole range of university reforms would be appreciated and secure under him. Eliot even managed to find favoring words for the concentration-distribution idea. His grounds for welcoming it were made clearer, however, in an address three months later. He then based his praise on the conclusion that "any young man going to Harvard College who could not find under this so-called new prescription all the freedom of choice of studies he needed had not wits enough to be worth a college education," and he also noted that liberal exceptions were to be made to the new rules.

In the address he gave before the alumni following Lowell's inauguration, Eliot attempted to define the purposes of American universities and colleges. One purpose, Eliot explained, was "to promote genuine, thorough, comprehensive scholarship." But with this quick obeisance to one of the central achievements of his administration, he hurried on to the second purpose: "to send forth into the American community an annual flood of young men who mean to serve their country and their race, who have enough of the keen sense of public duty, and who mean to respond to the great call of free institutions." Lowell and his allies may well have concluded that Eliot still missed their point. Instead of "floods of men," they preferred a phrase that emphasized quality. "Service" and "public duty" some of them accepted as collegiate aims, but not elevated above perpetuation of the cultural heritage. And a Barrett Wendell felt no need of qualifying his admiration for institutions with the adjective "free." [41]

IV

President Lowell refused to grant interviews to newspapermen, a break from the practice of his predecessor.[42] In other ways also a distinct turning inward came with the change in presidents, especially for the college. Lowell's praise for Eliot's achievement in reforming the professional schools by its very frequency emphasized his negative judgment on Eliot's program for the college. During Lowell's administration undergraduates were encouraged to consider themselves part of the community of Harvard College, a thing good in itself. Their intellectual and cultural acquirements were rarely described to them as preparation for a future vocation.

With the new requirements for concentration and distribution, the college departed from the principal institutional product of Eliot's individualism, the free elective system. It had served well in breaking the curricular lockstep and freeing departments to introduce advanced courses, but because it had cured some major institutional ills, Eliot tended to regard it as an educational panacea. He remained blind to less admirable concomitants—dilettantism, self-indulgence, and loss of any necessary connection in students' eyes between intellect and college courses. Those who came to Harvard valuing the A.B. chiefly as a symbol of social status could graduate without awakening to intellectual meaning in the collegiate experience. In this sense, traditional complaints about social snobbery at Harvard remained valid.

Eliot's faith in individualism might be judged antisocial had he not imagined the work ethic as virtually universal. For him, joy came through productive labor. Since man sought happiness, he would naturally seek the satisfactions of work, and the most fulfilling was that which helped others. Introspection showed Eliot precisely such motivations, and a good many other Americans believed in them. But there were other sources of happiness, especially for eighteen-year-olds, which equaled or exceeded work and preparation for work. Outside the university people were more likely to see the young men of Harvard pursuing less elevated pleasures, and a generation of Harvard fiction-writers and journalists publicized the nonintellectual side of the college.[43]

When the public listened to Eliot it heard him ringing the changes on the elective system's authentic emergence from American liberty. In an increasingly complex society, moreover, a great variety of differently trained individuals could be presented as a social necessity. Both democracy and industrial development were served by the elective system, and in its religious application—voluntary services—it testified to the workability of religious pluralism. Significantly, under President Lowell the elective system was reformed, not abolished. For all its shortcomings, it went far toward redeeming Eliot's pledge to build an American university.

Where did liberal education fit in Eliot's university? At one time he claimed that all Harvard College courses were liberal, and he rejected the test of utility until education became specifically professional. But his definition of liberal education was considerably different from the idea of prescribing the best from man's past cultural achievements. For Eliot any education was liberal that led to an open mind and broad sympathies. Much of high school and adult education he accordingly considered liberal.

It was fitting that he spelled out these ideas most fully before a huge educational convention. Just as the true gentleman became in Eliot's lexicon one who was also a democrat, so there was to be a "new definition of the cultivated man." The cultural side of a Harvard education, according to Eliot, was not esoteric, but part of a process widely shared among youth and adults. Even if not specifically prescribed, the ideal of broadened sympathies complemented the notion of specialization usually associated with Eliot's educational individualism.[44]

The elective system conveniently allowed simultaneous pursuit of ideals of culture, research, vocationalism, and mental discipline. Although eclectically embracing them all, Eliot cared most for mental discipline. In his rationale for the college, training the minds of the students held first place. His modifications of the theory of mental discipline were original and timely. It should mean, he argued, not symmetrical development of an all-around man, but the strengthening of a natural bent, the nurturing by formal education of what nature or early environment had already favored.

Some counterbalancing of Eliot's educational individualism came in the work of the professional schools. There the student must submit to prescription, he admitted, since the profession represented theory, skills, and ethics that superseded individual self-development. Professionalism was an idea of increasing importance in Eliot's educational and social thought. Like electivism, it was already institutionalized in Harvard University before he became president, but his theory of professionalism and the application of his administrative talents strengthened it immensely.

Americans have not always liked professionals or the institutions that train them. A Massachusetts farmer had complained in 1798 that the colleges were less sure to teach the principles of republicanism than the techniques for preserving the dignity and emoluments of a profession.[45] Eliot strived to focus public attention on the service the professional rendered. Much as he and his fellow Mugwumps had advocated a civil service improved by examinations for trained capacity, he argued that the higher standards which universities could set for the professions made practitioners more effective.

The stress on expertise in professionalism did not easily square with equalitarian notions of political democracy. The social dominance of professionals that marked Progressivism was bluntly advocated by Eliot: professionals were justifiably more truly directors of the society than were elected officials. The control suggested for the specially educated sounded like aristocracy, and it particularly roused suspicions when advocated by a member of the Eastern patriciate. In response, Eliot, who saw the "managerial" class as a distinct social entity, argued that under American conditions it would not be exclusively hereditary. This was good Brahmin doctrine. A major function of the American university was to render professional status accessible to individuals whatever their family background. The university would keep its costs low, aid the poor student, and broaden the range of suitable preparatory education. The state universities had many advantages over Harvard in pursuing this vision, but even with the handicaps of his institutional setting Eliot effectively sounded the theme of accessibility. Whatever the origins of the social managers, however, the control Eliot wanted them to assume undercut his older conception of America as full of "self-reliant freemen" and his faith in the people's ability to produce leaders like Lincoln.

Professionalism took such a central place in Eliot's thought that he forced the Graduate School of Arts and Sciences into the professional mold. Here, in a program whose participants usually justified it by ideals of truth for its own sake or of liberal culture, Eliot insisted on interjecting the notion of preparation for a special lifework. Of course such an interpretation made the graduate program easier to defend before the public. The new scholars, no matter how recondite their fields, could be honored as experts who gave service (even if the service was the rather mysterious affair of accumulating knowledge and teaching others to do likewise). Having defended the scholar's nonutilitarian standards in the 1890s, Eliot shifted to more worldly imagery after 1900. As Progressivism increased the governmental role of specialists, he spoke of scholars as if they were all aggressively concerned to improve American society.

Specialization is the term that represents the tendency of Eliot's educational reforms most completely. Almost immediately upon his accession to the presidency he divided administrative responsibilities among new deanships. Although the free elective system did not guarantee undergraduate specialization, it made the practice increasingly possible, and Eliot believed that it often occurred unconsciously. By freeing faculty from required elementary courses, the elective system succeeded brilliantly in encouraging their specialization. For both students and faculty the earned A.M. and the Ph.D. served the same purpose. Specialization in the professional schools was intensified by higher entrance standards and increased degree requirements.

It was part of Eliot's public task to show this specialization as a proper function for the American university, no matter how anti-equalitarian it seemed. He had asserted in the 1860s that an American university must be created, an institution not directly copied from other societies, but growing out of American conditions. In its accessibility, internal freedom, and willingness to concern itself with applications of knowledge, the university shaped by Eliot and his contemporaries suited a young industrial democracy. They could effectively appeal to nationalistic desires for achievement and the American ambition to refute Old World charges of inferiority. On these grounds even the specialists in abstruse and nonutilitarian fields could be defended.

Another mode of institutional justification was to picture the university as purposely diverging from dominant social goals. Human achievements that neither industrialism nor democracy advanced, such as theology and the fine arts ("poetry and philosophy," Eliot liked to say), were protected within the university. Eliot's metaphor of the storehouse had the merit of suggesting protection and preservation of what was not immediately demanded by the society. The storehouse was for "truth." That term proved remarkably elastic, making room for a great range of studies.

But accumulated truth concerned Eliot less than did active individuals well trained in their specialties. He scorned an older version of the American individual, the jack-of-all-trades. America needed not individuals who could do everything—that was a notion fit for savagery rather than civilization—but an aggregation of individuals whose varying skills were complementary. Eliot, well versed in Adam Smith's description of the division of labor, and vividly aware of the importance Darwinism attached to individual variation, sought to elaborate these ideas in educational theory. In restructuring American education, he built upon the principle that human variety, especially variety of minds, was a major social good.

America's President Eliot

The belief in progress in its most naïve form is still held by multitudes, especially in America. It may be doubted, however, whether in the future anyone of a distinction comparable to that of President Eliot will be able to hold it with the same bland confidence.

IRVING BABBITT (1929) [1]

To an exchange professor from Germany, the public excitement when Eliot announced his retirement in 1909 suggested that a change more important than that of the United States presidency was at hand. But popular interest was probably less aroused because Harvard was to have a new president than because President Eliot was at a turning point in his career. It was predictable that he would not drop from public sight. "Again and again," the German visitor remarked, "one hears or sees him characterized in America as 'our first private citizen' or as 'our greatest moral force as an individual.' " [2]

Eliot did not feel obliged to remove himself from all positions of responsibility at Harvard. Although as an Overseer from 1910 to 1916 he generally limited himself to providing information on past practice, that in itself could make change more difficult, given the clarity and logic of his explanations. In Lowell's opinion Eliot had erred in accepting the post of Overseer—and also in keeping his residence in Cambridge, where he was accessible to complainers. It was not unknown in faculty debate for a professor to support his position by reference to a recent visit with the president emeritus. In fatherly letters to his successor Eliot advised of the presidential duty to protect staff members who were "over-working or over-smoking," offered to counsel an obstreperous professor, and insisted that though the attitude of undergraduates toward their work was improving, the new awards of "artificial distinctions" were not the cause.[3]

His pension from the Carnegie Foundation for the Advancement of Teaching required Eliot's resignation from that body, where he had been chairman of the board, but there were other foundations which gave play to his abilities, notably the General Education Board and the Carnegie Endowment for International Peace. Besides education and world peace, his reform activities embraced civil service, municipal government, capital-labor relations, conservation, and sex hygiene. As his age advanced and the number of groups with which he was associated increased, it became clear that even his name alone was valuable, an imprimatur for good causes. Seeking to find unity in his burgeoning activities, Eliot noted that they were all "subjects of reform" and "all forwarded by voluntary associations." Finding many Harvard men similarly involved, he claimed proof that Harvard had taught "love of freedom, seconded by a profound purpose to serve free institutions and the country." [4]

Eliot supported these causes by traveling widely, a practice he had already developed during his presidency to a degree that caused criticism at Harvard. He sat in countless board and committee meetings and held himself ready to speak, often more than once a day. His most ambitious journey was a trip around the world in 1911–12, on behalf of the Carnegie Endowment. In 1917 he resigned some of his most demanding board memberships (he was then eighty-three), and increasingly he found his effective line of communication through letters to newspapers and magazine articles. It was chiefly thus that he propagated his pro-Allied, pro-League of Nations views during World War I and after.[5] When a volume of articles and addresses he had written between the ages of eighty and ninety appeared in 1924, the editor found the only problem to be an embarrassment of riches, and even then, the end was not yet.[6] Meanwhile, the press continued its attentions. If Eliot did not volunteer a statement on an issue of the day, some newspaperman sought one from him. The public seemed not to tire of Eliot's life story, and his aphorisms made good editorial leads.

Of these multifarious labors, one in which he became involved shortly after announcing his retirement, the Harvard Classics, was particularly controversial and significant. The project grew out of his broadening sense of what education should mean in America. Although the venture revived charges against him of cultural shallowness and commercial-mindedness, it met a success that reflected his wide following among the general public.[7]

Eliot had for some years urged the importance of continuing education beyond the period of formal schooling, especially when schooling ended early. Although he supported evening schools and free lectures, he dwelt particularly on self-education through good reading. The boom in correspondence schools and Chautauqua reading circles, he noted, indicated a general wish for better fare than daily newspapers. In some of his addresses Eliot urged good reading in conspicuously quantified terms. A five-foot shelf, he asserted, could hold all the books needed to give a liberal education, and fifteen minutes a day of reading would eventually encompass that end. These remarks caught the attention of Robert Collier of P. F. Collier and Son, a publishing house with a thriving book subscription department. He sent Norman Hapgood, editor of *Collier's Weekly* and a Harvard alumnus, to urge Eliot to select such a shelf of books. In his interview Hapgood stressed the derivation of the plan from Eliot's own public statements and argued that the name "Harvard Classics" would spread awareness of the university into distant regions and small towns and that it would associate Harvard with good reading. Eliot not only agreed to serve as editor, he won the support of the Harvard Corporation for the use of the university's name.[8]

The publisher's skill in advertising and subscription selling, the public's interest in Eliot, and the intriguing possibilities of a yet-to-be-formed list of books aroused wide attention. Among many criticisms some were as gentle as those of Mr. Dooley, who twitted "Charles," a bright-faced neophyte in the "univarsity iv th' Wicked Wurruld," with behaving like a typical freshman by telling people what books they should read; other objections were as bitter as that of an outraged patriot who denounced one selection (a somewhat inaccurate account of the Battle of Gettysburg) and in his remonstrance maligned Eliot as a slacker during the Civil War.[9] But in general the public welcomed another chance to be taught by its favorite schoolman and to associate itself with him. The sets sold far beyond original expectations.

The most elaborate criticism of Harvard's role in the enterprise came from John Jay Chapman, a Harvard graduate of 1884 and a relentless gadfly. Soon after advertisements for the project began to appear (promising Harvard crimson bindings and an "Eliot" watermark), Chapman sent an open letter to Eliot asking by what authority the name of Harvard was put to commercial use. Receiving no answer, he sent a similar letter to Henry L. Higginson. Then in a thoughtful appraisal of the affair, which admitted his own faulty tactics and "desire to give pain," Chapman interpreted it as part of the rise of business values in universities and their deepening allegiance to statistically measured success. He shrewdly appraised the motives of the three parties involved. "The spreading of the influence of Harvard, then, is what the trustees had in mind—the making of a little money and the doing of a great deal of good is what Dr. Eliot had in mind: the making of a great deal of money and the doing of a little good is what *Collier's* had in mind. But here is the point: Once launched, *Collier's* is in control."

Chapman granted that such popularized culture was justified in America and that bad taste in advertising would carry the books where good taste would not. But for Harvard to do the cultural spoon-feeding was, he maintained, an abandonment of its mission "to be a touchstone and a safe counselor to those who honor learning and who desire to be led toward her." Chapman broadened his critique to include the "booster" activities of alumni clubs and the drive for more students, and he urged businessmen on governing boards to yield their places to scholars and scientists.[10] The *Nation* joined the complaint: "To give the multitude to understand that fifteen minutes a day solemnly applied to the task of working off the set of books, inch by inch, will transform anybody into a man of liberal education, is to turn the whole idea of our colleges into ridicule; and a final touch of grotesqueness is added when the five-foot shelf, instead of being vaguely indicated or left to the imagination, is expressly prescribed, and arrangements duly made to supply it, the same for all comers, through the familiar machinery of the subscription coupon." [11]

The publisher was indeed in control in matters of form and presentation. Advertisements used Eliot's portrait, bindings bore the Harvard seal, the venture was puffed in the pages of *Collier's Weekly*, and Eliot found himself in the role of plaintiff in one of the lawsuits against piratical imitators. The contents of the first three volumes were chosen by a publisher's staff member (though with Eliot's eventual concurrence), and the retiring Harvard president found himself under pressure to decide on three or four volumes a month. He drew on the expertise of members of the Harvard faculty, and William A. Neilson, a professor of English who acted as assistant editor, poured vast energies into the venture. But while some professors cooperated, others objected much as Chapman had, and they voiced their disapproval in a Harvard faculty meeting.[12]

Eliot responded to critics in the careful phrases of his introduction (which appeared in the last volume, an oddity necessitated by the publishing schedule). He spoke of what could be gained by "careful and persistent" and "observant" readers. His selections, he claimed, offered to such readers the knowledge of literature essential to a cultivated man in the twentieth century. For Eliot, however, the most important attainment of a cultivated man remained "a liberal frame of mind or way of thinking." Properly used, his shelf of books could contribute to this quality also, leaving the reader's mind "enriched, refined, and fertilized." Although he avoided the term "liberal education" in the introduction, he had earlier maintained that such education need not be limited to the few.[13]

It was not a collection of the "greatest books" that Eliot sought to gather, but a record of human thought. His decisions ranged from the fruitful idea of an anthology of prefaces to the idiosyncratic inclusion of Manzoni's *I Promessi Sposi*. Far from being cultural pabulum, the series was generally judged to be excessively erudite, probably because Eliot drew on scholarly specialists for suggestions. His advice to readers included a plea for tolerance and a reaffirmation of progressive optimism. "The sentiments and opinions these authors express are frequently not acceptable to present-day readers, who have to be often saying to themselves: 'This is not true, or not correct, or not in accordance with our beliefs.' It is, however, precisely this encounter with the mental states of other generations which enlarges the outlook and sympathies of the cultivated man, and persuades him of the upward tendency of the human race." A reader's guide in the last volume outlined different courses of study that could be pursued through particular readings, thus applying the elective principle to the collection. Nor was the shelf presented as exclusive. Its use, Eliot hoped, would lead to serious reading of books not included in the Classics.[14]

Eliot's critics did not convert him. A decade after he decided to edit the series, he recalled the disapproval of Harvard graduates, but judged the Classics "a good and durable piece of work from the educational point of view." [15] He and Neilson edited a twenty-volume Harvard Classics Shelf of Fiction in 1917.

Although the Harvard Classics seem to have been a rather incongruous addendum to the Eliot administration, his admission reforms had been an attempt to make liberal education more widely accessible, and the Classics followed reasonably upon them. The chosen books, by their very nonutilitarianism, strengthened the idea of learning as good in itself, an idea that had been only a muted theme in Eliot's educational philosophy. Chapman noted correctly that the series bearing his university's name was to be cheap and popular.[16] But was Harvard the loser thereby? Culture is something that is not diminished by being shared. What was diminished, if anything, was the elitist connotation of a Harvard degree. After the name "Harvard" graced bookcases in middle class homes throughout the nation, fifty replicas of the Harvard seal proclaiming "Veritas" from the bindings, there was probably less certainty that a Harvard degree stood for highly esoteric attainments. But it is hard to imagine a case in which reading the Classics kept someone from attending college or made him less willing for his children to do so.

In an American tradition of popularization that extends from Franklin's almanacs to public television, Eliot's venture into mass-market publishing deserves an honorable place. Some purchasers, of course, sought only the prestige of possession and were not "careful and persistent" readers. Mr. Dooley satirized this aspect of the undertaking, assuring Mr. Hennessy that Eliot had the right idea with his five-foot shelf. "He real-izes that th' first thing to have in a libry is a shelf. Fr'm time to time this can be decorated with lithrachure. But th' shelf is th' main thing. Otherwise th' libry may get mixed up with readin' matther on th' table. Th' shelf shud thin be nailed to th' wall iliven feet fr'm th' flure an' hermetically sealed." Decades later, however, it seemed appropriate to Saul Bellow to include among the adventures of the well-meaning Augie March the perusal of a fire-damaged set of the Harvard Classics. The books found readers even beyond the ambitious middle and working classes Eliot had in mind— for example, Malcolm X during his term in Norfolk Prison. At the time of Eliot's death, a resident of Washington, D.C., sent to Harvard a copy of his poetic eulogy, which called to witness the Five-Foot Shelf, treasured in every clime by men "Who appreciate a great man's worth/Obeying his word read while in earth." [17]

Gradually Eliot's public role passed beyond what could properly be designated by the term "educator." Men used such words as "sage," "oracle," and "prophet" when they tried to describe his relationship to the mass of Americans. His university presidency was his first platform for reaching the public, but his influence far transcended that office. What Eliot said and how he said it were the secrets of his continuing ability to catch people's attention.

The question to be discussed was usually made clear in Eliot's title or opening phrase. His style was simple and direct, his language explicit, and generalizations demonstrated by example. Rather than a Latin epigram or an ornate figure, the reader found a quotation from Emerson, a homely autobiographical anecdote, or an observation of the behavior of everyday folk. If there was little humor, there was a refreshing outspokenness. One could imagine in reading Eliot's articles that he had made some readers angry. It widened his following when Samuel Gompers said, "He lives in an age he does not understand," or when Billy Sunday called him "so low-down he would need an aeroplane to get into hell." [18]

But by and large, Eliot's matter was as pleasing to Americans as his manner. He was saying what most Americans believed but did not articulate. He put the conventional wisdom into phrases of "lapidary inevitability." [19] Liberal individualism, expansive optimism, ethical idealism, faith in work and progress made up the ideological blend that motivated most Americans and held together their society. "The public," Eliot's biographer Henry James recognized, "expects eminent men to tell it over again the truths that are ancient and familiar." Hence the journalistic shrewdness of the headline, "Dr. Eliot Advocates Marriage." Hence the readership for "What Life Means to Charles W. Eliot: The Hopeful Creed of a Nonagenarian." Eliot's advice was often highly personal. If a man was in a profession he disliked, he should leave it. Young people should be less self-centered. Small items of considerateness made the mosaic of married happiness.[20]

Eliot did more than celebrate the obvious, however. He applied a familiar social philosophy, whose flexibility he helped reveal, to new problems: to industrial conflict (which might yield to profit-sharing), to nationwide prohibition (a justifiable encroachment on individual liberty, though the Volstead Act might well be amended to allow light beer), to the League of Nations (the United States was duty-bound to join and to promote world federalism).[21]

Special risks come from public acceptance of a sage. He may pontificate on matters about which he knows too little to render a worthwhile judgment. Even Eliot's remarkable gift for informing himself was inadequate to the range of matters on which he ventured opinions. It was ironic that one who had criticized the jack-of-all-trades phenomenon in America and encouraged specialization and professionalism should himself offer judgments on issues across the spectrum of human events, and should become, in Ralph Barton Perry's phrase, "adviser-at-large to the American people on things-in-general." [22]

There is danger, too, that the sage may rigidify public thought by continuing to affirm ideas whose time has passed. Irving Babbitt, in expounding the New Humanism, found Eliot a useful negative symbol. In Babbitt's eyes, he corrupted his fellow men by propagating the naturalistic sentimentalism of the nineteenth century. The multitudes, Babbitt maintained, continued to believe in a naïve doctrine of progress and in innate human goodness even when faced with such contrary evidence as World War I, and they clung to Eliot and his words because no other man of such obvious distinction any longer shared their confidence. Eliot was, accordingly, an unfortunate anachronism.[23]

Babbitt scoffed at Eliot's fundamental social belief: that man had an instinctual fellow-feeling which let him find his happiness through service to others, and that hence man could be trusted with liberty. But Eliot, in his support of universities and professions and in his increased willingness to embrace collective solutions to social problems, had passed beyond laissez-faire individualism. Objections to him as an extreme individualist might apply to his persistent advocacy of unqualified electivism and his complaint about labor union monopolism, but they no longer came to grips with most of his social and political programs. The Eliot of the twentieth century believed in organizational solutions to the problems of an industrial democracy, even though he urged "collectivism which does not suppress individualism."

Those who compared Eliot to earlier American heroes claimed to see in him the executive force of Washington, the practical wisdom of Franklin, the vision of Emerson, and the humanitarianism of Lincoln. Often he was called a Puritan, but always a Puritan with a difference—humanized, democratic, or liberal. Probably because the post-presidential years were nearer to them, writers of obituaries and two early biographies suggested that his seventeen years after leaving the presidency matched or exceeded the influence of his Harvard administration. Wondering who could replace him as public oracle, the *Christian Century* thought of Elihu Root, Henry Ford, and John Dewey, but rejected them all, concluding that Eliot's qualifications had been unique.[24]

Eliot's death on August 22, 1926, was followed by that of Rudolph Valentino a day later. *Time*, then in its infancy, ran the two obituaries under the heading "Heroes." For Eliot it repeated the now legendary tale of his university reforms and the even more familiar story of his old age, when he refused to "reminisce, dodder or preach plaintively." The briefer account of Valentino's death told of hysterical fans, a plan for perpetual preservation of the body, and a producer's million-dollar life insurance policy on the star.[25] The juxtaposition of the two lives provided an effective contrast of American values. But the paragon of old-fashioned virtues, though he never listened to the radio or saw films, had himself sought a mass audience, first through oratory and travel, then through the printed word. Perhaps Eliot, even more than the motion picture idol, had volunteered to be a national hero. In him Americans had wanted to embody their faith in progress, in the efficacy of work, and in human educability. He had accepted the call to be America's President Eliot.

Bibliographical Note

Included here are the most important sources used in the construction of this volume, as well as books that provide the logical next step for readers who wish to pursue various aspects of the subject.

Manuscript Collections

The principal source for this book was the Charles William Eliot Papers in the Harvard University Archives. The Papers, in nearly five hundred boxes, owes much to Eliot's orderly habits and justifiable sense of his significance. Besides family correspondence, the Papers includes many documents from his early career at Harvard. For the presidential period, there is little outgoing correspondence until the 1890s. From then on, both outgoing and incoming correspondence are quite complete. Also in the collection, filed in unnumbered boxes at the end, are many newspaper clippings. (Even more of these can be found in Eliot's file in the Biographical Collection of the Harvard University Archives.) Especially useful was the series of some nine hundred articles and addresses by Eliot, many in manuscript. Although this series is not complete, it allowed study of his less permanent and less popular utterances, some of which were never published, others of which were understandably bypassed in anthologies of his writing. A good many fugitive items published by official Harvard bodies are preserved in the Eliot Papers.

The Abbott Lawrence Lowell Papers, also in the Harvard Uni-

versity Archives, contains valuable correspondence between critics of Eliot's regime and reveals Eliot's rather distant relations
with his successor.

The Records of the Overseers of Harvard College, in the Archives, is particularly useful for its evidence of alumni resistance
to policies of the university administration.

Other collections and items in the Harvard Archives are best
pursued through the shelflists. The "Private Journal of John
Langdon Sibley of Harvard University Library," a detailed daily
account of Harvard affairs which reaches into the early years of
the Eliot presidency, deserves particular mention.

Various collections in the Houghton Library, Harvard University, include letters to and from Eliot. I list here those from
which more than one item was cited:

Edwin Lawrence Godkin Papers
Thomas Wentworth Higginson Papers
Charles Eliot Norton Papers
John Tetlow Papers

In the Manuscript Division, Sterling Library, Yale University,
various letters show the relations of Harvard with its friendly
rival. The Brush Family Papers is especially valuable for many
letters of Eliot, his friends, and his enemies to George Jarvis
Brush of the Sheffield Scientific School. The Whitney Family Papers contains correspondence of William Dwight Whitney, who
declined an invitation to Harvard, and Josiah Dwight Whitney,
who accepted.

In the Manuscript Division, Milton Eisenhower Library, Johns
Hopkins University, advice and information shared by university
presidents, including Eliot, can be traced in the Daniel Coit Gilman Papers.

The William Barton Rogers Papers, in the Archives of the
Massachusetts Institute of Technology, and the minutes of
M.I.T. faculty meetings, in the Registrar's Office, both shed light
on a phase of Eliot's career somewhat scanted in the Eliot Papers.

A few glimpses of Harvard can be caught in the Presidential
Collection, Special Collections, University of Chicago.

Official and Semiofficial Publications
of Harvard University

Second only to the Eliot Papers in providing the central strand of this study was the *Annual Report of the President of Harvard University*. Eliot elevated the status of such reports through his openness and boldness in controversy. Often summarized in the press, they were an important avenue to the general community. Although each report is a survey of the completed year, Eliot usually emphasized a particular theme, such as the elective system or the elevation of professional education. Appended to his report were the reports of the treasurer, various deans, and heads of special branches of the university. The reports of Dean LeBaron R. Briggs highlighted aspects of the university that found little place in the president's own report.

The *Harvard University Catalogue* is a monument to the rationalizing processes of the Eliot administration and the curricular expansion under the elective system.

The *Harvard Graduates' Magazine*, founded in 1892, was remarkably inclusive during the Eliot years. In it can be found statements by Eliot and his opponents in the Harvard community, reports of alumni gatherings, and a quarterly review of university affairs, written for some years by Albert Bushnell Hart and later by other faculty members. Though directed toward alumni, the magazine revealed the stance of the university toward the general public.

The *Harvard Monthly* (1885–1917), a student-controlled periodical, often invited contributions from faculty and alumni. Its editorials gave the reactions of serious students to Eliot's policies.

The survivor among various student newspapers, the *Harvard Crimson*, was strongly oriented toward athletics in its early days. On that issue it differed from Eliot, but it was not given to controversy with the administration.

Valuable aids in identifying Eliot's contemporaries at Harvard are the *Harvard University Quinquennial Catalogue of the Offi-*

cers and Graduates (of which I used the 1930 edition), *Historical Register of Harvard University, 1636–1936* (Cambridge, 1937), and the biographical sketches in various class reports.

Books by Charles W. Eliot
Eliot's *American Contributions to Civilization and Other Essays and Addresses* (New York, 1897) shows the educator reaching out into social philosophy and policy. His next book, *Educational Reform: Essays and Addresses* (New York, 1898), published when he was most deeply concerned with the lower schools, extends well beyond university matters. Liberal optimism suffuses both volumes. *Report of the Committee on Secondary School Studies Appointed at the Meeting of the National Educational Association, July 9, 1892* (Washington, D.C., 1893) was the work of Eliot more than of any other person. Eliot's stock-taking as he left office appears in *University Administration* (Boston, 1908).

The biography of his son, *Charles Eliot: Landscape Architect* (Boston, 1902), includes Eliot's detailed interpretation of one individual's education. The son's interest in conservation and the early stages of city planning helped expand the father's sympathy for collective forms of social action as he traced various programs in the biography. Further evidence of Eliot's modification of his earlier social theory appears in the brief *The Conflict between Individualism and Collectivism in a Democracy* (New York, 1910).

Publishers' eagerness to turn Eliot's addresses into short volumes indicated his growing following among Americans. The most important examples for this study are *More Money for the Public Schools* (New York, 1903), *Four American Leaders* (Boston, 1906), and *Education for Efficiency* (Boston, 1909).

A Late Harvest: Miscellaneous Papers Written between Eighty and Ninety (Boston, 1924), includes important reminiscences, as does *Harvard Memories* (Cambridge, 1923). Eliot approved for posthumous publication the essays on education and other subjects in William Allan Neilson (ed.), *Charles W. Eliot: The Man and His Beliefs*, 2 vols. (New York, 1926).

Books about Charles W. Eliot
One biography of Eliot appeared while he was still living, Eugen
Kuehnemann, *Charles W. Eliot: President of Harvard University*
(May 19, 1869–May 19, 1909) (Boston, 1909). The author, a
German scholar who had taught two years at Harvard as an exchange
professor, was an ardent admirer of the university's president.
Three biographies appeared at two-year intervals after Eliot's
death. Edward H. Cotton, *The Life of Charles W. Eliot* (Boston,
1926), pays more attention to Eliot's interest in lower schools
than the other biographies, but is valuable chiefly for showing the
full development of an Eliot legend. Henry Hallam Saunderson,
Charles W. Eliot: Puritan Liberal (New York, 1928), laden with
quotations, seeks to establish Eliot's continuity with Channing
and Emerson.

The major biography is Henry James, *Charles W. Eliot: Presi-*
dent of Harvard University, 1869–1909, 2 vols. (Boston, 1930),
one of the finest examples of the life-and-letters form of biography. James, the son of a Harvard professor and a student there at
the apex of Eliot's power, wrote with a participant's understanding, though his use of manuscripts was careful and thorough. The
tracing of the man's psychology and his influence on others is
deft and sure. James fails to do justice to Eliot's critics, however,
and he scarcely mentions Eliot's efforts in secondary education.
The work includes a "Bibliography of Eliot's Principal Writings."

Raymond Henry Fisher, "Charles W. Eliot's Views on College
Education in the Light of Present Trends" (Ph.D. dissertation,
University of Illinois, 1935) suggests the drop in Eliot's influence
and reputation during the 1930s.

Histories of Harvard University
In editing *The Development of Harvard University since the In-*
auguration of President Eliot, 1869–1929 (Cambridge, 1930),
Samuel Eliot Morison performed a lasting service to historians by

having departmental representatives write of their own parts of the university, thus drawing on memory and oral tradition as well as the written record. Morison himself contributed essays on the curriculum, government and administration, and the history department. Although part of a broader survey, the portions dealing with the Eliot years in Morison's *Three Centuries of Harvard, 1636–1936* (Cambridge, 1936) provide a stimulating interpretation. On the professional schools and related studies I found guidance in the following: Thomas Francis Harrington, *The Harvard Medical School: A History, Narrative and Documentary, 1782–1905*, 3 vols. (New York, 1905); Arthur E. Sutherland, *The Law at Harvard: A History of Ideas and Men, 1817–1967* (Cambridge, 1967); George Huntston Williams (ed.), *The Harvard Divinity School: Its Place in Harvard University and in American Culture* (Boston, 1954); Melvin T. Copeland, *And Mark an Era: The Story of the Harvard Business School* (Boston, 1958); and Arthur G. Powell, "The Study of Education at Harvard University, 1870–1920" (Ph.D. dissertation, Harvard University, 1969).

An important book that shows the way to a more sophisticated curricular history is Paul Buck (ed.), *Social Sciences at Harvard, 1860–1920: From Inculcation to the Open Mind* (Cambridge, 1965). Daniel Walker Howe, *The Unitarian Conscience: Harvard Moral Philosophy, 1805–1861* (Cambridge, 1970), illuminates major influences on Eliot during his youth.

Histories of American Higher and Secondary Education
Frederick Rudolph, *The American College and University: A History* (New York, 1962), has been a dependable support throughout the writing of this book; its bibliography is highly instructive. Early in the planning of this book I read Laurence R. Veysey, *The Emergence of the American University* (Chicago, 1965), in dissertation form. His work has affected my undertaking in many ways, some too subtle for formal notice. To single out one of many contributions, I commend his fresh conception of

liberal culture as a coherent educational movement. For guidance concerning the early, largely vain efforts toward university building in America, I have relied on Richard J. Storr, *The Beginnings of Graduate Education in America* (Chicago, 1953).

Richard Hofstadter and Walter P. Metzger, *The Development of Academic Freedom in the United States* (New York, 1955), gains in significance as the years pass; it is far more inclusive than the title suggests. For the disquiet in the colleges while Eliot and others were creating universities, see George E. Peterson, *The New England College in the Age of the University* (Amherst, Mass., 1964). The best history of the elective system is R. Freeman Butts, *The College Charts Its Course: Historical Conceptions and Current Proposals* (New York, 1939), and its bibliography is detailed. I learned much about efforts to connect scholarship with public affairs from Jurgen Herbst, *The German Historical School in American Scholarship: A Study in the Transfer of Culture* (Ithaca, 1965). On the economic necessities that tied science and education to the rest of society, see both Merle Curti and Roderick Nash, *Philanthropy in the Shaping of American Higher Education* (New Brunswick, N.J., 1965), and Howard S. Miller, *Dollars for Research: Science and Its Patrons in Nineteenth-Century America* (Seattle, 1970).

A model collection of original sources is Richard Hofstadter and Wilson Smith (eds.), *American Higher Education: A Documentary History*, 2 vols. (Chicago, 1961).

Of various studies of American secondary education the most relevant for this book have been Edward A. Krug, *The Shaping of the American High School* (New York, 1964); James McLachlan, *American Boarding Schools: A Historical Study* (New York, 1970); and Theodore R. Sizer, *Secondary Schools at the Turn of the Century* (New Haven, 1964). An anthology, Edward A. Krug (ed.), *Charles W. Eliot and Popular Education* (New York, 1961), includes a clarifying introduction. Walter B. Kolesnik, *Mental Discipline in Modern Education* (Madison, 1958), is a history of an often-misrepresented idea important in both secondary and higher education.

The America of Eliot's Day

Among recent interpretive histories of the period of Eliot's major influence, I have found Robert H. Wiebe, *The Search for Order, 1877–1920* (New York, 1967), the most cogent. Samuel P. Hays, *The Response to Industrialism, 1885–1914* (Chicago, 1957), also helps place Eliot in context. It is harder to see Eliot's activities in Ray Ginger, *Age of Excess: The United States from 1877 to 1914* (New York, 1965).

On religious developments I benefited particularly from James Ward Smith and A. Leland Jamison (eds.), *Religion in American Life*, vol. 1, *The Shaping of American Religion* (Princeton, 1961); Franklin Hamlin Littell, *From State Church to Pluralism: A Protestant Interpretation of Religion in American History* (Garden City, 1962); and Alvin Packer Stauffer, "Anti-Catholicism in American Politics, 1865–1900" (Ph.D. dissertation, Harvard University, 1933).

Science in America is ably treated in George H. Daniels, *American Science in the Age of Jackson* (New York, 1968); Daniel J. Kevles, "The Study of Physics in America, 1865–1916" (Ph.D. dissertation, Princeton University, 1964); and Nathan Reingold (ed.), *Science in Nineteenth-Century America: A Documentary History* (New York, 1964).

On economic affairs two volumes by Edward Chase Kirkland were useful: *Dream and Thought in the Business Community, 1860–1900* (Ithaca, 1956), and *Industry Comes of Age: Business, Labor, and Public Policy, 1860–1897* (New York, 1961). Business developments that had certain parallels in university life can be traced in Alfred Dupont Chandler, *Strategy and Structure: Chapters in the History of the Industrial Enterprise* (Cambridge, 1962), and in Thomas C. Cochran and William Miller's classic *The Age of Enterprise: The Social History of Industrial America* (New York, 1942). Much historical murkiness is swept away in Irwin Unger, *The Greenback Era: A Social and Political History of American Finance, 1865–1879* (Princeton, 1964).

Among the many political histories of the Gilded Age and Progressive Era, I gratefully single out two that bear with special directness on Eliot: Geoffrey Blodgett, *The Gentle Reformers: Massachusetts Democrats in the Cleveland Era* (Cambridge, 1966), and John G. Sproat, *"The Best Men": Liberal Reformers in the Gilded Age* (New York, 1968).

Autobiographies and Biographies of Eliot's Contemporaries

For the lives of fellow university presidents rich in social and educational context, see Nicholas Murray Butler, *Across the Busy Years: Recollections and Reflections*, 2 vols. (New York, 1939); G. Stanley Hall, *Life and Confessions of a Psychologist* (New York, 1923); Emma Rogers (ed.), *Life and Letters of William Barton Rogers*, 2 vols. (Boston, 1896); Walter P. Rogers, *Andrew D. White and the Modern University* (Ithaca, 1942); and *Autobiography of Andrew Dickson White*, 2 vols. (New York, 1905).

Faculty members essentially sympathetic with Eliot's program can be studied in Thomas Nixon Carver, *Recollections of an Unplanned Life* (Los Angeles, 1949); A. Hunter Dupree, *Asa Gray, 1810–1888* (Cambridge, 1959); Paul H. Hanus, *Adventuring in Education* (Cambridge, 1937); Ralph Barton Perry, *The Thought and Character of William James . . .*, 2 vols. (Boston, 1935); and Bliss Perry, *And Gladly Teach: Reminiscences* (Boston, 1935). More often in disagreement with Eliot were the subjects of the following: Edward Lurie, *Louis Agassiz: A Life in Science* (Chicago, 1960); Henry Aaron Yeomans, *Abbott Lawrence Lowell, 1856–1943* (Cambridge, 1948); George Santayana, *Persons and Places*, 3 vols. (New York, 1944–1953); and M. A. DeWolfe Howe, *Barrett Wendell and His Letters* (Boston, 1924). A personal supporter of Eliot who had some opposing educational ideals is presented in Rollo Walter Brown, *Dean Briggs* (New York, 1926). It is chiefly for their revelations about Harvard student life that I have used George A. Gordon, *My Education and Religion: An Autobiography* (Boston, 1925); Robert Grant, *Fourscore: An*

Autobiography (Boston, 1934); and *All Our Years: The Auto-biography of Robert Morss Lovett* (New York, 1948).

For the careers of three men thoughtfully critical of Eliot's policies, see *Charles Francis Adams, 1835–1915: An Autobiography* (Boston, 1916); Edward Chase Kirkland, *Charles Francis Adams, Jr., 1835–1915: The Patrician at Bay* (Cambridge, 1965); Richard B. Hovey, *John Jay Chapman: An American Mind* (New York, 1959); M. A. DeWolfe Howe, *John Jay Chapman and His Letters* (Boston, 1937); *I Remember: The Autobiography of Abraham Flexner* (New York, 1940); and *Abraham Flexner: An Autobiography* (New York, 1960).

The subjects of the following were public men or free-lance intellectuals more or less in the Harvard milieu: Harold Francis Williamson, *Edward Atkinson: The Biography of an American Liberal, 1827–1905* (Boston, 1934); Milton Berman, *John Fiske: The Evolution of a Popularizer* (Cambridge, 1961); Rollo Ogden (ed.), *Life and Letters of Edwin Lawrence Godkin*, 2 vols. (New York, 1907); and Tilden G. Edelstein, *Strange Enthusiasm: A Life of Thomas Wentworth Higginson* (New Haven, 1968).

Periodicals

Statements by Eliot and others concerned with educational issues can be found particularly in the following: *Andover Review, Atlantic Monthly, Century Magazine, Educational Review, Forum, Independent, Nation, New England Magazine, North American Review, Outlook, Science, Scribner's Magazine*, and *World's Work*.

Published proceedings of the Association of American Universities, the Association of Colleges and Preparatory Schools of the Middle States and Maryland, and the National Education Association are often revealing because they include the give and take of face-to-face debate as well as formal addresses.

Among Boston newspapers, the *Advertiser* and *Evening Transcript* were likely to express the views of the Harvard administration. More willing to embarrass the university were the *Herald* and the *Traveller*. The presence of a great many clippings in the Eliot Papers and other collections of the Harvard Archives allowed a use of newspaper sources that would otherwise not have been feasible.

Notes

GUIDE TO SPECIAL ABBREVIATIONS AND USAGES IN NOTES

AAU	*Association of American Universities Journal of Proceedings and Addresses*
ACPSMSM	*Association of Colleges and Preparatory Schools of the Middle States and Maryland Proceedings of the Annual Convention*
AR	*Annual Report of the President of Harvard University* (Parenthetical year is the last half of the academic year covered.)
clpg., unident. clpg.	clipping, unidentified clipping
CWE	Charles W. Eliot
DAB	*Dictionary of American Biography*
EP	Charles W. Eliot Papers, HUA
EPA	Addresses and articles by Eliot in EP (The number following is that used in the special card index to these documents.)
HGM	*Harvard Graduates' Magazine*
HL	Houghton Library, Harvard University
HUA	Harvard University Archives
HUC	*Harvard University Catalogue* (Parenthetical year is the last half of the academic year covered.)
MHS	*Massachusetts Historical Society Proceedings*
NEA	*National Education Association Journal of Proceedings and Addresses*
OR	Harvard University Overseers' Records, HUA
YU	Manuscript Division, Sterling Library, Yale University

All letters to or from Eliot are in EP, unless otherwise noted.

"Cambridge" refers in all cases to Cambridge, Massachusetts.

Unless otherwise noted, italics in quotations are in the original.

Where several citations in one note may cause confusion, I have included catch phrases in parentheses, without quotation marks.

PREFACE

1. Henry James, *Charles W. Eliot: President of Harvard University, 1869–1909* (Boston, 1930); Samuel Eliot Morison, *Three Centuries of Harvard, 1636–1936* (Cambridge, 1936); Morison (ed.), *The Development of Harvard University since the Inauguration of President Eliot, 1869–1929* (Cambridge, 1930).

2. Edward A. Krug, *The Shaping of the American High School* (New York, 1964); Theodore R. Sizer, *Secondary Schools at the Turn of the Century* (New Haven, 1964).

3. Frederick Rudolph, *The American College and University: A History* (New York, 1962), esp. ch. 14, "The Elective Principle"; Laurence R. Veysey, *The Emergence of the American University* (Chicago, 1965), 87; Frederic Cople Jaher, "The Boston Brahmins in the Age of Industrial Capitalism," in Jaher (ed.), *The Age of Industrialism in America: Essays in Social Structure and Cultural Values* (New York, 1968), esp. 217; Barbara Miller Solomon, *Ancestors and Immigrants: A Changing New England Tradition* (Cambridge, 1956), ch. 9, "The Minority with Faith."

4. "Inaugural Address as President of Harvard College," in CWE, *Educational Reform: Essays and Addresses* (New York, 1898), 34–35.

CHAPTER I, *Harvard's Mr. Eliot*

1. James, *Eliot*, I:71.

2. For family background, see ibid., vol. I, ch. 1; Mary Eliot Gould, "Samuel Atkins and Mary Eliot: A Memory Sketch by Their Oldest Daughter," typescript, HUA (HUG1359.235). For his pre-collegiate education, see CWE, "Charles William Eliot," *Report of the Harvard Class of 1853* (Cambridge, 1913), 95–96. See also CWE, *Harvard Memories* (Cambridge, 1923), 91, 96–97. The two cousins were Edward C. Guild and Arthur T. Lyman.

3. Quoted in James, *Eliot*, I:30. On the Brahmins: George M. Fredrickson, *The Inner Civil War: Northern Intellectuals and the Crisis of the Union* (New York, 1965), 29; Paul Goodman, "Ethics and Enterprise: The Values of the Boston Elite, 1800–1860," *American Quarterly* 18(1966): 437–51.

4. CWE, *Four American Leaders* (Boston, 1906), 122–23; Robin W. Winks, "Introduction," *An Autobiography of the Reverend Josiah Henson* (Reading, Mass., 1969), xiii; CWE to [his father?], Feb. 24, [1851] (abolitionist press); CWE to Carleton Hunt, Sept. 10, 1907; David Donald,

Charles Sumner and the Coming of the Civil War (New York, 1960), 185–86.

5. [Samuel A. Eliot], "Our Schools and Colleges," six articles from the Boston *Advertiser*, 1848, undated clpgs., HUA (HUA848.23); [idem], *A Letter to the President of Harvard College by a Member of the Corporation* [Boston, 1849], 10–11, 22–23; "Treasurer's Statement," 3–4 (in AR [1853] with separate pagination); Samuel A. Eliot to Theodore Dwight Woolsey, June 28, 1848, in T. D. Woolsey Papers, YU. On the founding of Lawrence Scientific School, see Howard S. Miller, *Dollars for Research: Science and Its Patrons in Nineteenth-Century America* (Seattle, 1970), 74–87.

6. CWE, "How I Have Kept My Health and Working Power Till Eighty" [1914], in CWE, *A Late Harvest: Miscellaneous Papers Written between Eighty and Ninety* (Boston, 1924), 4–5; James, *Eliot*, I:15; Henry P. Walcott, remarks, MHS, 60(1926–27):3; Francis Greenwood Peabody, "Charles William Eliot" HGM 35(1926–27):240; CWE, "[Address at] Dinner of Latin School Association, Nov. 13th, 1878," EPA 26.

7. *Addresses at the Inauguration of Jared Sparks, LL.D., as President of Harvard College, Wednesday, June 20, 1849* (Cambridge, 1849), 43–46, 52–54; AR(1849), 9–10, (1850), 11–12.

8. AR (1850–53), passim; HUC(1850–53), passim; *Charles Francis Adams, 1835–1915: An Autobiography* (Boston, 1916), 24–31; *The Education of Henry Adams: An Autobiography* (Boston, 1918), ch. 4; William Everett, "Harvard College in 1855," *Harvard Monthly* 3(1886–87):51.

9. Morison, *Three Centuries*, 264–65; Solon I. Bailey, "Astronomy, 1877–1927" in Morison (ed.), *Development of Harvard*, 292–93; AR(1850), 8–9.

10. Samuel A. Eliot, "Treasurer's Statement," 1 (in AR[1850]); "Faculty Records [of Lawrence Scientific School, 1848–1871]," MS volume, HUA (UAV513.30) [hereinafter, LSS Faculty Records], 1857–58.

11. Boston *Evening Traveller*, May 3, 1850; AR(1855), 11–33.

12. "Remarks of Mr[.] Boutwell," Boston *Post*, June 19, 1850; Morison, *Three Centuries*, 201; S. A. Eliot, "Treasurer's Statement," 1 (AR[1850]); ibid., 1–2 (AR[1852]); ibid., 2 (AR[1853]).

13. The report of a special committee of the Massachusetts House of Representatives ordered on January 16, 1850, "to consider and report what legislation, if any, is necessary to render Harvard University more beneficial to all the people of the Commonwealth," was printed, including a minority report, as *Harvard University, April, 1850*, Massachusetts House Document 164. See esp. pp. 3, 14. See also *A Memorial concerning the Recent History and the Constitutional Rights and Privileges of Harvard College; Presented*

by the President and Fellows to the Legislature, January 17, 1851 (Boston, 1851); Morison, *Three Centuries*, 286–89. On Boutwell and Massachusetts politics, see Donald, *Sumner*, 189–95; Tilden G. Edelstein, *Strange Enthusiasm: A Life of Thomas Wentworth Higginson* (New Haven, 1968), 107–9.

14. Massachusetts *Spy*, Nov. 27, 1850; Morison, *Three Centuries*, 290–93.

15. CWE to Thomas Wentworth Higginson, March 31, 1896, T. W. Higginson Papers, HL; CWE, "Eliot," *Report of the Harvard Class of 1853*, 96–97.

16. James C. White, "An Undergraduate's Diary," HGM 21(1913): 428; Morison, *Three Centuries*, 216–17; "President Eliot's Response" HGM 3(1894–95):71.

17. CWE to James Walker, Dec. 25, 1859; [CWE?], "Notes on [lectures on Christian evidences by] Dr. Walker," MS, EP; CWE to Carleton Hunt, Sept. 10, 1907 (on Bowen). For the theory and practice of Walker and his associates, see Wilson Smith, *Professors and Public Ethics: Studies of the Northern Moral Philosophers* (Ithaca, 1956); Daniel Walker Howe, *The Unitarian Conscience: Harvard Moral Philosophy, 1805–1861* (Cambridge, 1970).

18. CWE to T. W. Higginson, March 31, 1896, Higginson Papers; CWE, *Harvard Memories*, 15–16; CWE to Theodore Tebbets, March 14, 1852; CWE, "Reminiscences of Peirce," *American Mathematical Monthly* 32(1925):1–4; James Clarke White, "Class of 1853—Biographical Sketches," MS notebook, HUA (HUD253.794) (on Carroll).

19. Cooke to CWE, Dec. 27, 1859; AR(1850), 29, (1851), 31–32; White, "An Undergraduate's Diary," HGM 21:427; Lyman C. Newell, "Josiah Parsons Cooke," DAB 4:387–88; "Address of Francis Humphreys Storer [on Cooke]," *Proceedings of the American Academy of Arts and Sciences* 30(1894–95):528–30; "Address of Charles William Eliot [on Cooke]," ibid. 531.

20. CWE to T. W. Higginson, March 31, 1896, Higginson Papers. Eliot called his experience unique, but other students had similar experiences. His classmate James C. White pursued botany and ornithology informally under the direction of Asa Gray, and Tutor Francis J. Child met students in the evening for the study of early English texts. (White, "An Undergraduate's Diary," HGM 21:642–44).

21. CWE to his father, Jan. 5, 1851; CWE to Theodore Tebbets, March 14, 1852.

22. White, "An Undergraduate's Diary," HGM 21:428; AR(1851), 13, 6; CWE to his father, July 27, Aug. 8, [1852]; James, *Eliot*, I:53–55.

23. Adams Sherman Hill, "President Eliot as an Undergraduate," *Harvard Crimson*, March 21, 1904; CWE to Theodore Tebbets, June 27,

1852; H. K. Oliver, Jr., to CWE, Sept. 29, 1851, Class of 1853 "Secretary's File," HUA (HUD253.505).

24. CWE to Theodore Tebbets, March 3, 1853; White, "Class of 1853—Biographical Sketches."

25. CWE, "Eliot," *Report of the Harvard Class of 1853*, 97; CWE to Theodore Tebbets, Jan. 29, 1854; CWE, "The Full Utilization of a Public School Plant," NEA (1903), 242–43.

26. CWE to Theodore Tebbets, Feb. 11, 1852; Samuel A. Eliot to Charles Eliot Norton, May 27, Sept. 3, 1846, Charles Eliot Norton Papers, HL; CWE to Tebbets, March 3, 1853. Another nephew, Samuel Eliot (Harvard A.B. 1839), was directed into business by Charles's father, but left it for teaching (Gould, "Samuel Atkins and Mary Eliot," [see n. 2, above]).

27. For the attitudes of others, see Fredrickson, *Inner Civil War*, 29–35.

28. CWE to his mother, March 16, 1854, EP (the entire letter is printed in James, *Eliot*, I:60–66).

29. James Mills Peirce, "President Eliot as an Instructor," *Harvard Crimson*, March 21, 1904; CWE to Theodore Tebbets, March 13, 1856; Eliot, *Harvard Memories*, 117–18; *Orders and Regulations of the Faculty of Harvard College, Passed in Conformity with the Authority Given by the Laws of the College*, May 1849 (copy in HUA [HUA849.3]); Henry James [I] to Henry James [II], [1869], in Ralph Barton Perry, *The Thought and Character of William James* (Boston, 1935), I:106; William James to Alice James, Oct. 19, 1862, in ibid., 214; James, *Eliot*, I:68.

30. CWE to William James, May 20, 1894; CWE, "The 1858 Races—Origin of Harvard's Colors," HGM 8 (1899–1900):465–66; Robert Bruce Gelston to CWE, July 30, [1858]; CWE to Gelston's father, [Aug. 1858], (draft).

31. CWE, "Eliot," *Report of the Harvard Class of 1853*, 98; Eliot, *Harvard Memories*, 86, 89; Peirce, "Eliot as Instructor," *Harvard Crimson*, March 21, 1904; "Meeting of a Joint Committee of Overseers and Faculty on the Subject of Annual Examinations" [March 4, 1857], MS in CWE's hand, EP; William W. Goodwin, "Recollections of President Felton," HGM 17 (1908–09):653. Written examinations had recently been used by reformers in the Boston public schools (Harold Schwartz, *Samuel Gridley Howe, Social Reformer, 1801–1876* [Cambridge, 1956], 129–30).

32. "Prepared for the Faculty, but not read," MS in CWE's hand [about May 1, 1858], EP; HUC (1859), 30; AR (1860), 45, (1861), 23, (1862), 19. The course comprised crystallography, qualitative analysis, and mineralogy. For Cooke's expansionism, see AR (1856), 5–6; CWE, "Address," *Proceedings of AAAS*, 30:536–40.

33. Adams Sherman Hill to CWE, June 12, [1859]; Edward Everett Hale, "A Group of Presidents," HGM 4(1895–96):566; "Construction of the Tabular View, February & March 1856," proofsheets with CWE's revisions, EP; Frederick Winsor to CWE, Aug. 31, 1858; Francis Gardner to CWE, July 6, 1859; Amos A. Lawrence to CWE, June 22, [1858]; Walker to CWE, May 1, 1856; CWE to Felix Flügel, March 5, 1861 (copy); printed proposal for a Harvard Club, July 10, 1855, with notes by CWE, Dec. 26, 1855, EP; Eliot, *Harvard Memories*, 116; AR(1856), 4–5.

34. Eliot, *Harvard Memories*, 66–69; James, *Eliot*, I:71; AR(1853), 9; vote of Harvard Corporation, Feb. 26, 1859, copy, EP; Edward Pearce, Jr., to CWE, March 3, 1865; F. H. Storer to CWE, July 14, 1865.

35. CWE to Theodore Tebbets, Nov. 25, [1855]; Henry James [I] to Henry James [II], [1869], in Perry, *James*, I:106.

36. CWE to Charles Eliot Norton, Sept. 12, 1859; CWE to Theodore Tebbets, March 13, 1856.

37. The description in James, *Eliot*, I:104, considerably underestimates Storer's scientific sophistication. See C. A. Browne, "Francis Humphreys Storer," DAB, 18:94–95; CWE and Frank H. Storer, "On the Impurities of Commercial Zinc . . . ," *Memoirs of the American Academy of Arts and Sciences* n.s. 8(1861):57–96. For other joint publications, see Lewis William Fetzer, "In Memoriam: Francis Humphreys Storer," *Biochemical Bulletin* 4(1915):13.

38. CWE to George J. Brush, April 20, 1860, Brush Family Papers, YU; Storer to CWE, July 31, 1860; CWE to C. E. Norton, Sept. 10, 1860, Norton Papers.

39. Brush to CWE, July 9, 1860; Edward Twisleton to CWE, April 21, 1860; Wolcott Gibbs to CWE, Nov. 3, 11, 1861; George H. Daniels, "The Process of Professionalization in American Science: The Emergent Period, 1820–1860," *Isis* 58(1967):154.

40. CWE to Sarah P. Pratt, Feb. 21, 1862; G. T. L. [George Theodore Lyman?] to CWE, March 5, 12, April 3, 1862.

41. CWE to Theodore Tebbets, March 13, 1856; CWE to C. E. Norton, Sept. 18, 1860, Norton Papers; J. P. Cooke to G. J. Brush, June 20, 1857, Brush Papers.

42. James, *Eliot*, I:73–77.

43. Edward Lurie, *Louis Agassiz: A Life in Science* (Chicago, 1960), 275–77; A. Hunter Dupree, *Asa Gray, 1810–1888* (Cambridge, 1959), 253–55; J. P. Cooke to G. J. Brush, June 30, 1859, Brush Papers; F. H. Storer to CWE, July 14, 1865 (on Huntington). For Cooke's natural theology, see his *Religion and Chemistry, or Proofs of God's Plan in the Atmosphere and Its Elements* (New York, 1864).

44. CWE to James Walker, Oct. 28, 1859 (draft); vote of Harvard

Corporation, Oct. 29, 1859, copy, EP; Walker to CWE, Dec. 8, [1859]; J. P. Cooke to CWE, Dec. 27, 1859.

45. CWE to President and Fellows of Harvard College, May 18, 1863 (draft); CWE to Francis B. Crowninshield, Dec. 12, 1862 (draft); Edward Pearce, Jr., to CWE, Feb. 28, 1861 (citing Cooke on prospects). On Horsford, see Miller, *Dollars for Research*, 82–83; I. Bernard Cohen, "Harvard and the Scientific Spirit," *Harvard Alumni Bulletin* 50(1947–48): 397–98.

46. Morison, *Three Centuries*, 302–3; Robert S. Rantoul, "Prefatory Note," *Report of the Harvard Class of 1853*, p. vii.

47. Peirce, "Eliot as Instructor," *Harvard Crimson*, March 21, 1904; diary of Arthur Lincoln, quoted in Nathan Appleton, "Harvard College during the War of the Rebellion," *New England Magazine*, 10(1891):9; CWE to Theodore Lyman, Aug. 5, 1861, in James, *Eliot*, I:91–93.

48. James, *Eliot*, I:89–91; William Rogers to CWE, Sept. 25, Nov. 12, 1862 (quotas); LSS Faculty Records, Nov. 4, 1862; W. Steffens to CWE, Dec. 12, 1862 (military school); CWE to Henry Wadsworth Longfellow, Aug. 28, 1862, H. W. Longfellow Papers, Houghton Library (outfit); Francis H. Brown, *Harvard University in the War of 1861–1865* . . . (Boston, 1886), 11–12 (Eustis's service).

49. CWE to G. J. Brush, Dec. 18, 1860, Brush Papers; John A. Lowell to CWE, April 26, 1862; CWE to F. B. Crowninshield, Dec. 12, 1862 (draft).

50. William Dallam Armes (ed.), *The Autobiography of Joseph LeConte* (New York, 1903), 128–29; Lane Cooper, *Louis Agassiz as a Teacher* (Ithaca, 1945), passim; vote of Harvard Corporation, enclosed in Amos Lawrence to CWE, Oct. 21, 1861.

51. LSS Faculty Records, Nov. 5, Dec. 3, 17, 1861; John A. Lowell to CWE, April 26, 1862. Pressure for such introductory study was applied in 1855 by President Walker, but the plan was voted down at that time (LSS Faculty Records, April 20, May 4, 1855).

52. The general program which Eliot set up for his two departments, besides requiring attendance at the previously optional lectures in chemistry, physics, botany, and anatomy given in the academic department, added recitations in algebra, trigonometry, physiology, mineralogy, and political economy. Eliot apparently taught most of the new recitations himself, but his classmate Edward Pearce, Jr., was added to the staff in 1862 and probably took over the mathematics (Pearce to CWE, Sept. 7, 1862; HUC[1861], 74–75, [1862], 75–76, [1863], 73–75).

53. LSS Faculty Records, Sept. 30, Nov. 4, 11, 1862; James, *Eliot*, I:95; CWE, "Speech at Faculty Club[,] Institute of Technology," EPA 700.

54. CWE to his mother, Feb. 2, 1865; LSS Faculty Records, Nov. 11,

18, Dec. 2, 1862; Dupree, *Gray*, 314–17. In 1865, Agassiz, worried by the growth of Sheffield, pushed for a plan similar to Eliot's (Jeffries Wyman to CWE, June 25, 1865).

55. Louis Agassiz to Benjamin Peirce, "9th" [1870?], Benjamin Peirce Papers, HUA.

56. Lurie, *Agassiz*, 300–301. For a valuable comparison of the promotional styles of the two Lawrence professors, see Miller, *Dollars for Research*, ch. 3, "The Personal Equation."

57. CWE, *Harvard Memories*, 19–20; Lurie, *Agassiz*, 320; William G. Land, *Thomas Hill: Twentieth President of Harvard* (Cambridge, 1933), 124–25. The Overseers at first refused to assent to Hill's election, by a vote of nine to sixteen. He was said—correctly—to lack "practical business talent" and to plan to use Harvard for educational experiments. (OR, May 22, 1862; Boston *Courier* [1863], clpg, HUA[HUA863.2]).

58. Richard J. Storr, *The Beginnings of Graduate Education in America* (Chicago, 1953), 67–68; Lurie, *Agassiz*, 323–25; Benjamin Peirce, *Working Plan for the Foundation of a University* ([Cambridge], 1856), passim; LSS Faculty Records, Jan. 6, March 3, 1863; James, *Eliot*, I:96n.

59. Merle Curti and Roderick Nash, *Philanthropy in the Shaping of American Higher Education* (New Brunswick, N.J., 1965), 63. The first occupant of the Rumford chair, in his effort to name the area set out by the donor, gave a new and lasting meaning to the term "technology" (Dirk J. Struik, *Yankee Science in the Making* [Boston, 1948], 170.)

60. CWE to Francis B. Crowninshield, Dec. 12, 1862 (draft). As part of his strategy to get Storer installed, Eliot asked Brush to give Storer's dictionary of solubilities "a strong puff" in the *American Journal of Science* (CWE to G. J. Brush, Feb. 12, 1863, Brush Papers).

61. Francis B. Crowninshield to CWE, Jan. 24, 1863; CWE to Thomas Hill, Jan. 31, 1863; CWE to Nathaniel Silsbee, Feb. 17, 1863. The Lawrence Scientific School had from the beginning relied on such pieced-out salaries, but it was undeniably a weakness in the institution (LSS Faculty Records, Sept. 14, 1849; Abbott Lawrence to Samuel A. Eliot, Sept. 20, 1849, copy in ibid.).

62. CWE to Anne Lyman, Feb. 12, 1863; CWE to Joseph Coolidge, Feb. 13, 1863; CWE to Arthur Lyman, Feb. 17, 1863; CWE to President and Fellows, May 13, 1863 (draft); Land, *Hill*, 155–58. For an unattractive precedent for this sort of familial support, see the case of Karl Follen (Morison, *Three Centuries*, 254).

63. J. R. Lowell to E. Rockwood Hoar, Jan. 26, 1863, James Russell Lowell Papers, HL; Cooke to G. J. Brush, July 7, 1863; Brush to Josiah D. Whitney, June 30, 1863; Storer to Brush, Feb. 22, July 25, 1863; CWE to Brush, June 26, 1863, all five in Brush Papers.

64. CWE, "Eliot," *Report of the Harvard Class of 1853,* 104; Brush to CWE, June 23, 1863; CWE to Brush, June 26, 1863, Brush Papers.

65. CWE to Felix Flügel, Feb. 6, 1863 (copy, great war); CWE, "Speech at Institute of Technology," EPA 700; Fredrickson, *Inner Civil War,* 72–73.

66. Mary E. Parkman to CWE, July 12, 1863; Theodore Lyman to CWE, Aug. 9, 1863; James, *Eliot,* I:113; CWE to Brush, Sept. 29, 1863, Brush Papers.

67. CWE to his mother, Nov. 13, 1863, May 21, 1865; James, *Eliot,* I:146–49. For his view of expatriates, see also CWE to [B. G. Northrop], April 5, 1873, in Birdsey Grant Northrop, *Education Abroad, and Other Papers* (New York, 1873), 14–15.

68. CWE to his mother, April 20, 1864, Nov. 13, Dec. 10, 1863; CWE, remarks, ACPSMSM(1896), 121. One could scarcely get farther from the truth than the allegation of Abraham Flexner that while in Europe Eliot "was hardly more than a casual tourist" (*Abraham Flexner: An Autobiography* [New York, 1960], 267).

69. CWE to his mother, Oct. 6, 30, Nov. 6, 16, 21, 27, Dec. 22, 1864, Jan. 1, March 8, 1865. Precisely what projects he pursued in the laboratory is unknown, since his detailed accounts were in letters to Storer that were enclosed with those to his mother, but not preserved.

70. CWE to his mother, Oct. 6, 1864, Aug. 27–29, Jan. 1, 1865.

71. James, *Eliot,* I:139; CWE to his mother, Nov. 16, April 1, 1864.

72. CWE to his mother, Nov. 16, 1864, May 11, 21, 1865; CWE, *More Money for the Public Schools* (New York, 1903), 119.

73. CWE to C. E. Norton, Jan. 28, 1864, Norton Papers; CWE to his mother, June 11, Jan. 12, 1865.

74. CWE to Francis G. Peabody, Jan. 1, 1865; CWE to C. E. Norton, Jan. 28, 1864, Norton Papers; CWE to his mother, Dec. 3, 1863, April 20, 1864; CWE to Arthur Lyman, April 18, 1865, quoted in James, *Eliot,* I:145–47.

75. CWE to his mother, Aug. 31, 1864.

76. CWE to his mother, Apr. 20, 1864, Jan. 1, 1865, Oct. 30, 1864; Gray to CWE, March 19, [1865?]; Miller, *Dollars for Research,* 121; Dupree, *Gray,* 342–43.

77. Francis B. Crowninshield to CWE, April 10, 1865; CWE to Crowninshield, May 5, 1865 (copy). Eliot himself recounted the story in a letter to William A. Richardson, Aug. 12, 1889, and in CWE, "Eliot," *Report of the Harvard Class of 1853,* 105. For accounts by others, see Edward S. Martin, "President Eliot," *Harper's Magazine* 153(1926):785; Edward H. Cotton, *The Life of Charles W. Eliot* (Boston, 1926), 65–66; "President Eliot as Builder of Harvard," *American Review of Reviews* 74(1926):422.

78. CWE to his mother, May 6, 11, 1865. On the concept of the transcendent Yankee, see William R. Taylor, *Cavalier and Yankee: The Old South and American National Character* (New York, 1961), 106–8. The contrast with Alexander Agassiz, who made a fortune in copper mining, was not lost on Eliot. He recalled a meeting when he was "a low-salaried but contented professor" with young Agassiz, who declared he was going to make money before devoting himself to a career as a naturalist (CWE, "Alexander Agassiz," HGM 18[1909–10]:598). Eliot also had an offer, which he doubtless did not take seriously, to go west with his friend Edward Pearce and get a claim on a mine which the two would develop, Pearce on the spot, Eliot back east handling the business affairs (Pearce to CWE, March 3, 1865).

79. CWE to his mother, April 21, May 6, 1865.

80. Rogers to CWE, June 6, 1865; Struik, *Yankee Science*, 350–55; Samuel C. Prescott, *When M.I.T. Was "Boston Tech," 1861–1916* (Cambridge, 1954), 32–35; Emma Rogers (ed.), *Life and Letters of William Barton Rogers* (Boston, 1896), vol. I, chs. 5–7; vol. II, 77.

81. Rogers, *Rogers*, II:163–64, 110–12, 156–57; Rogers to CWE, July 17, June 6, 1865; Charles C. Smith, "Memoir of John Amory Lowell, LL.D.," MHS, n.s. 12(1897–99):124; A. A. Lawrence, "William Johnson Walker," DAB, 19:366 (on the alienated alumnus).

82. Rogers, *Rogers*, II:140–48, 163–64; Prescott, *When M.I.T.*, 39, 71; CWE, "Speech at Institute of Technology," EPA 700.

83. CWE to his mother, June 20, 1865, to Rogers, June 20, 1865 (copy); Lowell to CWE, July 7, 1865; Gurney to CWE, June 13, 1865.

84. Storer to CWE, July 14, 1865; CWE to his mother, Aug. 2, 1865.

85. CWE, "Francis Humphreys Storer (1832–1914)," *Proceedings of the American Academy of Arts and Sciences* 54(1918–19):416; "Records of the Faculty of the School of the Massachusetts Institute of Technology," Registrar's Office, M.I.T. [hereinafter, M.I.T. Faculty Records], Oct. 27, 1866; [CWE], "Draper's Chemistry," *Nation* 2(1866):503 (tools in hand); CWE to G. J. Brush, March 18, 1867, Brush Papers.

86. *First Annual Catalogue of . . . the Massachusetts Institute of Technology* (1866), 27, 14.

87. James, *Eliot*, I:164–65; Storer to CWE, May 3, 1868; CWE, "Storer," *Proceedings of AAAS* 54:416; CWE to Brush, March 18, 1867, Brush Papers (painfully minute); *Second Annual Catalogue of . . . M.I.T.* (1867), 13. A second, less significant textbook, *Compendious Manual of Qualitative Chemical Analysis*, was published by the two colleagues in 1869. For Eliot's views on textbooks, see his review of William G. Peck's *Elements of Mechanics, Atlantic Monthly* 5(1860):637–38.

88. CWE, "Speech at Institute of Technology," EPA 700; Storer to

William Barton Rogers, May 3, 1868, W. B. Rogers Papers, Archives, Massachusetts Institute of Technology; Storer to CWE, May 10, 1868 (on Henck); M.I.T. *Catalogue* (1866), 20; M.I.T. Faculty Records, Oct. 28, 1865.

89. CWE to Wendell Phillips Garrison, June 10, 1866, W. P. Garrison Papers, HL; M.I.T. *Catalogue* (1866), 24, (1868), 12, (1869), 12; CWE, "The New Education: Its Organization," *Atlantic Monthly* 23(1869):359–60.

90. M.I.T. Faculty Records, Oct. 28, 30, 1865, Dec. 22, 1866, Jan. 18, March 7, Oct. 10, 1868; Storer to CWE, May 10, 1868; George B. Emerson to W. B. Rogers, Nov. 30, 1868, Rogers Papers (long lessons).

91. CWE to W. P. Garrison, June 10, 1866, Garrison Papers; J. P. Cooke to CWE, April 10, 1865; Gurney to Eliot, June 13, 1865; CWE to his mother, Feb. 22, July 12, 1865 (both on Hill). For Eliot's later sympathetic appraisal of Hill, see CWE, *Harvard Memories*, 20, and CWE, "Discussion," *School and Society* 15(1922):78–79.

92. AR(1868), esp. 8, 11, 16–20.

93. *Annual Report of the President of Columbia College* (1869), 14–25; Hugh Hawkins, *Pioneer: A History of the Johns Hopkins University, 1874–1889* (Ithaca, 1960), 3–4; Edward Waldo Emerson and Waldo Emerson Forbes (eds.), *Journals of Ralph Waldo Emerson* (Boston, 1914), 10: 197, quoted in Walter P. Rogers, *Andrew D. White and the Modern University* (Ithaca, 1942), 4. On this postwar ferment, see Rogers, *White*, ch. 1, and Rudolph, *American College*, ch. 12.

94. Jacob Bigelow, *An Address on the Limits of Education, Read before the Massachusetts Institute of Technology, November 16th, 1865* (Boston, 1865), esp. 16–18; Frederic Henry Hedge, "University Reform: An Address to the Alumni of Harvard, at Their Triennial Festival, July 19, 1866," *Atlantic Monthly* 18(1866):296–307.

95. John Fiske, "Considerations on University Reform," *Atlantic Monthly* 19(1867):460–61, 464; Thomas Wentworth Higginson, "A Plea for Culture," *ibid.*, 31, 36; [Francis Parkman], "The Tale of the 'Ripe Scholar,' " *Nation* 9(1869):558–60.

96. *Historical Register of Harvard University, 1636–1936* (Cambridge, 1937), 37. The Corporation was rumored to be unenthusiastic about the change, perhaps out of fear of losing a claim on state financial support (Ephraim Gurney to CWE, June 13, 1865). A similar plan in the early 1850s had been rejected by a combination of Harvard supporters who wanted "the prestige of State patronage and control" and Harvard opponents who feared unqualified Unitarian control (Boston *Daily Advertiser*, April 18, 1864; *The State of the Colleges*, Massachusetts Senate Document 134 [1854]).

322 · Notes to Pages 41-45

97. OR, April 18, 1867, Feb. 11, 1869; *Report to the Board of Over-seers of Harvard College on the Condition, Needs, and Prospects of the University* (Cambridge, 1869), 6–11, 59, 61, 63, 65–71, 74–76. At this time some students, after passing Harvard admission examinations, would re-turn to a preparatory school, especially Phillips Exeter, for the equivalent of the freshman year. See "Private Journal of John Langdon Sibley of Har-vard University Library [1846–1882]," HUA (HUG1791.72) [hereinafter, "Sibley's Private Journal"], Oct. 1, 1870.

98. OR, Oct. 7, 1868, Jan. 7, 11, Feb. 25, March 10, 1869; CWE, "Remarks of President Elliott [sic], of Harvard College, Cambridge, before the Trustees of the Johns Hopkins University, Baltimore, June 4, 1874," EPA 11 (saucy); CWE to James T. Fields, Nov. 10, 1868, Fields Papers, Huntington Library, San Marino, Calif. Eliot later claimed to have intro-duced the term "new education" (CWE to L. P. Sanders, March 24, 1898). For examples of its use in the sense he intended (education without the ancient languages), see "University Influence," *Nation* 8(1869):450–51; *Annual Report of the President of Columbia College* (1870), 63. By mid-1869 Eliot declared himself "getting heartily sick" of the phraseology of "new and old education" (CWE to G. J. Brush, July 1, 1869, Brush Papers). See also James C. Austin, *Fields of* The Atlantic Monthly: *Letters to an Editor, 1861–1870* (San Marino, Calif., 1953), 166–67.

99. CWE, "New Education," *Atlantic Monthly* 23:204, 206–11. For Gibbs's rejoinder, see his letter to the editor, Feb. 19, 1869, in ibid., 514.

100. Ibid., 363, 214, 218, 364–67. The remarks on American economic potential reflected observations made during Eliot's second visit to Europe, when he was associated with William Barton Rogers in drawing up a re-port for Massachusetts on the Paris Exposition of 1867. Although because of Rogers's illness the report never appeared, Eliot's draft of certain parts, written during 1867–1868, survives (CWE, "Criticism of the Classification," MS, EP, box 454).

101. CWE, "New Education," *Atlantic Monthly* 23:216, 208, 215n. For support of Eliot's view that professions were losing status, see Daniel C. Calhoun, *Professional Lives in America: Structure and Aspiration, 1750–1850* (Cambridge, 1965), passim.

102. CWE, "New Education," *Atlantic Monthly* 23:366 (few prizes). Eliot viewed his election as a case of the educational profession receiving its own prizes (CWE to G. J. Brush, May 21, 1869, Brush Papers).

CHAPTER II, *From College to University*

1. CWE, "The Aims of Higher Education," in CWE, *Educational Reform*, 225.

2. OR, April 7–May 19, 1869, Oct. 7, 1868; Boston *Advertiser*, Feb. 26, 1869; "Rusticus" to editor, ibid., [Jan. 2, 1869?], clpg. in HUA (HUA869.2). As arrangements worked out, early in 1870, the new officer (called the dean) absorbed the functions previously assigned to the regent and some presidential duties directly involving undergraduates (OR, Jan. 22, Feb. 5, 1870; "Sibley's Private Journal," Feb. 17, 1870).

3. A. P. Peabody to Francis E. Parker, Feb. 12, 1869, Misc. Ser., Overseers Reports, HUA; "University Reform" to editor, Boston *Advertiser*, [Jan. 2, 1869?], clpg. in HUA (HUA869.2); [John Fiske], "The Presidency of Harvard College," *Nation* 7(1868):547–48; Milton Berman, *John Fiske: The Evolution of a Popularizer* (Cambridge, 1961), 72. Fiske was urged to write the article by E. L. Godkin and James Russell Lowell (Martin Duberman, *James Russell Lowell* [Cambridge, 1966], p. 455n20).

4. James, *Eliot*, I:191–92; Martin Duberman, *Charles Francis Adams, 1807–1886* (Boston, 1961), 336; CWE to G. J. Brush, May 21, 1869, Brush Papers. Fiske's article ruled out giving the presidency to a Boston business-man or trying to have Harvard compete with polytechnical schools.

5. William James to Henry Bowditch, May 22, 1869, in Perry, *James*, I:296; S. Kneeland to Mrs. William B. Rogers, April 28, 1869; John D. Runkle to Mrs. W. B. Rogers, April 8, 1869 (both in Rogers Papers); "Sibley's Private Journal," March 18, April 15, May 13, 1869. For a list of objections supposedly voiced by the Overseers, see ibid., April 21, 1869. William A. Richardson, an Overseer in 1869, recalled youth as a major objection (Richardson, "How President Eliot Was Elected," HGM 7[1898–99]:535–37).

6. Henry P. Walcott, remarks, MHS 60(1926–27):4; James, *Eliot*, I:193–94, including quotation from Lyman's diary.

7. James Bradley Thayer's diary, quoted in James, *Eliot*, I:195; "Sibley's Private Journal," Feb. 8, 1870 (Walker takes lead).

8. "Inaugural Address as President of Harvard College," *Educational Reform*, 1; James, *Eliot*, I:225–28, including Fiske quotation.

9. "President Eliot's Response," HGM 3(1894–95):74; AR(1878), 3; Oliver Wendell Holmes to J. L. Motley, April 3, 1870, quoted in HGM 5(1896–97):381 ("festina lente"); CWE, *Harvard Memories*, 69. For the traditions of the Harvard Corporation, see Walter Muir Whitehill, *Boston in the Age of John Fitzgerald Kennedy* (Norman, Okla., 1966), 143–54.

10. James L. Pennypacker, " 'We are Seven,' " HGM 12(1903–4):715; CWE to J. H. Clifford, April 22, 1870, Misc. Ser., Overseers Reports, HUA; "Alumni Dinner," unident. clpg., [1872], EP.

11. CWE, "New Education," *Atlantic Monthly* 23:365–66; Holmes to J. L. Motley, Dec. 22, 1871, quoted in HGM 5(1896–97):382; Godkin to Charles Eliot Norton, Feb. 17, 1870, in Rollo Ogden (ed.), *Life and Letters*

of *Edwin Lawrence Godkin* (New York, 1907), I:294; "Harvard Rejuvenated," *Independent* 23(1871):4.

12. [Thomas Wentworth Higginson?], "Young Harvard," New York *Tribune*, Feb. 17, 1872; John Jay Chapman, "President Eliot," *Memories and Milestones* (New York, 1915), 169–70; Barrett Wendell, "De Praeside Magnifico," HGM 18(1909–10):16; CWE, "Inaugural," *Educational Reform*, 34; Bliss Perry, *And Gladly Teach: Reminiscences* (Boston, 1935), 226.

13. CWE to Kuno Francke, Oct. 28, 1908 (business); CWE to Paul H. Hanus, Dec. 27, 1907 (politics); G. H. Palmer, "Eliot the Man," *Harvard Illustrated Magazine* 10(1909):192; Arthur Twining Hadley, quoted in James, *Eliot*, II:172–73.

14. CWE to his mother, Oct. 30, 1864; CWE, "New Education," *Atlantic Monthly* 23:216. On the romantic conception of the university, see Richard J. Storr, "The Public Conscience of the University," *Harvard Educational Review* 26(1956):77.

15. CWE, "New Education," *Atlantic Monthly* 23:216, 208; CWE, "The Aims of Higher Education," *Educational Reform*, 228 (quoting Cornell). Cornell's exact words are not known. The phrasing used in the motto of Cornell University is slightly more elaborate than Eliot's version (Morris Bishop, *A History of Cornell* [Ithaca, 1962], 74).

16. AR(1872), 34; CWE to Edward C. Towne, Aug. 1, 1895, quoted in James, *Eliot*, II:87–88.

17. Charles H. Haskins, "The Graduate School of Arts and Sciences, 1872–1929," in Morison (ed.), *Development of Harvard*, 452; AR(1870), 10–11; CWE, "New Education," *Atlantic Monthly* 23:206. Abolition of the "in course" A.M. had been recommended by a special committee of the Overseers shortly before Eliot's election.

18. CWE to G. J. Brush, June 24, 1869, Brush Papers; CWE to William Dwight Whitney, June 9, 1869, Whitney Family Papers, YU; Haskins, "The Graduate School," in Morison (ed.), *Development of Harvard*, 453; "Amicus Curiae" to editor, Aug. 27, 1869, in *Nation* 9(1869): 189–90; HUC(1870), 101–3; Josiah Royce, "Present Ideals of American University Life," *Scribner's Magazine* 10(1891):381; Francis G. Peabody, "The Germ of the Graduate School," HGM 27(1918–19):176–81; AR(1872), 13–17. Eliot's willingness to change from the University Courses brought him closer to the position of Louis Agassiz, who had objected to holding the lectures in Boston. But in Agassiz's opinion, the advanced age of American undergraduates precluded a successful postgraduate department (Agassiz to Benjamin Peirce, "9th," [1870?], Peirce Papers).

19. AR(1872), 17–18, (1873), 24–25; HUC(1872, 2nd ed.), 10–11 in second pagination; CWE, "[Speech at Harvard Club], New York, Feb. 21,

1872," EPA 6; CWE to John Gorham Palfrey, June 6, 1873, J. G. Palfrey Papers, HL (on honoraries). The A.M. continued to be given as an honorary degree, like the LL.D., though more modest.

20. AR(1872), 19; CWE, *University Administration* (Boston, 1908), 151.

21. AR(1872), 18; HUC(1873), 138–39, 141–42; W. W. Goodwin, "The Growth of the Graduate School," HGM 9(1900–1901):173–74 [similarly, Hugo Münsterberg to CWE, Aug. 30, 1894]; Herbert Weir Smyth, "The Classics, 1867–1929," in Morison (ed.), *Development of Harvard*, 52; Robert Grant, *Fourscore: An Autobiography* (Boston, 1934), 102–3.

22. Edward Channing to CWE, Aug. 17, 1888; Charles Loring Jackson to CWE, Jan. 26, 1888 (on fellowships); "Fellowships," HUC(1882), 211–14; AR(1874), 21–22; CWE to James B. Angell, Feb. 29, 1896 (on hiring students). The opening of Johns Hopkins had stimulated Eliot to seek improvement of graduate work (AR[1877], 20–21); ten years later a student editorial cited Johns Hopkins in its call for further Harvard encouragement of graduate work (*Harvard Monthly* 4[1887]:208).

23. James Mills Peirce, "The Graduate Department," in AR(1890), 115–18; Clement L. Smith, "The College," ibid., 59; HUC(1891), passim; James, *Eliot*, II:345; AR(1905), 36, (1908), 22. Faculty support for the three-year A.B. began at this time, partly out of a desire to encourage graduate study (Royce, "Present Ideals," *Scribner's Magazine* 10:387). For an optimistic editorial on the graduate school, see *Harvard Monthly* 10(1890):159–61.

24. Hugo Münsterberg to CWE, Aug. 30, 1894. After 1897 Harvard allowed any Ph.D. or S.D. who had faculty approval to teach for four months either gratuitously or for a fee which he collected himself. The program did not flourish (AR[1897], 44–45; Albert Bushnell Hart, "The Present and the Future," HGM 4[1895–96]:83; A. B. Hart, "The Spring Quarter," HGM 6[1897–98]:21; G. H. Palmer to CWE, Nov. 9, 1898).

25. CWE to Francis P. Keppel, Oct. 8, 1904 (cf. Veysey, *American University*, 96). There is an element of truth in the exaggerated statement of Nicholas Murray Butler that Eliot "never cared much for what has come to be known as the graduate school" (Butler, *Across the Busy Years: Recollections and Reflections* [New York, 1939], I:144). See also Eliot's comments enclosed in C. G. Child to Charles R. Van Hise, June 1, 1907, Van Hise Papers, University of Wisconsin Archives, Madison.

26. CWE, "New Education," *Atlantic Monthly* 23:215n; CWE, "Inaugural," *Educational Reform*, 13.

27. AR(1902), 45, (1905), 41–42; James, *Eliot*, I:263; Morison, *Three Centuries*, 393; James McCosh, *The New Departure in College Education: Being a Reply to President Eliot's Defense of It in New York, Feb. 24, 1885*

(New York, 1885), 5; W. R. Harper, "The Educational Progress of the Year 1901–2," NEA(1902), 365–66. Eliot's own position was somewhat modified by his advocacy of the three-year A.B., though he maintained that this meant no diminution in the amount of study in the bachelor's program.

28. CWE to Jerome D. Greene, April 5, 1920, in James, *Eliot*, II:295 (criticizing Fellows); ibid., I:265 (whatever sacrifice).

29. James, *Eliot*, I:293; CWE, "Oliver Wendell Holmes," *Late Harvest*, 35 (professor's mouth).

30. James, *Eliot*, I:280; CWE, "Langdell and the Law School," *Late Harvest*, 47–48; Sydney E. Ahlstrom, "The Middle Period (1840–80)," in George Huntston Williams (ed.), *The Harvard Divinity School: Its Place in Harvard University and in American Culture* (Boston, 1954), 111–13.

31. "President Eliot's Response," HGM 3(1894–95):73 (fight); CWE to [Henry J. Bigelow?], March 15, 1871 (draft) . (mercenary); O. W. Holmes to J. L. Motley, April 3, 1870, quoted in HGM 5(1896–97):382 (Bigelow's question); CWE, "Holmes," *Late Harvest*, 37 (thumb), 34 (clinical work); James, *Eliot*, I:288–89; AR(1871), 18–22. See also James Clarke White, *Sketches from My Life, 1833–1913* (Cambridge, 1914), 151–52.

32. CWE, "Inaugural," *Educational Reform*, 9–10; AR(1870), 16 (on salaries); CWE, *Harvard Memories*, 27 (on dilution); CWE, "James Russell Lowell," *Late Harvest*, 26–27.

33. Barrett Wendell to A. Lawrence Lowell, July 20, 1916, Abbott Lawrence Lowell Papers, HUA; CWE, remarks before Associated Harvard Clubs, HGM 12(1903–4):455; CWE to Josiah P. Cooke, April [25], 1871; Albert Bushnell Hart, *Studies in American Education* (New York, 1895), 12 (Yale and Cornell); Morison, *Three Centuries*, 372–73; anonymous faculty member, letter in J. McKeen Cattell, *University Control* (New York, 1913), 70 (without the advice). Leading faculty advisers, in order of probable influence, were Ephraim Gurney, Charles F. Dunbar, Cooke, Alexander Agassiz, and William W. Goodwin.

34. CWE to C. E. Norton, March 16, 1870, Norton Papers; CWE, "American Education since the Civil War," *Late Harvest*, 124–26; "Arthur Richmond Marsh," *Harvard College Class of 1883 Secretary's Report: No. III* (n.p., 1890), 65; A. R. Marsh to CWE, June 1, 1890.

35. Eliot to Brush, Nov. 2, 8, 1869, Brush Papers; Daniel C. Gilman to Edward E. Salisbury, Sept. 30, Nov. 10, 1869, E. E. Salisbury Papers, YU (on Whitney).

36. Robert L. Church, "The Economists Study Society: Sociology at Harvard, 1891–1902," in Paul Buck (ed.), *Social Sciences at Harvard, 1860–1920: From Inculcation to the Open Mind* (Cambridge, 1965), 24–25; CWE, "Charles Franklin Dunbar," HGM 8(1899–1900):477; Frank William Taus-

sig, "Economics, 1871–1929," in Morison (ed.), *Development of Harvard*, 187–89. Adams Sherman Hill also came to the faculty from journalism. E. L. Godkin declined an appointment in history.

37. CWE to Theodore Tebbets, March 14, 1852; CWE, "Langdell and the Law School," *Late Harvest*, 45–56; Henry Adams to CWE, July 3, 1870; *Education of Henry Adams*, 293–94; Edward H. Hall, "James Bradley Thayer," HGM 10(1901–2):509. On Adams, see also Ephraim Gurney to CWE, Aug. 20, [1870].

38. *Harvard University Quinquennial Catalogue of the Officers and Graduates, 1636–1930* (Cambridge, 1930), 640–41. I do not count Jesse Walter Fewkes, a Ph.D. of 1877 who became assistant in charge of radiates at the Museum of Comparative Zoölogy.

39. Two notable appointments of Europeans came in 1892, Hugo Münsterberg and William James Ashley.

40. CWE to T. W. Higginson, April 20, 1872, Higginson Papers (research); CWE, "New Education," *Atlantic Monthly* 23:214 (research), 365 (routine duties); E. W. Gurney to William D. Whitney, Nov. 16, 1869, Whitney Papers.

41. CWE, "Remarks before Hopkins Trustees," EPA 11; C. L. Jackson to CWE, Jan. 11, 1888; CWE to Edwin H. Hall, April 14, 1881, E. H. Hall Papers, HL; Hawkins, *Pioneer*, 288–89; P. W. Bridgman, "Edwin Herbert Hall," DAB, 22:273; E. H. Hall to CWE, Sept. 23, 1884.

42. Hugo Münsterberg to CWE, Jan. 26, 1898; Hugh Hawkins, "Three University Presidents Testify," *American Quarterly* 11(1959):116–17; idem, "Charles W. Eliot, Daniel C. Gilman and the Nurture of American Scholarship," *New England Quarterly* 39(1966):300–301.

43. AR(1905), 6.

44. C. L. Jackson to CWE, July 13, [1901]; AR(1901), 34–35; CWE to George E. Woodberry, July 29, 1903, G. E. Woodberry Papers, HL (on one large class). See also James B. Conant, *My Several Lives: Memoirs of a Social Inventor* (New York, 1970), 27–28.

45. CWE, "Inaugural," *Educational Reform*, 15; CWE, "The New Definition of the Cultivated Man" [1903] in William Allan Neilson (ed.), *Charles W. Eliot: The Man and His Beliefs* (New York, 1926), I:191; CWE, *Harvard Memories*, 65–66; CWE to Mark H. Liddell, Dec. 29, 1903 (literature spoiled).

46. AR(1890), 36, (1904), 50, (1905), 11–14. The first increase raised professors' maximum salaries from $3,000 to $4,000; the second, from $4,000 to $4,500. The law school maximum ran somewhat higher. At least two significant published complaints preceded the Teachers' Endowment: J. Williams White, "Problems of Higher Education," HGM 7(1898–99):

341–48; "From a Graduate's Window," HGM 12(1903–4):198–200. For a detailed account relating Harvard salaries to changing price levels, see Seymour E. Harris, *Economics of Harvard* (New York, 1970), 140–45.

47. Charles R. Lanman to Daniel C. Gilman, May 10, 1880, C. R. Lanman Papers, HUA; "Statutes of the University," HUC(1888), 25–26; CWE, "The Right of Continuous Employment, and Its Conditions" [1892], EPA 48; Julian Lowell Coolidge, "Mathematics, 1870–1928," in Morison (ed.), *Development of Harvard*, 251; "University Notes," HGM 2(1893–94):442–43; William R. Thayer, "Review of the Third Quarter," ibid., 529–30.

48. Francis Bowen, remarks, *Proceedings of the Harvard Club of New York City at Their 12th Annual Dinner, Held at Delmonico's February 21st, 1878* (New York, 1878), 14–15; AR(1897), 17, (1899), 12–13, (1907), 7–8; A. B. Hart, "The Interests of the College," HGM 7(1898–99): 552–53. Before the retirement system went into effect, professors taught well beyond seventy: Francis Bowen retired in 1889 at age seventy-seven, Joseph Lovering in 1888 at seventy-four.

49. Charles R. Lanman diary, May 20, 1880, C. R. Lanman Papers, HUA; "Rules for Granting Leave of Absence on Half Pay," broadside on plan adopted by the Corporation, May 31, 1880, copy in HUA (HUA-880.2); CWE to David Starr Jordan, Sept. 7, 1904; AR(1880), 19, (1901), 13.

50. William E. Story to Daniel C. Gilman, July 26, 1880, D. C. Gilman Papers, Manuscript Division, Johns Hopkins University Library; William Cook to Moorfield Storey, Feb. 28, 1881, EP; Charles Loring Jackson to CWE, Jan. 26, 1888 (all on community abuzz); AR(1896), 17. The new professors were Frederick D. Allen, Charles R. Lanman, and Crawford H. Toy.

51. "From a Graduate's Window," HGM 7(1898–99):182–83.

52. AR(1907), 98–100.

53. Francke, "Emperor William's Gift to Harvard University," HGM 12(1903–4):221; Palmer, remarks, HGM 15(1906–7):70; Palmer, "From Professor Palmer," HGM 16(1907–8):227; William Henry Schofield, "Department of Comparative Literature," HGM 14(1905–6):769–72.

54. Morison, *Three Centuries*, 355, 386; William R. Thayer, "Nathaniel Southgate Shaler," HGM 15(1906–7):4–7 (routine men).

55. CWE, "Inaugural," *Educational Reform*, 30–31; Francis Bowen to CWE, March 3, 1870 (a rather obsequious letter granting the Corporation's right to decide the matter and reporting, "The publication is effectually suppressed"); Richard Hofstadter and Walter P. Metzger, *The Development of Academic Freedom in the United States* (New York, 1955), 395; F. W. Taussig, "Economics, 1871–1929," in Morison (ed.), *Development of*

Harvard, 187–88. The reason the episode is so well known is that Eliot himself later recounted it. His recollection was that Bowen suppressed one chapter before publication (CWE, "Academic Freedom," *Science* n.s. 26[1907]:7). The volume, *American Political Economy: Including Strictures on the Management of the Currency and the Finances since 1861* (New York, 1870) bears a preface dated Feb. 24, 1870. Bowen may have suppressed something, but he still included a slap at the likely redemption at par in gold of bonds purchased with depreciated greenbacks (p. 352) and a plan for "contracting and paying a National Debt only in the form of *short annuities*, not exceeding twenty-five years in duration" (pp. 409ff.). Like the financial conservatives on the Harvard Corporation, Bowen was strongly in favor of rapid resumption of the gold standard (Irwin Unger, *The Greenback Era: A Social and Political History of American Finance, 1865–1879* [Princeton, 1964], 128–30); thus, the label of "Greenbacker," applied in Morison, *Three Centuries*, 350, is inappropriate. In fact, Bowen wanted the greenbacks publicly burned.

56. CWE to E. L. Godkin, Aug. 27, 1870, E. L. Godkin Papers, HL.

57. CWE to Adolf von Harnack, Feb. 2, 1893 (in refusing, Harnack declared he had freedom of work and speech at Berlin [Harnack to CWE, Feb. 14, 1893]); CWE to Ira N. Hollis, July 21, 1893 (on newspapers); CWE to Francis Rawle, Oct. 13, 1900 (on Bryan); J. Franklin Jameson to CWE, Aug. 13, 31, Sept. 2, 1897 (all on Andrews); Walter C. Bronson, *The History of Brown University, 1764–1914* (Providence, 1914), 462–67.

58. CWE to Jordan, Oct. 31, 1905; CWE, "Academic Freedom," *Science* 26:4.

59. CWE, "Academic Freedom," *Science* 26:7, 6, 4.

60. Cattell, *University Control*, 37–38; "The A.A.U.P.'s 'General Declaration of Principles,' 1915," in Richard Hofstadter and Wilson Smith (eds.), *American Higher Education: A Documentary History* (Chicago, 1961), II:863–64. Jacob Gould Schurman, president of Cornell from 1892 to 1920, spoke even more emphatically than Eliot in support of academic freedom (Bishop, *Cornell*, 322–23, 336).

61. Veysey, *American University*, part 2, "The Price of Structure, 1890–1910." On Harper specifically, see the more sympathetic treatment in Richard J. Storr, *Harper's University: The Beginnings* (Chicago, 1966).

62. A. B. Hart, "Ten Years of Harvard," HGM 11(1902–3):63–64; Morison, "Government and Administration, 1869–1929," in Morison (ed.), *Development of Harvard*, p. xxxiv; Royce, "Present Ideals," *Scribner's Magazine* 10:385–86; CWE, "The Unity of Educational Reform" [1894], *Educational Reform*, 332–34.

63. James to CWE, July 3, 1891 (having found himself on four committees, James suggested that more power be given to committee chairmen); Briggs, quoted in Rollo Walter Brown, *Dean Briggs* (New York, 1926), 118; C. L. Jackson to CWE, June 23, [1901?], June 2, 1903 (serious interruption); similarly, H. C. G. von Jagemann to CWE, July 6, 1899. A call for administrative experts to take over some of the faculty's duties is included in John Williams White's revealing article, "Problems of the Higher Education," HGM 7(1898–99):341–48.

64. AR(1903), 8, (1906), 11–12.

65. CWE to G. J. Brush, Jan. 13, 1875, Brush Papers; CWE to Richard H. Jesse, Dec. 28, 1904; CWE, "The University President in the American Commonwealth" [1911], in Neilson (ed.), *Eliot*, I:233.

66. Briggs, in AR(1905), 61; Thomas Nixon Carver, *Recollections of an Unplanned Life* (Los Angeles, 1949), 133; A. B. Hart, "University Happenings," HGM 5(1896–97): 248–49; CWE, "Speech at Institute of Technology," EPA 700; AR(1906), 13 (high value; similarly, CWE, "Academic Freedom," *Science* 26:11).

67. Briggs, quoted in Brown, *Dean Briggs*, 275; Perry, *And Gladly Teach*, 239–40. For Eliot's opinion of one individual's role in faculty meetings, see CWE to A. Lawrence Lowell, June 25, 1909, A. L. Lowell Papers. For a lively summary of a faculty meeting, see Barrett Wendell to A. L. Lowell, Nov. 22, 1905, ibid.

68. Morison, "Government and Administration," in Morison (ed.), *Development of Harvard*, p. xxxv; A. B. Hart, "The Half-Way Point," HGM 5(1896–97):389 (little Faculties); AR(1890), 10–11, (1900), 10. Cf. Mark Beach, "Professional versus Professorial Control of Higher Education," *Educational Record* 49(1968):267–68.

69. F. W. Taussig, "President Eliot's Administration," HGM 17 (1908–09):388 (in person); Taussig, "The Administrator," *Harvard Illustrated Magazine* 10(1909):194 (to engineering); Bolles to CWE, Jan. 10, 1889; Bolles, "A Review of the Academic Year, 1891–92," HGM 1(1892–93):101–2; Bolles, "An Administrative Problem," HGM 3(1894–95):1–8; William R. Thayer, "Frank Bolles," HGM 2(1893–94):366–72.

70. Boston *Post*, March 2, 1892; AR(1901), 47; James, *Eliot*, II:133–34; J. D. Greene, "Fluctuations of University Enrollment," HGM 17(1908–09):261–66; Greene, "Taxation of College Property," ibid., 368–69.

71. AR(1907), 337–40. Eliot felt the creation of the committee as something of a challenge (AR[1906], 9–10). Further recognition that organizational elaboration was causing institutional congestion appeared in simultaneous discussions in the Faculty of Arts and Sciences. The idea of a presidential cabinet or council of deans was "almost unanimously distrusted . . . as tending to the establishment of a new authority which would

incline toward excessive conservatism." But in fact the four deans of Arts and Sciences did act informally with the president to present projects to the faculty (AR[1907], 337). On bureaucratism, see Robert H. Wiebe, *The Search for Order, 1877–1920* (New York, 1967), chap. 6, "Revolution in Values."

72. Cattell, *University Control*, 23–25, 65–84, 67 (quotation).

73. G. H. Palmer to William James, [Dec. 25, 1900], in Perry, *James*, I:436 (question); CWE, "Undesirable and Desirable Uniformity in Schools" [1892], *Educational Reform*, 285.

74. James, *Eliot*, I:334–37, 342; quotation from CWE to Lyman, July 13, 1877, ibid., 336.

75. James, *Eliot*, I:309–10; Morison, *Three Centuries*, 359; William James to Alice James, Oct., 1887, quoted in Perry, *James*, II:679.

76. AR(1894), 242–43 (tribute); William James to CWE, May 19, 1894; James, *Eliot*, II:89.

77. Charles H. Grandgent, *The New Word* (Cambridge, 1929), 170–81.

CHAPTER III, *The System of Liberty*

1. *University Administration*, 131–32.

2. Morison, *Three Centuries*, 90; Rudolph, *American College*, 162–63.

3. "Original Papers in Relation to a Course of Liberal Education," *American Journal of Science and Arts* 15(1829):308–09, 328–30, 299, 313.

4. Rudolph, *American College*, 125–27.

5. David B. Tyack, *George Ticknor and the Boston Brahmins* (Cambridge, 1967), 99–126; Morison, *Three Centuries*, 228–38.

6. Rudolph, *American College*, 112–16; Eliot, "New Education," *Atlantic Monthly* 23:213–14.

7. Bronson, *Brown*, 279–82, 296–97, 324; Russell H. Chittenden, *History of the Sheffield Scientific School of Yale University, 1846–1922* (New Haven, 1928), I:55–61; CWE, "New Education," *Atlantic Monthly* 23:214 (loose); CWE to James B. Angell, July 11, 1899 (in advance). Eliot's fullest appraisal of Wayland's experiments appeared in "[Address on the Elective System and of Francis Wayland as One of the Originators Thereof: At Brown University]" [1885?], EPA 34.

8. Bishop, *Cornell*, 75, 324–25; R. Freeman Butts, *The College Charts Its Course: Historical Conceptions and Current Proposals* (New York, 1939), 187–88; Veysey, *American University*, 86.

9. David Starr Jordan, "The Policy of the Stanford University," *Educational Review* 4(1892):2–5; Orrin Leslie Elliott, *Stanford University: The First Twenty-five Years* (Stanford University, 1937), 70–72, 509–17.

10. "Faculty," in Paul Monroe (ed.), *A Cyclopedia of Education* (New York, 1911), 2:569–70; Ernest N. Henderson, "Formal Discipline," ibid., 2:642–47; McCosh, *New Departure*, 8.

11. Walter B. Kolesnik, *Mental Discipline in Modern Education* (Madison, Wis., 1958), 89.

12. Occasionally, his lists were longer but expressed the same tendency, as when he named six "essential constituents of education": "We must learn to see straight and clear; to compare and infer; to make an accurate record; to remember; to express our thought with precision; and to hold fast lofty ideals" (CWE, "Unity of Educational Reform," *Educational Reform*, 322). See also Thomas Reid, *Essays on the Intellectual Powers of Man*, ed. James Walker (Cambridge, 1850), esp. 26–29.

13. "Original Papers," *American Journal of Science* 15:300; CWE, "New Education," *Atlantic Monthly* 23:214. On this dichotomy, see also Edward A. Krug, *American High School*, 445; Michael B. Katz, *The Irony of Early School Reform: Educational Innovation in Mid-Nineteenth Century Massachusetts* (Cambridge, 1968), 125–28. At times Eliot added "character" as a third educational aim (CWE, "The Function of Education in Democratic Society" [1897], *Educational Reform*, 402).

14. CWE, "Inaugural," *Educational Reform*, 6; E. L. Youmans, *The Culture Demanded by Modern Life* . . . (New York, 1891 [originally published 1867]), 23, 2; Krug, *American High School*, 99–100.

15. Thorndike and Woodworth, quoted in Geraldine Jonçich, *The Sane Positivist: A Biography of Edward L. Thorndike* (Middletown, Conn., 1968), 273. As widely interpreted, Thorndike's "Connectionism" supported a curriculum of precise content with direct application. But Thorndike himself warned against such extreme specificity and at times spoke like the old-style mental disciplinarians. See Jonçich, *Sane Positivist*, 268–80; Geraldine Jonçich, "Science: Touchstone for a New Age in Education," in Jonçich (ed.), *Psychology and the Science of Education: Selected Writings of Edward L. Thorndike* (New York, 1962), 23–26; Kolesnik, *Mental Discipline*, 65–68, 43–44. The landmark article is E. L. Thorndike and R. S. Woodworth, "The Influence of Improvement in One Mental Function upon the Efficiency of Other Functions," *Psychological Review* 8(1901):247–61, 384–95, 553–64.

16. Burke A. Hinsdale, "President Eliot on Popular Education," *Intelligence* 13(1893):53. The quotations are from the article that stirred Hinsdale's criticism, "Wherein Popular Education Has Failed" [1892], in CWE, *American Contributions to Civilization and Other Essays and Addresses* (New York, 1897), 215.

17. Kolesnik, *Mental Discipline*, 46–49. For Eliot's view see note 19, below.

18. A. Lawrence Lowell, *At War with Academic Traditions in*

America (Cambridge, 1934), p. vii; Kolesnik, *Mental Discipline*, 20–21. The statement in Butts, *The College Charts Its Course*, 205, "Those who held to mental discipline generally opposed the elective system," is misleading since nearly all educators involved in the controversy "held to mental discipline."

19. CWE, "New Education," *Atlantic Monthly* 23:359. The same notion of method appears in a discussion of chemistry and physics in 1872, in which Eliot argued that only by "observation and experiment" could a student "acquire any just conceptions of the processes, methods and results" of these sciences. "If the bare facts of chemistry and physics are unprofitable husks, the theories and hypotheses of those sciences are not much better mental food when separated from the experimental data on which they rest" (CWE, "[Report of West Point Board of Visitors]" [1872] EPA 7).

20. CWE, "New Education," *Atlantic Monthly* 23:218 (pill); CWE, "Inaugural," *Educational Reform*, 1 (dwarfed faculties), 13 (concentration); CWE, "Liberty in Education" [1885], ibid., 138–41 (bent); Morison, *Three Centuries*, 342.

21. "Can School Programmes Be Shortened and Enriched?" [1888], *Educational Reform*, 167 (artificial hardness); "Republican Education" [1904], EPA 161 (pupil's will); similarly, "Wherein Popular Education Has Failed," *American Contributions*, 229; "Address to New Students, October 1, 1906," HGM 15(1906–7):223 (your interest).

22. "Is a Classical Education a Practical Education?" [1894] EPA 52; CWE, "The Unity of Educational Reform" [1894], *Educational Reform*, 322; CWE, "The Solid Satisfactions of Life," HGM 14(1905–6):214; "Republican Education," EPA 161; "New Definition of the Cultivated Man," Neilson (ed.), *Eliot*, I:199–203. In a letter to W. H. Smiley, Oct. 31, 1894, Eliot reserved judgment on the question, "Are all subjects equivalent for general education?"

23. "New Education," *Atlantic Monthly* 23:210, 214.

24. "Inaugural," *Educational Reform*, 11–14 (revelation); "Speech at New York Harv[ard] Club in Feb[ruary] 1870," EPA 3 (costly); CWE to Thomas W. Higginson, April 20, 1872, Higginson Papers (college proper).

25. "Liberty in Education," *Educational Reform*, 138 (group system); on Overseers' committee see p. 41, above.

26. "Inaugural," *Educational Reform*, 13; James Mills Peirce, in AR(1893), 127; W. W. Goodwin, "Growth of the Graduate School," HGM 9:173.

27. "Inaugural," *Educational Reform*, 3; CWE, "Undesirable and Desirable Uniformity in Schools," ibid., 282–83. Student judgment of teachers is hinted at in AR (1902), 24.

28. CWE, *Charles Eliot: Landscape Architect* . . . (Boston, 1902),

17, 28–29; Hofstadter and Metzger, *Development of Academic Freedom,* 397–99; CWE, "Academic Freedom," *Science* n.s. 26:7–10.

29. "[Experience with a College Elective System]" [1895], EPA 62 (reformation); *University Administration,* 173, 162.

30. For the period 1825–1877 the best history is AR(1884), 6–30. For the entire Eliot era, see Morison, "College Studies, 1869–1929," in Morison (ed.), *Development of Harvard,* pp. xxxix–l; Morison, *Three Centuries,* 345–46.

31. CWE, *Harvard Memories,* 27–28. See also James Russell Lowell, "Oration," *A Record of the Commemoration, November Fifth to Eighth, 1886, on the Two Hundred and Fiftieth Anniversary of the Founding of Harvard College* (Cambridge, 1887), 218–25, 232–34; Edgar B. Wesley, *NEA: The First Hundred Years: The Building of the Teaching Profession* (New York, 1957), 97–102.

32. HUC(1873), 65, (1874), 80; AR(1875), 15; George Herbert Palmer, "The New Education" [1885], in G. H. and Alice Freeman Palmer, *The Teacher: Essays and Addresses on Education* (Boston, 1908), 173 (first college).

33. HUC(1899), 419, (1900), 435. Morison, *Three Centuries,* 346, erroneously cites 1897 as the year when themes and forensics were dropped. Earlier, those who made high grades in English courses could avoid them.

34. Henry James [III], class of 1899, "Student Life," HGM 7(1898–99):558. Thus early did Eliot's biographer express his sympathy with his future subject.

35. HUC(1873), 60, 64, (1885), 77, 85–86; AR(1875), 15. The vestigial requirement for seniors was four "forensics" (written exercises).

36. AR(1881), 25; CWE, *University Administration,* 162 (infinite); Palmer, "New Education," Palmer and Palmer, *The Teacher,* 178–98.

37. On the controversy, see Butts, *The College Charts Its Course,* part 3, "The Elective Principle Wins the Day," and the descriptive bibliography, 430–35. For early support of Eliot, see F. A. P. Barnard to CWE, May 27, 1871.

38. Andrew F. West, *A Review of President Eliot's Report on Elective Studies* (New York, 1886 [reprinted from the *Independent*]), 11–12; Butts, *The College Charts Its Course,* 218–19.

39. West, *Review,* 8, 4, 14, 13; Thomas Jefferson Wertenbaker, *Princeton, 1746–1896* (Princeton, 1946), 304–5.

40. Besides his annual reports, see "What Is a Liberal Education?" [1884], *Educational Reform,* 89–122; "Liberty in Education," ibid., 125–48; "The System of Elective Studies in American Colleges" [1885?], EP, box 349. For a later summary defense, see CWE, "Educational Changes and Tendencies," *Journal of Education* 34(1891):403.

41. J. M. Crafts (president of M.I.T.) to CWE, Nov. 25, 1899; CWE to Albert Stickney, April 1, 1891; Timothy Brosnahan, *President Eliot and Jesuit Colleges* ([Boston?], [1900?]), 27–34.

42. CWE to James B. Angell, May 22, 1903; similarly, CWE, *More Money*, 113. For the actual case at Yale, see George Wilson Pierson, *Yale: College and University, 1871–1937*, vol. I, *Yale College: An Educational History, 1871–1921* (New Haven, 1952), esp. 195.

43. CWE, "[The Condition of American Education]" [1901], EPA 103; *University Administration*, ch. iv.

44. CWE to Daniel C. Gilman, Dec. 8, 1885, Gilman Papers; CWE, remarks, AAU(1904), 38–39; CWE, *University Administration*, 133–34.

45. West, *Review*, 13; *University Administration*, 162–64. So thoroughly did the practice die out that even the name "group system" came to designate something quite different, a technique of guaranteeing student course distribution among broad fields or groups (Russell Thomas, *The Search for a Common Learning: General Education, 1800–1960* [New York, 1962], 97).

46. William Goodell Frost to editor of the *Nation*, Jan. 23, 1882, reprinted in Hofstadter and Smith (eds.), *American Higher Education*, II:734; "Liberty in Education," *Educational Reform*, 142–45 (one mind); CWE to S. M. Macvane, June 18, 1897 (skeptic). The Cornell plan also required that twenty hours be given to concentration in one of twelve areas (Bishop, *Cornell*, 393).

47. George Santayana, *Persons and Places* (New York, 1944–53), vol. I, *Background of My Life*, 196 (geology); CWE, "Liberty in Education," *Educational Reform*, 143–44 (mature student).

48. George T. Ladd, *Essays on the Higher Education* (New York, 1899), 101.

49. "Liberty in Education," *Educational Reform*, 128–32 (similarly, AR[1881], 12); "Remarks before Hopkins Trustees" [1874], EPA 11.

50. CWE, *University Administration*, 134–35, 137; "Liberty in Education," *Educational Reform*, 136 (prevailing tendency); "Academic Freedom," *Science* n.s. 26:8 (to specialize early). Eliot admitted the undesirability of "extreme specialization" and frequently cited the results of a study of 1884–85 showing that only 8 per cent of Harvard College undergraduates specialized to a high degree (defined as taking at least two-thirds of three years' work in a single department); the same situation, he claimed with evident satisfaction, still prevailed in 1908 (AR[1885], 33, [1900], 12; *University Administration*, 155).

51. CWE, "Speech at New York Harv[ard Club]" [1870], EPA 3; Palmer, "New Education," Palmer and Palmer, *The Teacher*, 185. "Second-year honors" appears to have begun as a sop to the classics and mathematics

departments, an effort to attract students to these departments as they lost their required status; of the 181 members of the class graduating in 1885, 92 won honorable mention, but only 12 won honors or highest honors (AR[1885], 38–39, 185–87, 198–99; HUC[1885], 107–10; Ephraim Gurney, in AR[1872], 54).

52. AR(1900), 14–15.

53. "Liberty in Education," *Educational Reform*, 144 (conquests); "The Condition of American Education" EPA 103.

54. CWE to Thomas Goodell, Jan. 1, 1907.

55. "New Education," *Atlantic Monthly* 23:214; "Inaugural," *Educational Reform*, 13; AR(1885), 49. See below, pp. 201–3.

56. CWE to Henry S. Pritchett, July 13, 1907; "Original Papers," *American Journal of Science* 15:317; McCosh, *New Departure*, 14n2.

57. "Inaugural," *Educational Reform*, 8–9; Thomas Thacher (of Yale) to D. C. Gilman, Nov. 17, 1881, Gilman Papers; F. C. Lowell, "The President's Report for 1886–87," *Harvard Monthly* 6(1888):11.

58. "Inaugural," *Educational Reform*, 17; Charles T. Burnett, *Hyde of Bowdoin: A Biography of William DeWitt Hyde* (Boston, 1931), 38; Chapman, *Memories and Milestones*, 169, 171; James, *Eliot*, I:311–13.

59. Grant, *Fourscore*, 95, 87; William Lawrence, "A Call to Harvard Men," HGM 13(1904–05):5; Barrett Wendell, "Recollections of Harvard (1872–1917)," MS, HUA (HUG1876.10).

60. AR(1904), 14 (essential element); CWE, quoted in New York *Tribune*, Feb. 21, 1886.

61. William Coolidge Lane, "The University during the Past Six Years," 13–14, offprint from *Second Triennial Report of the Secretary of the Class of 1881 of Harvard College*, copy in HUA (HUA887.48); Morison, *Three Centuries*, 403; Charles Francis Adams, *Three Phi Beta Kappa Addresses . . .* (Boston, 1907), 137.

62. Brown, *Dean Briggs*, 96–98; Morison, "Government and Administration," in Morison (ed.), *Development of Harvard*, p. xxxv; Morison, *Three Centuries*, 402–03; J. Donald Adams, *Copey of Harvard: A Biography of Charles Townsend Copeland* (Boston, 1960), esp. 108; Veysey, *American University*, 225–26.

63. Morison, *Three Centuries*, 316–17, 420–22; Van Wyck Brooks, "Harvard and American Life," *Living Age* 259(1908):645; George Santayana, "A Glimpse of Yale," *Harvard Monthly* 13(1892–93):92–93; Barrett Wendell, "Social Life at Harvard," *Lippincott's Magazine* 39(1887): 152–59; Hart, "Some Aspects of Harvard's Growth," HGM 4(1895–96):402; Hart, "The University: The End of the Year," HGM 16(1907–8):66. A good example of an isolated student is Maroni, the butt of the

author's humor in Owen Wister, *Philosophy 4: A Story of Harvard University* (New York, 1903).

64. CWE, *University Administration*, 142; AR(1902), 58–59, (1906), 50–51; "College Students as Rumsellers," *Our Day* 9(1892):98–103 (D.K.E. scandal).

65. "Major Higginson's Gift—the Harvard Union," HGM 8(1899–1900):239; R. B. Merriman, "The Winter Quarter," HGM 13(1904-5):439–40; idem, "The Autumn Quarter," HGM 14(1905-6):260; Francis G. Peabody "Phillips Brooks House," HGM 9(1900–1901):540; AR(1900), 115.

66. William James, "The True Harvard," HGM 12(1903-4):7; similarly, Daniel Gregory Mason, "At Harvard in the Nineties," *New England Quarterly* 9(1936):69.

67. Morison, *Three Centuries*, 332; James, *Eliot*, I:242, 244; Robert Grant, "Harvard College in the Seventies," *Scribner's Magazine* 21(1897): 565; editorial, *Harvard Monthly* 3(1886):40.

68. "Liberty in Education," *Educational Reform*, 147–48 (ancient fiction); "Report of West Point Board of Visitors," EPA 7 (monastic discipline); CWE, address to Harvard Club, reported in *Swiss Times*, March 17, 1873; George Santayana, "The Spirit and Ideals of Harvard University" [1894], in James Ballowe (ed.), *George Santayana's America: Essays on Literature and Culture* (Urbana, Ill., 1967), 61; AR(1888), 9; HUC(1887), 90–91.

69. George Herbert Palmer, "Necessary Limitations of the Elective System" [1887], in Palmer and Palmer, *The Teacher*, 260, 263; Morison, "College Studies," in Morison (ed.), *Development of Harvard*, xliv; AR (1890), 16; Frank Bolles to CWE, Jan. 24, 1889; CWE to Albert Stickney, April 13, 1889; Ferdinand Bôcher to CWE, Nov. 18, 1889.

70. Dean Byron S. Hurlbut, in AR(1904), 112–13.

71. CWE, "[Address at Unitarian Festival]" [1880], EPA 29; "Academic Freedom," *Science* n.s. 26:9; G. H. Palmer, "New Education," in Palmer and Palmer, *The Teacher*, 182.

72. "Inaugural," *Educational Reform*, 16–17; "The Solid Satisfactions of Life," HGM 14(1905-6):214 (spotless reputation); Lord, quoted in Rudolph, *American College*, 139; "University Notes," HGM 2(1893-94): 601 (suggested regimen); CWE, remarks, HGM 18(1909–10):66–67 (good manners); L. B. R. Briggs, in AR(1900), 117 (transparency).

73. "Liberty in Education," *Educational Reform*, 140.

74. HUC(1893), 197, (1894), 210; W. M. Davis, "The Question of Seminars," HGM 11(1902-3):363–70; Clarence A. Brodeur to CWE, April 3, 1889; Henry James, "Student Life," HGM 7(1898-99):409–10. For sympathetic descriptions of paid cramming seminars, see Robert Morss Lovett,

All Our Years (New York, 1948), 38–39; John Corbin, "A Worm's-Eye View," *Saturday Review of Literature* 7(1931):890.

75. Rudolph, *American College*, ch. 18, "The Rise of Football"; Veysey, *American University*, 276–77; AR(1906), 45.

76. Morison, *Three Centuries*, 410–11; AR(1882), 16–19, (1887), 27; CWE, quoted in Rudolph, *American College*, 380; Thomas W. Higginson to CWE, March 28, 1896 (similarly, Adams, *Three Phi Beta Kappa Addresses*, 140–41). In 1895 and 1896 Harvard and Yale did not meet in football (AR [1901], 15).

77. Lodge, remarks, HGM 5(1896–97):67; AR(1898), 14–15, (1897), 40.

78. Rudolph, *American College*, 375–77; Roosevelt, summarized address, in G. H. Dorr, "Student Life," HGM 4(1895–96):592; CWE to Theodore Roosevelt, Dec. 2, 12, 1905; Columbus (Ohio) *State Journal*, April 23, 1908.

79. CWE to Theodore Roosevelt, July 14, 1908; CWE to Byron S. Hurlbut, July 13, 1908. For the texts of both telegrams, see Brown, *Dean Briggs*, 176n.

80. Lowell, "Inaugural Address," *At War*, 33 (similarly, Andrew Fleming West, *Short Papers on American Liberal Education* [New York, 1907], 110); CWE, "The Condition of American Education," EPA 103; CWE, "The 1858 Races—Origin of Harvard's Colors," HGM 8(1899–1900):465–67; Briggs, in AR(1908), 121; Morison, *Three Centuries*, 414–15.

81. Rudolph, *American College*, 443, 446–47; John W. Burgess, "The American University . . . ," in Burgess, *Reminiscences of an American Scholar: The Beginnings of Columbia University* (New York, 1934), 351–54; Jesse, quoted in Krug, *American High School*, 164. On the college-shortening movement, see ibid., 163–68.

82. For challenges to both these assertions, see E. B. Andrews, "Time and Age in Relation to the College Curriculum," *Educational Review* 1(1891):135–36; Arthur M. Comey, "The Growth of New England Colleges," ibid., 209–19.

83. AR(1887), 16–17, (1888), 12–13, (1900), 98. For an account of the question that goes well beyond the medical context, see Thomas Francis Harrington, *The Harvard Medical School: A History, Narrative and Documentary, 1782–1905* (New York, 1905), III:1273–1312.

84. A. B. Hart, "Actualities of the Three Year A.B. Degree," HGM 10(1901–2)201–7; Morison, *Three Centuries*, 370–71; CWE to W. W. Goodwin, Dec. 16, 1890. Eliot's best history and rationale for this program appears in AR(1902), 24–28. He also complained of long training for the Ph.D. and suggested shorter theses (AR[1901], 22–23).

85. AR(1898), 34–36, (1907), 28, (1908), 18, (1902), 32; CWE, remarks, AAU(1902), 43; Ephraim Emerton, "Personal Recollections of Charles William Eliot," HGM 32(1923–24):347.

86. CWE, *Four American Leaders*, 34–35; CWE, quoted in Valentine H. May, "Associated Clubs," HGM 14(1905–6):130; "The Three Years' Course" [report of a committee of the Associated Harvard Clubs], ibid., 580–87; AR(1902), 27.

87. AR(1905), 32 (obscure conditions); AR(1906), 16 (board and lodging). Extra tuition was a financial measure, not an attack on the three-year degree. In a simultaneous poll, 89 out of 124 members of the faculty agreed that the taking of "additional" courses should not be discouraged (AR[1906], 14).

88. Morison, *Three Centuries*, 370; AR(1908), 16–17; Krug, *American High School*, 168. For both sides of the discussion at Harvard, see "The Month," *Harvard Monthly* 11(1890–91):204–7; William James, "The Proposed Shortening of the College Course," ibid., 127–37 (in favor); S. M. Macvane, "The Three Years' Course," ibid., 12(1891–92):1–13 (against); Edwin H. Hall, "College Work and the A.B. in Three Years," HGM 9(1900–1901):330–37 (in favor).

89. CWE to Thomas Goodell, Jan. 1, 1907; CWE, "The Length of the College Course," HGM 12(1903–4):178.

90. Lawrence, "A Call to Harvard Men," HGM 13(1904–5):5; "President Eliot's Jubilee," HGM 12(1903–4):591–93; R. L. Groves, "Student Life," HGM 17(1908–9):305.

CHAPTER IV, *Christo et Ecclesiae?*

1. Charles A. Blanchard, "The Purpose of Higher Education," proof-sheets, EP.

2. *Autobiography of Andrew Dickson White* (New York, 1905), I:318, 366–67; Rogers, *White*, 72–84; Hawkins, *Pioneer*, 68–71; Franklin Hamlin Littell, *From State Church to Pluralism: A Protestant Interpretation of Religion in American History* (Garden City, 1962), 107–11.

3. Stow Persons, "Religion and Modernity, 1865–1914," in James Ward Smith and A. Leland Jamison (eds.), *Religion in American Life*, vol. I, *The Shaping of American Religion* (Princeton, 1961), 372–73; Arthur Meier Schlesinger, "A Critical Period in American Religion, 1875–1900," MHS 64(1930):523–47.

4. Ralph Barton Perry, "Charles William Eliot: His Personal Traits and Essential Creed," *New England Quarterly* 4(1931):18; CWE to G. H. Palmer, May 19, [1894], in *Harvard Crimson*, Dec. 15, 1926; Francis Green-

wood Peabody, "Charles William Eliot," HGM 35(1926–27):247; "Some Reasons Why the American Republic May Endure" [1894], *American Contributions*, 64.

5. James, *Eliot*, II:54–55, 299–300. Eliot's fullest statement of his religious views is "The Religion of the Future" [1909], in Neilson (ed.), *Eliot*, II:576–603.

6. Ezra S. Gannett to CWE, July 3, 1871; CWE to William Robertson Smith, Feb. 23, 1880 (draft); Morison, "Government and Administration," in Morison (ed.), *Development of Harvard*, xxviii; G. H. Palmer to CWE, Aug. 22, 1894; Hofstadter and Metzger, *Development of Academic Freedom*, 352.

7. James, *Eliot*, I:197.

8. Theodore Lyman to CWE, Oct. 20, 1869.

9. Edward Everett Hale to CWE, Oct. 20,1869.

10. CWE to Joseph May, Aug. 16, 1895; CWE, "New Education," *Atlantic Monthly*, 23:215n; CWE, "On the Education of Ministers" [1883], *Educational Reform*, 71.

11. W. T. Reid to CWE, Aug. 20, 1890; Justin Winsor to CWE, Jan. 23, 1890; Morison, *Three Centuries*, 362; T. E. St. John to CWE, Dec. 9, 1888, and enclosed clpg.; CWE to E. Winchester Donald, Feb. 3, 1897; Donald to CWE, Feb. 2, 4, 1897; CWE to William James, Aug. 2, 1902; John Trowbridge to CWE, April 29, 1886. A copy of the tract is in EP.

12. "New Education," *Atlantic Monthly*, 23:366.

13. McCosh, *New Departure*, passim. For Eliot's address at this first encounter, see "Liberty in Education," *Educational Reform*, 125–48.

14. CWE, "What Place Should Religion Have in a College? Read before the XIX Century Club of New York, February 3, 1886," EPA 36. James, *Eliot*, I:317–18, quotes the address without being able to identify it; significantly, it seemed to him to have the ring of the 1870s. See also *Officers, Members and Constitution of the Nineteenth Century Club and a List of the Lectures and Discussions before the Club since Its Formation* [New York, 1889], 33.

15. "Aims of Higher Education," *Educational Reform*, 235–39.

16. Blanchard to "Dear Sir," April 14, 1891, enclosing proofsheets of "The Purpose of Higher Education," EP; CWE to Blanchard, April 18, 29, 1891; Blanchard to CWE, April 21, May 2, 1891.

17. Hofstadter and Metzger, *Development of Academic Freedom*, 209–53.

18. CWE, answers to Bureau of Education questionnaire, 1876, EP; CWE to Joseph R. Putnam, Sept. 15, 1869 (draft); AR(1871), 32; James, *Eliot*, I:373; CWE to T. W. Higginson, April 20, 1872, Higginson Papers.

19. Francis G. Peabody to CWE, Nov. 9, 1900; Morison, *Three Cen-*

turies, 417; CWE to Arthur L. Thayer, Nov. 3, 1907; *Colorado Sun,* March 11, 1892; *Deseret Evening News,* March 17, 1894; Frank Bolles to CWE, April 14, 1892; Samuel A. Eliot to CWE, March 22, 1892; Boston *Evening Transcript,* [March, 1892], clpg., EP.

20. CWE to William A. Richardson, Jan. 30, 1890.

21. "Address at the Inauguration of Daniel C. Gilman" [1876], *Educational Reform,* 43, 46.

22. "What Place Should Religion Have in a College?" EPA 36.

23. "Three Results of the Scientific Study of Nature" [1877], *American Contributions,* 238.

24. CWE to Raymond Weeks, Feb. 18, 1908; James Freeman Clarke to [CWE], Feb. 5, 1870. For an analysis of the relationship between religious leaders and the universities at this juncture, see Hofstadter and Metzger, *Development of Academic Freedom,* ch. 7, "Darwinism and the New Regime." The Fiske affair is treated in ibid., 338n. A fuller account appears in Berman, *Fiske,* 71–80.

25. John W. Craig to CWE, April 20, May 21, 1886; CWE to Münsterberg, Nov. 6, 1908.

26. "An Urban University" [1896], *Educational Reform,* 397; AR (1882), 29–30; George A. Gordon, *My Education and Religion: An Autobiography* (Boston, 1925), 293.

27. For detailed accounts of the divinity school in Eliot's day, see Williams (ed.), *Harvard Divinity School,* and William Wallace Fenn, "The Theological School, 1869–1928," in Morison (ed.), *Development of Harvard,* 463–71.

28. Levering Reynolds, Jr., "The Later Years (1880–1953)," in Williams (ed.), *Harvard Divinity School,* 170–71 and passim; AR(1878), 36–37; CWE to W. W. Fenn, Nov. 13, 1900.

29. Littell, *From State Church to Pluralism,* 108–9. Charles F. Dunbar, dean of the Faculty of Arts and Sciences, could say of the divinity school in 1894 that it had "taken its place as a University Faculty, devoted to the advancement of theological science and the impartial training of seekers after truth" (Dunbar, "President Eliot's Administration," HGM 2[1893–94]:466).

30. CWE to Crawford H. Toy, Nov. 5, 1908.

31. Bishop, *Cornell,* 141–42, 193–94; Hawkins, *Pioneer,* 69. A related problem, the university church, saw Eliot contemplating abolition as early as 1869, but attaining his aim only in 1882 after the retirement of Andrew P. Peabody. See William A. Richardson to CWE, July 24, 1869; A. P. Peabody to CWE, June 25, 1875; AR (1882), 21.

32. AR(1873), 9.

33. CWE, *University Administration,* 61–63 (easily stirs); Alexander

V. G. Allen, *Life and Letters of Phillips Brooks* (New York, 1900), 2:614–15 (abandonment); "What Place Should Religion Have in a College?" EPA 36 (short service). Eliot's uncharacteristic rigidity on this question at this time may be related to troubles other reforms—notably widening the elective system and modifying admission standards—were bringing him.

34. AR(1881), 18; Palmer to CWE, May 25, 1882 (similarly, anonymous alumnus, "Cause and Effect at Harvard," *Nation* 41[1885]:377); Edward Atkinson to CWE, Jan. 28, 1884 (shocked father); Francis G. Peabody, "Voluntary Worship," in Morison (ed.), *Development of Harvard*, p. li (remnant): Odin Barnes Roberts, "Religious Reform at Harvard," HGM 14(1905–6):231 (on Garrison).

35. Peabody, "Voluntary Worship," in Morison (ed.), *Development of Harvard*, lii–liiii, lvi.

36. CWE to Brooks, Nov. 5, 1881, Phillips Brooks Papers, HUA; CWE, *University Administration*, 62. Although the practice at Cornell might have been cited as comparable, Peabody seems to have had the English example of dean and canons in mind.

37. This inference is based on Peabody, "Voluntary Worship," in Morison (ed.), *Development of Harvard*, p. li, and the fact that his election was simultaneous with the adoption of new statutes for the chair (CWE to Peabody, April 23, 1886, in "Papers belonging to the Plummer Professor and the Preachers to the University," scrapbook, HUA [HUA-1676.571]).

38. CWE to Brooks, May 22, 1891, Brooks Papers; Allen, *Brooks*, II:613–18; AR(1886), 6; *Congregationalist*, Jan. 26, 1888; Boston *Herald*, Dec. 11, 1887.

39. In AR(1896), 11–13, Eliot assessed the program at the end of its first decade. Even in the first year under the new plan, a student had urged his fellows to face the disagreeable fact that "two [sic] many empty benches stare Dr. Brooks and the other University preachers in the face each morning" (letter to the editor, *Harvard Crimson*, May 24, 1887). At Yale the critical alumnus observed "men reading newspapers, wearing sweaters, and in other ways showing no interest in, or respect for, the service" (Francis Woodman to CWE, Nov. 4, Dec. 27, 1901). Yale abolished compulsory chapel in 1926, during a period when the practice was widely called into question (Ralph Henry Gabriel, *Religion and Learning at Yale: The Church of Christ in the College and University, 1757–1957* [New Haven, 1958], 226–28; Rudolph, *American College*, 75–77).

40. W. H. P. Faunce to CWE, Dec. 15, 1897; Melville M. Bigelow to CWE, June 27, 1892; William Rainey Harper to C. F. Aked, March 25, 1896; F. G. Peabody to Harper, Oct. 8, 1901; last two in President's Papers, Special Collections, University of Chicago Library.

41. William Reed Bigelow, "Harvard's Better Self," *New England*

Magazine 9(1890–91):504–11; D. N. Beach, "Religion and University Life: The Experiment at Harvard," *Andover Review* 9(1888):597–604; Peter J. O'Callaghan, "Catholics at Harvard," *Catholic Family Annual for 1895*, 74–80. Catholic and Jewish students had been exempt from morning prayers upon request for many years. For a succinct account of the reform of morning prayers, set in the context of student life under Eliot, see Morison, *Three Centuries*, 366–68. For a brief account of this and other religious problems of the university by an English observer, see George Birkbeck Hill, *Harvard College by an Oxonian* (New York, 1895), ch. 3.

42. Gordon, *My Education and Religion*, 285; William Lawrence, *Fifty Years* (Boston, 1923), 42–43.

43. CWE to George Wigglesworth, Nov. 12, 1908. For the long-range results of this reform, see Ben W. Heineman, Jr., "Indifferent Majority Confronts Organized Religion at Harvard," *Harvard Crimson*, Dec. 13, 1963.

44. CWE, "Is a Classical Education a Practical Education?" [1894], EPA 52.

CHAPTER V, *The University and Democracy*

1. "[Speech at] Dinner of the New England Society in the City of New York," EPA 175.

2. James, *Eliot*, I:58; Robert P. Clapp (ed.), *Exercises in Celebrating the Two Hundred and Fiftieth Anniversary of the Settlement of Cambridge, Held December 28, 1880* (Cambridge, 1881), 94; Philip Putnam Chase, "Some Cambridge Reformers of the Eighties, or Cambridge Contributions to Cleveland Democracy in Massachusetts," *Cambridge Historical Society Publications* 20(1927–29):36; "Sibley's Private Journal," Nov. 10, 1870 (very forward).

3. Geoffrey Blodgett, *The Gentle Reformers: Massachusetts Democrats in the Cleveland Era* (Cambridge, 1966), esp. 3–4, 92–93; Chase, "Some Cambridge Reformers," *Cambridge Historical Society Publications*, 20:40; Moorfield Storey, remarks, MHS 60(1926–27):13; T. W. Higginson, "Introduction," in Charles Theodore Russell, Jr. (ed.), *Speeches and Addresses of William E. Russell* (Boston, 1894), p. xiv.

4. In 1864, though outside the country, he was strongly for Lincoln (James, *Eliot*, II:271). See also CWE to Theodore Tebbets, Aug. 3 [1856].

5. Chase, "Some Cambridge Reformers," *Cambridge Historical Society Publications*, 20:44; Raymond L. Bridgman, *The Independents of Massachusetts in 1884* (Boston, 1885), 6, 9, 11; Blodgett, *Gentle Reformers*, 9. In 1872 Eliot had leaned toward the early efforts of the Liberal Republicans (CWE to Isaac C. Collins, Oct. 20, 1873).

6. CWE to Charles Eliot Norton, Aug. 23, 1884; CWE, untitled MS,

labeled "Written for the Advertiser about Oct 25th 1884, but not sent," EP; A. A. Hayes (angered alumnus) to CWE, Oct. 13, 1884.

7. CWE, "New Party Platform" [1884], MS filed with R. H. Dana to CWE, Oct. 20, 1887. Eliot later made it clear that he favored pensions for all public officials, including teachers; it was veterans' pensions that troubled him ("A Republican Becomes a Democrat" [1889], EPA 44).

8. "Republican Becomes a Democrat," EPA 44.

9. Blodgett, *Gentle Reformers*, 20, 41, 69, 74–80; Richard M. Abrams, *Conservatism in a Progressive Era: Massachusetts Politics, 1900–1912* (Cambridge, 1964), 92.

10. CWE, quoted in Boston *Journal*, Oct. 18, 1892; AR(1894), 43.

11. Boston *Evening Transcript*, March 22, 1892; Brooklyn *Eagle*, March 27, 1892; CWE to C. E. L. Wingate, Sept. 29, 1896; CWE to Francis Leon Grisman, Sept. 29, 1896; CWE to T. W. Higginson, Aug. 31, 1896, quoted in Blodgett, *Gentle Reformers*, 224.

12. Oscar F. Cooper, "Student Life," HGM 9(1900–1901):220; George F. Washburn to CWE, Oct. 8, 1900; Gardiner M. Lane to CWE, Sept. 27, 1900; CWE, "Political Principles and Tendencies," *Outlook* 66(1900):457–60; CWE to Harrison O. Apthorp, Aug. 20, 1900; CWE to Thomas M. Osborne, Sept. 4, 1900.

13. CWE to William James, Jan. 24, 1901, in Perry, *James*, I:434; Blodgett, *Gentle Reformers*, 270; R. B. Merriman, "The University: The Spring Quarter," HGM 15(1906–7):627–28; CWE to Margaret Stuart, July 4, 1908. According to the Boston *Advertiser*, Oct. 14, 1904, Eliot's decision for Roosevelt would swing many "Harvard independents" and Cleveland Democrats.

14. CWE to Theodore Roosevelt, Sept. 27, 1906, July 14, 1908, June 12, 1904. For a suggestive interpretation of Eliot's connections with both Presidents, see E. Digby Baltzell, *The Protestant Establishment: Aristocracy & Caste in America* (New York, 1964), ch. 6, "The Aristocratic Counterattack on Caste: President Eliot and the Two Roosevelts."

15. New York *World*, Dec. 18, 1907; CWE to George Ledlie, Dec. 26, 1907; CWE to Jacob Schiff, July 4, 1908; James, *Eliot*, II:229–30.

16. CWE, "Wherein Popular Education Has Failed," *American Contributions*, 233 (on Mill); CWE, "Introduction," Herbert Spencer, *Essays on Education, Etc.* (London, 1911), vii–xvii; CWE, introductory comment to Spencer's "Specialized Administration," *Forum* 55(1916):709–16; CWE, "Emerson," *Four American Leaders*, esp. 118–19. See also William Boyd, "President Eliot and Herbert Spencer," *Harvard Teachers Record* 4(1934):33–36; Hazen C. Carpenter, "Emerson, Eliot, and the Elective System," *New England Quarterly* 24(1951):13–34.

17. "President Eliot's Remarks," Boston *Evening Transcript*, May 28, 1880.

18. *Four American Leaders*, 28–29; CWE, summarized remarks, HGM 6(1897–98):51; "Speech at City Dinner in Memorial Hall, July 3, 1875," EPA 14 (fierce passions); "[Speech at] Dinner of the New England Society in the City of New York" [1905], EPA 175 (human thought).

19. "The Proposed Taxation of Churches" [1874], EPA 10; "Address to New Students," HGM 15(1906–7):223 (world); "Congregationalism and Education" [1899], EPA 90.

20. "Speech at City Dinner," EPA 14; "Equality in a Republic" [1896], *American Contributions*, 168 ("unnatural"; see also CWE, "Wise and Unwise Economy in Schools," *Atlantic Monthly* 35[1875]:719); "Some Reasons Why the American Republic May Endure" [1894], *American Contributions*, 60; CWE to Frank Buffington Vrooman, Feb. 5, 1897.

21. "[Speech at] Latin School Dinner" [1876], EPA 18 (golden age); "Academic Freedom," *Science* n.s. 26:10 (human government).

22. "The Working of American Democracy" [1888], *American Contributions*, 89–90; CWE to E. L. Godkin, Nov. 30, 1899, Jan. 26, 1900 (both in Godkin Papers); "Wherein Popular Education Has Failed" [1892], *American Contributions*, 204–7. Cf. C. Edward Merriam, *A History of American Political Theories* (New York, 1903), 328–29.

23. CWE to Edward S. Joynes, Dec. 18, 1875; CWE to R. Burnham Moffat, Sept. 14, 1904 (cf. Blodgett, *Gentle Reformers*, 32); James, *Eliot*, II:211, 271; "Five American Contributions to Civilization" [1896], *American Contributions*, 22; John G. Sproat, *"The Best Men": Liberal Reformers in the Gilded Age* (New York, 1968), 253–54.

24. "American Democracy," HGM 10(1901–2):505 (no class); "The Working of American Democracy," *American Contributions*, 97 (public schools); CWE to Gertrude M. King, Jan. 19, 1903 (temporary majorities); "Academic Freedom," *Science* n.s. 26:2 (imagination); CWE to his mother, April 9, 1868 (honor).

25. "The Needful Powers and Qualities of a Statesman" [1881], EPA 29.2 (prejudices); "Speech at City Dinner," EPA 14 (men of education); CWE to William James, Feb. 6, 1900, in Perry, *James*, I:433; "Speech at a Dinner of the Society of Architects" [1873?], EPA 8 (both, durable families).

26. "New Americans" [1902], EPA 119; CWE, *The Conflict between Individualism and Collectivism in a Democracy* (New York, 1910), 46–47 (sports); "American Democracy," HGM 10:507 (up and down). See also James McLachlan, *American Boarding Schools: A Historical Study* (New York, 1970), 207–8.

27. "Address of President Eliot," on the occasion of the visit to Harvard of Grand Duke Alexis, unident. clpg. [1872], EP (hereditary culture); CWE to Daniel C. Gilman, June 18, 1883, Gilman Papers (grease the wheels); CWE, remarks, AAU(1902), 42 (control by professions). On

the aristocracy of culture, see John Higham, *History* (Englewood Cliffs, N.J., 1965), 15. A broader context for Eliot's efforts to relate democracy and various levels of education is provided in Rush Welter, *Popular Education and Democratic Thought in America* (New York, 1962), esp. ch. 12 and ch. 14.

28. Chapman, "President Eliot," *Memories and Milestones*, 165–67, 172, 184; similarly, Irving Babbitt, "President Eliot and American Education," *Forum* 81(1929):1, 4.

29. CWE to Isaac C. Collins, Oct. 20, 1873; "The Proposed Taxation of Churches," EPA 16.

30. CWE, "[Speech at] Dinner of the New England Society in the City of New York" [1905], EPA 175; "Paper for the Boston Central Labor Union 7 Feb. [19]04," EPA 143 (greatest good); CWE, remarks, HGM 13(1904–5):99 (increased dependence); "Republican Education" [1904], EPA 161; CWE to George Ledlie, Dec. 26, 1907 (incompetent administration). Cf. Wiebe, *Search for Order*, chs. 5–6.

31. CWE, *Conflict*, 101; CWE to A. V. Dicey, Oct. 2, 1911, in James, *Eliot*, II:214. On Eliot's Progressivism, see Eugen Kuehnemann, *Charles W. Eliot: President of Harvard University (May 19, 1869–May 19, 1909)* (Boston, 1909), 74–76.

32. CWE, *Conflict*, 2–5, 109–10; CWE, *The Wise Direction of Church Activities toward Social Welfare* [American Unitarian Association Department of Social and Public Service, Social Service Series, Bul. No. 11], (Boston, n.d.), 13–14. See also "Pres[ident] Eliot Declares against Socialism," Boston *Globe*, Dec. 23, 1908.

33. "Paper for the Boston Central Labor Union" and stenographic record of question period following [1904], EPA 143; CWE to Jacob Schiff, Aug. 16, 1907 (more threatening); Marguerite Green, *The National Civic Federation and the American Labor Movement, 1900–1925* (Washington, D.C., 1956), 111–12, 175–76; Joseph Warren to Ralph Easley, Dec. 20, 30, 1907, EP; Rowland Hill Harvey, *Samuel Gompers: Champion of the Toiling Masses* (Stanford University, 1935), 128–31; CWE to George Ledlie, Dec. 26, 1907; CWE, *Conflict*, 30 (does not suppress).

34. "Republican Education," EPA 161 (freedom to choose); "The Teacher's Conscience" [1882], EPA 31 (mere selfishness).

35. "Motives for Voluntary Enlistment" [1898], EPA 80. See also "The Function of Education in Democratic Society" [1897], *Educational Reform*, 414.

36. Rudolph, *American College*, 254 (shabbiest); CWE to [McCosh?], [1873]; McCosh to CWE. Feb. 4, 12, March 10, 1873; CWE, "New Education," *Atlantic Monthly* 23:209. See also CWE, remarks, NEA (1873), 44.

37. CWE, "A New Step for Massachusetts," Boston *Advertiser*, March 24, 1879; "The Exemption from Taxation" [1874], *American Contributions*, 302; CWE to "Dear Sir," March 11, 1876.

38. CWE to Folwell, March 19, 1870; "Remarks before Hopkins Trustees" [1874], EPA 11; CWE, "The Relation of Government to Education in the United States down to 1882," MS, EP, box 349; CWE, remarks, HGM 16(1907–8):75.

39. CWE, "National University," NEA(1873), 107–20 (reprinted several times, at least once in the 1890s); David Madsen, *The National University: Enduring Dream of the USA* (Detroit, 1966), 67–88; CWE to C. E. Norton, Aug. 25, 1873, Norton Papers; CWE to Isaac C. Collins, Oct. 20, 1873; C. E. Taylor to CWE, Dec. 24, 1894.

40. CWE, "National University," NEA(1873), 117–19.

41. "Discussion of Dr. Eliot's Report on National University," NEA(1873), 122, 128, 126–27; J. W. Hoyt, "A National University," NEA(1874), 175; Andrew D. White, "A National University," ibid., 68.

42. Edgar B. Wesley, *Proposed: The University of the United States* (Minneapolis, 1936), 17; Alexander Agassiz to CWE, Sept. 4, 1889; William Pepper to CWE, Sept. 17, 1889; CWE to Henry Baldwin, April 25, 1889.

43. CWE to Hoyt, Jan. 1, 1896; Hoyt, "Reply to the Views of the Minority," U.S. Senate (54th Cong., 1st Sess.) Report 429, Part 3, esp. pp. 8–9. At the turn of the century Eliot served on an NEA committee on the national university, headed by William Rainey Harper. The committee sought to undercut the plan by a private program to facilitate scholarly use of government resources in Washington (Madsen, *The National University*, 104–10; Nicholas Murray Butler to CWE, July 19, 28, 1898).

44. Veysey, *American University*, 110; CWE to R. H. Jesse, May 12, 1908 (similarly, *Conflict*, 55); CWE to L. A. Stout, April 10, 1891; "President Eliot's Speech," HGM 18(1909–10):132.

45. CWE, remarks, AAU(1906), 60; Charles R. Van Hise, remarks, HGM 17(1908–9):72–75; CWE, remarks, ibid., 594.

46. William C. Lawton to CWE, May 27, 1891.

47. "The Aims of Higher Education," *Educational Reform*, 233–34.

48. Carol F. Baird, "Albert Bushnell Hart: The Rise of the Professional Historian," in Buck (ed.), *Social Sciences at Harvard*, 132–33, 162–63; Carver, *Recollections of an Unplanned Life*, passim.

49. *Record of the Commemoration, November Fifth to Eighth, 1886*, 15, 38–41, 267–71, 224 (Lowell quotation).

50. Ferdinand Bôcher to CWE, May 11, 1892; "The Aims of Higher Education," *Educational Reform*, 231; unident. clpg., San Bernardino news-

paper, EP; Benjamin Standish Baker, "Advertising a University: The College 'Drummer' in Various Forms," unident. Boston newspaper, Feb. 25, 1903, EP, box 134.

51. Frank Bolles, "Progress of the Year," HGM 1:578; Edward Cummings, "The Harvard Exhibit at the World's Fair," HGM 2(1893–94):50–63; A. B. Hart, "Mid-Year Retrospect," HGM 3(1894–95):348; Cummings to CWE, Aug. 27, July 14, 1893; V. Mott Porter, "St. Louis," HGM 12(1903–4):655–56; "Harvard Exhibit at the World's Fair," HGM 13(1904–5):205–6; "The Harvard Exhibit at St. Louis," ibid., 262–69; *Harvard Bulletin* 7(Jan. 25, 1905):1. Most of the Chicago exhibits were shipped to the Atlanta Exposition in 1895 (Hart, "The Present and the Future," HGM 4[1895–96]:85–86). See also George Santayana, "Spirit and Ideals of Harvard," in Ballowe (ed.), *George Santayana's America*, 57–58.

52. Henry Adams to CWE, June 12, 1892; Emerton, "Personal Recollections," HGM 32:349; James, *Eliot*, II:106–7; Martin Brimmer to CWE, Dec. 11, 1882; E. E. Hale to CWE, May 15, 1883 (both favoring the degree; the vote was 11 to 15 [OR, 12:45–47]); M. A. DeWolfe Howe, *Portrait of an Independent: Moorfield Storey, 1845–1929* (Boston, 1932), 166–67; undated clpg., Boston *Globe* [1884], HUA (HUA881.52A).

53. CWE to C. E. Norton, Feb. 20, 1901; Henry P. Walcott to CWE, Dec. 14, 1900; Hammond Lamont to CWE, April 29, 1901; Howe, *Moorfield Storey*, 177; CWE, quoted in Boston *Journal*, June 6, 1901; A. B. Hart, "Reflections and Predictions," HGM 9(1900–1901):516; George F. Hoar, remarks, HGM 10(1901–2):75; Theodore Roosevelt, "Three College-Bred Americans," HGM 11(1902–3):1–5.

54. CWE to G. J. Brush, Feb. 29, 1872, Brush Papers. For a later similar complaint, see CWE to editor, Boston *Evening Transcript*, Feb. 16, 1904.

55. CWE to T. W. Higginson, April 20, 1872, Higginson Papers. The article, "Young Harvard," appeared in the New York *Tribune*, Feb. 17, 1872.

56. Charles Loring Jackson to CWE, Jan. 26, 1888; G. H. Palmer to N. S. Shaler, March 27, 1890, EP; Frank Bolles, "Opening of the Academic Year, 1892–93," HGM 1(1892–93):247; William R. Thayer, "Frank Bolles," HGM 2(1893–94):366–72; Lovett, *All Our Years*, 66.

57. CWE to Byron S. Hurlbut, Aug. 13, 1895; William R. Thayer to CWE, Aug. 6, 1900; G. V. S. Michaelis to CWE, Oct. 9, 1900.

58. Herbert Small to CWE, May 1, 4, Dec. 4, 1901; Jerome D. Greene to Alice L. Wait, Nov. 25, 1902, EP.

59. Jerome D. Greene to Leo F. Wormser, May 28, 1904; folder on "Publicity," EP, box 239; Greene to Alice L. Wait, Nov. 25, 1902; Greene,

"Fluctuations of University Enrolment," HGM 17(1908–9):261–66; O. D. Skelton (of the University of Chicago) to "Secretary of the Faculty," Sept. 27, 1905 (all letters in EP).

60. Veysey, *American University*, part 2, "The Price of Structure"; CWE, remarks, HGM 18(1909–10):66.

61. Louis E. Reber, *University Extension in the United States* (Washington, D.C., 1914), 6–8, 17; CWE to Edmund J. James, Nov. 21, 1892; CWE to H. W. Caldwell, Oct. 29, 1907; A. B. Hart, "University Participation—a Substitute for University Extension," *Studies in American Education*, 53–55; Edward Weeks, *The Lowells and Their Institute* (Boston, 1966), 72, 83, 125.

62. David B. Potts, "The Prospect Union: A Conservative Quest for Social Justice," *New England Quarterly* 34(1962):347–66, esp. 355; Allen Davis, *Spearheads for Reform: The Social Settlements and the Progressive Movement, 1890–1914* (New York, 1967), 43; CWE, "A Healthy, Natural Life" [1903], EPA 141.

63. J. D. Greene to Arthur A. Ballantine, Nov. 2, 1903, EP; CWE, statement acknowledged in Arthur A. Ballantine to CWE, Sept. 17, 1904; Barrett Wendell to CWE, May 4, 1894; CWE to Frank Buffington Vrooman, Feb. 5, 1897.

64. "An Urban University," *Educational Reform*, 397–98; "The Condition of American Education," EPA 103. Cf. Sproat, "*Best Men*," 271.

65. CWE, *Conflict*, 80; CWE, "[Speech at] Dinner of the New England Society in the City New York" [1905], EPA 175.

66. Samuel Haber, *Efficiency and Uplift: Scientific Management in the Progressive Era, 1890–1920* (Chicago, 1964), ix–x, 116; CWE, *Education for Efficiency* (Boston, 1909), 1; Krug, *American High School*, 274. See also Veysey, *American University*, 116–18.

CHAPTER VI, *Who Should Have a College Education?*

1. HGM 3(1894–95):68.

2. "Equality in a Republic," *American Contributions*, 162–63 (more unlike); "Undesirable and Desirable Uniformity in Schools," *Educational Reform*, 280 (equality of condition). On the range of meanings given "democracy" in relation to higher education, see Veysey, *American University*, 62–66.

3. "Silence Dogood, No. 4," in Leonard W. Labaree (ed.), *The Papers of Benjamin Franklin* (New Haven, 1959–   ), 1:14–18; Morison, *Three Centuries*, 286–93.

4. "Inaugural," *Educational Reform*, 21–22, 19, 20, 38.

5. See above, pp. 108–10. See also E. E. Grinnell to CWE, Jan. 21,

1882. In 1891 an alumnus of 1859 complained of "the solemn feminine importance attached to twopenny social distinctions," but he declared these had been an aspect of the college even in his student days (John C. Gray to CWE, Dec. 25, 1891).

6. Saltonstall, quoted in Springfield *Weekly Republican*, July 9, 1886; Aleck Quest, "The Fast Set at Harvard University," *North American Review* 147(1888):548; HUC(1888), 147; [Chicago *Daily News?*], July 13, 1886, clpg., EP, box 74; editorial, Boston *Advertiser*, [July, 1886], clpg. filed with W. E. Barrett to CWE, July 6, 1886; AR(1904), 18, 347.

7. AR(1887), 13, (1897), 48; CWE to C. F. Adams, May 27, 1904 (see also CWE to Adams, June 9, 1904); AR(1905), 24; Edward C. Kirkland, *Charles Francis Adams, Jr., 1835–1915: The Patrician at Bay* (Cambridge, 1965), 199.

8. "Pres. Eliot's Address," HGM 12(1903-4):167–68; "The Character of a Gentleman" [1904], EPA 155.

9. For a good survey of admission, see Arthur G. Powell, "The Study of Education at Harvard University, 1870–1920" (Ph.D. dissertation, Harvard University, 1969). A third reform was the shift from testing for information to testing for developed capacity (e.g., AR[1877], 9–12).

10. G. H. Palmer, "Erroneous Limitations of the Elective System" [1886], in Palmer and Palmer, *The Teacher*, 204.

11. AR(1874), 8. From the 159 entering I have subtracted the four who came from other colleges, whose secondary background is not given. I have fused the categories "endowed schools" and "private schools," although Eliot believed the former gave "near gratuitous education to poor boys." For additional data on the sources of Harvard freshmen, see McLachlan, *American Boarding Schools*, 205–6.

12. Sizer, *Secondary Schools*, 35. For a full treatment of data on secondary schools in this period with careful attention to the question of reliability, see ibid., ch. 3.

13. "Inaugural," *Educational Reform*, 10, 8; J. M. Peirce, in AR(1897), 93–100; Edwin C. Broome, *A Historical and Critical Discussion of College Admission Requirements* (New York, 1903), 45–46, 56–58; AR(1887), 12; McLachlan, *American Boarding Schools*, 228–29.

14. McCosh, *New Departure*, 7–8; AR(1877), 58; Kirkland, *Adams*, 197. See also the letter from "A Conservative of the Old School" to editor, Boston *Evening Transcript*, March 23, 1877; *A Report in Regard to the Tone and Tendencies of Harvard University Made by a Committee of Students from Other Colleges Now Studying at Harvard* (Boston, 1889). Special students, allowed to take courses without being candidates for a degree, were reintroduced into Harvard College early in Eliot's administration. He saw the measure as expedient, given the inaccessibility of secondary

education for large portions of the population, but he warned of possible abuses ("The Gap between Common Schools and Colleges" [1890], *Educational Reform*, 201). At Lawrence, from 1880 to 1894, special students outnumbered regular students (Hector James Hughes, "Engineering and Other Applied Sciences in the Harvard Engineering School and Its Predecessors, 1847–1929," in Morison [ed.], *Development of Harvard*, 427).

15. AR(1874), 10–11; CWE to T. W. Higginson, Feb. 24, 1879, Higginson Papers; Broome, *College Admission*, 88–89; CWE to G. J. Brush, Dec. 9, 1883, Brush Papers.

16. Fritz K. Ringer, *The Decline of the German Mandarins: The German Academic Community, 1890–1933* (Cambridge, 1969), 24–40; AR(1883), 17; M. A. DeWolfe Howe, *Barrett Wendell and His Letters* (Boston, 1924), 53, 92; Bennett H. Nash to CWE, Oct. 19, 1875, Dec. 3, 1883.

17. AR(1886), 7–8; "Remarks before Hopkins Trustees" [1874], EPA 11; "Present Relations of Mass[achusetts] High Schools to Mass[achusetts] Colleges" [1884], EPA 33.

18. Frederic Allison Tupper, "Harvard and the Secondary Schools," HGM 4(1895–96):670; AR(1890), 6–7, (1900), 6–7; A. B. Hart, "Opening of the Academic Year," HGM 3(1894–95):206. The extreme restriction at Harvard is made apparent by the fact that in 1889–1890 only 3 per cent of high school students in the United States were taking Greek, and only 7 per cent of students in private secondary schools (Krug, *American High School*, 34).

19. AR(1897), 19; G. H. Palmer, "Erroneous Limitations," in Palmer and Palmer, *The Teacher*, 217. With the easier Lawrence requirements in mind Eliot could say in 1890 that Harvard was accessible to "any graduate of a good high school" (AR[1890], 20). At the scientific school, however, tinkering with admission requirements was as frequent as at the college. The number of optional subjects a candidate for Lawrence must choose was increased between 1898 and 1903 until the aggregate approximated that needed for admission to the college. But neither Greek nor (after 1888) Latin was required, and certain subjects not acceptable for college admission, such as shopwork and drawing, were accepted (N. S. Shaler, "The Scientific School," HGM 5[1896–97]:564–65; CWE, "The Length of the Baccalaureate Course and Preparation for the Professional Schools," NEA[1903], 500).

20. A. B. Hart, "The Harvard Reform in Entrance Requirements," *Educational Review* 18(1899):263–80; AR(1897), 18; CWE to Seth Low, Oct. 26, 1895. On the Committee of Ten, see Sizer, *Secondary Schools*, esp. 161; Krug, *American High School*, chs. 2–4.

21. Ephraim Emerton, "History and Government," HGM 4(1895–

96):445; A. B. Hart, "Evidences of Progress," HGM 7(1898–99):63–64. Earlier, fear of Overseer opposition had chilled faculty interest in the far simpler Stanford system, a "free list" of entrance subjects (Hart, "Harvard Reform," *Educational Review* 18:271).

22. A. B. Hart, "The Interests of the College," HGM 7(1898–99):547 (enable a boy); Hart, "Evidences of Progress," ibid., 67 (collegiate instruction); Hart, "Harvard Reform," *Educational Review* 18:280.

23. AR(1899), 6.

24. AR(1906), 16–20, 334–46; R. B. Merriman, "The Winter Quarter," HGM 14(1905–6):421; idem, "The University: The Spring Quarter," ibid., 656; J. G. Hart, "New Methods of Admission to Harvard," ibid., 587–93; L. B. R. Briggs, "The New Committee on Admission," HGM 15(1906–7):396–97.

25. AR(1907), 22–24; Edwin E. Slosson, *Great American Universities* (New York, 1910), 4–5; AR(1909), 24.

26. AR(1907), 20.

27. Wilson Farrand, "A Brief History of the College Examination Board," in *The Work of the College Entrance Examination Board, 1901–1925* (Boston, 1926), 21; Claude M. Fuess, *The College Board: Its First Fifty Years* (New York, 1950), 9; AR(1887), 4–5. In 1884 Eliot supported the plans of Principal John Tetlow to institute joint meetings of college and secondary school teachers. The result was the formation of the New England Association of Colleges and Preparatory Schools the next year, and its attention to admission questions helped create the Commission of Colleges in New England on Admission Examinations (Krug, *American High School*, 1–3, 363).

28. CWE, "A Wider Range of Electives in College Admission Requirements" [1896], *Educational Reform*, 386–87; Fuess, *College Board*, 15–17, 22–23.

29. "Discussion," ACPSMSM (1899), 78–82; 85–86; Fuess, *College Board*, 23–27; Nicholas Murray Butler, "How the College Entrance Examination Board Came To Be," in *The Work of the CEEB*, 4–5; Krug, *American High School*, 146–49; Butler, *Across the Busy Years*, I:198–200. The version of Eliot's remarks usually cited—that given by Butler in his autobiography, published forty years after the event—is considerably more acerbic and seems to me less characteristic of Eliot than the words appearing in the original *Proceedings*. See Hugh Hawkins, "The University-Builders Observe the Colleges," *History of Education Quarterly*, 11(1971):356–57.

30. Edwin H. Hall, "Admission Tests in Common," HGM 10(1901–2):526; AR(1901), 100, (1903), 90–91, (1904), 91, (1905), 98, 114–15; Krug, *American High School*, 150; Fuess, *College Board*, 38–49.

31. Krug, *American High School,* 151–53; Rudolph, *American College,* 282–84; Broome, *College Admission,* 17; Abraham Flexner, *The American College: A Criticism* (New York, 1908), 84n.

32. "Remarks before Hopkins Trustees," EPA 11; CWE, "The Gap," *Educational Reform,* 214–17; CWE, remarks, ACPSMSM (1899), 73.

33. "The Gap," *Educational Reform,* 205–6, 213, 217. But even such support was qualified. Speaking at the University of Minnesota in 1909, Eliot maintained that any admission system without examinations was unsatisfactory ("President Eliot in Minnesota," HGM 17[1908–9]:583–84).

34. "The Gap," *Educational Reform,* 213–15. Later, schools using this system joined in the New England College Entrance Certificate Board and granted approval to schools whose graduates performed satisfactorily in member colleges. Harvard still held aloof (Krug, *American High School,* 156–57; A. B. Hart, "Quarterly Ruminations," HGM 9[1900–1901]: 356–57). One aspect of the certificate system, the inspection of schools, appealed to Eliot. Between 1892 and 1896 Harvard sent inspection teams on invitation to private schools, which then received a confidential report. For the rise and fall of this undertaking see CWE, "The Schools' Examination Board of Harvard University," HGM 1(1892–93):8–13; A. B. Hart, "The Opening of the Year," HGM 7(1898–99):227; Paul H. Hanus, *Adventuring in Education* (Cambridge, 1937), 136–38; Arthur G. Powell, "The Education of Educators at Harvard, 1891–1912," in Buck (ed.), *Social Sciences at Harvard,* 249–50.

35. Krug, *American High School,* 155; Draper, "State Universities of the Middle West," *Educational Review* 13(1897):318–19; William C. Collar, "The Action of the Colleges upon the Schools," ibid. 2(1891):438. For evidence of alumni pressure for Harvard to inspect schools and admit by certificate, see *Relations of Harvard University to Schools of Secondary Education: Second Report of Committee of Associated Harvard Clubs* (n.p., 1906).

36. Krug, *American High School,* 152–63; Broome, *College Admission,* 116–25.

37. "Mr. Choate's Address of Presentation," HGM 3(1894–95):68; Solomon, *Ancestors and Immigrants,* 99–102, 186–88; CWE, quoted in Pittsburgh *Chronicle,* Dec. 16, 1905. In comparison with the IRL, Eliot was indeed tolerant, but both Solomon and Oscar Handlin, *Race and Nationality in American Life* (Boston, 1957), 49, are overgenerous in their praise of Eliot's view of ethnic minorities.

38. CWE to Bruce L. Keenan, Aug. 9, 1907; CWE to Bliss Perry, Oct. 20, 1900; William R. Thayer, "Germanization, Oxfordization, and Critics," HGM 16(1907–8):283.

39. CWE to S. A. Steel, Oct. 25, 1901.

40. Solomon, *Ancestors and Immigrants*, 191, 183; CWE, "Wise and Unwise Economy," *Atlantic Monthly* 35:713–14; CWE, "An Average Massachusetts Grammar School" [1890], *Educational Reform*, 193; CWE, "Brief of an Address before Principals and Other Teachers of Boston Schools . . ." [1894], EPA 52.2.

41. CWE, *More Money*, 36–37; Solomon, *Ancestors and Immigrants*, 183.

42. CWE, quoted in Indianapolis *News*, March 11, 1909; Charleston *News and Courier*, March 10, 1909; CWE, telegram, copy enclosed in J. D. Greene to "City Editor," March 14, 1909. Other reactions can be found with EPA 279 and among clpgs. on CWE, box 9, Biographical Collection, HUA.

43. Blodgett, *Gentle Reformers*, ch. 6, "The City: Efforts at Cooperation," and pp. 259, 261, 53–55; James, *Eliot*, II:163–64.

44. Morison, *Three Centuries*, 198, 257. In 1894 Bonaparte addressed Harvard students on the role of the Catholic Church in the United States (Scott F. Hershey, "Papal Harvard," unident. Chicago magazine, 1894, copy in EP, box 135).

45. "The Exemption from Taxation," *American Contributions*, esp. 325 (to legislate); "The Proposed Taxation of Churches" [1874], EPA 10; John J. Williams to CWE, April 2, 1875; "Five American Contributions," *American Contributions*, 18–21. He bluntly opposed efforts to add a religious amendment to the Constitution, telling one of its supporters that his reference to "Christian" practices and values should in candor use the term "Protestant" (CWE to D. McAllister, Dec. 26, 1872).

46. Katherine E. Conway and Mabel Ward Cameron, *Charles Francis Donnelly: A Memoir* (New York, 1909), 38–39, 223; Robert H. Lord, John E. Sexton, and Edward T. Harrington, *History of the Archdiocese of Boston* . . . (New York, 1944), III:116, 132; Alvin P. Stauffer, "Anti-Catholicism in American Politics, 1865–1900" (Ph.D. dissertation, Harvard University, 1933), 258, 267; CWE to D. C. Gilman, Dec. 2, 1893; CWE to a Catholic correspondent, Dec. 6, 1893; CWE, "[Religion in the Public Schools]" [1886] with accompanying clpgs. and correspondence, EPA 35.

47. Clifford K. Shipton, *Biographical Sketches of Those Who Attended Harvard College in the Classes 1690–1700* [*Sibley's Harvard Graduates*, vol. 4] (Cambridge, 1933), 52; CWE to Keane, June 17, 1890; Keane to CWE, June 19, Oct. 25, 1890.

48. Frank Bolles, "A Review of the Academic Year 1891–92," HGM 1:105; Ephraim Emerton to CWE, Dec. 8, 1890; CWE to Thomas Dwight, Nov. 6, 1903; CWE to Edward W. Hooper, Jan. 1, 1895; Francis J. Child to CWE, two letters, "Sunday night" and "Oct 15" [1895 or 1896?]; CWE to A. C. McGiffert, Dec. 23, 1908.

49. William R. Thayer, "Review of the Third Quarter," HGM 2(1893–94):531; James W. Gallivan, "Catholic Sons of Harvard," *Donahoe's Magazine* (November 1894), 510, 499; John J. Ryan, "The St. Paul's Catholic Club," *Harvard Alumni Bulletin* 17(1914–15):264–67; "Saint Paul's Catholic Club Scrapbook," HUA; Peter J. O'Callaghan, "Catholics at Harvard," *Catholic Family Annual for 1895*, 76, 78 (copy in HUA).

50. Hershey, "Papal Harvard" (see n. 44, above); Peter E. Hogan, *The Catholic University of America, 1896–1903: The Rectorship of Thomas J. Conaty* (Washington, D.C., 1949), 73n; HUC(1899), 520–21, 525; James Barr Ames to CWE, May 25, 1900; Roche to CWE, June 19, 22, 1893; CWE to Roche, June 20, 1893, in Boston *Pilot*, July 1, 1893.

51. David R. Dunigan, *A History of Boston College* (Milwaukee, 1947), 168–72; CWE to J. Havens Richards, Aug. 4, 1893, quoted in Joseph T. Durkin, *Georgetown University: The Middle Years (1840–1900)* (Washington, D.C., 1963), 192; J. H. Richards to CWE, July 16, Sept. 21, 1893; CWE to Thoms J. Conaty, Oct. 24, 1898; CWE to James Higgins, Jan. 13, 1899; HUC(1898), 508; T. J. Conaty to Timothy Brosnahan, Dec. 20, 1899, quoted in Hogan, *Catholic University*, 73; Mullan to CWE, Jan. 11, 1900.

52. CWE, "Recent Changes in Secondary Education," *Atlantic Monthly* 84(1899):443.

53. Bliss Perry to CWE, Jan. 17, 1900; Perry, *And Gladly Teach*, 170–71; Dunigan, *Boston College*, 174, 160, 165; Timothy Brosnahan, *The Courses Leading to the Baccalaureate in Harvard College and Boston College* (Woodstock, Md., [1900], reprinted from *Sacred Heart Review*, Jan. 13, 1900), esp. 7–8.

54. CWE to W. G. R. Mullan, June 2, 1900.

55. CWE to George V. Leahy, Jan. 17, 1900; CWE to John O'Brien, Feb. 14, 1900; Blodgett, *Gentle Reformers*, 229–30; CWE to W. W. Oliver, May 20, 1878.

56. *Is East Cambridge a "Whitechapel" Town?* ([Cambridge?], 1903), pamphlet published by the *Sacred Heart Review*, copy in EP; CWE, quoted in Memphis *Commercial Appeal*, Feb. 19, 1909; Montgomery *Advertiser*, March 9, 1909; Jerome D. Greene to John D. Merrill, March 13, 1909, EP; CWE, enclosure in J. D. Greene to "City Editor," March 14, 1909.

57. The quoted phrase is from Eliot's letter to Mullan, June 2, 1900, which so described the experience of Catholic students at Harvard.

58. Morison, *Three Centuries*, 198, 417, 422; CWE to Fleischer, Nov. 14, 1901; Jacob H. Schiff to CWE, April 29, 1902; James Mott Hallowell to CWE, May 17, 1902.

59. Unident. clpg., Feb. 13, 1904, EP; CWE to William A. Hazel, Aug. 25, 1905; CWE to Monroe Trotter, May 5, 1909; Edwin B. Craig-

head, "A Voice from the South," *Harvard Illustrated Magazine* 10(1909): 202. See also William P. Few, "President Eliot and the South," *South Atlantic Quarterly* 8(1909):184–91.

60. CWE to Theodore Roosevelt, Sept. 27, 1906 (concerning C. F. Adams's "Reflex Light from Africa," *Century* 72[1906]:101–11); CWE to Monroe Trotter, April 30, May 5, 1909; CWE to C. E. Norton, Feb. 20, 1901 (from Bermuda).

61. CWE to Charles Kohler, March 11, 1904; CWE to Bliss Perry, Oct. 20, 1900; CWE, quoted in Boston *Globe*, Feb. 15, 1907.

62. Gilbert T. Stephenson, *Race Distinctions in American Law* (New York, 1910), 163–64, quoting CWE, in Boston *Evening Transcript*, Feb. 15, 1907. A version of Eliot's remarks with slightly different wording appeared in the Boston *Globe*, Feb. 15, 1907.

63. Stephenson, *Race Distinctions,* 164; Jerome D. Greene to Ray Stannard Baker, Sept. 27, 1907, R. S. Baker Papers, Library of Congress; CWE to Byron S. Hurlbut, Aug. 13, 1895; CWE to Bruce L. Keenan, Aug. 9, 1907 (but Japanese students, Eliot observed, were admitted to social clubs).

64. CWE to C. F. Thwing, Jan. 31, 1923.

65. Articles on "Commencement," HGM 5(1896–97):57, 9(1900–1901):57, 12(1903–4):68. The introduction was by former Governor and Secretary of the Navy John D. Long.

66. CWE to B. T. Washington, Sept. 7, 1906. See also CWE, "What Uplifts a Race," *Harvard Bulletin* 8(April 25, 1906):1–2; CWE, "Problems of the Negro," Boston *Evening Transcript*, Feb. 17, 1904; R. R. Moton, "Charles W. Eliot and the Humanistic Attitude," *Harvard Teachers Record*, 4(1934):38–39.

67. Eleanor Flexner, *Century of Struggle: The Woman's Rights Movement in the United States* (Cambridge, 1966), 80; "Inaugural," *Educational Reform*, 22–24; T. W. Higginson, "Harvard vs. the West," *Woman's Journal*, Jan. 8, 1870; James Freeman Clarke to T. W. Higginson, Nov. 18, 1873, Higginson Papers (citing the "Satan" epithet of Julia Ward Howe).

68. "Remarks before Hopkins Trustees," EPA 11; James, *Eliot*, I:330; CWE, "Address at Smith College" [1879], EPA 27; W. A. Neilson, "Biographical Study," in Neilson (ed.), *Eliot*, vol. I, p. xxii. CWE, quoted in Alice Payne Hackett, *Wellesley: Part of the American Story* (New York, 1949), 136.

69. J. F. Clarke to T. W. Higginson, Nov. 18, 1873, Higginson Papers (Eliot winked); AR(1870), 29–30, (1878), 40, 148–49; Harrington, *Harvard Medical School*, III:1217–46, esp. 1229, 1235; Arthur Gilman (ed.), *The Cambridge of Eighteen Hundred and Ninety-Six . . .* (Cambridge,

1896), 178. A questionnaire answered by candidates for Overseer in 1886 showed only James Freeman Clarke favoring admission of women to the college, though there was much support for admitting them to the medical school (Morison, *Three Centuries*, 360). Eliot's support for admitting women to the medical school was qualified by his recommendation of separate laboratories and separate teaching of "delicate subjects."

70. A. B. Hart, "How the University Goes On," HGM 7(1898–99): 399–404; Slosson, *Great American Universities*, 26–27; Lucy Allen Paton, *Elizabeth Cary Agassiz: A Biography* (Boston, 1919), ch. 10, "The Passing of the Harvard Annex, 1893–1894."

71. Paton, *Agassiz*, 250, 409–12; CWE, remarks, HGM 4(1895–96): 98–99; "President Eliot's Address," HGM 9(1900–1901):229.

72. CWE, "The Higher Education for Women," in Neilson (ed.), *Eliot*, I:160–67; CWE, *More Money*, 120–21; CWE, remarks, HGM 7(1898–99):416 (desirable training); "President Eliot's Radcliffe Address," HGM 11(1902–3):76 (emancipation).

73. M. Carey Thomas, "The 'Bryn Mawr Woman'" [1899], in Barbara M. Cross (ed.), *The Educated Woman in America* . . . (New York, 1965), 142; CWE, "The Condition of American Education," EPA 103. In a later counteraccusation of pessimism, President Thomas recalled Eliot's dire prediction about student self-government when he first visited Bryn Mawr (Edith Finch, *Carey Thomas of Bryn Mawr* [New York, 1947], 332).

74. CWE, "Higher Education for Women," in Neilson (ed.), *Eliot*, I:160–67; CWE to "Dear Sir," [July, 1899], HGM 8(1899–1900):74.

CHAPTER VII, *Utility and Its Limits*

1. *Educational Reform*, 1.

2. Rudolph, *American College*, 32; Rush, "To Friends of the Federal Government: A Plan for a Federal University," in Hofstadter and Smith (eds.), *American Higher Education*, I:156. Aside from vocational training and creation of techniques applicable to agriculture and industry, there was another sort of utility which college men themselves often called for, the training of citizens and public leaders. For such political concerns, see above, ch. 5, "The University and Democracy."

3. Rudolph, *American College*, 248–49; Edward Danforth Eddy, Jr., *Colleges for Our Land and Time: The Land-Grant Idea in American Education* (New York, 1957), 13–18, 23–24.

4. Curti and Nash, *Philanthropy in the Shaping of American Higher Education*, 76–80.

5. *Annual Report of the President of Columbia College* (1870), 36–

64; George E. Peterson, *The New England College in the Age of the University* (Amherst, Mass., 1964), 17n17, ch. 3, "The Confusing Shape of New England Reality"; Veysey, *American University*, ch. 1, "Discipline and Piety."

6. *Educational Reform*, 1–2 (similarly, "Education in Its Relations to Business Affairs" [1890], EPA 45); CWE, "New Definition of the Cultivated Man," in Neilson (ed.), *Eliot*, I: 191 (on Arnold).

7. CWE to "Dear Sir," [1874?] (draft, on tariff); CWE, "An Urban University" [1896], *Educational Reform*, 396; "Aims of Higher Education," ibid., 231–33; Samuel Thurber. "Opening Remarks by the President," *Academy* 7(1892): 191.

8. CWE, quoted in James, *Eliot*, II: 106–7 (above all); CWE, "Family Stocks in Democracy" [1890], *American Contributions*, 151 (way bill); CWE to M. A. Mikkelsen, Feb. 27, 1897 (principal service). Eliot called himself a utilitarian in a letter to his mother, Aug. 18, 1865.

9. *Educational Reform*, 12 (enthusiastic work); CWE, *University Administration*, 147–48.

10. An example of such a life led by a Harvard alumnus appears in Santayana, *Persons and Places*, I: 224–30. The quotation is hypothetical.

11. Ibid., II, *The Middle Span*, 175.

12. CWE to M. A. DeWolfe Howe, June 5, 1923, Mark Antony DeWolfe Howe Papers, HL.

13. CWE, "Liberty in Education," *Educational Reform*, 139; "Aims of Higher Education," ibid., 226; Hughes, "Engineering," in Morison (ed.), *Development of Harvard*, 420, 428–29. In 1908 Eliot clearly presented engineering as properly a postgraduate study, albeit one that could be aided by undergraduate studies in mathematics and physics (*University Administration*, 147).

14. CWE, "Unity of Educational Reform," *Educational Reform*, 338; CWE, "The Elements of a Liberal Education," *Educator-Journal* 8(1908): 499.

15. CWE, "Education in Its Relations to Business Affairs" [1890], EPA 45.

16. "Aims of Higher Education," *Educational Reform*, 224; similarly, CWE, "Educational Changes and Tendencies," *Journal of Education* 34(1891): 393.

17. CWE to "My dear Sir," Jan. 10, 1873. Cf. Raymond H. Merritt, *Engineering in American Society, 1850–1875* (Lexington, Ky., 1969), 175.

18. "Medical Education of the Future," *Educational Reform*, 366–67; Wiebe, *Search for Order*, 145–63.

19. John Jay Chapman to Elizabeth Chanler, March 18, [1898], in M. A. DeWolfe Howe, *John Jay Chapman and His Letters* (Boston, 1937), 175; Veysey, *American University*, ch. 2, "Utility."

20. Arthur E. Sutherland, *The Law at Harvard: A History of Ideas and Men, 1817–1967* (Cambridge, 1967), 174–77; Ephraim Gurney to CWE, [1883]. As a replacement for Oliver Wendell Holmes, Jr., who had recently resigned, Gurney preferred the older Joseph H. Choate, who had experience as a practicing attorney, over the younger, Langdell-trained William A. Keener. Keener won the place.

21. Gray to CWE, Jan. 3, 1883; AR(1874), 26–27; Sutherland, *Law at Harvard*, 184; Kuehnemann, *Eliot*, 31. For Eliot's recollection of the controversy, see "Langdell and the Law School," *Late Harvest*, 48–49. Similarly, in the divinity school in 1869 two out of three faculty members were also pastors of churches. A few years later, none was (Fenn, "Theological School," in Morison [ed.], *Development of Harvard*, 463).

22. James, *Eliot*, I:279 (quoting Bigelow), II:63 (teaching of medical science); AR(1874), 26–27, (1881), 29–30 (impossible to separate), (1888), 16–18 (dental school).

23. Frederick C. Shattuck, "The Medical School, 1869–1929," in Morison (ed.), *Development of Harvard*, 568–69; William Morton Wheeler, "The Bussey Institution, 1871–1929," ibid., 508–17; AR(1901), 26–27; Stanley F. Morse, "The Bussey Institution: Harvard's Agricultural School," *Country Gentleman*, April 15, 1909. For the better fortunes of the veterinary school at the University of Pennsylvania, where some state aid was received, see Edward Potts Cheyney, *History of the University of Pennsylvania, 1740–1940* (Philadelphia, 1940), 309–10, 373.

24. William Morris Davis and Reginald Aldworth Daly, "Geology and Geography, 1858–1928," in Morison (ed.), *Development of Harvard*, 308–9; Hughes, "Engineering," ibid., 417; *Harvard University Quinquennial Catalogue* (1930), 803–4.

25. CWE, "Harvard Law School?" [1882], EP, box 349; CWE, remarks, AAU(1903), 42.

26. *Atlantic Monthly*, 23:210, 214–15.

27. AR(1870), 68, (1871), 42–43; CWE to J. D. Whitney, Jan. 31, 1870 (build up). I find no evidence to support the assertion that pressure from the Lawrence family initiated Eliot's overture to M.I.T. (Curti and Nash, *Philanthropy in the Shaping of American Higher Education*, 68). For the rapid decline of interest at M.I.T. in the merger, as the degree of control Eliot wanted for the Harvard governing boards became clear, see the following: J. D. Runkle to W. B. Rogers, Jan. 27 (copy), Feb. 22, 1870, Feb. 20, 1871; Edward Atkinson to Rogers, July 28, 1870 (all in Rogers Papers); W. B. Rogers to CWE, Feb. 7, 1870. For later merger efforts by Eliot, and a briefly successful one by his successor, see Prescott, *When M.I.T.*

28. Josiah P. Cooke to CWE, Jan. 27, 1871. Wolcott Gibbs's "Plan for the Reorganization of the College and Professional Schools" (MS, EP)

is similar, as is the plan of Louis Agassiz referred to in Alexander Agassiz to J. D. Whitney, [March, 1870?], Whitney Papers.

29. H. L. Eustis, "Remarks on a Plan for Uniting the Schools of Applied Science in Harvard College," Jan. 27, 1871, MS, EP. A similar reference to the primacy of teaching at Harvard had appeared in Eliot's inaugural (*Educational Reform*, 27).

30. CWE, draft of a statement to the Lawrence family, March 23, 1871, EP, box 89.

31. AR(1872), 31; Hughes, "Engineering," in Morison (ed.), *Development of Harvard*, 416.

32. Charles Loring Jackson, "Wolcott Gibbs," *Harvard Alumni Bulletin* 32(1929–30):958–60; James, *Eliot*, I:296.

33. AR(1871), 24–26, (1872), 30; Hughes, "Engineering," in Morison (ed.), *Development of Harvard*, 420.

34. Gibbs to O. N. Rood, March 21, 1869; B. A. Gould to Gibbs, July 8, 1871, both in Wolcott Gibbs Papers, Franklin Institute, Philadelphia; CWE to Brush, May 19, 1871, Brush Papers.

35. After the change, in fact, Gibbs entered a very productive period of research (C. L. Jackson, "Wolcott Gibbs, 1822–1908," *American Journal of Science* 37[1909]:256. Eliot knew that Gibbs was about to come into a sizable fortune and could easily bear the expense in a private laboratory. When Gibbs first heard of Eliot's election to the presidency, he felt that he might be forced to resign. Yet he stayed, declining an invitation from Johns Hopkins in 1875 (Gibbs to O. N. Rood, March 21, 1869, Gibbs Papers; James, *Eliot*, II:25).

36. "I wish to acknowledge the courtesy and consideration with which you met, in 1871, my strong desire to consolidate the chemical laboratories, and to strengthen the department of physics. At the time, I supposed that the changes suggested were on the whole not disagreeable to you; but in later years the thought sometimes occurred to me that the change in the nature of your work for the University had caused you some regrets. If my later thought was correct, I have only the more reason to express to you my obligations for your considerate action in the matter" (CWE to Gibbs, Jan. 21, 1888). Gibbs's response of January 23, 1888, a pleasant letter of thanks and good wishes, made no reference to the events of 1871. At the time these letters were exchanged Eliot was being enlightened on the importance of research by Charles Loring Jackson, who may have spoken directly of the Gibbs case (Jackson, "Chemistry, 1865–1929," in Morison [ed.], *Development of Harvard*, 259–60).

37. AR(1872), 75–76, 30.

38. Gibbs to G. J. Brush, Jan. 26, 1875, Brush Papers; Hughes, "Engineering," in Morison (ed.), *Development of Harvard*, 419–21, 426; AR

(1886), 16, (1887), 107; *Record of the Commemoration, November Fifth to Eighth, 1886*, 26–28; Dunbar, "President Eliot's Administration," HGM 2(1893–94):472.

39. Hughes, "Engineering," in Morison (ed.), *Development of Harvard*, 423–24; N. S. Shaler to CWE and Fellows, Oct. 19, 1893; AR (1893), 10–11.

40. AR(1892), 22–23 (new programs), (1894), 20 (advantages); CWE to Henry P. Walcott, Sept. 1, 1897.

41. Alexander Agassiz to CWE, March 3, 1902.

42. The last Lawrence degree was actually granted in 1910; the degree of C.E. was last granted in 1888 (AR[1906], 20–22; Hughes, "Engineering," in Morison [ed.], *Development of Harvard*, 428–29; *Harvard University Quinquennial Catalogue*, [1930], 804).

43. CWE to Theodore W. Richards, June 18, 1908 (my memory); AR(1892), 36 (students of science); CWE, "Character of the Scientific Investigator," in Neilson (ed.), *Eliot*, I:128–29 (not discreditable); AR (1893), 27 (graduate school).

44. Edwin H. Hall to CWE, July 21, 1886; James W. Harris to "Sir," Feb. 19, 1878, EP (the letter was composed by Eliot); Cooke to CWE, Aug. 13, 1890.

45. C. M. Woodward to CWE, Sept. 9, 1896; Hamlin to CWE, Dec. 16, 1896.

46. James W. Harris to "Sir," Feb. 19, 1878, EP; W. H. Forbes to CWE, April 19, 1881; CWE to W. H. Forbes, April 21, [1881]; Shaler to CWE, Aug. 21, 1900.

47. Miller, *Dollars for Research*, passim; *Endowment Funds of Harvard University, June 30, 1947* (Cambridge, 1948), 393–94.

48. Denver *Republican*, [Feb. 1891], clpg. in EP, box 448. Eliot's inaugural, however, had carefully distinguished a university presidency from a business position: "A university cannot be managed like a railroad or a cotton-mill" (*Educational Reform*, 27).

49. *Endowment Funds of Harvard*, 403; CWE to William Rainey Harper, June 7, 1902, President's Papers, University of Chicago.

50. Harris, *Economics of Harvard*, 208–9, 227; C. J. Bonaparte, remarks, HGM 15(1906–7):58–59; James Ford Rhodes to CWE, Feb. 7, 1902 (a long, sympathetic appraisal of Rockefeller's career, evoked by Eliot's inquiry); Chapman to William James, Feb. 13, 1907, in Howe, *Chapman*, 227; *The Harvard Medical School, 1782–1906* ([Boston?], 1906), 180–81; Harrington, *Harvard Medical School*, III:1173, 1193–95.

51. CWE, "Exemption from Taxation," *American Contributions*, 303–4; AR(1893), 46.

52. CWE, *More Money*, 191–92; OR, March 11, April 9, 1868. A

fund collected from Boston businessmen remained for many years under a separate board of trustees. In 1878, after a decade of inactivity, the fund began to support lectures at Harvard by such "sound" economists as Simon Newcomb (CWE to "Dear Sir," April 16, 1876 [draft], EP, box 86; AR[1879], 44–45). For the fund's ultimate disposition, see *Endowment Funds of Harvard*, 62.

53. Taussig, "Economics," in Morison (ed.), *Development of Harvard*, 187–88; Unger, *Greenback Era*, ch. 4, "The Hard Money Interest."

54. Kansas City *Times*, March 5, 1891; Kansas City *Star*, March 16, 1891; St. Louis *Republican*, March 10, 1891; unident. clpg. from St. Louis newspaper, EP, box 448.

55. CWE to David Starr Jordan, June 4, 1901.

56. CWE to Dexter A. Hawkins, June 14, 1883 (teachers free); F. W. Taussig to "Dear Sir," Feb. 20, 1890, printed copy, EP; C. F. Dunbar to CWE, March 25, 1890; Boston *Herald*, Dec. 22, 1890; *American Economist* 5(1890):91; CWE, "Why the College Professors are Tariff-Reformers" [1891?], EPA 46. Eliot's hiring of the English economist William James Ashley in 1892 may have been partly motivated by hopes that he would represent the protectionist position. Probably more important, however, was the expectation that Ashley, an economic historian, would counter the highly theoretical cast of the department (Church, "The Economists Study Society," in Buck [ed.], *Social Sciences at Harvard*, 68–71).

57. Blodgett, *Gentle Reformers*, 74–76; Frederic Cople Jaher, "Boston Brahmins," in Jaher (ed.), *Age of Industrialism*, esp. 200; John Jay Chapman to Henry James, Dec. 23, 1930, in Howe, *Chapman*, 449 (throwing the college); Henry L. Higginson to CWE, March 24, 1896.

58. Hofstadter and Metzger, *Development of Academic Freedom*, 451–58; Irvin G. Wyllie, "The Businessman Looks at the Higher Learning: The Evolution of His Present Attitude," *Journal of Higher Education* 23(1952):298; Veysey, *American University*, 266–67; Edward C. Kirkland, *Dream and Thought in the Business Community, 1860–1900* (Ithaca, 1956), 102; Edward Atkinson to CWE, March 6, 1890 (for an opposite view of Harvard versus M.I.T., expressed in 1879, see Jaher, "Boston Brahmins," in Jaher [ed.], *Age of Industrialism*, 216).

59. CWE to Oscar Ely, Feb. 12, 1897 (thorough mental training; similarly, CWE to R. T. Crane, Sept. 12, 1901); Curti and Nash, *Philanthropy in the Shaping of American Higher Education*, 74; "Associated Harvard Clubs at Cincinnati," *Harvard Bulletin* 5(Dec. 17, 1902):1; CWE to Charles F. Thwing, Nov. 16, 1904. The volume praised was Thwing's *College Training and the Business Man*.

60. J. D. Greene to James G. Jones, Nov. 5, 1901, EP; T. N. Carver to J. D. Green[e], March 20, 1902, EP; Carver to CWE, Jan. 22, 1903.

61. "What Is a Liberal Education?" [1884], *Educational Reform*, 120; CWE, remarks, AAU(1904), 42.

62. "George Bridge Leighton," *Harvard Class of 1888: Fiftieth Anniversary Report* (Cambridge, 1938), 196–97; Leighton, "Higher Education in Railway Management," HGM 3(1894–95):481–85; various letters of Leighton to CWE, esp. July 28, [1895], Oct. 4, 1895, March 2, April 10, Nov. 10, 1896, Apr. 22, 1897; Baldwin to CWE, Dec. 26, 1895; Baldwin to N. S. Shaler, March 24, 1896, EP; CWE to Leighton, March 13, 1896; HUC(1897), 106, (1898), 346.

63. CWE, "Commercial Education," *Educational Review* 18(1899): 423, 420; A. C. Coolidge to CWE, Dec. 2, 1899, quoted in Melvin T. Copeland, *And Mark an Era: The Story of the Harvard Business School* (Boston, 1958), 3; CWE to Edmund J. James, Feb. 7, 1907; CWE to A. C. Coolidge, July 14, 1907 (excellent training). On the founding, see also Wallace B. Donham, "The Graduate School of Business Administration, 1908–1929," in Morison (ed.), *Development of Harvard*, 533–35.

64. Copeland, *And Mark an Era*, 17, 20, 341, 9–11; CWE, remarks, AAU(1904), 42; Chapman, quoted in Richard B. Hovey, *John Jay Chapman: An American Mind* (New York, 1959), 304; CWE to E. C. Patterson, March 5, 1908 (quite agree).

65. CWE, "Aims of Higher Education," *Educational Reform*, 246.

66. See p. 201, above.

CHAPTER VIII, *Reform in the Lower Schools*

1. CWE to Louis F. Post, Feb. 4, 1908.

2. Charles De Garmo, "Report of the Committee of Ten from the Point of View of Educational Theory," *Educational Review* 7(1894):275; I. L. Kandel, *History of Secondary Education: A Study in the Development of Liberal Education* (Boston, 1930), 497; Sizer, *Secondary Schools*, 1–5.

3. Alexander James Inglis, *The Rise of the High School in Massachusetts* (New York, 1911), 15–18, 35, 99–100. Most high schools offered Latin, as did Boston English after 1876 (ibid., 102).

4. CWE to John D. Philbrick, Oct. 5, 1869. Cf. AR(1874), 10–11.

5. CWE, remarks, NEA(1873), 44.

6. Katz, *Irony of Early School Reform*, 19, 53, 80–93 (see also Elmer Ellsworth Brown, *The Making of Our Middle Schools: An Account of the Development of Secondary Education in the United States* [New York, 1926], 314–18); McCosh, remarks, NEA(1873), 49.

7. Brown, *Middle Schools,* 356–59; Samuel Thurber, "Election of Studies in Secondary Schools: Its Relation to the Community," *Educational Review* 15(1898):431; CWE to Edward S. Joynes, Dec. 18, 1875.

8. CWE, "Wise and Unwise Economy," *Atlantic Monthly* 35:718–20.

9. "Rough Notes of Remarks at Meeting of Classical and High School Teachers Association" [1876], EPA 16.

10. *Educational Reform,* 8–9.

11. "[Address at Phillips Academy]" [1878], EPA 24.

12. AR(1900), 6–7; Powell, "Education at Harvard," 24.

13. Samuel Thurber, "Opening Remarks by the President," *Academy* 7(1892):190; CWE, *Requirements for Admission to Colleges and Scientific Schools: An Address delivered before the Schoolmasters' Association of New York and Vicinity, February 8, 1896* (n.p., 1897), 3; CWE, "National University," NEA(1873), 111; CWE, "Wise and Unwise Economy," *Atlantic Monthly* 35:716; CWE, "Teachers' Tenure of Office," *Educational Reform,* 49–58. Eliot proposed a curriculum for the Boston Latin School in 1875 and one for the Chelsea High School in 1884 (CWE, "Course of Study for the Public Latin School of the City of Boston," EP; C. R. Allen to CWE, Jan. 29, 31, 1903; Sizer, *Secondary Schools,* 80).

14. "Relation of Government to Education in the United States down to 1882," MS, EP, box 349.

15. EPA 33.

16. CWE, remarks, ACPSMSM(1896), 79 (feeble minority); CWE to John Tetlow, July 20, 1904, John Tetlow Papers, HL; John Tetlow, "The Colleges and the Non-Classical High School" [1896], MS, Tetlow Papers; Krug, *American High School,* 1–3.

17. AR(1886), 7–8; J. A. Beatley, remarks, *Educational Review* 13(1897):463–64.

18. *Educational Reform,* 152–54. Eliot's proof of such a decline was highly dubious, as were his generalizations about the rising age of college students. See Arthur M. Comey, "The Growth of New England Colleges," *Educational Review* 1(1891):209–19; W. Scott Thomas, "Changes in the Age of College Graduation," *Popular Science Monthly* 63(1903):159–71.

19. "An Average Massachusetts Grammar School" [1890], *Educational Reform,* 179–94 (including self-effacement, pp. 179, 194); "Shortening and Enriching the Grammar-School Course" [1892], ibid., 253–69; "The Gap," ibid., 197–219; G. I. Aldrich, "The Forty-Sixth Meeting of the Massachusetts State Teachers' Association," *Educational Review* 1(1891):161–62; Boston *Traveller,* March 1, 1892 (both criticisms); CWE, "The Unity of Educational Reform" [1894], *Educational Reform,* 315–19.

20. William C. Collar, "The Action of the Colleges upon the Schools," *Educational Review* 2(1891):425; Sizer, *Secondary Schools,* 39–

40; Flexner, *American College*, ch. 3, "The College and the Secondary School"; CWE, quoted in Denver *Republican*, Feb. 25, 1891.

21. Tetlow, "The Colleges and the Non-Classical High School" [1896], Tetlow Papers; editorial, *Educational Review* 4(1892):203–4; Krug, *American High School*, 35–37; Butler, *Across the Busy Years*, I:17, 196; CWE, "Undesirable and Desirable Uniformity," *Educational Reform*, 299–300. On the basis of documents closer to the event, it seems safe to say that Butler exaggerated his own role as initiator of the committee, at the expense of Eliot's.

22. Sizer, *Secondary Schools*, 181; Thurber, "Opening Remarks," *Academy* 7:190.

23. CWE, *More Money*, 91–93. The development of such institutions is examined in McLachlan, *American Boarding Schools*.

24. CWE, *More Money*, 150–53; "The Grammar School of the Future" [1893], *Educational Reform*, 310; "Undesirable and Desirable Uniformity," ibid., 297.

25. *Report of the Committee on Secondary School Studies Appointed at the Meeting of the National Educational Association, July 9, 1892* (Washington, D.C., 1893), 51.

26. The students in Western high schools were actually from a broad social range. The absence of immigrants and their children from high schools may have led Eliot to exaggerate their class barriers nationwide. See Sizer, *Secondary Schools*, 52–53.

27. CWE, "Recent Changes in Secondary Education," *Atlantic Monthly* 84(1899):434 (Boston pattern); AR(1890), 20; CWE, "Full Utilization of a Public School Plant," NEA(1903), 243; CWE, ["The Elementary Schools, the High Schools, and the Colleges"] [1894], EPA 53; CWE, remarks, ACPSMSM(1896), 86–87.

28. *Report of the Committee*, 6. The next question, "At what age should this differentiation begin, if any be recommended?" could apply only if Question 7 were answered affirmatively. Thus, the unanimity of the conferences against such differentiation was probably not foreseen. According to the *Report*, the response went against "a very general custom" (p. 17).

29. Ibid., 17, 44 (trifling exceptions: e.g., third year English was a four-period subject for those in the English program, a three-period one for those in the Classical program), 38, 22; CWE, "The Fundamental Assumptions in the Report of the Committee of Ten (1893)," *Educational Review* 30(1905):329 (simplification and economy).

30. CWE, "Can School Programmes Be Shortened and Enriched?" *Educational Reform*, 156; CWE, "Recent Changes," *Atlantic Monthly* 84:433, 437; "The Condition of American Education," EPA 103; CWE,

"Fundamental Assumptions," *Educational Review* 30:330–33; *Report of the Second Conference of Schoolmasters concerning the Relations between Preparatory Schools and the Scientific School of Harvard University* ([Cambridge?], [1901]), 5–6, copy in HUA (HUE49.97.75).

31. CWE, "Undesirable and Desirable Uniformity," *Educational Reform*, 296–97 (cf. Krug, *American High School*, 204–5); CWE, "Wherein Popular Education Has Failed," *American Contributions*, 222; CWE to Joseph A. Sneed, July 17, 1886 (not inconsistent); CWE, remarks, ACPSMSM (1896), 86.

32. In a call for more historical studies, for example, Eliot spoke of them in distinctly informational terms: "that [students] may learn how, as a matter of fact, arts came into being, commerce was developed by one city or nation after another, great literatures originated and grew up, new industries arose, fresh discoveries were made, and social conditions were ameliorated." This was clearly not drum and trumpet history, but it was knowledge, not mental training, that Eliot was advocating. He seems to have been unaware that he had justified this subject for the just-rejected motive of "giving information rather than of imparting power" ("Wherein Popular Education Has Failed," *American Contributions*, 231, 223). For a similar defense of modern languages with no regard to its implications, see CWE, "Commercial Education," *Educational Review* 18:418.

33. CWE, "Recent Changes," *Atlantic Monthly* 84:436, 441. Knowledge appears in 1903 as one of the four elements in Eliot's "New Definition of the Cultivated Man," in Neilson (ed.), *Eliot*, I:197–99.

34. De Garmo, "Report of the Committee," *Educational Review* 7:279; James M. Taylor, "The Report of the Committee of Ten," *School Review* 2(1894):195.

35. CWE to [Oscar D. Robinson], Oct. 24, 1893, in Robinson, "The Work of the Committee of Ten," *School Review* 2(1894):368–69 (cf. Sizer, *Secondary Schools*, 143); *Report of the Committee*, 41, 47, 50.

36. Krug, *American High School*, 292; Thurber, "Election of Studies," *Educational Review* 15:433.

37. Krug, *American High School*, 176; Hall, "The High School as the People's College," NEA(1902), 268. For elaborate comment by Hall on college domination, see his *Adolescence: Its Psychology* . . . (New York, 1904), II:514–27.

38. "Inaugural," *Educational Reform*, 12, 3–5; CWE, "New Education," *Atlantic Monthly* 23:361; "Liberty in Education" [1885], *Educational Reform*, 129, 135; CWE to Joseph A. Sneed, July 17, 1886. On the unlikelihood that secondary schools would provide adequate general education, see Thomas, *Search for a Common Learning*, 26.

39. *Report of the Committee,* 44–48; "Report of the Committee on College-Entrance Requirements," NEA (1899), 661.

40. "The Unity of Educational Reform," *Educational Reform,* 325–27 (first three); CWE, *Four American Leaders,* 84; "[Address at] Harvard Teachers Association" [1903], EPA 128; CWE, "Recent Changes," *Atlantic Monthly* 84:440 (on Stanford); Münsterberg to CWE, Jan. 25, 1899.

41. Inglis, *Rise of the High School,* 102; CWE, "A Wider Range of Electives in College Admission Requirements" [1896], *Educational Reform,* 389; Krug, *American High School,* 192, 135–36; A. F. Nightingale, "Reform of College Entrance Requirements," *Educational Review* 14(1897): 39–40; CWE, *More Money,* 90–91; CWE to Seaver, Oct. 18, 1900; Seaver to CWE, Aug. 27, 1902 (showing Eliot's later approval of the reform).

42. Krug, *American High School,* 195–97; CWE, "Undesirable and Desirable Uniformity," *Educational Reform,* 284 (welcomed); "The Unity of Educational Reform," ibid., 326 (imperfect application); CWE to W. R. Harper, June 7, 1902, President's Papers, University of Chicago; CWE, *University Administration,* 161–63. On this drive against parallel courses, see Brown, *Middle Schools,* 384–85.

43. AR (1897), 19; "The Condition of American Education," EPA 103; "Undesirable and Desirable Uniformity," *Educational Reform,* 291.

44. CWE, "Wherein Popular Education Has Failed," *American Contributions,* 231 (all-important); AR (1887), 8; "Unity of Educational Reform," *Educational Reform,* 315. On Harvard's program to aid secondary schools before 1890, see Powell, "Education at Harvard," ch. 1.

45. CWE, "Wise and Unwise Economy," *Atlantic Monthly* 35:712–13; "Undesirable and Desirable Uniformity," *Educational Reform,* 286; CWE, "Tendencies of Secondary Education," *Educational Review* 14(1897):426; *More Money,* 143; "Fundamental Assumptions," *Educational Review* 30:329; "An Average Massachusetts Grammar School," *Educational Reform,* 191–93.

46. Hart, *Studies in American Education,* 31; editorial, *Educational Review* 7(1894):516–18; John T. Prince, "The Grading and Promotion of Pupils," ibid., 15(1898):234–36, 242–45; CWE, "Tendencies of Secondary Education," ibid., 14(1897):427; *Report of the Second Conference of Schoolmasters,* 6.

47. CWE, "Undesirable and Desirable Uniformity," *Educational Reform,* 286. On the later movement, see Krug, *American High School,* ch. 13; Raymond E. Callahan, *Education and the Cult of Efficiency: A Study of the Social Forces that Have Shaped the Administration of the Public Schools* (Chicago, 1962).

48. "Can School Programmes Be Shortened and Enriched?" *Educational Reform,* 153–54; Krug, *American High School,* 165; *I Remember:*

The Autobiography of Abraham Flexner (New York, 1940), 81–82; CWE, "Undesirable and Desirable Uniformity," *Educational Reform*, 296.

49. *Report of the Committee*, 42–43, 38. Eliot himself said, "I believe that the best criterion for determining the value of each subject [for college admission purposes] is the time devoted to that subject in schools which have an intelligent programme of studies." He declared this system superior to that then in use at Harvard, under which subjects were weighted by whether they had one- or two-hour admission examinations ("A Wider Range of Electives in College Admission Requirements," *Educational Reform*, 380–81).

50. "Fundamental Assumptions," *Educational Review* 30:333, 336. In his answer to Hall, Eliot dwelt on the qualifying phrases in the *Report*. It is probable, however, that many of these qualifications were added by committee members other than Eliot. Hall would have been harder to answer if he had drawn from Eliot's own views, especially his defense of subject election.

51. Krug, *American High School*, 161–62; CWE, "Fundamental Assumptions," *Educational Review* 30:329. For an unsympathetic assessment of the time units, see Dietrich Gerhard, "The Emergence of the Credit System in American Education Considered as a Problem of Social and Intellectual History," *American Association of University Professors Bulletin* 41(1955):647–68.

52. Krug, *American High School*, 169, 284; "The Condition of American Education," EPA 103; CWE, "Commercial Education," *Educational Review* 18:417–18.

53. "Full Utilization of a Public School Plant," NEA(1903), 243 (understand principles); CWE, "Tendencies of Secondary Education," *Educational Review* 14:418; Lawrence A. Cremin, *The Transformation of the School: Progressivism in American Education, 1876–1957* (New York, 1961), 33–34; CWE, "Fundamental Assumptions," *Educational Review* 30:330.

54. On this movement, see Krug, *American High School*, ch. 10, and Cremin, *Transformation of the School*, ch. 2. Eliot sided with Hanus and the new commission against the State Board of Education in a struggle settled only in 1909 by a merger of the two bodies (CWE to Hanus, Dec. 27, 1907; Hanus, *Adventuring in Education*, 171–72).

55. CWE to J. G. Croswell, Aug. 31, 1906; CWE, *An Address Delivered at the Second Annual Conference of No-License Workers of Massachusetts, Boston, 29 October, 1908* (Boston, [1908]), 8; CWE, *Lawlessness: An Address Delivered before the Civic Forum in Carnegie Hall, New York City, December 12, 1908* (New York, 1909), 4, 27.

56. CWE, "Labor Unions from the Educator's Point of View" [1902], EPA 118; CWE to J. K. Turner, Feb. 6, 1908; Boston *Evening Transcript*, Nov. 28, 1908.

57. "Industrial Education as an Essential Factor in Our National Prosperity," *National Society for the Promotion of Industrial Education Bulletin*, No. 5 (1908):9–14.

58. For Eliot's concept of the "automatic" worker, see *More Money*, 48–49. In this address of 1902 he urged more schooling as a corrective, but implied that the students would voluntarily remain in schools if enough money were spent to improve them. See also his argument in "The Full Utilization of a Public School Plant," NEA (1903), 243, that evening schools could teach young workers "to understand principles as well as practice; and to escape from the contracting influence of automatic repetition."

59. "President Eliot's Democracy," *The Public* 10(1908):1083–84; CWE to Post, Feb. 4, 14, 1908; Post to CWE, Feb. 7, 12, 1908. The assertion in Krug, *American High School*, 226n35, that Eliot did not seek to justify himself after this address, is mistaken. For a similar exchange on the address, see the Cleveland *News* account of it as a "freakish utterance" and the defense of Eliot by an admirer, J. K. Turner. According to Turner's interpretation of Eliot's plan, manual training in the elementary schools (which Eliot had long supported and which Massachusetts law required in large towns and cities) would reveal to the child his abilities and thus help him choose an appropriate trade school (Turner to CWE, Feb. 4, 1908, and enclosed clpg.; CWE to Turner, Feb. 6, 1908). See also Boston *Globe*, Jan. 24, 1908.

60. CWE, "Education for Trades and Trade in a Democracy" [1908], EPA 236; CWE, "The Elements of a Liberal Education," *Educator-Journal* 8(1908):498–505, esp. 499, 501, 504. Eliot made no reference to the vocational guidance movement then emerging in Boston, though recognition of it would have strengthened his case.

61. CWE to Eben S. Draper, Jan. 22, 1909; CWE, *More Money*, 157–58; similarly, CWE, "Full Utilization of a Public School Plant," NEA (1903), 245.

62. "Elements of a Liberal Education," *Educator-Journal* 8:501 (four classes); "Educational Reform and the Social Order," *School Review* 17(1909):217.

63. Krug, *American High School*, 244.

64. *Report of the Committee*, 54–55.

65. On summer schools: CWE to James B. Angell, Nov. 19, 1895, Feb. 8, 1899; AR(1874), 32, (1875), 38–39; Shaler to CWE, Sept. 1, 1894; on Lawrence: James, *Eliot*, I:295, AR(1880), 39; on Hall: AR(1881), 39;

Hall to CWE, April 10, 1882; G. Stanley Hall, *Life and Confessions of a Psychologist* (New York, 1923), 216–18; Dorothy Ross, *G. Stanley Hall: The Psychologist as Prophet* (Chicago, 1972), 112–13.

66. For a careful account and interpretation of these developments, see Powell, "Education of Educators," in Buck (ed.), *Social Sciences at Harvard*, 225–34; further details are given in Powell, "Education at Harvard," ch. 1.

67. CWE, "Unity of Educational Reform," *Educational Reform*, 332; CWE, remarks, ACPSMSM(1896), 120–21; CWE, *More Money*, 102–3; Frank A. Hill to CWE, Nov. 7, 1895; CWE, "Tendencies of Secondary Education," *Educational Review* 14:425. For sources of Eliot's low opinion of the normal schools, see G. Stanley Hall to CWE, April 10, 1882; E. Hunt to CWE, Sept. 3, 1892. See also A. W. Edson, "The Massachusetts Public-School System," *Educational Review* 16(1898):453–57.

68. Hart, *Studies in American Education*, 73. For the continuation of these in-service courses and their eventual shift to "cultural" extension courses, see Powell, "Education at Harvard," 83, 124.

69. Hanus, *Adventuring in Education*, 87–93, 101, 108–9, 112; Powell, "Education of Educators," in Buck (ed.), *Social Sciences at Harvard*, 235.

70. Hanus to CWE, March 4, 31, April 10, 22, 1891; Powell, "Education of Educators," in Buck (ed.), *Social Sciences at Harvard*, 263; CWE to Hanus, Feb. 18, 1906, quoted in Powell, "Education at Harvard," 202.

71. CWE, quoted in Denver *Republican*, Feb. 25, 1891; Hanus, *Adventuring in Education*, 145–47; Wendell to CWE, Feb. 1, 1899; CWE to Charles F. Thwing, Feb. 14, 1900.

72. CWE to Caskie Harrison, Aug. 9, 1894 (a priori determinations); CWE, "An Average Massachusetts Grammar School," *Educational Reform*, 182; CWE, "The Report of the Committee of Ten," *Educational Review* 7(1894):105 (first research); Powell, "Education at Harvard," 159.

73. CWE to Hanus, Aug. 3, 22, 1903, quoted in Hanus, *Adventuring in Education*, 214–16; CWE, "Report of Speech at Dinner to Celebrate Starting of Graduate School of Education, 17 Feb. 1920," EPA 697. Eliot may have seen danger in the fact that one so scornful of education courses as Barrett Wendell was willing to have them at Harvard if offered in a separate school, where they would not aspire to the status of the Faculty of Arts and Sciences (Wendell to CWE, Feb. 1, 1899).

74. Powell, "Education of Educators," in Buck (ed.), *Social Sciences at Harvard*, 272–74.

75. CWE, remarks on Radcliffe, HGM 12(1903–4):625; P. J. Eaton, "Associated Clubs," HGM 13(1904–5):479; Hugh Shepherd, "Associated Clubs Convention," HGM 16(1907–8):721.

76. William C. Lane, "The University during the Last Five Years,"

HGM 1(1892–93):51; "Harvard Teachers' Association," HGM 2(1893–94):273–74; Hanus, *Adventuring in Education*, 134–35, 228; "Dr. Eliot and the Harvard Teachers Association," *Harvard Teachers Record* 4(1934):3.

77. CWE, "The Elementary Schools, the High Schools, and the Colleges," EPA 53; CWE to Charles F. Thwing, Dec. 14, 1894; "A Conference of American Universities on Problems Connected with Graduate Work: The Call," AAU(1901), 11.

78. CWE to John Eaton, Jan. 9, 1904; CWE to C. E. Norton, Aug. 25, 1873, Norton Papers (stupid volume); Harris to CWE, Jan. 15, 1896.

79. J. D. Greene to F. G. Peabody, Feb. 28, 1903, EP; B. I. Wheeler to CWE, July 21, 1903; "Minutes of the Annual Business Meeting," NEA (1903), 24–28; "Report of the President," NEA yearbook (1903), 41–42, offprint in EP; "The Boston Meeting of the N.E.A.," *Intelligence* 23(1903): 507; CWE to Baker, April 1, 1904; Krug, *American High School*, 167; Richard Whittemore, *Nicholas Murray Butler and Public Education, 1862–1911* (New York, 1970), 102–3.

80. E. P. Seaver to CWE, Aug. 27, 1902; CWE to John Eaton, Jan. 9, 1904; J. M. Peirce to J. D. Greene, June 13, 1903, EP; George P. Baker, "Summer Quarter," HGM 12(1903–4):49–50; "Harvard and the N.E.A. Convention," ibid., 177; AR(1903), 17.

81. Wesley, *NEA: The First Hundred Years*, 104, 328–31, 335; Butler, *Across the Busy Years*, I:195; Krug, *American High School*, 214, 437–38. Eliot was consulted on the charges of discrimination against women and protection of trust funds (Irwin Shepard to CWE, Oct. 13, 1910). He objected vigorously to the NEA's drive for a million-dollar endowment because a 15 per cent commission was to go to the chief fund-raiser ([CWE] to A. E. Winship, April 10, Sept. 19, 1913; [CWE] to Thomas W. Bicknell, Jan. 9, 1913).

82. CWE to L. P. Sanders, March 24, 1898.

83. Timothy L. Smith, "Progressivism in American Education, 1880–1900," *Harvard Educational Review* 31(1961):168–93; Cremin, *Transformation of the School*, 3–8.

84. For criticism: Krug, *American High School*, 19; Sizer, *Secondary Schools*, 20. For praise: William H. Maxwell, "Professor Hinsdale on the City School Superintendent," *Educational Review* 7(1894):187; Tetlow, "The Colleges and the Non-Classical High School," MS, Tetlow Papers.

85. E.g., remarks at Pittsburgh Central High School, reported in Boston *Globe*, May 30, 1905; remarks at Boys' High School, Brooklyn, reported in Troy (N.Y.) *Times*, April 2, 1908.

86. E. Hunt to CWE, April 14, 1891 (frustrated superintendent);

Walter F. Drost, *David Snedden and Education for Social Efficiency* (Madison, Wis., 1967), 36; editorial, *Educational Review* 7(1894):207; John E. Bradley, "The Report of the Committee of Ten from the Point of View of the Smaller Colleges," ibid., 372; editorial, Springfield *Republican*, March 17, 1904. For similar appraisals, see Krug, *American High School*, 215–16; Krug, "Charles W. Eliot and Popular Education: An Introduction," in Krug (ed.), *Charles W. Eliot and Popular Education* (New York, 1961), 22–23.

87. Thurber, "Opening Remarks," *Academy* 7:190–91.

88. "The Condition of American Education," EPA 103; "Republican Education," EPA 161; "Full Utilization of a Public School Plant," NEA (1903), 245–47; CWE, "A Better Chance for the Children of the Slums," *Outlook* 86(1907):769–70; "New Definition of the Cultivated Man," in Neilson (ed.), *Eliot*, I:189–204.

89. James, *Eliot*, II:185; CWE to Oswald Garrison Villard, Feb. 7, 1918, O. G. Villard Papers, HL; Cremin, *Transformation of the School*, 280; Krug, *American High School*, 344; Patricia Albjerg Graham, *Progressive Education: From Arcady to Academe: A History of the Progressive Education Association, 1919–1955* (New York, 1967), 23–24.

CHAPTER IX, *The Resurgence of Collegiate Concerns*

1. "President Eliot's Response," HGM 3(1894–95):74.

2. Youmans, *Culture Demanded by Modern Life*, 54; Babbitt, "Academic Leisure," HGM 15(1906–7):258–59.

3. The quotation from Arnold appears in Veysey, *American University*, 186, in the section "Definitions of 'Culture,'" which identifies and analyzes this academic movement. See also Rudolph, *American College*, ch. 21, "Counterrevolution." For the parallels in German professorial thought, see Ringer, *Decline of the German Mandarins*.

4. C. F. Adams, "A College Fetich," *Three Phi Beta Kappa Lectures*, 5–48, and "Some Modern College Tendencies," ibid., esp. 119–20, 124; F. C. Lowell to "Dear Sir," April 1, 1886, in *Circular Sent to the Candidates for Overseers [and] Replies* (n.p., n.d.), copy in EP, box 74 (see also F. C. Lowell, "The President's Report for 1886–87," *Harvard Monthly* 6:7–15); Slosson, *Great American Universities*, 27 (thick of the fight); William C. Lawton to CWE, July 11, 1896 (strife); Münsterberg to CWE, Jan. 25, 1899 (see also Münsterberg, "Philosophy at Harvard," HGM 9[1900–1901]:481).

5. Brown, *Dean Briggs*, 60; various letters of Wendell to CWE, esp. Feb. 18, 1893; Howe, *Wendell*, passim.

6. Howe, *Wendell*, 193 (shared with Eliot); Wendell to E. S.

Martin, June 20, 1909, in ibid., 200 (scholarship; specialized training); ibid., 198–99 (classical dinner); Wendell to CWE, Oct. 29, 1900 (wasteful).

7. Howe, *Wendell*, 137, 268, 181; Brown, *Dean Briggs*, 56–63.

8. Howe, *Wendell*, 81, 31, 125, 131 (quotation); "Literary Notes," HGM 13(1904–5):335.

9. Howe, *Wendell*, 118, 120, 137, 132; Brown, *Dean Briggs*, 60.

10. Wendell, "De Praeside Magnifico," HGM 18(1909–10):15–18; Howe, *Wendell*, 201–2.

11. Byron S. Hurlbut, in AR(1902), 120 (just man); Briggs, in ibid., 103 (pushing blindly); Briggs, "Some Old-Fashioned Doubts about New-Fashioned Education," *Atlantic Monthly* 86(1900):467, 469, 470; Briggs to CWE, May 6, 1901. On the humanizing functions of the early deanships, see Rudolph, *American College*, 435.

12. Briggs, remarks, HGM 9(1900–1901):66.

13. For biographical detail, see Henry Aaron Yeomans, *Abbott Lawrence Lowell, 1856–1943* (Cambridge, 1948); for his early essays and addresses on education, see Lowell, *At War*.

14. Lowell, *At War*, 155–56 (practice); Lowell, "Dormitories and College Life," HGM 12(1903–4):526 (earning bread); Lowell, remarks, MHS, 60(1926–27):11; Lowell, "Athletics and Distinction in Life," HGM 12(1903–4):330–33; Yeomans, *Lowell*, 66–67.

15. "Dormitories and College Life," HGM 12:525; Lowell to Henry S. Pritchett, April 16, 1902, in Yeomans, *Lowell*, 524 (both on graduate school); Lowell to President and Fellows, [Dec. 9?, 1901], in ibid., 57 (essential function).

16. Lowell, remarks, HGM 18(1909–10):69; "President Lowell's Speech," ibid., 133–34; "Dormitories and College Life" [1904], HGM 12:528; "Inaugural," *At War*, 42. On the side of aesthetics and development of "taste," Lowell was relatively divorced from the advocates of liberal culture. He belonged to the later, intellectualized stage of that advocacy, rather than its misty *fin-de-siècle* phase (see Veysey, *American University*, ch. 4, "Liberal Culture").

17. "Inaugural," *At War*, 35 (cohesion); "Address to His Students," HGM 17(1908–9):579 (good fellowship); remarks, HGM 18:68 (poverty). On student council: ibid., 69; Yeomans, *Lowell*, 81, 329; Briggs, in AR(1908), 99.

18. AR(1901), 10, 83–89, (1902), 27; Briggs, in AR(1902), 100–102; Yeomans, *Lowell*, 72–73.

19. Briggs, in AR(1904), 95.

20. For the full report, see "Report of the Committee on Improving Instruction in Harvard College," HGM 12(1903–4):611–20. The figures on study time excluded graduate students and students who left the uni-

versity in 1902 by graduation or otherwise. More important, they excluded sixty-seven and one-half courses, those with laboratories and those requiring theses (term papers), because of ambiguity in responses. These represented about one-fifth of all courses, including many of the smaller ones and quite possibly those where students on independent projects may have been inspired to devote a great deal of out-of-class time to the course. There was thus a definite skewing of the survey toward the large lecture courses. But these courses had been the original cause of complaint, and most of the findings of the committee were directed specifically to them.

21. AR(1902), 27.

22. Ibid., 22–24.

23. G. H. Palmer, "Necessary Limitations of the Elective System" [1887], in Palmer and Palmer, *The Teacher*, 248–49.

24. B. S. Hurlbut, in AR(1905), 120. On Eliot's ideal workday, see p. 112, above.

25. AR(1904), 13. Geology 4 was stiffened up and restored to credit-giving status the next year (AR[1905], 97).

26. AR(1904), 95; Yeomans, *Lowell*, 80.

27. Jordan, "An Apology for the American University," NEA (1899), 221; Hyde, "The Educational Progress of the Year 1902–1903," NEA(1903), 339; Hurlbut, in AR(1906), 13. Such a curricular scheme existed in some high schools (Hanus, *Adventuring in Education*, 159), and had even been suggested as an ideal by Eliot in 1903, though without limiting the free elective system ("New Definition of the Cultivated Man," in Neilson [ed.], *Eliot*, I:197).

28. Yeomans, *Lowell*, 121–35. For details of the new plan, see AR(1909), 45–50; "New Rules for Electives," HGM 18(1909–10):400–401; W. B. Munro, "The Winter Quarter," ibid., 453–54; Lowell, remarks, ibid., 576–81. For the committee's conclusions, see "Report of the Committee Appointed to Consider How Tests for Rank in College May Be Made a More Generally Recognized Measure of Intellectual Power," ibid., 478–84.

29. AR(1900), 12–13; Pierson, *Yale*, I:251, vol. I, ch. 14, "Retrospect: A New System on Old Principles," esp. 266; Veysey, *American University*, 118–20, 241–42, 249–50.

30. A. B. Hart, "New Problems and Changes," HGM 10(1901–2):235–37; R. B. Merriman, "The Autumn Quarter," HGM 14(1905–6):251–53; New York *World*, Oct. 16, 1905; Springfield *Republican*, March 17, 1904; Brooks, "Harvard and American Life," *Living Age*, 259:644. The total enrollment on Oct. 15, 1904, was 4,086. Dean Hurlbut attributed the decline to improved state universities and easier admission at colleges using the certificate system (AR[1908], 104).

31. The figure of 60 per cent excludes professional schools (AR[1904], 50). In 1909 tuition income at Harvard still paid a relatively high percentage of the institution's cost of instruction (Slosson, *Great American Universities*, x, 4).

32. AR(1904), 50. Eliot bluntly reviewed this period of decline in his last report (AR[1908], 10).

33. Slosson, *Great American Universities*, 19; J. H. Gardiner, "The Future of Harvard College," HGM 13(1904–5):406–7; William Lawrence, "Teachers' Endowment Fund of Harvard College," ibid., 621; AR(1906), 14–16.

34. C. F. Adams, *Three Phi Beta Kappa Lectures*, esp. 115–24; editorials in *Harvard Monthly* 40(1905):80–81, 45(1907):49–50, 45(1908):207; Yeomans, *Lowell*, 66 (going to hell). See also C. F. Adams, *Autobiography*, 36; Kirkland, *Adams*, 128, 199.

35. CWE, remarks, HGM 13(1904–5):74; Babbitt, "The Humanities," *Atlantic Monthly* 89(1902):770–79; CWE, "Address to New Students, October 1, 1906," HGM 15(1906–7):221–22; CWE to Carleton Hunt, Sept. 10, 1907.

36. CWE to L. B. R. Briggs, July 31, 1903 (guidance); AR(1908), 7–8 (high scholarship). See also James, *Eliot*, II:144; CWE, *University Administration*, 149.

37. "Major Higginson's Gift—the Harvard Union," HGM 8(1899–1900):239 (university spirit); "President Eliot's Address," HGM 10(1901–2):216–18 (opportunity); "President Eliot's Commencement Speech," HGM 15(1906–7):30 (enlarge the organization); Slosson, *Great American Universities*, 507; AR(1907), 53–54; CWE, *Harvard Memories*, 74 (know by name).

38. Adams, *Copey*, 35; Yeomans, *Lowell*, 123; AR(1908), 18. For another defense of the three-year degree, arguing revealingly that it would get students "into real work a year earlier," see Dean Hurlbut's comments, in AR(1908), 108–9.

39. "Inaugural," *At War*, 35, 45, 33, 43.

40. Wilson, "The Spirit of Learning," HGM 18(1909–10):6; "De Praeside Magnifico," ibid., 15–18.

41. CWE, remarks of Oct. 6, 1909, HGM 18(1909–10):283–84; CWE, remarks of Jan. 26, 1910, ibid., 583.

42. Louis Lyons, quoted in Yeomans, *Lowell*, 199.

43. E.g., Charles M. Flandrau, *The Diary of a Freshman* (New York, 1901); Waldron Kintzing Post, *Harvard Stories: Sketches of the Undergraduate* (New York, 1896); William Dana Orcutt, "Clubs and Club-Life at Harvard," *New England Magazine* 12(1892):81–98; Edward S. Martin, "Undergraduate Life at Harvard," *Scribner's Magazine* 21(1897):531–53.

44. CWE, "Elements of a Liberal Education," *Educator-Journal*

8:499–500; CWE, "New Definition of the Cultivated Man," in Neilson (ed.), *Eliot,* I:189–204.

45. William Manning, "The Key of Libberty," ed. S. E. Morison, *William and Mary Quarterly,* ser. 3, 13(1956):226.

EPILOGUE: *"America's President Eliot"*

1. Irving Babbitt, "President Eliot and American Education," *Forum,* 81:2.

2. Kuehnemann, *Eliot,* 1–4.

3. James, *Eliot,* II:184; Yeomans, *Lowell,* 291; Conant, *My Several Lives,* 91 (recent visit); CWE to Lowell, June 25, 1909, July 11, 1910, Nov. 30, 1914, A. L. Lowell Papers.

4. James, *Eliot,* II:185, 192, 189; *The Changing Years: Reminiscences of Norman Hapgood* (New York, 1930), 53–54; CWE, remarks, HGM 18(1909–10):584 (voluntary association).

5. Thomas N. Perkins to A. L. Lowell, Feb. 9, 1912, A. L. Lowell Papers (criticism of travel); James, *Eliot,* II:185, 215–19; Cotton, *Eliot,* ch. 22, "The World War."

6. M. A. DeWolfe Howe, "Introduction," in CWE, *Late Harvest,* vii.

7. Neilson, "Biographical Study," in Neilson (ed.), *Eliot,* I:xix–xx; Cotton, *Eliot,* 270–77.

8. CWE, "Some Reasons Why the American Republic May Endure," *American Contributions,* 48; CWE, "Fundamental Assumptions," *Educational Review* 30:332; CWE, "Full Utilization of a Public School Plant," NEA(1903), 242; Kuehnemann, *Eliot,* 56–57; Hapgood, *Changing Years,* 50–52; William Patten, "Memorandum Re Harvard Classics" (mimeographed), EP, box 405. Eliot's original statement referred to a three-foot shelf and ten minutes a day (CWE, quoted in Atlanta *Journal,* March 16, 1909).

9. Finley Peter Dunne, *Mr. Dooley Says* (New York, 1910), "Books," 134–35; Edward O. Skelton to CWE, July 28, 1910, A. S. Webb Collection, YU; Boston *Traveller,* April 20, 1910 (both on Gettysburg).

10. John Jay Chapman, "The Harvard Classics and Harvard," *Science* n.s. 30(1909):440–43.

11. [Fabian Franklin], "The American College and American Culture," *Nation* 89(1909):321–22.

12. James, *Eliot,* II:194; Margaret Farrand Thorp, *Neilson of Smith* (New York, 1956), 123.

13. CWE, "The Editor's Introduction to the Harvard Classics," *The Harvard Classics* (New York, 1909–10), 50:3–4; Krug, *American High School,* 294n.

14. CWE, "Editor's Introduction," *Harvard Classics*, 50:7, 10.

15. CWE to M. A. DeWolfe Howe, March 21, 1919, Howe Papers, HL.

16. Chapman to Henry L. Higginson, Aug. 16, 1909, in New York *Times*, Aug. 19, 1909.

17. Dunne, *Mr. Dooley Says*, 136–37; W. E. Harris, "Charles W. Eliot Emeritus," enclosed in Harris to F. W. Hunnewell, May 10, 1927, A. L. Lowell Papers. *The Adventures of Augie March* (New York, 1953), 92; *The Autobiography of Malcolm X* (New York, 1965), 187.

18. Manchester (New Hampshire) *Union*, quoted in HGM 18(1909–10):591 (on Gompers); Upton Sinclair, *The Goose-Step: A Study of American Education* (Pasadena, Calif., 1923), 103 (Sunday).

19. Edward K. Rand, "Humanist and Friend," *Harvard Alumni Bulletin*, 45(1942–43):233.

20. James, *Eliot*, II:190; Chicago *News*, April 11, 1908 (headline); "What Life Means," *Current Opinion*, 76(1924):696–97; John B. Kennedy, "Dr. Eliot Looks Ahead: An Interview with Dr. Charles W. Eliot," *Collier's Weekly* 77(1926):9 (advice).

21. "The Road to Industrial Peace," *Late Harvest*, 151–68; Kennedy, "Dr. Eliot Looks Ahead," *Collier's Weekly* 77:9; "The Next American Contribution to Civilization," *Late Harvest*, 268–94.

22. Perry, "Eliot," *New England Quarterly* 4:18.

23. Babbitt, "President Eliot and American Education," *Forum* 81:2, 5–6.

24. Editorial, *Christian Century* 43(1926):1075; similarly, Edward S. Martin, "President Eliot," *Harper's Magazine* 153(1926):788.

25. *Time* 8(Aug. 30, 1926):9.

Index

The subentries "cited" and "quoted" are used when the name of the person referred to appears in the relevant note, but not in the text.

ABBREVIATIONS

CWE	Charles W. Eliot
HC	Harvard College (undergraduate academic division of Harvard)
HC plus year	year of graduation from Harvard College, to distinguish individuals with the same name
HU	Harvard University
LSS	Lawrence Scientific School

A.B., 7, 56, 211, 256, 277, 278; as requirement for professional schools, 59; for scientific course at Union College, 83; changed requirements for, at Brown, 83-84; at Cornell, 84; at Stanford, 85; said to be threatened by CWE, 106; requirements for, 113; CWE's emphasis on, 119; admission standards for, 177; professional courses counted toward, 202; higher standards for, 273; as status symbol, 285. *See also* bachelor's degree; three-year degree

A.M., 256, 288; "in course" ended, 54, 54n17; earned, established at HU, 55. *See also* M.A.

Abbott, Lyman, 137
abolitionists, 4, 8
Academic Council, 55
academic freedom, 65, 72n60; CWE's support of, 70-72; and Bowen's book, 70n55; for students, 94, 112-13; relation of, to science and religion, 130-31; and divinity training, 131; and economic policy controversies, 217-18
academies, 224; free admission to, 172n11; CWE stresses, as preparatory institutions, 225-26; and higher college standards, 227-28;